Y0-CZS-348

Audrey Cohen College
5 0664 01006154 9

LB 1576 F43 1993
Finn, Patrick J.
Helping children learn language arts

DATE DUE

AUDREY COHEN COLLEGE LIBRARY
75 Varick St. 12th Floor
New York, NY 10013

LB
1576
F43
1993

HELPING CHILDREN LEARN LANGUAGE ARTS

Patrick J. Finn

State University of New York at Buffalo

With the editorial assistance of Mary E. Finn

Longman
New York & London

Helping Children Learn Language Arts

Copyright © 1993 by Longman Publishing Group.
All rights reserved.

No part of this publication may be reproduced,
stored in a retrieval system, or transmitted
in any form or by any means, electronic, mechanical,
photocopying, recording, or otherwise,
without the prior permission of the publisher.

Longman, 10 Bank Street, White Plains, N.Y. 10606

Associated companies:
Longman Group Ltd., London
Longman Cheshire Pty., Melbourne
Longman Paul Pty., Auckland
Copp Clark Pitman, Toronto

Senior acquisitions editor: Laura McKenna
Sponsoring editor: Ray O'Connell
Development editor: Virginia Blanford
Production editor: Dee Amir Josephson
Text design: Betty Sokol
Cover design: Joseph DePinho
Photos: Christina V. Bogan
Production supervisor: Richard Bretan

Library of Congress Cataloging in Publication Data

Finn, Patrick J.
    Helping children learn language arts / Patrick J. Finn.
        p.   cm.
    Includes bibliographical references and index.
    ISBN 0-8013-0049-5
    1. Language arts (Elementary)—United States. 2. Reading (Elementary)—United States—Language experience approach.
I. Title
LB1576.F43   1993   92-8759
                                                          CIP

1 2 3 4 5 6 7 8 9 10-HA-9594939291

To Molly and Amy. What a pair!

Contents

To Think Abouts   xi

Preface   xiii

1   A Holistic, Collaborative, Integrated Approach to Teaching Language Arts   1

Introduction: The Relationship Between Teachers' Beliefs and Practices   2
TO THINK ABOUT: Autonomy in the Classroom   3
Two Contrasting Approaches   3
TO THINK ABOUT: Underlying Assumptions in Teaching   3
Issues That Define Approaches   10
Summary   13
   For Review and Discussion   14
   For Further Reading   14

2   Support for a Holistic, Collaborative, Integrated Approach to Teaching Language Arts   16

Introduction: A Social View of Learning   18
An Interactional View of Language Acquisition   18
   Activity   21
Parent-Child Interactions That Facilitate Development   22
Homes, Communities, and Language   27
   Activity   31
Oral Language at School   38
TO THINK ABOUT: Teacher/Student Collaboration   42
Integrating the Language Arts   44
   Activity   46
Summary   47
   For Review and Discussion   50
   For Further Reading   51

3   Understanding Oral Language   52

Introduction   54
A Communication Model   54
TO THINK ABOUT: Culture and Communication   55
   Activity   56

v

Focusing on Listening   58
   Activities   70, 72
Conversation   68
Discussion   73
   Activities   74, 76, 78, 79
Supporting Formal Speaking and Listening in the Classroom   80
Summary   85
   For Review and Discussion   87
   For Further Reading   87

4 Oral Language: Small-Group Discussion, Cooperative Learning, and Conflict Resolution   90

Introduction   92
Small-Group Discussion   92
TO THINK ABOUT: Teacher Talk: Directive or Collaborative   99
Lesson Plan: Disputes and Discussions   104
Lesson Plan: Potholes   104
Cooperative Learning   105
Conflict Resolution   113
Lesson Plan: Alliterative Name Games   114
Lesson Plan: Classroom Yellow Pages   114
Lesson Plan: Active Listening   116
Lesson Plan: The Description Game   117
Lesson Plan: Recognizing Methods of Decision Making   118
   Activities   118, 120
Summary   121
   For Review and Discussion   124
   For Further Reading   124

5 Oral Language: Focus on Function   126

Introduction   128
The Informative Use of Language   128
Lesson Plan: Photographic Field Trip   130
Lesson Plan: Listening to Directions   130
Lesson Plan: An Interview   130
Lesson Plan: Meeting Martians   131
Persuasive Language   132
Lesson Plan: Responding to Commercials   134
Lesson Plan: Scarce Resources   135

Lesson Plan: Problem Puppets   135
Lesson Plan: Frames of Reference   136
Lesson Plan: My Bike   136
Communicating Emotions, Feelings, and Attitudes: The Affective Function of Language   137
Lesson Plan: "Getting Into" a Part   140
Lesson Plan: Stereotypes   140
Lesson Plan: More Stereotypes   141
Lesson Plan: Mixed Signals   141
Lesson Plan: Reading Signals   141
Lesson Plan: Put-Downs   142
Lesson Plan: Affirming Statements   142
Creating With Language: The Imaginative Function of Language   143
Engaging in Social Transactions: The Ritualistic and Transactional Functions of Speaking and Listening   144
Lesson Plan: Folk Gestures   146
Lesson Plan: Manners   146
Lesson Plan: What Do You Say, Dear? What Do You Do, Dear?   147
Lesson Plan: Changing Times   147
Combining Functions   147
Lesson Plan: Create Checklists   148
Summary   149
For Review and Discussion   150
For Further Reading   151

6 Approaches to Teaching Reading   152

Introduction   154
The Concept of Emergent Literacy   154
TO THINK ABOUT: Underlying Assumptions in Emergent Literacy   160
TO THINK ABOUT: Reflections on the Writing Process Approach   162
TO THINK ABOUT: Reflections on the Language Experience Approach   165
TO THINK ABOUT: Reflections on the Individual Reading Program Approach   167
   Activity   170
TO THINK ABOUT: Reflections on Reading Conferences   170
TO THINK ABOUT: Reflections on Reading Workshops   171
The Traditional Concept of Reading Readiness   172
TO THINK ABOUT: Underlying Assumptions—Reading Readiness vs. Emergent Literacy   176
TO THINK ABOUT: Underlying Assumptions: The Phonics Approach   177
Basal Reading Programs   177
   Activity   179
Summary   182
   For Review and Discussion 183
   For Further Reading 184

7 Methods, Lessons, and Strategies in Teaching Reading — 186

Introduction   188
Concepts Related to Print   188
The Vocabulary of Reading Instruction   189
  Activity   190
Concepts Related to Storybooks   191
  Activity   192
Word Recognition   193
  Activities   196, 199
Metalinguistic Awareness   199
  Activities   200, 203
Metacomprehension   203
  Activities   204, 205
Comprehension   206
  Activities   212, 213, 214, 220
Summary   221
  For Review and Discussion   223
  For Further Reading   223

8 Approaches to Teaching Writing — 224

Introduction   226
What We Know About Writers and Writing   226
  Activity   228
TO THINK ABOUT: The Audience's Role in Communication   236
  Activity   238
The Process Approach to Teaching Writing   239
  Activity   248
Contrasting Modes of Instruction   248
  Activities   250, 253
Summary   253
  For Review and Discussion   254
  For Further Reading   255

9 Methods, Lessons, and Strategies for Teaching Writing — 256

Introduction   258
The Prewriting Stage   258
  Activity   262
TO THINK ABOUT: Discussion and Prewriting   262
  Activity   264

The Writing Stage   265
Lesson Plan: The Green Monster   268
The Rewriting Stage: Revising   269
TO THINK ABOUT: "Tidy" and "Messy" Writing—the Revision Process   274
　Activity   278
The Rewriting Stage: Editing   278
The Sharing/Publishing Stage   282
Summary   284
　For Review and Discussion   286
　For Further Reading   287

10 Language as Magic: The Language and Literacy Rich Classroom   288

Introduction   290
The Imaginative and Affective Use of Language in Early Childhood   290
What Can Happen in the Classroom   292
Teaching the Spoken Arts and Creative Dramatics   293
Lesson Plan: Focusing on Storytelling   294
Lesson Plan: Criteria for Storytellers   295
Lesson Plan: Practicing Storytelling   295
　Activity   297
Lesson Plan: Suggestions to Facilitate Role Playing   302
Lesson Plan: Objects   302
Using Creative Dramatics to Teach   307
Children's Literature   309
　Activity   312
TO THINK ABOUT: Detachment and Communication   317
Language Across the Curriculum: Using Thematic Units   324
　Activity   327
Summary   327
　For Review and Discussion   330
　For Further Reading   330

11 Grammar, Syntax, Usage, Handwriting, and Spelling   332

Introduction   334
Grammar, Syntax, and Usage   334
Handwriting   350
Spelling   356
Summary   365
　For Review and Discussion   367
　For Further Reading   368

12 Teaching Language Arts in the Multicultural Classroom
by Jean V. Yepes
370

Introduction: The Increasingly Diverse Student Population   372
Second Language Acquisition   374
Effective Language Arts Programs for Culturally Diverse Students   378
Structuring the Class to Help English as a Second Language Students   379
   Activities   380, 381, 382, 383
TO THINK ABOUT: Sharing Cultures   384
Strategies for Fostering Language Development in the Multicultural Classroom   385
Language Arts as a Way of Empowering Culturally Diverse Students   390
   Activities   395, 396
Summary   397
   For Review and Discussion   398
   For Further Reading   398

References   401

Glossary   415

Index   421

To Think Abouts

Autonomy in the Classroom   3
Underlying Assumptions in Teaching   3
Teacher/Student Collaboration   42
Culture and Communication   55
Teacher Talk: Directive or Collaborative   99
Underlying Assumptions in Emergent Literacy   160
Reflections on the Writing Process Approach   162
Reflections on the Language Experience Approach   165
Reflections on the Individual Reading Program Approach   167
Reflections on Reading Conferences   170
Reflections on Reading Workshops   171
Underlying Assumptions—Reading Readiness vs. Emergent Literacy   176
Underlying Assumptions: The Phonics Approach   177
The Audience's Role in Communication   236
Discussion and Prewriting   262
"Tidy" and "Messy" Writing—the Revision Process   274
Detachment and Communication   317
Sharing Cultures   384

Preface

Over a thirty-year teaching career, I have both observed and participated in the evolution of a holistic, collaborative, integrated approach to teaching language arts. This approach is the latest manifestation of an abiding impulse in education to base teaching methods on what I will call "rationalist" (sometimes called "cognitivist" or "constructivist") beliefs about the way human beings learn—particularly about the way we learn language and literacy. Hillocks (1986) traces some aspects of the holistic, collaborative, integrated approach to Rousseau. Many antecedents of this approach can be seen in the Progressive movement early in this century. Jeanette Veatch proposed a holistic, collaborative, integrated approach to teaching reading in the 1950s.

I believe that this approach keeps reappearing because of its essential rightness. Compared with traditional, skills emphasis approaches, it is more consistent with the way children acquire language and literacy before school age and outside school. Based on what we know about language and society, it empowers students, giving them the language skills needed to get on with their agendas.

I believe that in the past this approach has failed to become the predominant mode of teaching for two reasons. Proponents have not made enough of an effort to explain why teachers ought to adopt the approach. They have relied too much on explaining how it works and on infecting others with their enthusiasm. In this book I present a narrative of the way children acquire language and literacy. I try not to present a course in linguistics or learning theory but to present enough information so that the reader can understand why the holistic, collaborative, integrated approach is desirable.

Proponents have also too often emphasized the newness of the approach, sometimes insisting that it is categorically different from traditional methods of teaching and organizing the curriculum. They condemn the use of any material or methods identified as traditional. This can overwhelm both new teachers and experienced teachers who may be interested in making a gradual transition.

True, I state my bias toward the holistic, collaborative, integrated approach and treat this approach much more fully. True, I believe that there is a fundamental difference between the way skills emphasis teachers and holistic, collaborative teachers perceive teaching and learning. But I also discuss both approaches and acknowledge the accommodations possible between the two.

Furthermore, I present topics in a traditional format. There are chapters devoted explicitly and distinctly to oral language (speaking and listening), reading, written composition, and the "magical" language arts—choral reading, drama, poetry, and literature. Grammar, syntax, usage, handwriting, and spelling are treated separately and explicitly. As each new topic is treated I stress the relatedness of the areas of language arts from a teaching and learning point of view. After each topic is introduced, I discuss it from an integrated language arts perspective. Therefore, the book preserves that sense of order that many find attractive about the way language arts has been presented traditionally and moves to a new kind of order that grows out of the holistic, collaborative, integrated approach.

The idea that students represent many cultures is introduced in the context of language and literacy acquisition in the early chapters. In the last chapter, Jean Yepes informs us that multiculturalism is yet one more reason why the holistic, collaborative, integrated approach is desirable for teaching language arts in the elementary school. It suggests ways of using this approach in classrooms where children with different native languages and different cultures are present.

HOW THIS BOOK IS ORGANIZED

In chapter 1, I introduce two teachers—Michael, a teacher who uses a traditional skills emphasis approach, and Laura, a teacher who uses a holistic, collaborative, integrated approach. Commenting on their differing behaviors and attitudes, I point out the issues that define these two approaches.

In chapter 2, I present a narration of language acquisition and derive the characteristics of parent-child interactions that facilitate development. I then discuss how communities influence the way in which people use language and the differences between children's language experiences at home and in school. The purpose of this chapter is to show that the holistic, collaborative, integrated approach to teaching language arts in school reflects the kinds of interactions that seem to facilitate a particular kind of language behavior outside school. That particular kind of language behavior appears to facilitate literacy and school discourse practices. The holistic, collaborative, integrated approach continues these kinds of language related interactions with children who find them in their homes and introduces such interactions to children who are not accustomed to them.

Chapters 3, 4, and 5 deal with oral language. Chapter 3 introduces a communication model and the concept of communicative stress. I try to "unpack" the global notion of teaching and learning about oral language by discussing, in turn, listening, conversation, discussion, and speaking in a formal setting. In chapter 4, I discuss three topics that relate to the use of oral language in a small group setting—small group discussion, cooperative learning, and conflict resolution. In chapter 5, I discuss oral language from the standpoint of *use* (to inform, persuade, and so on). Numerous lessons in this chapter help to clarify the concept of language use and give practical suggestions for teaching oral language from this perspective as well.

Chapter 6 and 7 deal with reading. In chapter 6, I discuss emergent literacy (a concept consistent with the holistic, collaborative, integrated approach) and approaches to teaching reading that are consistent with it. I then discuss reading readiness (a concept consistent with the skills emphasis approach to teaching language arts) and approaches to teaching reading that are consistent with it. I finally discuss basal reading programs. In chapter 7, I present methods, lessons, and strategies for teaching aspects of reading. These include concepts related to print and story books, word recognition, metalinguistic awareness, metacomprehension, and comprehension.

Chapters 8 and 9 deal with written composition. The first part of chapter 8 describes the process known as "the writing cycle" and it describes the dimensions on which student writers can be expected to develop. The second part of chapter 8 deals with a holistic, collaborative, integrated approach to teaching writing—the process approach. Two other approaches are presented as well, the presentational mode, a directive, skills emphasis approach, and the environmental mode, an approach that is similar to cooperative learning. Chapter 9 presents many lessons and strategies organized under stages in the writing cycle.

Chapter 10 deals with the imaginative and effective uses of language. At this point when all the elements have been introduced, the *integrated* feature of the holistic, collaborative, integrated approach can finally be fully discussed. The final section in chapter 10 presents the concept of language across the curriculum, or the integrated perspective of teaching in the elementary school.

Chapter 11 deals with the form of language—grammar, syntax, and usage. It deals with aspects of form that are associated with writing—handwriting and spelling. Methods of teaching these important aspects of the language arts curriculum in the context of using language are presented.

Chapter 12, the final chapter, deals with an important factor in the present school scene. The presence of children whose native tongue is not English and whose culture is not that of the mainstream is becoming the rule rather than the exception. This chapter, written by Jean Yepes, discusses the challenges and opportunities presented by this situation.

ACKNOWLEDGMENTS

I am grateful to many people for their help in getting this book written. Nancy Myers and Pat Glinski typed cheerfully through many revisions. Laura Palka suggested ideas for lessons. Leslie Bookbinder and Gay Church worked on the bibliography. Gay Church assisted with permissions.

All the photographs were taken by Christina V. Bogan at the Red Jacket Academy, a Buffalo Public School, and the Fisher Price Endowed Early Childhood Research Center at the State University of New York at Buffalo. I am grateful to the faculty and students involved, especially Camille Boczar at Red Jacket and James Hoot at the Early Childhood Research Center. I wish to express my appreciation to the following reviewers, whose helpful suggestions and insight contributed greatly to the development of this book:

Peter Afflerbach, Emory University
Howard Blake, Temple University

Marguerite Bumpus, University of Rhode Island
Byron Byars, University of Arkansas
Maryanne Doyle, University of Connecticut
Susie Emond, Saginaw Valley State University
Shirley Ernst, Eastern Connecticut State University
Mary Renck Jalongo, Indiana University of Pennsylvania
Julie Jensen, University of Texas at Austin
Ann Nagel, University of San Diego
Driek Zirinsky, Boise State University

I am especially grateful to my wife, Mary Finn. Although her field is not language arts, we have developed many of the same ideas about education over many years. Many of *our* ideas appear in this book. Crediting her with editorial assistance, as we have done on the title page, most definitely understates her contribution. I could not have written this book without her.

CHAPTER 1

A Holistic, Collaborative, Integrated Approach to Teaching Language Arts

Introduction: The Relationship between Teachers' Beliefs and Practices
TO THINK ABOUT: Autonomy in the Classroom
Two Contrasting Approaches
TO THINK ABOUT: Underlying Assumptions in Teaching
Issues That Define Approaches
Summary
For Review and Discussion
For Further Reading

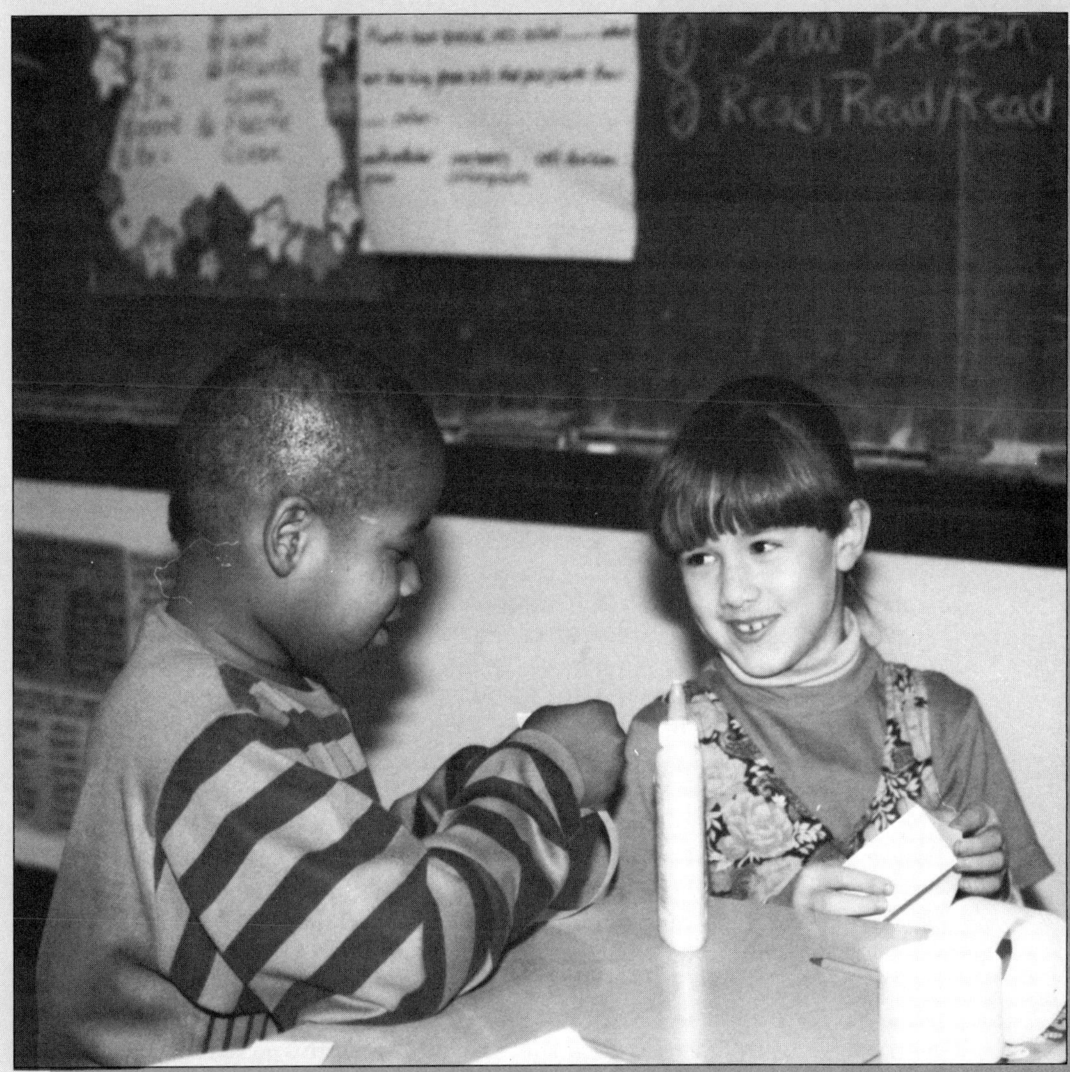
Read Read/Read

INTRODUCTION: THE RELATIONSHIP BETWEEN TEACHERS' BELIEFS AND PRACTICES

This book addresses three major areas of language arts education: the curriculum (*what* is taught), the methods of teaching (*how* it is taught), and the *beliefs* that determine both curriculum and methods.

As a teacher you will have plenty of guidance, if not outright direction, about *what* to teach. State and local curriculum planners, school boards, and administrators will lay out plans; parents, fellow teachers, textbook publishers, and students will all offer ideas. You will probably be given more suggestions about what to teach than you can possibly cover in any school year. These same sources may also give you suggestions about *how* to teach. As a result, you will constantly need to make decisions, to choose what you will teach and how you will teach. Those decisions will be based on what you believe.

Suppose you are a fifth-grade language arts teacher. There is universal agreement that spelling is a subject for which you are responsible, but opinion diverges significantly on exactly what and how to teach under the rubric of spelling. Should you give the students a list of spelling words? How many words? Which words? Or will you refrain from supplying lists and instead assign words that individual students misspell in their writing assignments as "spelling words"? Will you test students by reading the lists aloud, or by having students write them from memory? Or will you have students write paragraphs containing these words as you dictate? Will you teach spelling rules, or just ask students to memorize lists?

If you must make all these decisions about teaching spelling—a subject most people think of as well defined, uncomplicated, and straightforward—imagine the decisions you are faced with in teaching less well defined, more complex, and multifaceted subjects like reading, writing, literature, and drama.

In some schools, teachers have a great deal of autonomy; they seem to teach whatever they want and however they want. Such teachers have an enormous obligation to make intelligent decisions about curriculum and methods, and so they need to reflect on the validity of the beliefs that motivate their decisions. Even in these laissez-faire systems, however, teachers are often called upon to explain and defend what they are doing, and they must be able to articulate and defend the validity of their beliefs.

Many teachers have, or feel they have, much less autonomy. They feel obliged to cover the material in the curriculum guide or textbooks and to use methods prescribed by principals or school boards. However, even these teachers are responsible in the end for the decisions that affect their classrooms. Teachers who believe that their teaching could be made more effective by changes in curriculum or in methods have an obligation to make their concerns known and to argue as skillfully as they can for the changes they feel are needed. In order to do this, they must clearly understand the beliefs that motivate them, and they must be able to articulate and defend these beliefs.

Teachers sometimes go wrong in one of two ways:

They do not reflect, and so they are not clear about their beliefs; their decisions may be inconsistent as a result.

They accept a system of beliefs that does not stand up to observation and experience, and so they consistently make less than optimal decisions.

In this chapter I will describe two approaches to teaching language arts, examine the beliefs that motivate these two approaches, and indicate which of these two approaches I recommend. In chapter 2 I will present the evidence that has convinced me to favor one approach over the other.

TO THINK ABOUT

Autonomy in the Classroom

Based on your experience as a teacher (or as an elementary-school student who observed language arts teachers at first hand for at least eight years), respond quickly and informally to the following questions.

1. How much autonomy do you believe language arts teachers have in determining the curriculum and methods in their classrooms?
2. Have you observed teachers who were given prescribed curricula and/or methods which they felt were not in the best interest of their students? How did they respond? How should teachers address this problem?
3. Have you observed teachers defending decisions they made autonomously? How should teachers defend such decisions?

Understanding: Your beliefs regarding what you teach and how you teach are as important as what you teach and how you teach.

TWO CONTRASTING APPROACHES

Michael Knight and Laura Morgan are fourth-grade teachers.[1] Each has been teaching fourth grade for about ten years. Michael and Laura have very different beliefs, and as a result they teach different things and use different methods. The following excerpts are taken from interviews in which these two teachers were asked about their language arts programs.

TO THINK ABOUT

Underlying Assumptions in Teaching

As you read the statements made by Michael and Laura, try to discover the underlying assumptions that result in such different teaching styles. See if you discover all or

---

[1] Michael and Laura are fictitious personages whose responses were created to represent two points of view that are widely held among teachers.

some of the three characteristics that I will identify as dividing these two teachers in the discussion later in this chapter.

You may want to read this discussion first and return to the following interviews. This will enable you to take note of the statements the teachers make that reveal these characteristics.

Michael—A Skills Emphasis Approach

On Teaching Speaking and Listening
There is so much to teach in speaking, like pronunciation and grammar and speaking in front of a group—you know, public speaking. I pretty much stick with the textbook because there is so much to teach I'd never cover it all otherwise.

I recently taught a lesson to get the students to think about the importance of speaking distinctly and listening carefully. They worked in pairs—a sender and a listener. The sender read a list of words and the listener wrote down what she or he heard. The lists were made of words that sound like other words like *graft* and *cost* (which sound similar to *raft* and *cast*). The interesting part was that the sender and listener were seated back to back so the listener could not see the speaker and all the senders were reading different lists at the same time. This gave me an opportunity to talk about not only the importance of speaking distinctly and listening carefully, but also the things that make listening difficult, like noise and not looking at your listener.

The program also has exercises for practicing listening to visualize, listening for rhythm, tone, and mood; listening for main ideas, for bias, for details, and a lot of things like that. I don't even cover all of it in a year because there is so much to cover in

Laura—A Holistic, Collaborative, Integrated Approach

On Teaching Speaking and Listening
We do a lot of small groups and cooperative learning [see chapter 4] so they get a lot of practice in speaking and listening. It takes a lot of effort for them to learn to work in small groups. You've got to see to it that silent children contribute and that they listen and respond to each other instead of everyone talking to themselves. It takes a lot of work.

Of course in small groups they get practice in conversation as well and one student often has to tell the rest of the class what his or her group did or what they came up with. And then they are addressing a large group. A lot of times small-group projects can easily become panel discussions or reports. So you have talking and listening in a lot of situations. This gives them the experience of talking to a large audience with the security of being part of a panel.

It's hard to talk about listening and speaking separately. All the small-group activities I just talked about involve listening and talking. When students give reports in a fairly formal situation, I mean prepared reports on projects they've done, we talk about listening—getting the main idea and so on, sort of note taking on an informal level. Of course, whenever we have reading and writing that there is just not enough time to cover the listening strand of the program every week.

On Teaching Reading

I have my class divided into three groups for reading and I use different levels of the reader for the three groups according to ability. I use a second-grade reader, a fourth-grade reader, and a fifth-grade reader in the three groups.

In my two top groups I begin by introducing new words and supplying background information for the story. Then I ask a few questions that the students will be able to answer by reading the story. All of this is in the teacher's guide. After they've read the story silently, I ask the students to read orally those portions of the text that answer the questions that were posed before reading. Then we cover other comprehension questions through discussion and sometimes through further oral reading from the text. There are also questions to get at the students' feelings about the story.

Afterward, the kids work on some skill, like dividing words into syllables or recognizing common prefixes and suffixes. They usually write these lessons while I'm teaching the other groups. This calls for a lot of correcting of papers, but some of the brighter kids help with that so it's manageable.

In the low group I start with reviewing some letter-sound generalization, such as the sound usually represented by the letters *ch*. The following story always has words that demonstrate the rule. Then I proceed pretty much in the same way as I do in the higher groups. Since I use the same basal for all three groups the lessons are

a videotape or a skit or play, we're talking about listening.

On Teaching Reading

I used basal readers (the usual three groups) for the first five years I taught. That's how I was taught to teach reading and that's how I did it, and I always thought it was pretty successful. Then I started to experiment with reading workshops.

Students read from books they bring from home or the library or the classroom library. Sometimes they read books "published" by their classmates from the classroom library. [See Figure 1.1] They write responses to what they are reading in the form of a letter to me once a week. I have brief conferences with them individually where they do a little oral reading and talk about the books. I try to help them with problems as they arise and plan ways to share their books with the class. These workshops often begin with a short lesson where I talk about things of general interest to the class.

Of course, I try to stay alert for times students are having trouble with word recognition in reading conferences. The other day one of my brighter students was pronouncing *tagged* "tay-ged" and I talked a little about syllable division and inflectional endings and so on with words like *tagged, ripped,* and *hopped.* I know she caught on and I think she'll remember it. If I had taught a ten-minute lesson to the entire class on the rule for doubling final consonants when adding *-ed* simply because it came next in the teacher's

Figure 1.1 Typical "published" books in a second-grade writing process classroom. (*Source: We Went to Como Park*, by Kevin McMullen. Reproduced by permission of Patricia McMullen; *Me and Bonnie*, by Rebecca Onello. Reproduced by permission of Cynthia Onello; and *Our Charlotte's Web Book*, by Alyssa Hulse and Nichol Mroz. Re-

quite similar. There's just a little less phonics in the higher-level books.

On Teaching Writing

I teach penmanship every day for about fifteen minutes. I just follow the lessons in the book. I keep after five or six kids who really need help. For the rest of the kids, I just look over their papers to see if they are doing the lessons carefully.

I have them write two or three times a week. For example, the week before Mother's Day we made Mother's Day cards. I used a technique the kids really

guide, I think it would have gone in one ear and out the other.

On Teaching Writing

I have writing workshop three days a week and basically use Graves's writing process approach [described in chapter 8].

I have conferences with each child every fifth or so school day. Each child has a folder and I look to see that he or she is producing each week. Then we look at one piece. The first thing I look for and comment on is what meaning the student wants to love. It's called "popcorn." I wrote the word *Mother* on the board in a circle and kids called out words that *Mother* made them think of, like *happy, nice, hugs, love,* and so on. [See Figure 1.2.] Then they each made a card with a picture and a message using words from the board. Of course, I went around to see if they were printing neatly and using the correct capitals and periods and so on. I didn't collect this, but I usually collect their writing and correct it.

I've got this great list of topics. Most of the time I give the students two or three to choose from. When I was teaching descriptive writing, for example, I suggested that each describe a big snake; a homeless, hungry dog; or a pet that the child owns.

I don't correct every paper they turn in because I don't have time. I probably correct more than half of them. It takes a long time to correct papers when you have twenty-seven kids. After I correct the papers I have the kids rewrite them and I put the ones that are really good and done neatly on the bulletin board.

When students have trouble with grammar I use grammar exercises or, if their punctuation is wrong, I use workbook exercises so they can work

relay to the reader. I try to make a statement summarizing the piece so the child knows I'm paying attention and am trying to understand.

Sometimes the child asks for help on a particular piece. I keep track of what the child wants to work on or what I want him or her to work on with a checklist stapled inside the folder. It could be opening sentences or paragraphing or complete sentences or whatever.

Students also conference with one another. They mostly try out what they've written on an audience. They listen, tell what they don't understand, and comment on inconsistencies. Again, it takes a lot of teaching to get them to do this effectively.

An important part of this is that they "publish" things at regular intervals. Publishing gives you a chance to make the really important point that spelling and punctuation and handwriting are important because if there are a lot of problems, the published piece fails. You know, the reader is distracted from the message by all the problems.

I think both the writing and reading workshops work because the students are choosing what they read

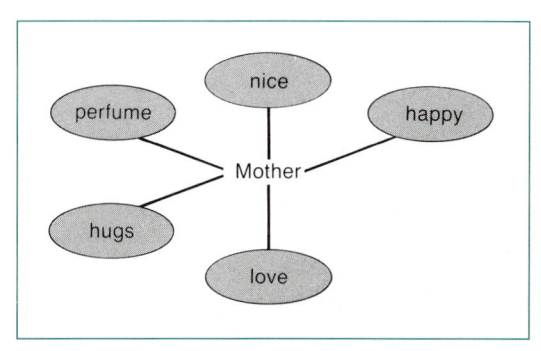

Figure 1.2 The "popcorn" technique

on it. It's a shame that there are not better diagnostic tests of writing. I mean with reading you can pinpoint just where a kid is, like in their level of comprehension or vocabulary, but in writing it's hard to assign a grade level. Of course you can spot kids who are not getting the lessons from the English book and give them extra lessons from the teacher's guide or workbook to reinforce their learning.

On Using Textbooks

There's so much for them to learn. I'd miss half of it if I didn't stick with the textbooks pretty much. I mean I don't do all of it. You'd need three years in fourth grade to cover everything the textbooks cover. But it's *activities* you skip, not *concepts* or *skills*.

But I do stick to the textbooks—the reader and speller and the English book—because there's so much to teach them and then getting it in the right order. I know there are teachers who don't use textbooks much, but I'd be worried that I didn't cover everything or that I was trying to teach something they weren't ready for.

It's so important that you don't ask kids to do things they are not ready for. I mean it's obvious that students should learn to spell short, frequent words before they learn long, rare words, but if I were to have my own spelling program, I wouldn't know what order to put many words in. The same in reading. You should teach the most frequent phonics rules first, but after a while, you're not sure which one to teach next. Textbooks put the skills students need into the right order.

Teacher's guides also give you good ideas to use with students who

and write about. The experts call it "ownership." I think it makes a big difference.

Once children believe they can write on anything (and they don't believe that at first), it's amazing what they think of to write about and how interested they are in what they are writing about.

On Using Textbooks

Sure I use the textbooks. Of all of them I use the spellers most religiously. I'm convinced that they'd learn to spell most of the words on their weekly spelling list through massive experience with reading and writing, but the parents expect a spelling program and I just don't think it would be worth the effort to try to convince them that we could do without it.

I've got six students using the handwriting workbooks they use in our district. These students' writing is just beyond the pale, so I see to it that they do regular practice.

I use the English books too. It's funny how in writing you suddenly notice that a lot of the students are having the same problem. I don't know whether they all start having the problem or you start noticing it. But when I see eight of them are having trouble with run-on sentences, or punctuating a series, or whatever, I form a group (sometimes the whole class) and use some of their sentences to demonstrate the problem and then I use lessons from the book.

I still use the basals occasionally. For example, I've been trying reciprocal teaching where the students are ahead of the others or who work faster than the others. They're often left with nothing to do but read a book. Teacher's guides often give you ideas about things they can do to reinforce the skills that the others are working on.

On Teaching Drama, Poetry, and So On

Oh yes, we have some dramatics, poetry, choral speaking, and even mime. I do it as enrichment with my top reading group. They don't need the drill in the basics or the review that the other two groups need, so I have them work on acting out a story or choral reading or something like that, especially when I have a teacher's aide who can supervise them.

Right now I have my top reading group rehearsing a play for Martin Luther King's birthday. They're really getting into it. They'll probably do it for the class and maybe we'll invite the other fourth-grade class.

On Students Learning from One Another

Sure, I have the brighter kids work with the slower ones. For example, I had two kids who did not recognize all of the Dolch sight words—in fourth grade! Each of them knew most words but got stuck on around fifteen of them. So I gave each of them a set of cards with their hard words and when one of the top group finished work early they'd work on these kids' hard words with them. You know, flash card style. By the middle of October, both these kids knew all 220 words.

I've tried to have some of the best readers work with poor spellers the same way—have them give them their

read parts of selections (usually nonfiction) and then practice summarizing, questioning, predicting what will come, and clarifying puzzling parts of the text. When a lesson calls for students' each having a copy of the same text, basals come in handy.

On Teaching Drama, Poetry, and So On

Oh yes, we have drama, puppetry, poetry, and all that. Language is magic. It's not just to convey information. It's magic. It seems to me that effective use of language is often the result of loving language. When you love a thing you pay attention to it. You want to know how it works and want to make it work better. So I think the students should all get liberal doses of theater, poetry, and literature, not after they have mastered skills, but as a method of getting them to want to master the skills.

On Students Learning from One Another

I'm tempted to say that's what it's all about; they learn everything from one another. But as a matter of fact, they learn a lot from me. Getting small groups to work takes a lot of very directive teaching from me. Besides that, I make a lot of assignments. I teach a lot of lessons to groups or to the whole class and I do a lot of direct teaching in conferences.

But they do learn a lot from one another. I have two girls right now. One is the best writer I've had in eleven years, and the other rarely writes a whole page, but I've seen each of them give the other useful words and then go over them. But I don't do that as much as I'd like because it's kind of complicated to find time when both of them have all their work finished at the same time. Weeks go by when I can't arrange it, so the poor spellers can't count on it. I haven't done it consistently enough to know how much good it does.

suggestions in student writing conferences. Something as simple as pointing out that one of them wrote *going* when she meant *goes* or when reading her story aloud the sentence she said was not the sentence she had written on the paper. That's exactly what I do when I'm trying to get them to edit.

ISSUES THAT DEFINE APPROACHES

These interviews are fairly bursting with provocative remarks. I will be returning to Michael and Laura again and again. For now, I want to address issues that seem to separate them.

❖ Directive Versus Collaborative Teaching Styles

Michael thinks of teaching in terms of lessons suggested by textbooks and taught with him in charge. Students talk to Michael, and Michael talks to students. They perform; he evaluates. Students do not talk to one another. Michael's next lesson is the next lesson in the book. He believes that if "we all keep after them [that is, teach them each lesson in the book] they'll be all right." Michael is consistently directive.

Laura is consistently collaborative. She encourages her students to try writing (as well as speaking, listening, and reading) and she tries to help them (work, labor, and collaborate with them) as they encounter problems. She places high importance on the children's being able to choose their reading material and their writing topics. She thinks of teaching, listening, and speaking in terms of what students learn in discussion with one another as much as with her. She emphasizes how children learn from one another in reading and writing.

But Laura is not nondirective. She acknowledges that you have to teach children to work in small groups and comments on how much work that takes. She suggests things for students to work on in their writing folder and she expects them to do so. However, it is important to notice that although Laura can be quite directive, much of her directive behavior originates in a collaborative situation.

Viewing Learner as Passive Versus Active

Directive and collaborative teaching styles arise from teachers' beliefs about the way humans learn. Directive teaching comes out of a tradition that views learners as subjects that are acted upon by teachers or the environment. According to this view teachers must decide what to teach next, and if they teach it right, the students will learn that thing. This tradition is closely identified with the stimulus-response-reward paradigm of learning. The teachers present stimuli, reward desired responses, and fail to reward (or punish) undesired responses. When only the desired response is elicited by the stimulus, learning has occurred.

Collaborative teaching comes out of a tradition that views learners as actors with curiosity, initiative, and the ability to select and organize stimuli in the environment and make sense out of it in order to accomplish some tasks that they have set for themselves. According to this view, teachers should observe learners and figure out what task they are trying to accomplish or what the learner is trying to organize and make sense out of in order to accomplish the task. Being more experienced than students (farther along the path of learning), teachers can help learners direct their attention to things they appear to have missed and help them organize and make sense of those aspects of the environment that will help them accomplish their task.

Michael's teaching is consistent with the idea that learners are essentially passive, whereas Laura's teaching is consistent with the belief that learners are essentially active.

Viewing Language Learning as a Teacher-to-Student Process Versus an Interactional Group Process

While Michael repeatedly refers to a teacher-to-student teaching model, where the possessor of knowledge imparts that knowledge to an individual who lacks it, Laura views learning as something that happens in social interactions. She believes that the knowledge, skills, and attitudes that are important in a literate society are sought by learners when, through social interaction, they become aware of them and of their usefulness. In this situation learners try their hand at what they see others doing around them. A teacher's job is to promote a classroom community where literacy skills will be valued and to recognize what the children are trying to do and collaborate with them in doing it.

Laura believes that students are motivated by their peers as well as by the teacher to "try literacy" through reading each other's writing and sharing their reading. Accomplished students as well as teachers collaborate with learners in mastering tasks—recognizing words, writing a story, or fixing a letter that is written backward. The accomplished student in one situation may be the learner in the next.

✤ Atomistic Versus Holistic Focus

Michael thinks of teaching language arts as teaching students language—not a foreign language but the students' own narrative tongue. Teachers who see their jobs as teaching children their native tongue tend to focus on pronunciation, usage, and vocabulary in oral language and on phonics, spelling, handwriting, grammar, usage, and punctuation in written language. These teachers focus on the *forms* of language rather than the *functions* that are performed with language.

Laura thinks of teaching language arts as teaching students to *use* their native language. The focus changes when teachers see their job as teaching children to use language rather than teaching them the forms of language. A teacher whose objective is to improve a student's ability to persuade others will focus on the effectiveness of the student's message rather than on his or her grammar and spelling. Laura does not ignore her students' grammatical usage, spelling, and so on. Nonstandard spelling and punctuation in a letter, for example, may make it less persuasive; so Laura works with students on spelling and punctuation. But it is seen as a secondary task. Teaching language—pronunciation, grammar, and so on, is always done in the context of improving a child's facility to use language—to persuade or to inform.

Michael starts each response by referring to form, and he focuses on form throughout his interview. He always refers to the effective use of language as something that results from getting the form correct. Laura begins her responses by referring to the effective use of language, and she focuses on the effective use of language throughout her interview. She always discusses attention to form as part of or something that grows out of attempting to use language effectively.

Focusing on form causes teachers to view language as bits and pieces—letters, sounds, words, and sentences at one level; handwriting, usage, spelling, and punctuation at another level; and reading, writing, speaking, and listening at yet another level.

When teachers respond to uses of language—to inform or to be informed, for example—what they notice first about a child's language is whether or not it is informative, not whether the words are pronounced correctly or if the periods are in the right place. Focusing on use results in a holistic approach to teaching language arts.

Michael's view of language is atomistic, and Laura's view of language is holistic. These views are reflected in their teaching.

Laura focuses on effective use of language. For her, attention to form (the bits and pieces) always grows out of attempts to use language effectively. This has come to be known as the top-down view of language and language arts teaching.

✤ Integration of the Language Arts

Michael and Laura are both interested in integrating the language arts. Anyone who has taught language arts or who has even thought about teaching it realizes that it is hard to separate listening and speaking in any but the most formal settings, and realizes that the tasks of speaking and writing have a great deal in common, as do the tasks of listening and reading.

But because of the way Michael and Laura view teaching language arts, there is a difference. Michael regards such things as teaching rhyming words—which might have application to writing poems, spelling, and listening—as integrating language arts. In other words, there are bits and pieces that appear in several areas of language arts, and to learn them in one area helps children to learn them in others. Laura regards the overlapping goals of effective comprehension and communication in oral and written language to be the source of integration of the language arts.

In terms of the categories developed in this discussion, Michael sees integration of the language arts in terms of form, atomistically, from the bottom. Laura sees integration of the language arts in terms of use, holistically, from the top. Throughout the remainder of this book, the word *integrated* in regard to the language arts program will be used in that sense.

Michael's and Laura's beliefs represent two traditions. Michael's beliefs result in a way of teaching language arts that is variously known as an atomistic, behaviorist, or **skills emphasis approach.** I shall refer to it as the skills emphasis approach. Laura's beliefs result in a way of teaching language arts that is variously known as a holistic, cognitivist, or meaning emphasis approach. Recently, the term **whole language** has been used to refer to a philosophy and approach that grows out of the tradition that Laura represents. However, I will refer to it as a **holistic, collaborative, integrated approach.**

Over the years the traditions represented by Michael and Laura have both influenced the teaching of language arts in the schools. Teachers who are aware of these two traditions see them at work in the curriculum, methods, and materials for teaching presented or suggested to them by boards of education, parents, fellow teachers, teacher preparation courses, principals, supervisors, textbook publishers, and students. It is up to each of us to reflect on what we are asked to do, what we do, and what we should do as teachers. How does our experience as teachers inform our beliefs about the nature of learning? Are our practices consistent with our beliefs? Schoen (1984) refers to this process as reflecting in action.

I recommend the holistic, collaborative, integrated approach, Laura's approach. I will explain why in the following pages. I hope readers will consider my arguments in light of their knowledge and experience and continue to reflect on their beliefs and practices and the consistency between the two as they teach language arts to children. I hope the following chapters will help readers to do this.

Summary

What you teach and how you teach reflect your beliefs about learning. In this chapter I presented two teachers with very different beliefs talking about what they teach and how they teach language arts. These teachers represent two approaches. Michael tends to be directive; he tends to view the learner as passively awaiting instruction; he views learning as a teacher-to-student process. Michael focuses on teaching the building blocks of language arts. As a result his teaching concentrates on the form of language arts such as letters, sounds, spelling, and punctuation. This is an atomistic approach.

Laura's teaching style is collaborative. She reponds to the learners' curiosity, initiative, and ability to organize and select stimuli in the environment in order to accomplish tasks they have set for themselves. Laura views learning as a collaborative group process. She focuses on students' ability to use language to inform and persuade. Her first concern is whether the child's language is effective—whether it is informative or persuasive—rather than on whether the child's pronunciation or spelling is correct. This is a holistic approach. Laura regards the overlapping goals of effective comprehension and communication in oral and written language to be the source of integration of the language arts.

Michael represents a skills approach to teaching language arts. Laura represents a holistic, collaborative, integrated approach to teaching language arts.

I endorse the holistic, collaborative, integrated approach to teaching language arts, and I urge the reader to begin to reflect on her or his beliefs about learning.

For Review and Discussion

1. Find examples in the interviews that show Michael to be directive and atomistic in his approach and Laura to be holistic and collaborative.

2. Whose style are you most comfortable with? Why? Write your responses to these questions and refer to them as you progress through this book. Note whether your answers change or whether you develop better reasons for your opinions.

For Further Reading

Ashcroft, L. (1987). Defusing "empowering": The what and the why. *Language Arts, 64,* 142–156.

Buckley, M. (1986). When teachers decide to integrate the language arts. *Language Arts, 63,* 369–377.

Canterford, B. (1991). The "new" teacher: Participant and facilitator. *Language Arts, 68,* 286–291.

Clarke, M. (1987). Don't blame the system: Constraints on "whole language" reform. *Language Arts, 64,* 384–396.

Crouse, P., & Davey, M. (1989). Collaborative learning: Insights from our children. *Language Arts, 66,* 756–766.

Fine, E. S. (1987). Marbles lost, marbles found: Collaborative production of text. *Language Arts, 64,* 474–487.

Sumara, D., & Walker, L. (1991). The teacher's role in whole language. *Language Arts, 68,* 276–285.

CHAPTER 2

Support for a Holistic, Collaborative, Integrated Approach to Teaching Language Arts

Introduction: A Social View
  of Learning
An Interactional View of
  Language Acquisition
  Activity
Parent-Child Interactions That
  Facilitate Development
Homes, Communities,
  and Language

  Activity
Oral Language at School
TO THINK ABOUT: Teacher/
  Student Collaboration
Integrating the Language Arts
  Activity
Summary
For Review and Discussion
For Further Reading

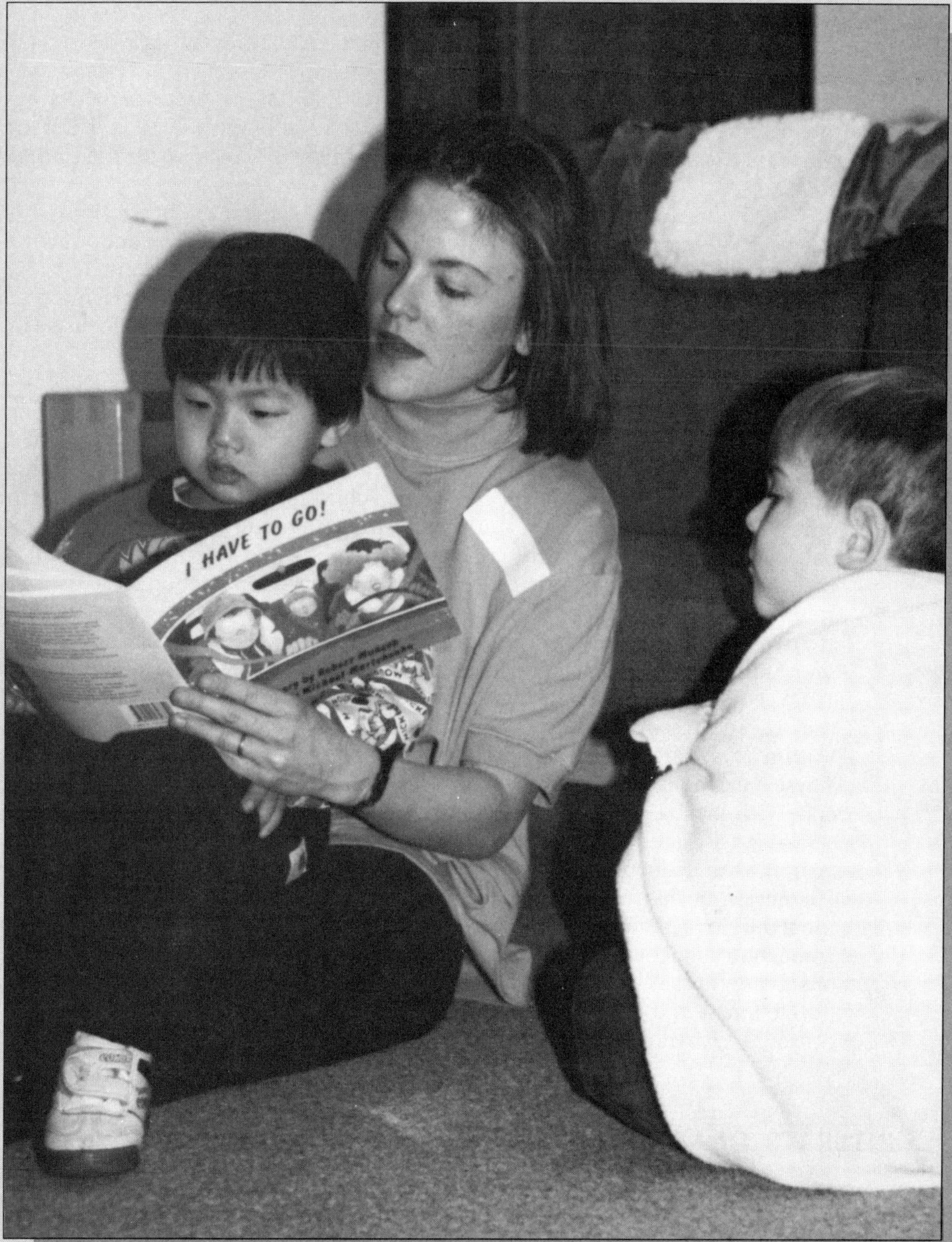
I HAVE TO GO!

INTRODUCTION: A SOCIAL VIEW OF LEARNING

The holistic, collaborative model of children's acquisition of knowledge and language is consistent with the ideas of Vygotsky (1896–1934), a Russian psychologist and educator who first became influential in America when his monograph *Thought and Language* was published in English in 1962. Later, in 1978, another collection of his essays was published as a book entitled *Mind and Society*.

According to Vygotsky, meaning develops in society in interaction with other persons and later becomes internalized by individuals. The act of pointing is an example. Extending one's finger may be a random or meaningless act; but if one extends a finger *at* something and intends to direct the attention of others toward the object, the act has meaning. Such meaning can only arise in interaction with others.

Vygotsky suggests that this meaning arises when a child tries unsuccessfully to grasp an object and the act is interpreted by others as the child's directing their attention. Soon the child associates his or her gesture with the resulting behavior of others, and the gesture takes on meaning. The crucial elements of this example are that meaning is not created in a child's mind and then conveyed to others; instead, meaning arises in social interaction and then becomes established in the child's mind. This is a central tenet of Vygotsky's cognitive theory: that interpersonal (social) processes become intrapersonal (mental) processes.

Vygotsky's theory of cognitive development and his theory of instruction stem from the idea that children can solve more difficult problems and employ more difficult concepts in collaboration with others than they can alone.

Vygotsky calls the difference between what children can do alone and what they can do in collaboration with others the **zone of proximal development.** Within this zone, new concepts are developing through social interactions. These concepts have not yet been internalized and, therefore, the child cannot cope with them alone.

Vygotsky defines *learning* as interaction with others in solving problems or dealing with concepts that one is not capable of solving or dealing with alone. His notion of *instruction* is to identify the child's zone of proximal development and to present problems and tasks to the child which he or she can work through in collaboration with peers or teachers. When children are then capable of solving this set of problems by themselves, they have reached a new level of development and the zone of proximal development will also have changed; they will have moved to a higher level.

AN INTERACTIONAL VIEW OF LANGUAGE ACQUISITION

In the following pages you will find an overview of what is known about language development. Observations of preschool children with their parents reveal that parents of children who tend to be successful in school appear to assume that their children are active learners and that learning is a collaborative, interactional process. They take a holistic, collaborative approach to their children's language and literacy development, focusing on the meaning rather than on the form of communication.

❖ Early Acquisition of Communication Strategies

Infants begin life as part of society. From birth, children appear to act out of a special relationship to other humans as distinct from all other objects in their new environment. Only hours after birth, children react differently to spoken language than to other sounds—even rhythmic sounds like music (Eimas et al., 1971). Infants show more interest in people than in inanimate objects (Snow, 1977). In the first several weeks of life, children show a preference for looking at human faces and respond differently to familiar and unfamiliar faces. Infants direct their earliest and most elaborate spontaneous behavior toward people (Trevarthen, 1979).

❖ Emergence of Conversation

The emergence of conversation can be traced to the first few weeks of life. From birth the parent is attentive to the gestures, vocalizations, and changes of gaze initiated by the child and responds to them. These "initiation-response interactions" are the beginning of conversation. Kadisha may fling her hands up near her face, and her mother imitates her and says, "Whoops!" Kadisha spits up milk, and her mother wipes her mouth saying, "What a little piggy!" In a further development, both parties begin to focus their attention on some aspect of the environment. The parent looks at the infant and, following the child's gaze, points at, touches, or picks up the objects the child is looking at. This kind of interaction is called a **proto-conversation.**

Parents use speech in their contributions to proto-conversation. In repeated "conversations" revolving around the routines of feeding, changing, and bathing, words are frequently matched with ongoing activities. These interactions of a child with his or her parents are obviously important to the development of the child's communicative ability. At the same time, the child is making other discoveries about communication.

❖ The Emergence of Meaningful, Intentional, and Conventional Communication

Meaningful but Unintentional Communication

The cries, gurgles, coos, and vocalization of newborn infants are undoubtedly instinctual. Although they may have no intentional meaning for the child, parents constantly watch for meaningful signs. When Anthony cries, does he need a clean diaper? Does he want to be held? Does he need to be burped? When Sarah coos, is she happy to see Mommy? Does she feel comfortable in her fresh diaper? Does she like being cuddled? Parents guess at the meaning of whatever signs they read in the child's behavior, and they act on their guesses. Mothers of very young infants often believe that they can distinguish between a cry of hunger, a cry of discomfort, and "just crying."

Researchers and observers (Buckhalt et al., 1978; Cross, 1977; and Gleason, 1977) describe this stage as one where the child communicates without intending to communicate. The adult imposes meaning on the sounds and behavior of the child and responds to these meanings with appropriate behavior. Child-initiated behaviors are followed by parental responses in regular and repeated patterns. Soon the child begins to act as if he or she has caught on to the relationship between behaviors he or she initiates and the response of the adult.

Meaningful and Intentional Communication

In time, a profound change occurs in these communication interactions between parents and children. Children cry *because* they want their diapers changed; they coo and smile *because* they feel warm and dry and safe in their mother's arms; they look from their mother's eyes to the toy on the floor *because* they want her to look there too. A great watershed in the development of language has occurred; the child *intends* to communicate. As early as six weeks, parents begin to interpret the child's facial expressions and changes of gaze as both meaningful and intentional.

Michael A. K. Halliday (1975), in a careful study of his own child, determined that Nigel learned to accomplish several different purposes, functions, or uses—at first through intentional communicative behavior, and later through language. For example, Nigel learned to get things done for himself (the instrumental function), to control the behavior of others (the regulatory function), and to initiate and maintain contact with others (the interactional function). Halliday identified a total of six uses of language. Since Halliday's study, several authors have proposed classification systems for the uses of language. The system used in this book was proposed by Wells (1973). It includes the following five uses: to inform, persuade, express emotion, imagine, and engage in transactions and rituals.

In discovering uses of communication and mastering them, children "learn how to mean." But they have not necessarily acquired language yet. Smiles, frowns, gestures, and vocalization may communicate, but they are not language.

The Emergence of Unconventional Language

Early communicative behavior relies heavily on vocalization. Language begins when a particular vocalization takes on a particular meaning (or meanings). When little Sarah begins to say *uh, uh* when she wants to be picked up and *ba* when she wants milk, another monumental event has occurred. She is using an arbitrary symbol to communicate meaning. The vocal signal *uh, uh* has no connection with the act it elicits, except that the child and caretaker have come to an unspoken agreement that *uh, uh* means "pick me up." That is language, in a sense, but there is one more hurdle to jump.

Although the child's communicative behavior is both meaningful and intentional, it is not conventional. Children are born into societies that have language. There are conventional symbols in each society for expressing meanings such as "pick me up" and "give me milk."

The Emergence of Language: Meaningful, Intentional, and Conventional Communication

Soon, however, children apparently notice that everyone around them has a set of agreed-upon arbitrary vocal symbols for certain meanings that is different from their own. Sarah abandons *uh, uh* in favor of *up* and *ba* in favor of *milk*. Her communicative behavior then possesses all the characteristics of human language. It is meaningful, intentional, and conventional. Another magnificent accomplishment for a twenty-four-month old!

ACTIVITY

Collect examples of infant communication that can be classified as:

1. meaningful but unintentional
2. meaningful and intentional (but not language)
3. unconventional language
4. conventional language

Collect examples of adult communications that can be classified as:

1. meaningful but unintentional
2. meaningful and intentional (but not language)
3. unconventional language
4. conventional language

Notice that proficient adults do not abandon forms of communication that they acquire early. Instead they acquire a greater range of communication options and exercise greater control over which options to use to get communication jobs done.

♣ Some Generalizations

Notice that as infants pass from unintentional but meaningful communication to conventional communication

- the process is collaborative rather than directive;
- the learner is viewed as active rather than passive;
- the focus is on use or function rather than form; and
- learning is viewed as holistic rather than atomistic.

The process described above is reenacted again and again in language learning throughout life. Children first learn what they can do with the functions of language, and they invent ways to accomplish these functions. Next, they discover that there are conventional ways of accomplishing the functions, and they adopt these conventions. The parent's job (and later the teacher's job) is

- to provide an atmosphere where communication is encouraged and where new functions of communication (and later language) are discovered, and
- to provide a model for conventional spoken language and help children adopt conventions when they are ready.

In a literate society children soon learn the use and function of writing, and they invent ways to accomplish these tasks. Next, they discover that there are conventional ways to do things with writing, and they adopt these conventions. The parent's job (and later the teacher's job) is

- to provide an atmosphere where written communication is encouraged and where new uses of written language are discovered, and
- to provide a model for conventional written language and help children adopt conventions when they are ready.

PARENT-CHILD INTERACTIONS THAT FACILITATE DEVELOPMENT

After the onset of language the process of developing communication skills continues. The following transcriptions of toddlers interacting with their parents provide further insights into children's language development. As you read each exchange, think about the following questions before proceeding to read the discussion that follows the transcription.

1. What can the child do with language?
2. How is the parent helping the child
   a. to communicate the matter at hand
   b. to learn more about effective communication?

Mark at Twenty-three Months
Present: Mark—aged twenty-three months; Helen—aged nine months; and Mother
[Mark is looking in a mirror and sees reflections of himself and his mother.]
  Mark: Mummy. Mummy.
Mother: What?
  Mark: There . . . there Mark.
Mother: Is that Mark?
  Mark: Mummy.
Mother: Mm.
  Mark: Mummy.
Mother: Yes that's Mummy.
  Mark: Mummy. Mummy.
Mother: Mm.

>   Mark: There Mummy. Mummy. There ... Mark there.
>   Mother: Look at Helen. She's going to sleep. (long pause)
>   *[Mark can see birds in the garden.]*
>   Mark: Birds Mummy.
>   Mother: Mm.
>   Mark: Jubs. (Mark's word for birds)
>   Mother: What are they doing?
>   Mark: Jubs bread.
>   Mother: Oh look. They're eating the berries, aren't they?
>   Mark: Yeh.
>   Mother: That's their food. They have berries for dinner.
>   Mark: Oh. (Wells, 1981, p. 102)

Mark's Performance

Mark initiates the conversation, introduces new topics, and responds to Mother's contributions. He has moved beyond the earliest stages of language use in that his language performs several functions at once. His whole conversation is transactional; it establishes and maintains contact. At times he is also informative. He has clearly begun to adopt the conventions of language. Most of his words are English words. He has begun to use more than one word per utterance and, therefore, syntax (word order) is present.

Parent's Role in Mark's Communication

Mark's mother's utterances are simple in form and restricted to topics arising from the immediate context. She particularly comments on topics Mark introduces. She follows the child's lead by asking questions, restating what Mark has said, and adding new information to support and extend the topics Mark has introduced. This practice is called "leading from behind" (Wells, 1981) or "scaffolding" (Applebee & Langer, 1984). Notice that when Mother introduces a topic ("Look at Helen."), Mark makes no response and she drops it.

Researchers (Garnica, 1977) have questioned mothers about their intention to teach their children in conversations like this. Mothers report that their aim is not to teach, but merely to communicate effectively. They speak in simple utterances so their children will understand. They question and rephrase to check on what the child means.

Although mothers do not consciously teach language, children undoubtedly learn from their parents' language. Parents' utterances are often conventional versions of what the child has just said or words matched to what the child has focused his or her attention on. Parents sometimes use words that may be new to the child (such as *berries*). It is typical for mothers to exaggerate stress on words like *berries* and to repeat them in situations like this.

Two months later Mark and his mother had the following conversation.

Mark at Twenty-five Months

> *[Mark has seen a man working in his garden.]*
>   Mark: Where man gone? Where man gone?

Mother: I don't know. I expect he's gone inside because it's snowing.
Mark: Where man gone?
Mother: In the house.
Mark: Uh?
Mother: Into his house.
Mark: No. No. Gone to shop Mummy.
[The local shop is close to Mark's house.]
Mother: Gone where?
Mark: Gone shop.
Mother: To the shop?
Mark: Yeh.
Mother: What's he going to buy?
Mark: Er—biscuits. [cookies]
Mother: Biscuits, mm.
Mark: Uh?
Mother: Mm. What else?
Mark: Er—meat.
Mother: Mm.
Mark: Meat. Er—sweeties. Buy a big bag sweets.
Mother: Buy sweets?
Mark: Yeh. M—er—man—buy. The man buy sweets. [Wells, 1981, p. 107]

Mark's Performance

Mark's utterances have improved in terms of becoming more conventional. They are longer and have taken on the subject-verb-object form. However, the most remarkable progress he has made is revealed by the topic. This conversation is not about something going on in the immediate context. The man, the store, the purchases, and the action are not present.

This conversation is imaginative as well. The researcher who collected this example refers to it as Mark's first story.

Parent's Role in Mark's Communication

Once again Mother's role is to scaffold or lead from behind. She takes his topic and, realizing he has invented a reason for the man's disappearance, she helps him to develop an account of a shopping trip by asking what the man bought. Meaning is therefore negotiated and the story is a collaborative effort.

This conversation demonstrates the development of language and thinking (cognition) on dimensions that will continue throughout life and that have special relevance to school and success in reading and writing. Mark has begun to talk about events that are not going on in the immediate environment, and he has begun to deal with literary forms—the story.

Mark at Twenty-eight Months

Mark: All right you dry hands.
Mother: I've dried my hands now.
Mark: Put towel in there.

Mother: No, it's not dirty.
Mark: Tis.
Mother: No, it isn't.
Mark: Tis. Mummy play. Play Mummy.
Mother: Well, I will play if you put the top on the basket.
Mark: All right. There. There. Play Mummy. Mummy come on. (Wells, 1981, pp. 24–25)

Mark's Performance

In this short exchange Mark successfully attempts to regulate his mother's behavior ("you dry hands") and to get her to do something for him ("Mummy play"). These are forms of persuasion. Although conditional clauses are thought to be cognitively complex, he responds appropriately to her conditional sentence ("I will play *if* you put the top down"). On the other hand, he does not supply articles (*the* towel), a task that seems so easy. But Mother does not correct his grammar. She sees his remark as a request or command and responds to it. Elsewhere in this conversation, Mark hands his mother a towel and makes an utterance that is a series of vowel sounds—not an English word. His mother interprets this to mean "Here you are," and responds appropriately.

Parent's Role in Mark's Communication

Mark's mother does not focus on his mistakes and failures. She focuses on the jobs Mark is attempting to accomplish with language and cooperates by responding in language and in action to his meaning.

The exchanges between Mark and his mother are typical of toddlers and parents in mainstream American homes. Children from such homes tend to do well in school. Notice that in all these exchanges

- Mark's mother is collaborative rather than directive;
- Mark is viewed as active rather than passive;
- Mark's mother focuses on the meaning rather than the form of Mark's language; and
- learning is viewed as holistic and top-down rather than atomistic and bottom-up.

❖ Nigel at Twenty Months

Halliday's son, Nigel, at twenty months, has been taken to the children's zoo. He has picked up a plastic lid that he is clutching in one hand while stroking a goat with the other. The goat, after the manner of its kind, starts to eat the lid. The keeper intervenes and says kindly but firmly that the goat must not eat the lid—it would not be good for the goat. Here is Nigel reviewing the incident after returning home, some hours later:

Nigel: Try eat lid.
Father: What tried to eat the lid?
Nigel: Try eat lid.
Father: What tried to eat the lid?
Nigel: Goat . . . man said no . . . goat try eat lid . . . man said no.

Then, after a further interval, while being put to bed:

Nigel: Goat try eat lid . . . man said no.
Mother: Why did the man say no?
Nigel: Goat shouldn't eat lid . . . (shaking head) good for it.
Mother: The goat shouldn't eat the lid: it's not good for it.
Nigel: Goat try eat lid . . . man said no . . . goat shouldn't eat lid . . . (shaking head) good for it. (Halliday, 1975, pp. 111–112)

Nigel's Performance

Here again we have a child who is talking about an event that has occurred in the past in a different location. He is trying his hand as a raconteur (a person skilled in relating stories), and he includes several elements of the narrative form: character, action, and motivation.

Parents' Role in Nigel's Communication

Applebee and Langer (1984) make the following observations about the role of Nigel's parents in his fledgling performance as a storyteller. This is an instance of "scaffolding"—where the novice puts language to a use that is new to him or her in contexts where the more skilled language user provides support. The structure provided by the skilled language user is gradually internalized by the novice, who eventually learns to engage in this new use of language conventionally and without outside support (or scaffolding). These authors make the following observations about Nigel's efforts at storytelling:

1. The parents' questions are embedded in the child's attempt to complete a task that he has undertaken but cannot complete successfully on his own; Nigel responds well to the questions because they serve his own intentions.
2. The questions are structured around an implicit model of appropriate structure for a story; they solicit information that will make the child's narrative more complete and better formed.
3. At times, the parents directly model appropriate forms that Nigel is in the process of mastering, recasting or expanding upon the child's efforts without "correcting" or rejecting what he has accomplished on his own.
4. Over time, the patterns provided by the parents' questions and models are internalized by the child and are used without external scaffolding in new contexts. In turn, the scaffolding the parents provide can be oriented toward the next steps in Nigel's growth as a language user. (Applebee & Langer, 1984, p. 184)

❖ Summary of Parent-Child Interactions That Facilitate Development

In homes of children who tend to be successful in school, the following five characteristics are typical of interactions between parents and their preschool children. This list is similar to Applebee and Langer's (1984, p. 185) five aspects of "natural language learning."

Intentionality. Children have an overall purpose that the parent recognizes, and the parent's efforts are motivated by the desire to help the child to accomplish this purpose.

Proximal Development. Children attempt to do things with language that they cannot quite accomplish on their own, but that can be accomplished with the help of an experienced language user.

Collaboration. The parent questions, expands, and recasts the child's efforts without rejecting what the child has accomplished on her or his own. The parent's responses are collaborative rather than evaluative.

Internalization. As the child gains facility with the use of language in question, the leading from behind or scaffolding on the part of the parent becomes unnecessary.

Continuous Development. As facility with a language use matures, new intentions to use language begin to emerge and the process continues.

I will refer to this list frequently since a holistic, collaborative, integrated approach to teaching language arts shares these characteristics.

HOMES, COMMUNITIES, AND LANGUAGE

Notice that in the previous section I stated five generalizations that were drawn from observing interactions of parents and toddlers in homes of children who tend to be successful in school. Heath (1983) studied parent-child interactions in two communities. (Heath's study actually included three communities. For the purposes of this discussion I will refer to her findings in only two of them.) In one community she found parent-child language interactions that are very similar to those of Mark and Nigel. Children from this community tended to do well in school from kindergarten onward. In the other community Heath found parent-child exchanges that were quite different. Children in this community tended to do less well in school; they tended to succeed at first but fall behind in middle grades.

Heath referred to these two communities as "Maintown" and "Roadville." Maintowners described themselves as "middle class," "mainstream," or "typical American families." Roadville was a community of fourth-generation blue-collar textile mill workers. The two communities were located within a few miles of each other. The following are typical of the kinds of conversations preschoolers engaged in with adults in their different communities (Heath, 1986, pp. 160–162).

Excerpt of Maintown dinner conversation with four-year-old Pat (who has spent the morning in the church nursery school with Mrs. L, the teacher):

Father: Pat, how did you like Mrs. L? Did she let you play with Robbie?
Pat: Me 'n Rob, we go to a zoo.
Father: You didn't go to a zoo: what are you talking about?
Mother: (starts giggling and looks at Pat) Tell daddy about the zoo.
Pat: Well, me 'n Rob, we got this plan, 'n we were gonna build a zoo for all the kids, so we took all the animals—
Father: Where'd you get the animals—and what did Mrs. L think?
Pat: Outta the toy box, and Rob went into the baby room to take the animals outta the cribs—
Father: But what did Mrs. L think?
Pat: Wait, lemme tell you what we did—we had this plan—we had it all worked out—we had decided—you know, we have this free time after the story and all—we were gonna build something *big*. It was gonna have a big gate, a park inside, parking lots, and lots of stuff. We sell tickets to people who wanted to come look at the animals and see our park. They could have picnics too.
Father: Did your plans work out? Those sound like pretty big plans for just one Sunday School class.
Pat: No, that old teacher of the babies, the one from the crib room, found out that Rob had taken the animals from the empty cribs. She came and took 'em all back, so we just had to pretend then, but that wasn't so fun.
Father: Has Rob been to the zoo?
Pat: And we were gonna have a petting part too, you know, where the babies are.
Father: What would you kids have done if the teacher hadn't come to get the lost animals?
Pat: We would have taken 'em back.

Excerpt of Roadville dinner conversation with four-year-old Sally, her mother, teenage brother, and ten-year-old sister.

Mother: Can you tell your brother what you helped Mr. Jones do today?
Sally: We went to get gas, 'n there was this cricket, and he was in a field. I found some sticks to make one.
Mother: But wait, wait, why did we go to the gas station?
Sally: Mr. Jones helped us?
Mother: Yes, but why did Mr. Jones have to help us? Come on, you know what happened.
Sally: We couldn't got to the store. The car broke, 'n I found a cricket.
Mother: What broke on the car?
Sally: The tire broke.
Mother: And did you help Mr. Jones fix the tire?
Sally: Yes. The cricket was fun, but I had to leave 'im: I took down the fence.
Mother: Well, let me tell you what happened to us . . . [At this point, Sally's mother tells the events of the day.]

The contrasts between Maintown and Roadville are astounding. Pat's father responds to her intentionality and proximal development. He is collaborative and supportive. Pat ignores his repeated questions about Mrs. L, and he does not insist on her answering them. On the other hand, Sally's mother introduces a topic—the story of a flat tire and help from Mr. Jones. She ignores Sally's topic, which was an episode involving a cricket. When Sally refuses to adopt her topic, the mother takes over the conversation, never even acknowledging Sally's topic, much less scaffolding, supporting, or collaborating with Sally's attempt to tell it.

Heath does not claim that all children from Maintown have interactions like Pat's all the time or that all Maintown children succeed at school. She does not claim that all children from Roadville have interactions like Sally's all the time or that all Roadville children do poorly in school. She does document strong tendencies in these directions, however.

What is it about the experiences of children like Mark, Nigel, and Pat that prepares them for school and fosters their success in school? Those who study the relationship between culture, thought, and language believe they have some answers to their questions and these answers shed light on the question of why Laura's holistic, collaborative approach is superior to Michael's atomistic, directive approach.

❖ The Habit of Using Explicit Language

When we are with our family and friends we naturally use implicit language. We rely on shared knowledge, feelings, and opinions when speaking to one another. For example, a man looks at a sweater on a chair in his living room and says to his wife, "Did you tell him what I said yesterday?" and she answers, "Yes. But he didn't do it." He says, "Don't feel bad. It's not your fault." Although this is a perfectly clear communication for the husband and wife, it leaves many unanswered questions for the outside observer. The two are relying on context (the sweater apparently identifies the person they are talking about), shared information, and shared feelings. This kind of language is engaged in by nearly everyone when dealing with others with whom they are intimate or at least familiar.

An explicit rendition of the conversation might go as follows.

Husband: Did you tell our son, Ricardo, who seems to have left his sweater on the chair again, that I said I would turn him out of the house if he did not call my cousin Juan and accept the job Juan offered him?

Wife: Yes, I told him, but he didn't do it. I feel somewhat responsible because I've spoiled Ricardo and now he's totally incompetent and without ambition.

Husband: Don't feel bad. I think he would have been incompetent and without ambition even if you hadn't spoiled him.

❖ Life Styles and Demands for Explicit Language

Research going back to Schatzman and Strauss's classic study (1955) has shown that there is a difference between the language habits and behaviors of mainstream, middle-class Americans and the language behaviors and habits of less affluent and less powerful groups. One major difference is that the language of people with economic and political power tends to be *explicit*, while the language of less affluent groups tends to be *implicit* (Bernstein, 1973).

❖ The Rise of School Discourse Practices

Adults from communities like Maintown tend to acquire facility with explicit language for several reasons. Their employment and lifestyles require them to correspond with people who are unfamiliar to them and who are far away. Under these circumstances they cannot be sure that their correspondents share their information, attitudes, and feelings. They must make clear their knowledge, their understanding of situations, their intentions, their reasons, and their expectations of the other. Because of their frequent necessity to communicate with strangers in writing, and on business rather than personal matters, their writing exhibits the characteristics of formal written language; it is explicit, not context-dependent, nonredundant, concise, impersonal, abstract, and expository (like an essay rather than a story). This kind of language is valued in school settings. These characteristics of language are what Gee (1985) refers to as **school discourse practices.**

Furthermore, the employment and lifestyles of Maintowners often bring them into face-to-face contact with strangers from different locations, professions, and cultures. Although they can rely on reference to immediate shared context, they still may not assume shared information, attitudes, and feelings, so their oral language must be quite explicit as compared with the example of the husband and wife. In fact, the habit of being explicit with strangers carries over to conversation with friends and family, and they are frequently more explicit than they need to be. We all know people who sound a bit stuffy and academic. Listen to such people and you will probably discover that they are sometimes explicit, not context-dependent, nonredundant, concise, impersonal, abstract, and expository in informal settings where such characteristics of language are unnecessary and sometimes out of place.

In contrast, the employment and life styles of less affluent people from communities like Roadville require much less written communication with strangers. Their more limited correspondence tends to be with family and friends, and it tends to retain the characteristics of informal spoken language. They are less likely to have frequent face-to-face contact with strangers from different locations, professions, and cultures.

The employment and life styles of people from communities like Roadville tend to promote habitual use of implicit language, language that depends on shared context, language with the characteristics of informal oral language. It is implicit, context-dependent, redundant, copious (the opposite of concise), personal, concrete, and narrative.

> **ACTIVITY**
>
> Take a topic such as sports, politics, or marriage. Develop two texts on this topic: one that is explicit, not context-dependent, nonredundant, concise, impersonal, abstract, objective, and expository (like an essay rather than a story) and another that is implicit, context-dependent, redundant, copious, personal, concrete, and narrative. Which of these sounds more like the language of the school, the language of textbooks, lessons, and lectures?

Other factors besides the employment and life styles of parents affect the degree to which explicit language is used in homes. Two such factors are styles of exercising authority and the degree to which conformity is demanded.

Explicit language arises when parents' style of exercising authority includes stating their reasons and discussing decisions with children. Authoritarian parents do not discuss their decisions. Their reasons are sometimes implied or understood, but rarely stated.

The use of explicit language also arises when nonconformity is tolerated, if not encouraged. Opinions, beliefs, and attitudes need to be stated clearly in homes where differences are acceptable. In homes where conformity is demanded, opinions, beliefs, and attitudes are assumed to be the same and need only be alluded to—implied, rather than stated.

Parents whose style of communicating with their children tends to be collaborative also tend to discuss and state reasons in exercising authority and to tolerate nonconformity to a certain extent. Parents whose style of communicating with their children tends to be directive also tend to be authoritarian and intolerant of nonconformity.

To a certain extent styles of exercising authority, tolerance of nonconformity, and economic status are related. More affluent parents are likely to be less authoritarian and more tolerant of nonconformity than less affluent parents. This is, of course, not an iron-clad rule, but there is a tendency for characteristics that promote habitual use of explicit language (and school discourse practices) to appear together in some homes and for characteristics that promote habitual use of implicit language (and other characteristics of informal spoken language) to appear in other homes. Therefore, many students arrive in school ready to continue to develop discourse practices with which they are already familiar, while other students arrive in school quite unprepared for the discourse practices they find there. Bernstein (1973) observed many years ago that some children experience language continuity from home to school while other experience language culture shock.

Compared with Laura's, Michael's style of teaching is more directive, more authoritarian, and more demanding of conformity. His style of teaching shares many of the characteristics of homes which promote habitual use of implicit language, language that depends on shared context, language with the characteristics of informal oral language.

Laura's style of teaching shares many of the characteristics of homes which promote school discourse practices. Her collaborative style of teaching shares authority and accepts nonconformity. Her style requires and depends upon communication among students in situations that demand explicit language.

Children who come from homes where they have repeated experiences like the examples involving Mark, Nigel, and Pat arrive at school ready to further develop their language on the model they have already embarked upon. Children from such homes tend to succeed in school. This seems to argue unequivocally for the holistic, collaborative approach to teaching language arts since this is the model employed in homes where explicit language is habitually used and where such language is routinely called for.

❖ Literacy and School Discourse Practices

Many teachers like Michael are quite aware that their job is to give students facility with language that is explicit, nonredundant, concise, impersonal, abstract, and expository, and yet they continue to use a skills emphasis, directive approach. They do so in the belief that teaching skills causes literacy and that literacy causes people to adopt and use school discourse practices automatically.

They are simply bewildered when students learn to read and write (in a mechanical sense), but continue to be unable to deal with written and spoken language that is explicit, nonredundant, concise, impersonal, abstract, and expository and continue to fail in school. Such teachers often assume that these students have not been made literate enough, and they teach them more phonics, spelling, and punctuation rules in a skills emphasis, directive approach.

Gee (1986) argues that literacy (the ability to read and write in a mechanical sense) may be necessary for acquiring facility with language that is explicit, nonredundant, concise, impersonal, abstract, and expository, but that literacy per se does not *cause* individuals or groups to acquire facility with such language. He cites many examples of times when the ability to read and write became fairly widespread in a society, but these language traits did not emerge. He believes facility with language that is explicit, nonredundant, concise, impersonal, abstract, and expository is inextricably bound up with the mainstream economic, social, and political system of Western democracies. Such facility gives individuals access to power, and exercise of power leads to greater facility with such language. It is no surprise that this facility is valued in the schools which are after all creatures of the dominant group in Western democracies.

Gee separates literacy from facility with school discourse practices. He believes we do a good job of teaching the former and a very poor job of teaching the latter. Children who learn school discourse practices in their homes learn to read and write and prosper in school. Children who do not learn school discourse practices in their homes also learn to read and write, but they do not prosper in school.

Children acquire school discourse practices when they are given many experiences in situations that demand school discourse practices. Learning phonics rules, how to form letters, and how to spell words as isolated skills does not put children into situations that demand school discourse practices. Asking children to find solutions to problems in small groups, to respond to stories with improvisations, to write papers on topics of their own choosing, and to hear the questions of teachers and other students regarding their papers are situations where students must use school discourse practices and where others can scaffold and support their sometimes tentative use of these communication skills. These are strategies used in a holistic, collaborative, integrated approach to teaching language arts. This is one more reason I recommend the holistic, collaborative, integrated approach to teaching language arts and why I am much less enthusiastic about skills emphasis, directive approaches.

✣ Dialect Difference

Perhaps the greatest breakthrough in the 1970s for teachers of culturally diverse students was the realization that children who speak a dialect of English other than standard English are not trying to speak standard English and failing because they are illogical or unintelligent or deprived. They are speaking a dialect that is as useful, logical, and consistent as standard English. Their problem, if they have one, is that the dialect of their home and community is not as prestigious as standard English. Standard dialects of English and other languages are not superior to nonstandard dialects. They have more prestige because they are used by segments of the community that have money and power. That is what makes these dialects *standard.*

This insight changes teachers' perceptions of their jobs. We are not trying to teach English to native speakers of English; we are trying to give them additional options in the use of language. There is plenty of evidence that standard English gets jobs (such as persuading or arguing) done better in many situations because the speaker is perceived as having money and power. Therefore, it is generally agreed that students who speak a nonstandard dialect should be encouraged to learn standard English as a second dialect. (Teaching standard usage will be taken up in chapter 10.)

Differences in Styles: Topic-Centered and Topic-Associating Discourse

A similar breakthrough came in the 1980s. Teachers have long observed that children from nonmainstream cultures do not tell stories and convey information like their middle-class mainstream counterparts. Michaels (1986) studied the "sharing-time stories" told by mainstream, middle-class children (stories she characterized as "topic-centered discourse") and those of less affluent nonmainstream children (stories she characterized as "topic-associating discourse"). The stories of children who engaged in topic-centered discourse tell about one important thing, whereas the stories of children who engaged in

Table 2.1 Two Types of Sharing-Time Stories

Topic-Centered Discourse	Topic-Associating Discourse
On a single topic or a series of closely related topics	A series of anecdotal episodes linked implicitly to a topic
Time, persons, places, and things specified explicitly	Shifts in time and place across segments are signaled by tempo, pitch, stress, and intonation—not stated explicitly in words
Begin by stating time, place, and focus followed by elaborating on the topic	Relationship between parts must be inferred by listener
Finishes with a punch line	To persons who do not understand this style, there seems to be no beginning, middle, or end
Stories are short and concise	Stories tend to be long and not very concise

topic-associating discourse tell a series of concrete anecdotes, without any explicit statement of the topic. Some of the contrasting features of these stories, which Michaels calls "topic centered" and "topic associating," are found in Table 2.1.

Gee (1985, p. 32) quotes a story by a seven-year-old girl that begins as follows:

1. Last
2. last
3. yesterday
4. when
5. uh
6. m' my father
7. in the morning
8. an' he
9. there was a hook
10. on the top o' the stairway
11. an' my father was pickin' me up
12. an' I got stuck on the hook
13. up there
14. an' I hadn't had breakfast
15. he wouldn't take me down
16. until I finished all my breakfast
17. cause I didn't like oatmeal either
18. an' then my puppy came
19. he was asleep
20. an' he was—he was
21. he tried to get up
22. an' he ripped my pants
23. an' he dropped the oatmeal all over him

The story goes on for another sixty lines and involves two further episodes, being late for school and going to the animal doctor.

The child's teacher interrupted the story as a failed attempt to tell a topic-centered story. She found the story incoherent, asked a few questions that did not make sense to the child, and finally told the child to sit down.

Gee, on the other hand, began his interpretation of this story with the assumption that no one under normal conditions fails to make sense when creating a narrative of his or her own experience. Presuming that the story makes sense, Gee discovered a fairly profound theme: Adults and institutions represent discipline, while children and puppies represent freedom; when in conflict, adults and institutions win. Once this theme is discovered, the child's entire narrative makes perfect sense.

❖ Responding to Topic-Associating Storytellers

The discourse practices of children reflect the discourse practices of their communities. Topic-associating stories are an embryonic form of language that is implicit, context-dependent, redundant, copious, personal, concrete, and narrative—that is the language characteristic of nonmainstream, less affluent communities. On the other hand, topic-centered stories are an embryonic form of language that is explicit, not context-dependent, nonredundant, concise, impersonal, abstract, and expository. Topic-centered stories have the beginnings of school discourse practices.

Facility with school discourse practices is probably necessary to function in centers of power and wealth in Western society. In order to have access to these centers of power people must have command of this kind of language. Therefore, analogous to teaching standard English to speakers of nonstandard dialect as a second dialect, teaching a topic-centered style to users of a topic-associating style as a second way of narrating one's own experiences is a responsibility of the schools.

We need to note one further analogy. It is generally agreed that before children will accept a teacher as an ally in their efforts to acquire standard English as a second dialect, the teacher must acknowledge that there is nothing inferior about the children's dialect. In like manner, for children to accept a teacher as an ally in their efforts to acquire discourse practices that lead to expository speaking and writing, the teacher must acknowledge that there is nothing inferior about the children's discourse practices. The problem is not that topic-associating children are trying to tell topic-centered stories and failing. The problem is that middle-class, mainstream teachers evaluate these stories and respond to them as if they are attempts to tell topic-centered stories. If teachers evaluated these stories by the correct standards they would realize that many of them are brilliant. Gee (1985) points out that elements of topic-associating stories appear in the works of James Joyce, Gertrude Stein, T. S. Eliot, and Virginia Woolf.

Several observers (Heath, 1983) have noted that topic-associating children have highly refined skills of inference and analogy that get them into trouble in the primary grades because they do not reflect the language style that teachers expect. These same characteristics are highly valued by the middle grades. The trouble is that many such youngsters are turned off school by the time they reach the middle grades because of their accumulated history of failure in language interactions with mainstream teachers.

This line of inquiry (how different communities make sense of their experience through narrativization and how these discourse strategies impact on teaching and learning language arts) is in its infancy. This will undoubtedly remain an area of intense study for years to come. The following is a summary of the insights gained so far.

- In nearly all cases, children recounting their own experiences make sense. If teachers do not understand such narratives, it is probably because of cultural-linguistic differences, *not* because the child is irrational, unintelligent, or deprived.

- Once we presume that children's narratives of their own experiences make sense, the meaning of many narratives becomes clear. Even when the meaning remains obscure, questions that probe for meaning are more productive than those that suggest a narrative lacks meaning. A teacher in a classroom where Michaels (1986) did her research commented, "You know, it's a whole lot easier to get *them* to make the connections clear, if you assume that the connections are there in the first place" (p. 115).
- Learning to give all young narrators what is due to them—acknowledgment that they make sense and that their way of making sense is highly prized—is a necessary beginning. However, all students should have access to both styles.
- Teachers should attempt to infer the topic or theme of topic-associating stories and state them explicitly for the child. "It would be nice to just play with your puppy and have fun, but your father and your teacher have rules they make you follow, don't they?"
- A criticism that is leveled against "sharing-time" techniques in the primary grades (and at the language arts program in general) is that children who learn school discourse practices in their homes and community are provided numerous opportunities to practice them in school, but children who do not learn these practices in their homes and communities are not taught them in school; they are identified early as failures.

The insights gained into this problem and the suggested solutions indicate the desirability of a holistic, collaborative approach to teaching language arts rather than an atomistic, directive approach.

❖ Approaches That Teach School Discourse Practices

There are two well-known programs that were devised explicitly to deal with students from cultures where nearly everyone can read and write, but where they do not engage in mainstream habits of using language (school discourse practices).

Cultural Journalism

Cultural journalism is an approach to teaching language arts, particularly writing, that is associated with Eliot Wigginton, who developed the approach in the early 1970s while teaching in a rural, poverty-stricken area in the mountains of Georgia. Wigginton recognized two problems. The folkways of the people, such as broom making, whittling (wood sculpting), and, yes, even moonshining (making corn alcohol), were disappearing without any written record, and Wigginton's high-school students needed some reason for pursuing literacy beyond the acquisition of basic skills. Gee would probably describe Wigginton's students as being able to read and write, but uninitiated into school discourse practices.

Wigginton addressed both problems by sending his students out into the community to interview older relatives and neighbors, and using a combination of writing, diagrams, and photographs, he helped them create a written and graphic record of the folkways of the area. The results were eventually published by Doubleday in six *Foxfire Books* between 1972 and 1980. Although the approach did not solve all the problems of all the students, it did enable many students to acquire many characteristics of mainstream language use. Wigginton describes his experience in *Sometimes a Shining Moment* (1985).

Students as Ethnographers

Shirley Brice Heath (1983) described a somewhat similar project in a fifth-grade classroom in a community that shared many characteristics with the one Wigginton described. The students, all minority boys, had scored at the second-grade level or below on standardized tests of reading. As they were studying plant life, Heath began by showing them a film of her work in a Latin American village where she, an anthropologist, had studied the life of the people, including their food and eating habits. Having aroused their interest she told the students that they could study the growing, preparing and eating of food in their own community—just as she had done in Latin America. They were to become ethnographers.

They were to imagine that they were outsiders working for a government agency (a concept familiar to the students) who wanted to know how food was grown in the area and whether the growing customs were scientifically sound. As ethnographers they were to participate, observe, interview, collect documents and artifacts, take photographs, and collect life histories.

The children started with a simple question: Who are the best farmers? They were immediately faced with the question of what they would use as evidence. They came up with two ideas. They asked around to discover who was mentioned frequently, and they looked in back copies of local weekly newspapers that frequently had stories on gardening, particularly at harvest time. They had both interviews and written sources to identify the best farmers. They were talking, listening, writing, reading, and learning about validity and reliability of evidence—fundamental questions in science.

This project continued for eight weeks under the direction of Heath and the science teacher. The final product was a student-written booklet on local farming practices and their scientific validity. The teacher set standards for contributions to this booklet that was used as the "science book" for the unit on plant life for students in fifth grade the following year. The criteria for writing to be included in the booklet were these:

1. Make statements and back them up with a source recognized by the scientific world.
2. Ask and answer questions briefly and precisely. Be direct.

3. Avoid telling stories about knowledge. Discuss items for their own sake, not in terms of your direct experience with them.
4. Use the vocabulary of science used in science books and by science teachers.

Items 2 and 3 are of special interest because the children were from a community where topic-associating discourse and implicit language were common and topic-centered discourse and explicit language were rare. One of the most remarkable incidents in the project was when two boys commented to the teacher and their classmates that it was hard to get many adults in the community to answer a direct question.

They had come to pay attention to the kinds of questions people in different situations in life asked and answered directly. When the unit test time drew near, they joked about the fact that they would be asked direct questions; on that kind of test they would not get by with telling a generalized story (Heath, 1983, p. 321).

In fact, on the standard unit test from the textbook, twelve students scored above 90 percent, eight in the 80s, and three in the 70s. None failed.

ORAL LANGUAGE AT SCHOOL

Although there is obviously variation in home environments and in parents' style and substance in talking with children, a number of characteristics emerge that describe the conversational experience of preschool children in the home.

1. Children initiate a majority of (but not all) conversations in which they take part in the home. Therefore, preschoolers are almost always talking about "their topics."
2. Conversation and topics of conversation arise spontaneously from the interest of the moment.
3. Parents engage in teaching behaviors ("What kind of tree is that?" "No, that's not bread. He's eating berries."), but they do not have a predetermined curriculum. They do not set out to teach particular facts or skills. They introduce facts or skills relevant to the child's interest and talk, partly to keep the conversation going on the child's topic.
4. Talk ranges over all of the child's and the family's shared experience, including the physical context, activities, social interaction, and emotional responses.

All of the qualities that appear in the oral language experience of preschool children in the home appear to some extent in the oral language that children experience in school; but there are important differences:

1. In school, teachers initiate the majority of exchanges that children take part in with the teacher; children are almost always asked to talk about the teacher's topic.

2. Although the teacher often introduces materials or activities so that topics will seemingly arise from the environment, the topic is usually planned. Unplanned topics spontaneously arising from the material or from events in the classroom are often sidestepped.
3. Compared to what happens in the home, establishing meaning in school is less often collaborative and more often directive. It is the teacher's meaning that will be established.
4. Teachers ask more questions to which they already know the answers. These are called display questions because their purpose is to enable students to display their knowledge.
5. Closed questions usually outnumber the open questions asked by the teacher. Closed questions are questions to which there is one correct answer. For example, "What is the capital of Vermont?" Open questions are questions that elicit opinions or to which there is no one correct answer. For example, "What do you think the man is buying at the shop?"
6. By middle grades, the "Teacher Initiation-Pupil Response-Teacher Feedback" or Question-Answer-Evaluate routine becomes the norm for in-school language exchanges.
7. The range of appropriate topics is limited by the school's curriculum and objectives. Topics become impersonal. Talk about feelings and emotions and expression of feelings and emotions are curtailed.

The contrasts between the characteristics of preschool conversation and in-school conversation raise an important question: Are children asked to do things with language in school that they have no experience of in their homes? Observations have shown that the answer to this question is clearly no. Children do not initiate all conversations at home. They do answer closed questions. In short, we can find examples of everything children are asked to do in school in their preschool talk. What does happen, however, is that a small part of their at-home repertoire suddenly becomes almost exclusively the kind of talk they are expected to take part in at school.

Teachers should bear in mind that children have different degrees of experience with the talk one finds in school, and therefore they will cope differently with the language roles that are set for them. Children who are not immediately successful in school are not necessarily nonverbal, nor do they necessarily need to be taught language. It is more likely that they need to be taught the way language is typically used in school. That is, they need to learn school discourse practices.

✤ Rosie and Teacher One

An exchange like the following was reported by Wells between five-year-old Rosie (who by age ten was clearly failing in school) and one of her kindergarten teachers. Rosie was making a calendar from one of the previous year's Christmas cards. The picture on the card showed Father Christmas (Santa Claus) skiing down a snowy mountainside. While Rose worked, the teacher tried to engage her in talk about this picture, although, initially, the teacher's attention was somewhat distracted by another child who had already finished her calendar (Wells, 1986, pp. 96–97).

> Teacher: [to Rosie] What are those things? [Pointing to Santa's skis.]
> Teacher: [referring to skis in picture] *D'you know* what they're called?
> [Rosie shakes her head.]
> What d'you think he uses them for? [Rosie looks at the card. The teacher turns to the other child's calendar.]
> It's very nice. After play, we'll put some ribbons at the top.
> Teacher: [to Rosie, pointing at the skis on the card] What's—what are those?
> [Rosie looks blank.]
> What d'you think he uses them for?
> Rosie: [rubbing one eye with the back of her hand] Go down.
> Teacher: Go down—yes, you're right; go on.
> [Rosie rubs both of her eyes with the backs of her hands.] What's the rest of it? [Puts down card.]
> You have a little think and I'll get—er, get the little calendar for you. I think you're sitting on—. Right. [Points to calendar.] Could you put some glue on the back there? [Rosie takes the calendar from the teacher.] He uses those to go down—[5-second pause]—Is it a hill or a mountain?
> Rosie: A hill.
> Teacher: A hill, yes. And what's on the hill?
> Rosie: Ice.
> Teacher: Yes. Ice. They're called skis.

Compare this conversation with the conversations between Mark and his mother concerning the birds and the neighbor who has "gone to the shop." Rosie's conversation differs from Mark's in that the teacher (adult)

- initiates the conversation
- introduces and insists upon her own topics
- asks closed questions
- asks display questions

In short, the teacher is unrelentingly directive.

✤ Rosie and Teacher Two

After she had finally finished making her calendar and been out to play, Rosie went to her reading teacher. The book she was reading was called *I Am Tall*. As she read, the teacher pointed to the words with a pencil. She had reached the page showing a picture of a chimney (Wells, 1986, p. 98).

> Rosie: I am tall said the—tower.
> Teacher: [correcting her] Chimney.
> Rosie: Chimbley.
> Teacher: [pointing at picture] It's a big factory chimney, isn't it?

Rosie: I don't like—
Teacher: [pointing at illustration with pencil] There's a lot of smoke coming out of the top.
Rosie: [pointing at picture of chimney] I don't like that one.
Teacher: You don't like it? [Rosie shakes her head.] Why not?
Rosie: I only like little ones.
Teacher: Have you got a chimney in your house? [Rosie nods emphatically.]
Child: And me.
Teacher: [to Rosie] D'you have smoke coming out of the top?
[Rosie nods emphatically.] Mm?
[Rosie nods her head again. The teacher turns the page, then closes the book.]
What's underneath the chimney, then, that makes the smoke come out?
Child: I know, fire.
Teacher: [to Rosie] Mm?
Rosie: Fire.
Teacher: Is it? Have you got a fire then?
Child: Miss, *can I have this one*?
Teacher: [to Rosie] *Which room's the* fire in? [Shifts gaze to other child.] Yes. [Looks back to Rosie.]
Rosie: In the front one.
Teacher: Is it? So it keeps you warm? Lovely.
Rosie: And I got a bed.
Teacher: Where's your bed?
Rosie: E's upstairs.
Teacher: Anybody else got a bed in your room?
Rosie: Carol got a bed—and Kelvin [very softly] and Carol.
Teacher: Uh-huh. What about Donna?
Rosie: Donna—we're sharing it.
Teacher: You're sharing with Donna, are you? [Rosie nods her head emphatically.] D'you have a cuddle at night?
Rosie: Yeh, and I—when I gets up I creeps in Mummy's bed.
Teacher: For another cuddle? [Rosie nods.] Oh that's nice! It's nice in the morning when you cuddle.

Rosie, who seems nonverbal in her conversation with Teacher One is talkative with Teacher Two. Rosie introduces the topic and the teacher collaborates in establishing Rosie's meaning. The teacher's questions are open and she seeks information rather than displays. Rosie undoubtedly emerges from this exchange with a feeling of satisfaction and success in contrast to the feelings of failure she must have experienced with Teacher One. In school, Teacher One's approach is more typical than Teacher Two's. Teacher Two's approach has more in common with a parent's approach.

Of course schools cannot simply reproduce the language patterns of the home. Most classrooms contain one teacher and many children, and the teacher has a curriculum to cover. The characteristics of school talk grow out of these pressures.

If we consider only the curriculum and the pupil-teacher ratio, the directive style of language that is characteristic of school makes excellent sense. However, there are other matters to consider. Children's interest, motivation, and feelings of self-esteem all work in their favor when they learn through the typical parent-child collaborative style of conversation. The directive approach, on the other hand, can be destructive of interest, motivation, and self-esteem. One solution to this problem is to permit and encourage collaborative, child-initiated talk when it facilitates curriculum goals.

❖ Supporting Collaborative Talk in the Classroom

Encouraging students to express their reactions to stories or to relate stories to their own experiences is a worthwhile activity in discussing literature, for example. Here teachers can follow the students' lead and avoid closed questions. Some classroom observers believe that teachers sometimes become so accustomed to the directive approach that they miss these opportunities and do not employ the collaborative conversational style even when it is appropriate. Rosie's conversations with her two teachers show that more collaborative conversation is often appropriate in a classroom, but that opportunities for collaborative conversation are often missed.

Throughout the remainder of this book there are numerous discussions of giving students ownership of the topic in teaching language arts and there are numerous examples of collaborative teaching approaches.

---TO THINK ABOUT---

Teacher/Student Collaboration

Reflect on Michael's and Laura's teaching styles. Which is likely to present more opportunities for establishing the child's meaning through collaborative efforts between the student and teacher?

❖ Collaborative Talk between Students

Six-year-old Elaine and Stuart are discussing on tape the snails in a glass-sided container in the classroom—part of a science project involving an older group of children (Ede & Williamson, 1980, pp. 121–123, 127–128). Initially the tape includes the teacher.

Teacher: Is that one asleep?
Stuart: Yes.
Teacher: What makes you think they're asleep?
Elaine: They're not moving.
Teacher: They're not moving. Can you find any that are moving?
Stuart: No.
Elaine: I don't think so.
Stuart: If this one moves, I'm going to put t'lid on again.
Teacher: You're going to put the lid on again?
Stuart: Yes, in case it bites me.
Teacher: I don't think it'll bite you.

Elaine: What will it do?
Teacher: See if you can count how many there are and have a look ever so closely 'cos I'm sure there's some that are hiding... I mean I can see one that's moving.

[Several pages later in the transcript.
Elaine and Stuart are now left alone.]

Elaine: Well, we've got to describe 'em. Well the shells... Kind of a browny colour, aren't they?
Stuart: Look at that shell moving.
Elaine: They make all slime behind 'em and I think... and I don't think they've got four eyes. (This is a continuation of her previous description)
Stuart: I don't think
Elaine: Well we'll have to have a close up... look.
Stuart: Have a close look. (A deliberately gruff voice, as he bends very close to the tank)
Elaine: Eh, shall I pick one up with this thingy and have a look then. Well it's very hard to see at the bottom. Look if that would just climb up
Stuart: Have a look in t'bottom. Go on just... yes pick it up, now pick it up more... look under t'bottom, see all them... thingies. (Sound of distaste in his voice) Put it down it's gonna bite you, it's gonna bite you. (Nervous laughter)
Elaine: No, they've only got two eyes. I say they've only got two.
Stuart: I say they've only got four...
Elaine: I say they've got two...
Stuart: Well/well them big 'uns must be the eyes.
Elaine: Well, we'll ask Mr. Godfrey.
Stuart: Them big 'uns/them big 'uns must be the eyes... No them big 'uns/them big 'uns must be the eyes, (shouts to make himself heard) them little 'uns must be the tabs (ears), or them little 'uns must be the eyes and them
Elaine: (Finally getting a word in edgeways) Look I/look don't let's argue, now I know that those big 'uns are the eyes, and I don't think the bottom ones are because I can't see nothink, believe me Stuart I can't see no dots in the others.
Stuart: I can't. (Screams) Get a magnifying glass. Wo, wo, wo (a sort of rhythmic singing).

Compare Elaine and Stuart's conversation with their teacher to their conversation without their teacher present. What is the teacher's contribution to the conversation? How does the children's talk change after the teacher leaves? Which conversation is directive? Which is collaborative?

Conversations like the one between Elaine and Stuart demonstrate that children as young as six are able to talk to one another in "the language of reasoned thinking which is so essential to children if they are to benefit from later schooling" (Phillips, 1985, p. 64). Children can formulate hypotheses, ask for clarification, and offer alternative suggestions if they disagree with what their peers say.

What can be learned from Elaine and Stuart is that there are a variety of ways that knowledge can be pursued and that communication skills can be exercised and developed. One of the things that must be considered is the likelihood that a topic determined by the teacher (acting for the school and society) will be adequately covered. Other things that must be considered are the interest, enthusiasm, motivation, and involvement of the learners. When the teacher is in control of the conversation and is directive, the topic is more likely to be covered in a methodological manner. When the teacher withdraws from the conversation or becomes collaborative and nondirective, the students' involvement and enthusiasm are likely to become heightened, but the topic may not be covered methodically or covered at all. As in many cases, good teaching requires finding a balance between two conflicting agendas.

INTEGRATING THE LANGUAGE ARTS

In the previous sections, I have tried to explain why Laura's holistic and collaborative approach to teaching language arts is desirable. In this last section I will address the reasons why teaching language arts should be integrated.

Teachers of language arts are not charged to simply teach children the isolated mechanical skills associated with speaking, listening, reading, and writing. If this is all that were expected of language arts teachers, Michael would do an excellent job. In fact, numerous teachers like Michael *do* do an excellent job of teaching these things. That is probably why children from Roadville tend to do well in the early grades and begin to fall behind in the middle grades.

Teachers of language arts must teach school discourse practices over and above the isolated, mechanical skills associated with speaking, listening, reading, and writing. When the teacher's ultimate aim is to teach school discourse practices, integrating speaking, listening, reading, and writing not only makes good sense. It becomes obvious that such an approach is necessary. In the following paragraphs, I will explain why this is so.

❖ School Success and Facility with School Discourse Practices

Children begin life by expressing meanings to parents who are eager to establish their child's meanings. The child's meanings always arise out of the immediate physical or psychological context and are supported by these contexts. When language emerges it is implicit and context-dependent.

As children grow older, their audiences become more distant, less familiar, less intimately connected. Their language must become more explicit if they are to make themselves understood. Their meanings may remain context-related, but their communication partners become less willing to collaborate in establishing the children's meanings. Furthermore, communication partners begin to insist on speaking about their own topics, at least part of the time. The child is required to understand other peoples' meanings. These meanings are less often merely references to previously established meanings, and they are less often derivable from the immediate context.

In school, these communication demands are intensified. Even teachers like Laura are far more directive than many parents of preschoolers. Children must learn to understand teachers, with whom they have no intimate connection, speaking about topics unrelated to the immediate physical and psychological context of the classroom. In turn, students must learn to make themselves understood by others, with whom they have no intimate connection, speaking about topics that are unrelated to the immediate physical and psychological context. The child, both as a listener and as a speaker, must learn to deal with explicit language.

Highly formal oral presentations begin to appear in the middle and upper grades. Teacher talk begins to take on the characteristics of prepared lectures, and students are required to deliver more formal oral presentations. Such formal speech is impersonal, accurate, explicit, and concise. As you will see, these are also the characteristics of professional, published writing.

Children's involvement with written language follows a similar pattern. Many children exhibit readinglike behavior long before they enter school. They recognize print on packages, for example, and will say that the toothpaste package says "brush your teeth" and that a McDonald's wrapper says "hamburger." Reading at this stage is recognizing print and relying entirely on the context for meaning. Words are often first recognized in books that have been shared with parents dozens of times so that recognition and meaning rely nearly entirely on context once again.

In school (or for many children before school) children learn that the meaning of print has some autonomy. Just as conversation partners begin to insist on their own meanings rather than continuously scaffolding the child's meaning, the child learns that print has its own meaning. But parents and teachers provide early experiences with print where context suggests the correct meaning and supports word recognition. The topic is familiar. The tone is intimate.

As children progress in school, however, the nature of the printed language they encounter changes. Context is less and less helpful, topics become less familiar, the tone becomes more distanced and formal. As the students move into the middle grades, the written language they encounter takes on characteristics that are associated with published, edited writing. Stubbs (1980) refers to the published, edited, written language as "institutional writing" which has the following characteristics:

- Institutional writing is public rather than private. It is not addressed to any individual and the identity of the author is unimportant. The focus is on the content.
- Institutional writing is accurate. Writers and editors check facts and reformulate statements after reflecting on their accuracy, precision, and consistency.
- Institutional writing is explicit. It is intended for a large audience with whom the author is not intimately acquainted. The author cannot gauge the reader's knowledge, beliefs, and opinions with the same accuracy as is often possible in speech. Therefore, in institutional writing, facts are stated explicitly, descriptions and explanations are detailed, and arguments are spelled out precisely.
- Institutional writing is nonredundant and concise rather than redundant and copious. Institutional writing is usually revised and edited both by

the author and by editors. This process eliminates redundancy. Each sentence makes its unique contribution to the discourse, whereas in spoken language repetition is common.

Teaching school discourse practices is teaching children to use language having the characteristics of institutional writing as a listener, speaker, reader, and writer.

> **ACTIVITY**
>
> Stubbs (1980) distinguishes between institutional writing and personal correspondence: Personal correspondence retains many similarities to spoken language that result from the personal relationship between the writer and receiver, their familiarity with the topic, the shared experiences they have had regarding the topic, and the informality of the language.
> Share a personal letter or note with a classmate. How much clarification is necessary for someone who is barely acquainted with the receiver of the letter to understand it?
> Rewrite the note so it can be clearly understood by your classmate. How many characteristics of institutional writing appear in the rewritten version?

❖ Integrating Language Arts Teaching

The Reading-Speaking Connection

School offers numerous opportunities to speak in situations where explicit language is necessary for effective communication. Teacher-student conferences and small groups of students working together on a well-defined task offer excellent opportunities for this kind of language. By making effective communication the objective and giving the child feedback on his or her success in reaching this objective (in small groups by simply encouraging children to ask for clarification of others' remarks), all children gain facility with the use of explicit language whether they are accustomed to hearing and using it outside school or not. Learning to use explicit language in speech will help children understand explicit language when they read.

The Reading-Writing Connection

As students encounter more and more institutional writing in their role as readers, their own writing should be developing the characteristics of institutional writing. By the middle grades, typical questions and comments from teachers and fellow students regarding a student's writing might be these:

- Are you sure it was over one hundred and twenty degrees every day during your visit to Florida? (Be accurate. Check your facts.)

- The boy in your story (a fantasy) is only two inches tall, but you say he went upstairs. How did he get upstairs? (Be consistent.)
- You say it was a big house. How big was it? How many rooms? How many stories? (Be more explicit.)
- You said three times that the movie was boring. Why don't you tell us why it was boring? (Do not be redundant. Be explicit.)

If things go well, students' reading comprehension is aided by what they learn as writers—that written language is accurate, explicit, and not redundant. At the same time they are encountering these characteristics more and more in their reading, which should help them to improve their writing.

Recently while teaching a writing workshop in an elementary school, I commented to the regular classroom teacher that one student was a particularly gifted writer. The teacher answered, "I know. She reads all the time." That may seem like a non sequitur, but there are few language arts teachers who would not understand and endorse the logic of the reply.

❖ The Essence of Teaching Language Arts

The essence of teaching language arts is not teaching such things as diction in speech, auditory discrimination in listening, the mechanics of forming letters in writing, or word recognition in reading. The essence of teaching language arts is teaching facility with school discourse practices, such as explicitness, which are typical of the language of institutional writing and public discourse. This is one more reason why a holistic, integrated approach to teaching language arts is desirable. Facility gained with school discourse practices

- through reading makes students better speakers, listeners, and writers.
- through writing makes students better speakers, listeners, and readers.
- through speaking makes students better listeners, readers, and writers.
- through listening makes students better speakers, readers, and writers.

When teachers focus on teaching school discourse practices as their ultimate goal in teaching language arts, everything connects.

Summary

Language acquisition develops in stages from "initiation-response" interactions, where parents respond to an action initiated by the child, to "proto-conversations," where both parent and child focus their attention on the same aspects of the environment. Vocalizations usually accompany these exchanges. Eventually the parent and child attach meaning to certain vocalizations, and the result is meaningful and intentional but unconventional communication. Finally the child will adopt the conventional, socially agreed-upon vocal symbols for certain meanings. The child's communicative behavior then possesses all the characteristics of human language: It is meaningful, intentional, and conventional.

In all these collaborative activities the parent's and the child's focus is on the use of language to accomplish some function. Form is a secondary consideration.

The examples of conversations between Mark and his mother show how some parents collaborate with a child's language initiatives. By following the child's lead, asking questions, restating what the child says, and adding new information to extend the topic the child has introduced, the parent teaches by leading from behind or providing scaffolding on which the child can build or expand his or her language use. The parent responds to the child's meaning or purpose in using language and does not focus or comment on incorrect form.

The samples of language between Nigel and his parents also indicate scaffolding—where the more skilled language user (parent) provides support for the attempts of the child to use language in new ways by asking questions and modeling appropriate forms. Over time the parent's pattern of questioning and modeling are internalized and can be used by the child in new contexts without parental scaffolding. Again the parents do not evaluate or reject the child's attempts but do what they can to help the child accomplish his or her purpose.

Observational studies have shown that in homes where children tend to be successful in school, there are five characteristics of parent-child interactions that facilitate development. They are intentionality, proximal development, collaboration, internalization, and continuous development.

The dialog between Sally and her mother shows a different pattern. Sally's mother does not support Sally's attempt to tell her story. Heath found such interactions typical in one of the communities she studied. Children in this community tended not to succeed in school.

Children from economically affluent and politically influential homes, such as Heath describes in Maintown, acquire the language habits of their parents whose employment and lifestyle requires the habitual use of explicit language. These parents' written as well as oral language tends to be concise, context-independent, and essaylike—the kind of language required in school. Gee describes these characteristics of language as "school discourse practices."

Children from less affluent and influential homes acquire the habit of using implicit language. The employment and life styles of their parents do not require much explicit language; their language relies on shared context and tends to be more personal, concrete, and narrative.

Authority styles may differ as well between the two types of homes, with accompanying linguistic differences. For example, authoritarian parents are less likely to state explicit reasons for requiring certain behavior and they may require greater conformity. Opinions, beliefs, and attitudes do not need to be explicitly stated in homes where conformity is expected. Parents who are collaborative give more reasons for exercising authority, are more willing to discuss their views, and will often tolerate greater nonconformity.

Schools tend to expect students to have explicit discourse habits when they arrive at the classroom. For children from homes that promote implicit language patterns, the language of the school will be something of a culture shock. These

SUMMARY

children especially will benefit from a classroom atmosphere that is supportive and collaborative and that provides linguistic and social interactions that promote the use of explicit language. Such a classroom has the characteristics of holistic, collaborative, and integrated teaching which are advocated in this text.

An important distinction has been noted by Gee between the ability to read and write and the facility with school discourse practices. Literacy skills per se (phonics, spelling, punctuation rules, and so on), taught in a skills emphasis, directive approach will not produce the facility with explicit, nonredundant, concise, impersonal, abstract, and expository language which is associated with economic, political, and social power. On the other hand, problem-solving in small groups, responding to stories with improvisation, writing papers on student-selected topics, and responding to questions from teachers and other students on those papers are activities that demand the use of school discourse practices.

It is important for teachers to understand that dialect differences are not the cause of failure to develop facility with school discourse practices. However, standard dialect is used by powerful, dominant culture groups and nonstandard dialect users should be encouraged to acquire standard English as a second dialect. Similarly, it is important that teachers recognize the value of topic-associating language styles while at the same time providing all students with access to the topic-centered style that makes meaning explicit and is compatible with school discourse practices.

Two approaches to encouraging explicit discourse practices are cultural journalism, such as that published in the *Foxfire Books* and students' ethnographies, such as those produced by Heath's students in a booklet on community farming practices. Both help students acquire many of the characteristics of mainstream language use.

There are differences between the oral language of the home and the school. Language use that has been only a small part of children's at-home repertoire suddenly becomes almost exclusively the kind of talk they are expected to take part in at school. For example, while most preschool talk is child-initiated, most in-school talk is teacher-initiated and topics are determined by the teacher. Teachers' questions ask students to display knowledge; they tend to be closed as opposed to open questions which elicit the students' opinions.

Collaborative teaching styles make school talk more like home talk. It is more likely to produce feelings of satisfaction and success on the part of the child for her conversational efforts. Students can also benefit from collaborating with each other, as the example of conversation between Elaine and Stuart shows.

As children grow and develop they spend more time in a variety of situations that are outside of the home. In order to be understood in new and different environments children need to use language explicitly and to understand meanings which may not refer to the immediate context or to shared knowledge. This facility with explicit language is particularly important as the child enters the middle grades, where formal oral and written presentations begin to dominate. Children must be able to understand the meaning being expressed without undue reliance on context. They must learn especially that the meaning of print has autonomy; they must be able to take meaning from published, edited written language such as that which Stubbs refers to as "institutional writing." And they must learn to produce writing that has these characteristics.

As students read more institutional writing they will have more experience listening to formal oral language discussion of the topics read, thereby integrating reading and listening skills. They will also be called on to speak on these topics themselves, thereby integrating reading and speaking skills. Their writing will become more like institutional writing as they are exposed to reading institutional writing, thereby integrating reading and writing skills.

Teaching language arts is teaching facility with school discourse practices. When teaching school discourse practices with a holistic, collaborative, integrated approach, everything connects.

For Review and Discussion

1. Give an example of something you've learned in collaboration or interaction with others.

2. Why is parental behavior that is collaborative and supportive compatible with the child's natural, actively exploratory mode of learning?

3. If the parent naturally focuses on the child's use or function of language, how does the child acquire correct form?

4. Can the parental method of teaching by leading from behind or scaffolding be used by classroom teachers? How would such a classroom differ from those where skills emphasis teaching dominates?

5. Think of times when implicit language was used inappropriately. What was the result? On the other hand, think of times when explicit language was used inappropriately. What was the result?

6. How does acquisition of school discourse practices differ from acquiring literacy? Give examples that show why being able to read and write does not assure one will succeed in school.

7. Do you agree that nonstandard dialect speakers and topic-associating storytellers should be taught standard English and topic-centered storytelling? Should standard dialect users and topic-centered storytellers be taught nonstandard usage? Why or why not?

8. What are the main differences between in-home and in-school conversations? How can teachers use questioning that reflects the home pattern? How can they teach proper responses to traditional in-school questioning to students who are less familiar with this kind of discourse?

9. What language-use changes occur in middle grades that make facility with explicit language a particularly important skill?

10. Explain the statement: Teaching school discourse practices demands integrating language arts instruction. Give examples.

For Further Reading

Baron, D., & Lovell, J. (1987). Bryan the brave: A second grader's growth as reader and writer. *Language Arts, 64,* 505–515.

Brookes, G. (1988). Exploring the world through reading and writing. *Language Arts, 65,* 245–254.

Clarke, M. (1990). Some cautionary observations on liberation education. *Language Arts, 67,* 388–398.

Dillard, J., & Dahl, K. (1987). Learning through teaching in a reading/writing classroom. *Language Arts, 63,* 692–697.

Fine, E. (1989). Collaborative writing: Key to unlocking the silences of children. *Language Arts, 66,* 501–508.

Greene, M. (1988). Research currents: What are the language arts for? *Language Arts, 65,* 474–480.

Harman, S., & Edelsky, C. (1989). The risks of whole language literacy: Alienation and connection. *Language Arts, 66,* 392–406.

King, R. (1989). Outlaws and artists: Naming the world in childhood. *Language Arts, 66,* 822–827.

Minns, H. (1988). Teacher inquiry in the classroom: "Read it to me now!" *Language Arts, 65,* 403–409.

Potter, G. (1989). Parent participation in the language arts program. *Language Arts, 66,* 21–28.

Power, B. (1989). Beyond "Geddenagrupe": A case study of three first grade collaborators. *Language Arts, 66,* 767–774.

Ridley, L. (1990). Enacting change in elementary school programs: Implementing a whole language perspective. *The Reading Teacher, 43,* 640–647.

Sanders, M. (1987). Literacy as "passionate attention." *Language Arts, 64,* 619–633.

Voss, M. (1988). "Make way for applesauce": The literate world of a three-year-old. *Language Arts, 65,* 272–278.

Walters, K., Daniell, B., & Trachsel, M. (1987). Formal and functional approaches to literacy. *Language Arts, 64,* 855–868.

Winterowd, W. R. (1987). Literacy: Kulture and culture. *Language Arts, 64,* 869–874.

CHAPTER 3

Understanding Oral Language

Introduction
A Communication Model
TO THINK ABOUT: Culture and
    Communication
Focusing on Listening
    Activity
Conversation
    Activities

Discussion
    Activities
Supporting Formal Speaking
    and Listening in
    the Classroom
Summary
For Review and Discussion
For Further Reading

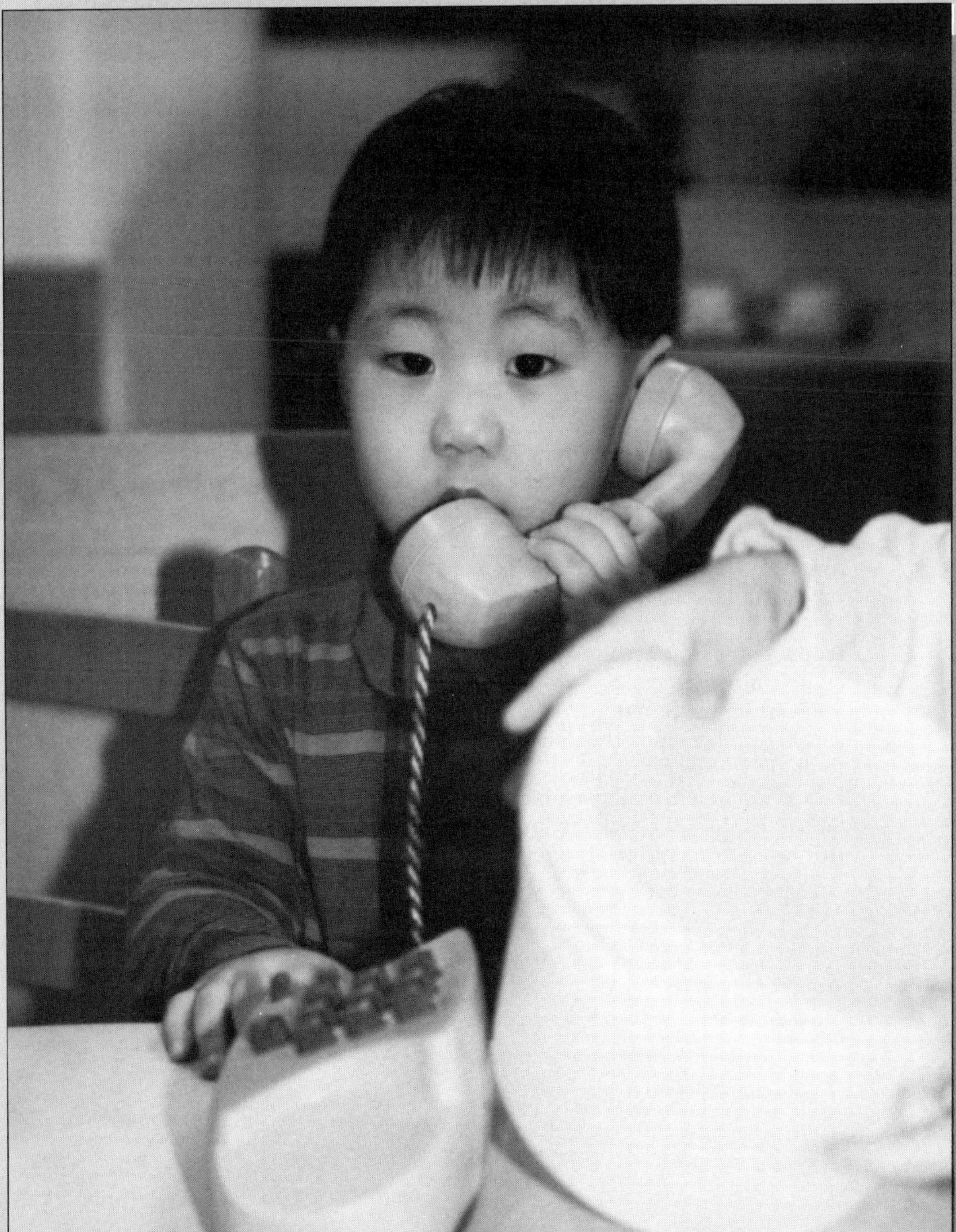

INTRODUCTION

The concepts of the **communication model** and **communicative stress** are introduced in this chapter to provide a framework for understanding oral language. These concepts are considered from both the speaker's and the listener's points of view and suggestions for improving the student's facility with oral language communication are derived from this framework. Finally, three formats for oral language are considered (conversation, teacher-led discussion, and speaking to an audience) and suggestions for improving the student's facility with oral language communication within each of these formats are presented.

A COMMUNICATION MODEL

Oral language communication involves a speaker, a listener, a topic, and a context or communicative setting. As each of these variables changes, the task of the speaker changes (see Figure 3.1).

The speaker's ability to use language effectively and appropriately depends on his or her ability to do two things: to understand the different demands of the various communicative settings and to produce the communication demanded. A speaker can go awry on either point. There was a *Time* story reporting that a football player said, "Lighten up, Sandy," to Supreme Court Justice Sandra Day O'Connor at a dinner party. His language was not appropriate or effective, probably because he did not properly understand the demands of the communicative setting.

Failure of appropriate and effective communication also results when the speaker understands the demands of the communicative setting, but is unable to produce the communication demanded through either lack of knowledge or lack of confidence. This sometimes results in spoken communication which fails to achieve its goals; it sometimes results in people remaining silent when they wish to and probably should speak.

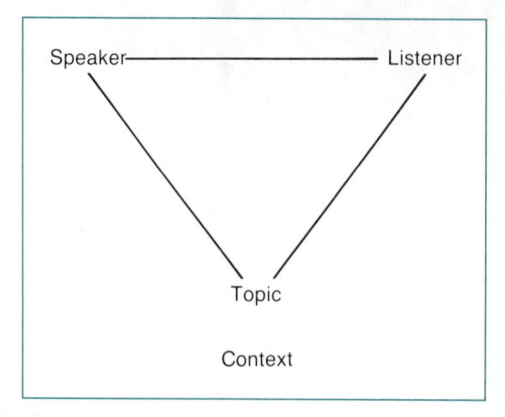

Figure 3.1

✤ Factors That Contribute to a Speaker's Communicative Stress

The Information Gap

Anderson and others (1984) introduced the concept of communicative stress to describe those factors that make it difficult for a speaker to perform well. These factors include, first, "the information gap," which is defined as the usefulness of the information the speaker is trying to impart to the listener. If the speaker is sure that the listener does not know the information and if the speaker knows the listener needs the information, the information gap does not add to communicative stress. It is easy for a ten-year-old to tell his school principal that the building is on fire; it may be very difficult for the child to chat with her about the weather.

The information gap as a communicative stress factor takes on special importance in the context of adult-child interactions. Much of what children say to adults is in response to what are known as "display" questions. The function of children's language in such cases is not to inform but to display their knowledge by saying what the adult knows and expects. Children are sometimes labeled nonverbal because they fail to respond to such questions. It is possible that they simply fail to understand the communication demands of the situations.

---TO THINK ABOUT---

Culture and Communication

As part of a test of language ability that was once widely used, the teacher would place a green block of wood on the table where it was clearly visible to both teacher and child and say, "Tell me about this."

What is a child to do whose culture teaches him or her that it is insulting to tell a person something that is obvious from context? From such a child's point of view, the reply, "It's green," implies that the child thinks that the teacher can see the block but needs to be told what color it is.

Such children do not need to learn how to speak. They have the capacity to say everything the teacher expects. They need to learn the communication demands of school situations that are in conflict with the communication demands of their homes and neighborhood.

Can you think of other examples of where a child who follows the rule "Don't say things that are apparent from context" appears to be nonverbal or unintelligent to teachers and others who understand the communication demands of display questions in the classroom?

Characteristics of the Listener

The second group of factors that contributes to communicative stress has to do with the listener. The listener's status in relationship to the speaker can introduce communicative stress. Children talk more easily to peers than to adults, and more easily to a familiar adult than to a strange adult. Sometimes the listener is actually a group of listeners, and most of us find it easier to talk to an individual than to a small group or a large audience. The behavior of the listener can also introduce stress. Some listeners are willing to let speakers work out what they are trying to say and to help them to work it out. Others interrupt, lose interest, or are critical.

Characteristics of the Topic

The topic can be a source of communicative stress. When speakers feel their own understanding of the topic is shaky, they will experience more stress while speaking. If the topic is difficult or complicated, speakers will experience more stress.

Characteristics of the Context

The context may be a source of stress. A person may feel quite at ease describing an incident in a lawyer's office but quite stressed describing the same incident to the same lawyer while on the witness stand.

Speaker-Listener Format

Conversation is probably the least stressful format. The formality of discussion may add some stress. Large-group discussions tend to be even more formal, and the size of the group may inhibit some people from contributing. Addressing an audience is perhaps the most stressful format.

Factors that contribute to communication stress are interrelated. The courtroom context may not be the only source of stress to the witness. The presence of the victim's family, the defendant, and newspaper and television reporters will all affect the level of stress.

ACTIVITY

Factors that contribute to communication stress for a speaker are outlined in Box 3.1. Imagine the worst case scenario for communication stress. The listeners have the information or do not need it (IB). There is a large group of listeners (IIA3). They are of higher status than the speaker (IIB3). They are strangers to the speaker (IIC3). They are hostile (IID2). The speaker's understanding of the topic is shaky (IIIA2). The topic is complex (IIIB2) and the context is threatening (IVB). It is a speaker/audience situation (VD). What situation might this scenario describe?

An example might be that a young scholar is delivering a paper on a complex subject to a group of eminent experts in the field. The speaker is not sure of what he or she is talking about and has nothing new to say. The audience is angry and the young scholar's career advancement depends on the outcome of this talk.

What would be the easiest case scenario? It is important information that the listener needs (IA). There is one listener (IIA1) of lower status (IIB1), and so on. What situation might this describe?

Invent a medium case scenario (some easy, some middling, some hard). What situation might it describe?

This activity should help you to understand the concept of communication stress and how these variables interact with one another. It will be helpful to share examples with your classmates.

I. The Information Gap—The importance of the information to the listener

   A. Easy—Important information that the listener needs
   B. Hard—Information that the listener has or does not need

II. Listener Characteristics

   A. Number
      1. One
      2. Small group
      3. Large group

   B. Status
      1. Lower status (younger, uninitiated)
      2. Equal status
      3. Higher status (older, professional)

   C. Familiarity
      1. Intimate
      2. Familiar
      3. Stranger(s)

   D. Behavior
      1. Shows interest, makes helpful suggestions, is supportive.
      2. Interrupts, is hostile, shows boredom, criticizes.

III. Characteristics of Topic

   A. Degree of Understanding
      1. Speaker's understanding is secure.
      2. Speaker's understanding is shaky.

   B. Degree of Complexity
      1. Uncomplicated
      2. Complex

IV. Characteristics of Context
   A. Familiar, supportive
   B. Unfamiliar, hostile, threatening

V. Speaker-Listener Format
   A. Conversation
   B. Small-group discussion
   C. Large-group discussion
   D. Speaker/audience

BOX 3.1 Factors That Contribute to Communication Stress for a Speaker

FOCUSING ON LISTENING

In our discussion of oral language, the focus thus far has been primarily on speech and expressive communication, which are, of course, only part of the oral language communication picture. Listening and receptive communication make up another important part of the picture.

The listening demands that children typically encounter in school are somewhat different from those they encounter at home. The school does not present an entirely new set of listening demands; but as with speaking, some listening demands that are present in the home are diminished; others gain a more dominant role, and some are transformed.

Box 3.2 summarizes the characteristics of the parent-child communication (referred to as the Parent-Child Register following Bryen, 1981) and shows the contrasting characteristics of the teacher-student communication. You will notice that the characteristics of the Parent-Child Register focus on the parents' language so that from the child's point of view this is a list of characteristics of the parents' language that the child deals with as a listener.

PARENT-CHILD REGISTER	TEACHER-STUDENT REGISTER
1. There is a high degree of responsiveness to a child's communicative signals, whether intentional or unintentional, verbal or nonverbal.	
2. Conversational model established early and used almost exclusively. As early as three months, mothers respond to burps and sneezes and make these topics of "conversation."	Because of the one-to-many teacher-student ratio and the need to accomplish curriculum goals, the first six characteristics of the Parent-Child Register all but disappear from the Teacher-Student Register.
3. Mothers talk constantly about what they perceive to be the child's wishes, needs, and intentions.	
4. The parent follows the child's interest in setting the topic.	
5. The child has a turn as speaker for every turn the parent takes. Turns are very short in duration.	
6. A special vocabulary characterized by phonologically simplified words ('*nana* for *banana*) and child's unique words (*Gunnie* for *grandmother*) is used.	

BOX 3.2 A Comparison of the Parent-Child Register with the Teacher-Student Register

BOX 3.2 *(continued)*

7. From twenty weeks on, the child shows interest in objects and events in the environment. Mother's references to child decrease and references to objects and other people increase.

8. The topic centers on the here and now—objects that are present, activities that are ongoing.

In primary grades the curriculum focuses somewhat on the child, but includes things and people in his or her immediate environment as well. As the child progresses through the grades, the focus moves to things and people that are not in the child's immediate environment, and that are not in his or her firsthand experience. Although good teachers continue to bring in concrete objects, diagrams, familiar examples, and so on, the topics of school language become increasingly more abstract and further removed from the student's immediate experience.

9. There is a high proportion of questions from the parent. This is a way of giving the child his or her turn.

A high proportion of questions from the teacher continues, and part of the function of the questions remains the same—to keep the discourse conversationlike, but new purposes are added and eventually dominate. Questions are used to check to see if the children are paying attention, to evaluate, and to guide children's thinking toward a conclusion (convergent questioning) or to encourage their own creative thought processes (divergent questioning).

10. Mother talks at a slower rate and with a higher pitch and exaggerates contours (highs and lows); this makes mother's speech accessible to the child.

11. Length of utterances is reduced; syntax is kept simple.

12. There is a great deal of redundancy (repetition and rephrasing).

As children progress through school the typical teacher's presentation changes from that of someone who is communicating with an individual with limitations of linguistic and cognitive capacity to that of a performer or a good public speaker. The primary object is no longer to make language accessible, but to present concepts and arguments clearly and to keep the students interested and attentive.

❖ Listening in School

A Typical Spelling Lesson

A fourth-grade teacher stands in front of a chalkboard facing a group of six students. The following words are written on the board:

Row 1	fun	bag	fat
Row 2	funny	baggy	fatty
Row 3	fruit	tear	rain
Row 4	fruity	teary	rainy
Row 5	sand	string	mess
Row 6	sandy	stringy	messy

The following exchange ensues:

Teacher: Which rows of words are root words, and which rows of words are root words plus suffixes?
Child 1: Rows one, three, and five are root words. Rows two, four, and six have suffixes.
Teacher: Let's circle the root words in row two. What letters will I circle in *funny*?
Pupil 2: F-u-n.
Teacher: Good. What letters will I circle in *baggy*?
Pupil 3: B-a-g-g-y.
Teacher: No, Sandra. I don't think you are listening. Andrew, what letters will I circle for the root word in *baggy*? . . . .

The lesson continues through Question-Answer-Evaluate sequences to establish a spelling generalization.

The Question-Answer-Evaluate format of this lesson is typical of the Teacher-Student Register. These are, of course, display questions. The teacher is not seeking information that he or she doesn't already have. This is not unlike most of the questions parents ask preschoolers. The difference is that the teacher is controlling the topic, and the lesson is abstract. The teacher is doing what he can here to make it easy for the children to listen; he is trying to make it a discovery lesson. He is using concrete examples. One hopes he is keeping things lively through pacing, tone of voice, expression, and body movements. But the fact is that it is his topic (or the school's topic).

❖ Factors That Contribute to the Listener's Communicative Stress

We introduced a communication model consisting of four elements (a speaker, topic, setting or context, and listener) in connection with communication stress from a speaker's point of view (see Figure 3.1). These same elements can be a source of support or difficulty from a listener's point of view.

The Speaker

Three sources of potential difficulty for the listener arise in connection with the speaker.

Coping with the Speaker's Language
Is the speaker's language—its level of complexity and vocabulary—within the listener's capacity? The business of the school is to increase students' capacity to deal with language and vocabulary so they will be able to comprehend the widest possible range of speakers. The entire language arts program, in fact the entire school program, can be said to be aimed at this goal in one way or another.

Coping with the Speaker's Ability to Take the Listener's Point of View
Speakers need to take the listener's point of view into consideration and supply the information the listener will need to understand what is being said. The listener needs to know when comprehension has gone awry because the speaker has not supplied enough information, and to ask the appropriate questions. This listening skill is most closely associated with informative language and will be discussed in chapter 5 under that heading.

Coping with Emotional and Judgmental Responses Evoked by the Speaker
A speaker may arouse feelings of alienation, mistrust, suspicion, and revulsion. On the other hand, a speaker may arouse feelings of sympathy, trust, credulity, and affection. Listening becomes a more difficult task when listeners must deal with feelings toward the speaker as well as understand what is being said.

These listening skills are closely associated with affective, persuasive, and informative language and will be treated in chapter 5 under those headings.

The Topic: Who Owns It?

Who has control of the topic is an important consideration in oral language communication. If it is the listener's topic, his or her knowledge about the topic and interest in it are more or less built in. If it is the speaker's topic (the typical situation for a student in school), two aspects can introduce difficulty: whether the listener is interested in the topic and whether the information is new or a restatement of what is already known.

The Context

A crucial factor in success in listening is sometimes the degree to which the message of the speaker is supported by the context. Children begin their language careers depending heavily on the context to decipher the meaning of what is being said to them. In early grades, the curriculum concentrates on the children and their immediate surroundings, so that school talk continues to refer to the here and now—ongoing activities and concrete things in the environment. Although teachers continue to use audiovisual aids and analogies to relate concepts to the immediate environment, topics become more abstract and less related to the here and now as children progress through school.

The Listener

Characteristics in listeners themselves can affect success in listening.

Support from Previous Knowledge
From a very early age, a listener's previous knowledge can either facilitate or hinder listening. Edgar Dale coined the term COIK (Clear Only If Known) to describe messages that are so poorly constructed that they can be understood only by persons who already know the information the speaker intends to convey (Steil et al., 1983). Communication between people who are intimately related over a long period of time often relies little on language alone; it relies heavily on implicit references to shared knowledge, experiences, and beliefs. Such communication is clear only because the message is already known to the listener.

Interference from Previous Knowledge
Possession of knowledge can also be a source of trouble. Messages that conflict with pre-established knowledge or beliefs are sometimes understood in such a way as to conform to those pre-established beliefs—that is, they are misunderstood.

Lack of Knowledge
Lack of knowledge is often a source of failure at listening: Effective listeners recognize when they have failed to understand because of a lack of knowledge on their part. The speaker may be at fault for misjudging the audience, but regardless of fault, it is up to the listener to recognize the breakdown and the reason for it. Flavell and others (1981) found that young children always tend to blame the listener when spoken communication fails. When they are speakers they blame the listener, and when they are listeners they blame themselves.

Effort
Finally, listening often takes effort on the part of the listener. In his best-selling book, *The Road Less Traveled*, psychoanalyst M. Scott Peck repeatedly returns to listening as the most important way to demonstrate attention, concern, understanding, and love for another person. Peck warns that while all listening takes effort, to *really* listen—to suspend all judgments and preconceived notions about what is being said—takes enormous effort.

The Interaction among Speaker, Topic, Context, and Listener

Listening is every bit as complex as speaking, and sources of difficulty frequently appear in combination. The first grader listens to a teacher who is familiar, trustworthy, understandable, and who talks about concrete things and ongoing activities. New information is likely to be compatible with what the child already knows and is not likely to elicit a strong negative emotional response. An eighth-grade girl who listens to a health education lecture from a representative of Planned Parenthood does not know the speaker, who may or may not be doing a good job of making the message clear. Some concepts may be new; they may be totally unrelated to the context of the classroom; and the student may find them threatening, in conflict with things she thinks she knows, and contrary to her beliefs. All this makes listening more difficult.

❖ Supporting Listening in the Classroom

Effective listening is learned through direct focused involvement in the act of listening itself. All language arts subjects and all school subjects afford opportunities for focused involvement in the act of listening. Good listening habits should be facilitated by the teacher and practiced by teachers and students throughout the school day.

The Russels (1979), in their now classic book on teaching listening, suggest that throughout the school day teachers do the following:

1. Call attention to the listening demands placed on students by ongoing activities.
2. Discuss topics of high interest and that elicit strong feeling.
3. Supply students with specific purposes for listening, such as looking for suspense, identifying sequence, responding to humor and so on.
4. Build in opportunities for students to respond (to take a turn as speaker). Unison responses in primary grades are especially appropriate.
5. Schedule time to talk about listening problems after a presentation. What was hard to understand; where did interest and attention lag; what note-taking would have been appropriate?
6. Avoid class activities that teach children not to listen, such as students' reading reports essentially copied from encyclopedias.
7. Help students to keep their attention focused by using audiovisual aids, diagrams, outlines, and so on.
8. Establish interesting listening centers.

Successful listening is the result of numerous attitudes, behaviors, and thought processes (see Box 3.3). Friedman (1986) proposes that a universe of listening activities can be defined by relating components such as those listed in Box 3.3 to the functions of language: to inform, persuade, express feelings, imagine, and ritualize. That is, each component of listening (attentiveness, understanding, evaluation, and emotional response and the sub-categories listed under them) can be considered from the standpoint of listening for information (the informative function), listening to arguments (persuasive function), and so on. The teacher can create a variety of listening opportunities in the classroom.

COMPONENTS OF ATTENTIVENESS

Receptive to others
Accepting
Open
Attuned to speaker

Gives full attention to speaker
Imposes own point of view minimally
Maintains external focus on speaker and message

COMPONENTS OF UNDERSTANDING

Actively selects and organizes input
Distinguishes essential from non-essential
Distinguishes personally relevant from irrelevant
Senses interrelatedness of concepts
Compares/contrasts

Classifies
Generalizes
Infers
Predicts
Hypothesizes

COMPONENTS OF EVALUATION

Weighs message against personal beliefs
Questions speaker's motives
Challenges speaker's ideas
Questions validity of message
Judges by standards of excellence
Wonders what has been omitted
Thinks of ways to improve on message

COMPONENTS OF EMOTIONAL RESPONSE

Cares/Does not care
Likes/Dislikes
Interested/Uninterested

Sensitive/Insensitive
Relaxes/Is on guard
Enjoys/Becomes angry

BOX 3.3 Attitudes, Behaviors, and Thought Processes That Promote Effective Listening

Make a "Friend Crest" (Primary Intermediate)

Ask the children what things they would like to know about their friends, such as their favorite game or what they like to do on Saturday. After several items of information have been suggested ask each child to chose four questions to ask a neighbor.

FOCUSING ON LISTENING 65

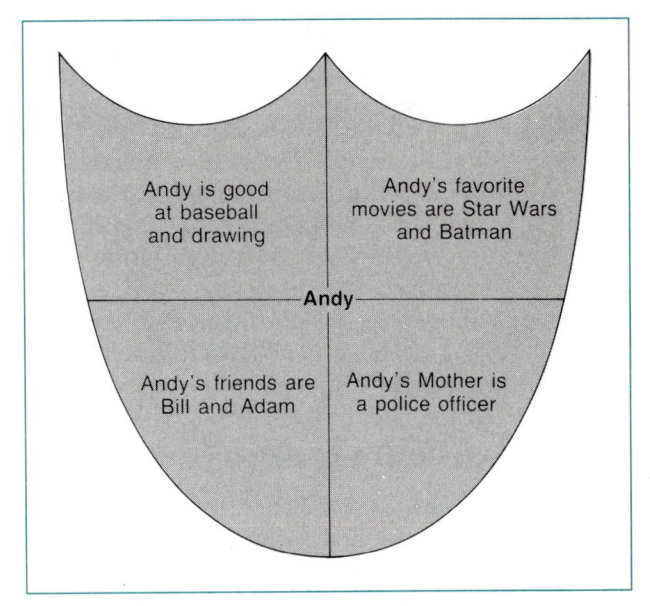

Figure 3.2

(Shield diagram containing:)
- Andy is good at baseball and drawing
- Andy's favorite movies are Star Wars and Batman
- Andy
- Andy's friends are Bill and Adam
- Andy's Mother is a police officer

Put the children into pairs. Direct them to ask their questions of their partner and make a "friend crest" for their partners such as the one in Figure 3.2.

Following Directions I

Pair the children off. Identify one child as the Direction Giver and the second as the Listener. Give the listener the construction-paper shapes seen in Figure 3.3; give the direction giver the completed picture in Figure 3.4. Tell the direction giver to tell the listener where to glue each shape to make the picture. Of course the listener may not see the completed picture, and the direction giver may not use the word *telephone* in giving directions. After the exercise is complete have the listener compare his or her picture with the original.

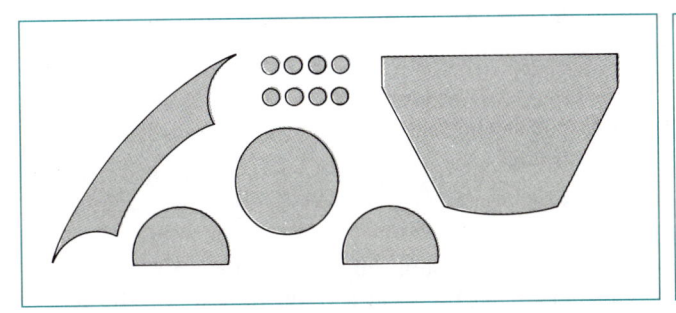

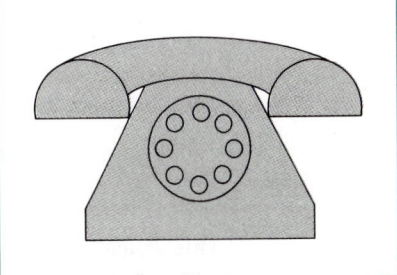

Figure 3.3

Figure 3.4

Variations and Embellishments
Identify Observers—students who can see both the original picture and the listener's picture as it evolves. Have observers discuss sources of difficulty after the listener completes the picture. Where were directions not explicit enough? Where did the listener fail to follow directions?

Have the listener and direction giver switch roles using different shapes to make a different picture after completing the exercise with the telephone.

Try the exercise in a situation where the direction giver can watch the listener carry out directions. Notice what happens when the two share the context. "Paste the little yellow circles around the edge of the big red circle" may become "Take the little circles and put them near the edge.—No, not there. A little higher."

Following Directions II

Give each child a sheet of paper and a crayon. Give them step-by-step directions like the following that are open to different interpretation.

1. Draw a large square on the paper.
2. Draw a triangle on the top of the square.
3. Draw a rectangle at the bottom of the square.
4. Add two squares next to the square.

Have the children compare their pictures with one another and discuss the many ways the directions were interpreted.

Variations and Embellishments
Show the children your version of what the picture should look like and decide what you should have said to make the directions clear. For example, "Draw a large square on your paper" might become "Draw a square about three inches on each side at the middle of the paper." Of course, even more explicit directions might be given.

Do the exercise over, but permit the children to ask questions at each step. An important part of listening is becoming aware of what information is needed to perform a task.

The same procedure can be followed with directions for playing a game, for following a recipe, or for traveling to some destination.

Listen to Channel 128 (Classroom Number) TV

Ask the students to write a newsy, descriptive advertisement, weather report, or sportscast such as the following.

> This delicious oversized chocolate bar contains only the finest assortment of nuts. Each piece is one-half ounce and the total bar weighs a whole three ounces. Yes, folks, that comes to six pieces of delicious candy in one bar—and

all for fifty cents. Look for it only in your local grocery store right in the express lane. It's the big bar in the pink-and-purple wrapper.

Have individuals read their efforts aloud. After the class listens, they try to remember as many facts and details as possible.

Listen to Local Book Reviews

Encourage students to jot down reactions to books they have read and to use these notes to record book reviews. Questions like the following might be supplied as a guide.

1. Did you like the book?
2. Was it funny? Scary?
3. Could the story have really happened?
4. Would a classmate probably like it?

Devote one side of an audiotape to each title. As further students read a book they can add their reviews to earlier recorded ones. Students should be encouraged to listen to recorded reviews as a way of selecting books.

The following is a sample review:

"This is Ben. I just finished reading *Curious George*. It was a really funny book with a funny little monkey. It didn't take me a long time to read, and I think everyone should read it as soon as they can."

Listening Like a Speaker

Have children watch and listen to professional speakers, such as TV newscasters, and make a list of rules for good speakers such as the following:

1. Speak loud enough, but not too loud.
2. Speak slowly enough, but not too slow.
3. Talk about interesting things.
4. Don't talk too long.
5. Sit (or stand) still.

Reflecting on a speaker's performance makes students' better listeners. It focuses their attention and helps them to see that effective communication takes good speaking as well as good listening.

Listening with a Purpose

Get into the habit of stating a purpose for listening to your students. For example, "Today I'm going to begin the book, *Hope for the Flowers*. Listen carefully because we're going to illustrate parts of the book once I'm finished."

✣ Establishing a Listening Center

A listening center can be started with a tape recorder and headphones. Teachers can record class summaries, math facts, and spelling assignments. Students can record book reviews, stories, unfinished stories, poems, journal entries, and interviews. Professional recordings of poetry, literature, journalism, and interviews can be made available. These tapes can be used in assignments and for recreation.

CONVERSATION

Conversation and discussion are similar forms of spoken discourse. The chief characteristic that distinguishes a discussion from a conversation is the extent to which participants adhere to a particular agreed-upon topic. In both conversation and discussion, participants need to follow certain rules or the discourse will be neither satisfying nor efficient. Everything said in the following section about conversations is also true of discussions.

✣ Rules of Conversation

Conversations are characterized by a number of rules that govern our participation and make it possible for meaning to be created collaboratively. Among these are turn-taking, cohesion, the given-new contract, and the cooperative principle.

Turn-Taking

People who have made a serious study of conversation observe that participants in a conversation follow rules which assure the orderly conduct of the exchange of speaker's and listener's roles. Of course, these are rules only in the implicit sense; that is, they explain the behavior of the people involved. The speakers may not be explicitly aware of them.

Some of the rules of turn-taking are described by Wells (1981) as follows:

1. Only one person has the role of the speaker at one time.
2. The person who is the speaker decides when there should be a change in speakers. Speakers employ subtle strategies to accomplish this. They look away from the listener while talking and look back at him or her when they are ready to cede their turn. They use pause fillers like "ah . . . ah . . ." to show that, although they have paused, they are not ceding their turn. They warn listeners that they are going to take a long turn with phrases like "For the following reasons . . ." or "Well, there is an explanation for that." This way they can keep the floor, and if interrupted they can regain it and finish their reasons or explanation before the topic can be changed.

3. In order for these strategies to work, the listener must pay attention and cooperate. The listening job is not only comprehending what is being said and getting ready to make a coherent response, it also is watching for cues for turns.

Cohesion

Conversation is marked by cohesion; that is, if all the turns are added together and seen as a whole (as a discourse) the parts seem to be related to one another and to the whole.

The most obvious way that conversations maintain coherence is that participants tacitly agree to talk topically. Sometimes the topic is formally and explicitly understood, as in a telephone conversation between a bank employee and a customer about a disagreement regarding the balance in the customer's account; the conversation may then be defined as a discussion. In more causal circumstances the topic may not be as clear or as rigidly adhered to.

The Given-New Contract

At times the connection of a speaker's contribution to the topic is not clear to an outsider, but may be obvious to the participants. For example, friends may be discussing plans for a party when one person says, "Mable Constable left yesterday for the West Coast." Is Mable a caterer who would probably be asked to prepare food for the party? Is she a person who would certainly have been invited? The listener automatically assumes that Mable's departure has something to do with the party plans and operates on the most likely connection unless the speaker stated a different connection explicitly. Clark and Haviland (1977) refer to this tacit agreement in a conversation as the **given-new contract.** The hearer presumes that "new" information is related to "given" information and that the most likely connection is the correct one. If the relationship is not likely to be clear, or if an incorrect relationship is likely to be assumed, the speaker states explicitly how the new is related to the given.

The Cooperative Principle

Besides talking topically, participants in a conversation establish and maintain cohesion by employing the **cooperative principle;** that is, speakers try to be informative, truthful, relevant, and clear; and listeners presume that speakers are being informative, truthful, relevant, and clear, and interpret what is said accordingly (Grice, 1975).

All the other characteristics (turn-taking, coherence, and the given-new contract) depend on the cooperation of those taking part. Conversation is always a collaborative effort. Speakers do whatever they can to ensure that their meaning will be available to the listener, and listeners make use of every cue to construct and interpret the speaker's intended meaning.

> **ACTIVITY**
>
> A. Role play a conversation where the rules of conversation are not followed.
>   1. Turn-Taking. Participants talk at the same time or begin to speak while the legitimate speaker is attempting to hold the floor.
>   2. Cohesion. Participants talk about unrelated topics.
>   3. Given-New Contract. Participants willfully misinterpret the obvious relationship between what is said and the topic.
>   4. The cooperative principle. Participants willfully refuse to be informative, truthful, relevant, or clear, or they refuse to act as if their conversation partners are informative, truthful, relevant, or clear.
> B. Ask your classmates to identify which rule(s) of conversation are being violated in each role play.
> C. Discuss ways this activity could be turned into lessons for primary, intermediate, and upper grades.
> D. If you are currently teaching elementary school, adapt this activity to your classroom. Share the results with your classmates.

❖ Developing Conversational Skills in the Classroom

McCroskey (1977) suggests that teachers become aware of their own oral communication behavior through such simple devices as a Verbal Activity Scale (see Box 3.4). If the results of the scale are inconsistent with your own perception of how talkative you are, McCroskey suggests using this scale as a way of broaching the topic with friends, and, if you teach older children, with your students. Teachers who discover that they are too talkative or too much inclined to silence would do well to consider the effect this example may have on their students.

In the middle and upper grades the Verbal Activity Scale can be administered to students and used as a starting point of discussion. Making students aware of their own inclination to be too talkative or too little inclined to talk may be a necessary starting point in your combined efforts to make students better conversationalists.

A video recording of "Sesame Street" or a family situation comedy (depending on the grade level) can serve as a focus of discussion about good conversation. A simple checklist of good conversation rules such as that in Box 3.5 can serve as a basis for evaluating conversations. A review of turn-taking, cohesion, the given-new contract, and the cooperative principle in this chapter will help you select conversations to view and help the class create a checklist.

Directions: The following ten statements refer to talking with other people. If the statement describes you very well, circle "1." If it somewhat describes you, circle "2." If you are not sure whether it describes you, or if you do not understand the statement, circle "3." If the statement is a poor description of you, circle "4." If the statement is a very poor description of you, circle "5." There are no right or wrong answers. Work quickly; record your first impression.

1 2 3 4 5	1. I enjoy talking.
1 2 3 4 5	2. Most of the time I would rather be quiet than talk.
1 2 3 4 5	3. Other people think I am very quiet.
1 2 3 4 5	4. I talk more than most people.
1 2 3 4 5	5. Talking to other people is one the things I like best.
1 2 3 4 5	6. Most of the time I would rather talk than be quiet.
1 2 3 4 5	7. I don't talk much.
1 2 3 4 5	8. Other people think I talk a lot.
1 2 3 4 5	9. Most people talk more than I do.
1 2 3 4 5	10. I talk a lot.

To obtain your VAS score, complete the following steps: (1) Add your scores for the following items: 2, 3, 6, 7, and 9. (2) Add your scores for the following items: 1, 4, 5, 8, and 10. (3) Add 30 to your score for step 1. (4) Subtract your score for step 2 from your score for step 3. Your score should be between 10 and 50.

(McCroskey, 1977, p.16)

BOX 3.4 Verbal Activity Scale

YES	NO	1.	One person speaks at a time.
YES	NO	2.	Speakers stay on the topic.
YES	NO	3.	Listeners try to understand speakers—they do not deliberately misunderstand.
YES	NO	4.	Speakers tell the truth.
YES	NO	5.	Listeners answer questions truthfully.

BOX 3.5 A Conversation Checklist

> **ACTIVITY**
>
> Work in small groups.
> A. Invent role plays of conversations that run into difficulties
>   1. because of factors that contribute to communication stress (Box 3.1).
>   2. because one participant does not understand the demands of the communicative setting.
> B. Ask your classmates to determine the source of the problem in the conversation your group presents.
> C. Discuss ways this activity could be turned into lessons for primary, intermediate, and upper grades.
> D. If you are currently teaching elementary school, adapt this activity to your classroom. Share the results with your classmates.

Teachers should work hard to separate the necessary classroom rule that says "No disruptive behavior" from the rule that says "No talking." Teachers should seize opportunities to converse with individual students in the way that the second of Rosie's teachers did (chapter 2). Many times during the school day, conversations between students can and should be permitted, and conversations between students should also be a deliberate part of the instructional program. Some specific lesson ideas follow.

Rules of Conversation I—Primary

Divide the class into small groups (approximately three students per group) and ask each group to discuss a familiar topic (for example, what I like to do at recess, good television shows, favorite toys). Post the following Rules of Conversation for students to think about:

1. Do I let each person talk?
2. Do I ask questions?
3. Do I add new ideas?
4. Do I listen?

Rules of Conversation II—Primary

Children in your class may be familiar with the Mister and Miss books (*Mr. Greedy, Mr. Nosy, Miss Bossy,* and so on). Each book portrays a character who has a behavior problem.

Create a character, Mr. Blabber Mouth, who does not wait his turn to talk in a conversation, and ask children to help you write a story about Mr. Blabber Mouth modeled on the Mister and Miss books. Write each child's contribution at the bottom of a sheet of paper and have that child draw an illustration on the page. Bind the pages to make a book to add to the class book center.

Repeat the process with other characters, like Mr. Silly, who doesn't stay on the topic.

Rules of Conversation III—Intermediate

Have students use puppets to demonstrate inappropriate rules of conversation. Make one puppet unable to focus on the topic, one unable to take turns, and so on. Then have the students create a similar conversation in which the puppets model appropriate conversation behavior. Follow this with a classroom discussion about why the second conversation was more efficient and satisfying than the first.

Intermediate-age youngsters might perform the puppet act for primary children and explain the importance of conversational rules.

Rules of Conversation IV—Primary/Intermediate/Upper

Role play to demonstrate rules of conversation. Divide the class into small groups. Ask each group to focus on one aspect of conversation—turn-taking, cohesion, and so on. Role play inappropriate behavior and follow this by role playing appropriate behavior. Present role plays to the class followed by discussion.

Videotapes of these role plays made in intermediate and upper grades might be shown to primary-age children followed by a discussion of good conversation behavior.

DISCUSSION

Conversation is marked by informality. The topic is easily changed. Participants may avoid giving their opinion or stating relevant facts simply to avoid unpleasantness. Conversations often serve no purpose except to pass the time.

Discussion, on the other hand, is a more formal kind of discourse. It has the following characteristics.

1. Discussion requires that *more than one point* of view be expressed.
2. Discussion is on a *particular topic,* subject, or question.
3. Discussion has the *purpose of improving knowledge, understanding, or judgment* regarding the topic, subject, or question. Sometimes, the purpose of discussion is to come to some agreement on what is correct, but its purpose may be simply to make alternatives clear.
4. Discussion requires that participants *respond* to each other. Several people can express different points of view on a topic but fail to respond to one another. This is not discussion.
5. Discussion requires that *participants be willing to be convinced* by others' statements and reason. A lawyer whose job is to refute the arguments of an adversary, no matter how compelling, is not willing to engage in discussion. (Bridges, 1979)

> **ACTIVITY**
>
> A. 1. Form five small groups. Select numbers from one to five from a hat so that each group has a number, but groups do not know the other groups' numbers.
>   2. Have each group create a role play of a discussion where one of the five characteristics of discussion proposed by Bridges (the number drawn by the group) is lacking. Ask other groups to identify the characteristic that is lacking.
> B. Adapt this activity for use in the middle or upper grades.
> C. If you are currently teaching elementary school, adapt this activity to your classroom. Share your results with your classmates.

❖ Stages and Procedures in a Discussion

For discussion to succeed, participants must abide by all the rules of conversation, but the need to talk topically is more strictly interpreted to mean that the speaker must not only stay on the topic but must pursue the more or less explicitly stated aims of the discussion. Furthermore, the speaker may not change the topic. As in conversation, it is the speaker's duty to be informative, truthful, relevant, and clear.

There are discernable stages in discussions, which include (1) identifying the topic or problem; (2) stating alternative responses and arguing their merits; and (3) moving to a decision or conclusion. The formality of these stages varies from setting to setting, but they are always present to some degree.

These stages are related to certain procedural questions, including these:

a) Who decides the topic and the purpose of the discussion?
b) How is traffic regulated? Who speaks, when, for how long?
c) How is progress of the discussion facilitated and monitored?
d) How is the discussion brought to an appropriate close at an appropriate time?

❖ Attitudes and Values Necessary for Discussion

Discussion depends on certain attitudes and values on the part of the participants that cannot be directly observed or monitored. Participants can pretend to be open to other points of view, for example, while being deliberately closeminded. For this reason, Bridges (1979) refers to the "moral disposition or principles" (p. 21) that participants must subscribe to to create an appropriate climate for discussion:

- Reasonableness: As stated above, a person in a discussion must be willing to listen to and be persuaded or affected by compelling reasons, arguments, evidence, insights, and imaginings of other participants.

- Peaceableness and orderliness: Participants must abide by rules such as "one person speaks at a time." In large groups, this principle may require a formal arrangement such as recognition by a chairperson.
- Truthfulness: Participants must refrain from lying, and they must also say what they believe to be true where it is relevant, even if it supports a point of view different from their own.
- Freedom: None of the participants should feel constrained from speaking. Participants should make an effort to encourage others to overcome constraints that arise from unequal status, such as between young people and adults, students and teachers, and laymen and experts.
- Equality: There must not be a presumption that one participant's contribution is more valid than any other's. Participants consider and respond to contributions at face value—regardless of the status or personal characteristics of the contributor.
- Respect for persons: This includes all the preceding attitudes and values.

While Bridges refers to the "moral culture" of discussion, Martin and her colleagues (1976), after analyzing hundreds of hours of tapes of children talking, cite "what one might call humanity, and certain social qualities and skills—concern, generosity, courtesy, [and] humility" as being essential to growth in oral language communication.

Teaching oral communication is not value-free. To teach discussion is to touch the moral principles that Bridges lists and the humanity that Martin observes. A classroom that values these principles and qualities is a classroom where discussion can be introduced and will flourish. A classroom where discussion is taught, used, and valued is a classroom where these principles and qualities will flourish.

❖ Using Discussion to Clarify Thoughts

Discussion encourages students to express themselves tentatively, haltingly, ungrammatically, and, with the collaboration of others, finally to get it right. What teachers and students often fail to realize is that talking can help us think. Students who seem unable to put their thoughts into words on paper may simply not have developed their thoughts well enough to put them into the kind of language we associate with written schoolwork. Discussion provides opportunities to clarify thinking and to practice putting thoughts into words. Studying recorded discussion helps students to see this process at work and, one hopes, to value the tentative, halting speech for what it is and what it accomplishes.

❖ Learning to Deal with Criticism

Discussion is an ideal format in which to learn how to disagree with a person's ideas without making negative comments about that person. Of course, people sometimes feel hurt and defensive simply because their ideas are not wholeheartedly endorsed. One of the objectives of discussion should be to help students learn to distance themselves somewhat from their own contributions to the discussion so that others can respond honestly without fear of hurting or offending the contributor. Adults learn to preface their remarks with such clichés as "This is just off the top of my head, but . . . ," or "I know I'm not making myself very clear, but . . . ," or "Let me just play the Devil's advocate."

People also learn to take criticism impersonally. Students can be helped to see that the tentative, half-formed language of discussion is the language of collaboration. Even their well-developed ideas can be expressed so that they can be examined and challenged. This is another form of collaboration. This process, like all toughening-up processes, can be done only through exercise.

Two more attitudes and values necessary for discussion, then, could be added to Bridges' list.

- Courage: Participants must speak up and say what they believe to be true and relevant.
- Resilience: Participants must not let their display of sensitivity to criticism silence others.

> **ACTIVITY**
>
> A. 1. Form seven small groups. Select numbers from one to seven from a hat so that each group has a number, but groups do not know the other groups' numbers.
>   2. Each group creates a role play of a discussion where one of the seven attitudes and values necessary for discussion (the number drawn by the group) is lacking: (1) Reasonableness; (2) Peaceableness; (3) Truthfulness; (4) Freedom; (5) Equality; (6) Courage; and (7) Resilience. Ask other groups to identify the attitude or value that is lacking.
> B. Adapt this activity for use in the middle or upper grades.
> C. If you are currently teaching elementary school, adapt this activity to your classroom. Share your results with your classmates.

❖ Conducting a Teacher-Led Discussion

Stanford (1977, pp. 119–131) suggests the following techniques for fostering good discussion:

1. Arrange seating so students can see and hear one another. A circle or semicircle is ideal. Children seated in clusters can be encouraged to turn to face speakers. Students seated in rows all facing the teacher is the least desirable arrangement for good discussion.

2. Redirect students' questions instead of answering them. Imagine that Vern Konczal's sixth grade is discussing how the class will commemorate Columbus Day and Lavelle says, "On television last night there was an American Indian saying that Indians would have been better off if Columbus hadn't found America. Do you think it was bad for Columbus to find America?" Vern's instinct is to defend Columbus on the basis of the good things that followed from his discovery, or to agree with the position Lavelle introduced, or to take a middle ground. But being a good discussion leader, Vern replies, "That's a very important question. Who has some ideas about that?"

   Vern (1) does not answer the question; (2) treats the question as important; and (3) does not imply a correct opinion (he does not say, "Who can tell Lavelle why Columbus's discovery was really good in the long run?").

3. Use redirection when the students are not listening to one another. If Vern had reason to believe that Dhanraj was not paying attention, he might say "Dhanraj, what do you think about that?" If Dhanraj says he did not hear Lavelle's question he would respond, "Ask Lavelle to repeat what he just said." Vern's refusal to repeat the question or to ask Lavelle to repeat it sends the message that students must listen to one another. The teacher is not a "switchboard."

4. Do not echo every contribution. Many teachers are in the habit of repeating what every child says before recognizing another child to make a response. This habit encourages students to ignore one another and listen only to the teacher.

5. Do not allow nonlisteners to make new contributions. When students' comments do not follow what has gone before, ask them to summarize what has been said so far before accepting their contribution. Ask previous speakers to comment on the accuracy of the summary. This establishes the idea that students must listen to others before they can contribute their own ideas.

6. Make linking statements. For example, "Both Lin and Hershel seem to be saying that men make better police officers because they are stronger, but Lin thinks women make good police officers anyway. Is that right?"

7. Model good discussion behaviors.
   a. Focus your attention on each speaker. Look at the speaker. Nod and utter "uh-huh." This does not signal agreement but understanding of what the speaker is saying and willingness to listen.
   b. Encourage the speaker to talk rather than seizing the opportunity to answer. "Can you tell me why you think that?" is a better response to an idea with which you disagree than immediately defending your idea.
   c. Do not be afraid of silence. When the speaker pauses, do not fill the silence with a response. Wait and indicate that you are willing to keep listening if the speaker has more to say.

❖ Teacher Neutrality in Teacher-Led Discussion

In general, teachers should not state their opinions in a classroom discussion. The status of teacher by reason of knowledge, age, and power is so overwhelming that the condition of equality which must be present in a discussion simply cannot exist when the teacher becomes one of the discussants.

On the other hand, children are sometimes frustrated when teachers refuse to state an opinion in a discussion, because they feel that the discussion is futile unless they find out what the teacher thinks. This can occur when it is not clear what kind of teacher-led discourse the class is involved in.

For example, in a teacher-directed lesson in arithmetic or spelling, the teacher may have a fact or generalization in mind and may be trying to help the students to state the fact or generalization. In this kind of inductive lesson, the teacher is looking for a correct answer, or at least some answers are closer to what the teacher is looking for than others. In a teacher-led discussion, the point is not to come to a correct solution, but to learn to use language to inform; persuade; express emotion; and negotiate new meanings, judgments, and attitudes in the moral climate of discussion.

Students need to understand the distinction between a teacher-directed lesson and a discussion. In a discussion, students need to know that although the teacher may have an opinion or a belief on the topic, he or she will not state it because the objectives of the discussion are different from the objectives of other teacher-led discourse.

❖ Reflecting on and Evaluating Discussion

People learn how to participate in discussion through a two-part process: *engaging in discussion* and *reflecting on the success of their discussions*. Such reflection can be brought about for students through teacher evaluation and comments or students' self-evaluation and comments. Evaluation and commentary can be done on the spot or through video- or audiotape recordings of discussions using checklists such as those in Boxes 3.6 and 3.7.

ACTIVITY

A. 1. Reflect on a recent teacher-led class discussion (or hold such a discussion for the purpose of this activity) and respond to the Student Self-evaluation Checklist in Box 3.6.
   2. Divide into small groups. Using the responses to the checklist discuss the seven attitudes and values necessary for discussion cited earlier in this chapter: reasonableness, peaceableness, truthfulness, freedom, equality, courage, and resilience.
B. Adapt this activity for use in the middle or upper grades.
C. If you are currently teaching elementary school, adapt this activity to your classroom. Share your results with your classmates.

ACTIVITY

A. 1. Reflect on a recent teacher-led class discussion (or hold such a discussion for the purpose of this activity) and respond to the Evaluation of the Teacher by Students or Others checklist in Box 3.7.
   2. Divide into small groups and share your evaluation of the teacher and arrive at recommendations for improvement by the teacher both as a discussion leader and as a person striving to improve the quality of discussion.
B. Adapt this activity for use in the middle or upper grades.
C. If you are currently teaching elementary school, adapt this activity to your classroom. Share your results with your classmates.

---

1. Did I have an idea or an opinion during the discussion that I did not express?
   If yes, was it because:
   a. I did not know how to say it. It wasn't clear enough so I was afraid I would not be able to make myself understood.
   b. I do not know enough about the topic.
   c. I am not used to discussions so I didn't know when to speak.
   d. My opinion might have gotten me into trouble with the teacher.
   e. I was afraid the others would have laughed.
   f. I didn't want to get into an argument with _____ (another member of the group). We argue about everything.
   g. I didn't want to give _____ (another member of the group) a chance to put me down.
   h. Everyone seemed to agree and I didn't want to disagree.
   i. My comment would have brought up a subject that would have hurt or embarrassed another person in the group.
   j. I didn't want to disagree with _____ (another member of the group) because he/she is a good friend.
   k. I didn't want to disagree with _____ (a group that I am a part of—for example, boys, black students, members of my home room).

BOX 3.6 Student Self-evaluation Checklist

In this chapter I have treated discussion primarily as a teacher-led classroom activity. However, much discussion in classrooms is conducted within small groups of students. I will treat small-group discussion in the next chapter. For the remainder of this chapter I will turn to oral language in a speaker-audience format.

A. Evaluation as a discussion leader
   1. a. Phrased discussion questions neutrally
      b. Implied the answers wanted (Cite an example.)
   2. Gave a fair hearing to all opinions expressed (If no, cite an example.)
   3. a. Assured that everyone was able to finish what he or she had to say
      b. Let louder or more assertive voices drown some people out (Cite an example.)
   4. a. Seemed willing to accept the outcome of the discussion
      b. Seemed to want one certain outcome (Explain.)
B. Evaluation as a teacher trying to improve the discussion
   1. Did the teacher do the following things? If yes, recall an example.
      a. Asked why someone held an opinion
      b. Asked how one point followed from another
      c. Asked how a point was related to the purpose of the discussion
      d. Asked whether one point contradicted another
      e. Asked for clarification of a point
      f. Asked for explanation
      g. Asked for an illustration or an example
      h. Asked for reason or evidence
      i. Asked students to comment on statements of other students
      j. Asked students if their opinions changed
      k. Asked students if they learned new facts
      l. Asked students if they formed new ideas
   2. Think of each example you recalled in 1 *a–l*. Do you think the student(s) to whom the teacher was talking felt the teacher was
      a. helping them say what they wanted to say
      b. helping them understand what others were saying
      c. helping them to compare their ideas and opinions with other people's ideas and opinions
      d. helping them learn new facts
      OR
      e. criticizing them for saying the wrong thing
      f. trapping them into admitting they were wrong
   3. If there are any examples of *e* or *f*, how could the teacher have shown the student that he/she meant to help them when it seemed like he/she meant to criticize or trap them.

BOX 3.7 *Evaluation of the Teacher by Students or Others*

SUPPORTING FORMAL SPEAKING AND LISTENING IN THE CLASSROOM

In the contemporary elementary-school classroom, we rarely find a student standing in front of the classroom reading a book report on *Tom Sawyer* or delivering a talk on his or her research on the invention of the microscope.

The formality of such reports is out of keeping with the atmosphere of modern classrooms and teachers have come to realize that such reports are counterproductive. It is generally conceded that book reports turn everyone off literature—both the speakers and their audiences.

Many other activities can and do serve the purposes of the traditional book report and are far more interesting and informative. In today's classroom, research projects are more likely to be shared by small groups of students with similar interests or students who are engaged in a project where the reported information might be relevant and used to further the project.

Still, students can be given experience in addressing the whole class or addressing small groups as a speaker, rather than as a participant in a discussion, in a number of ways.

❖ Introducing the Speaker-Audience Format

Show and Tell, Demonstrate and Evaluate, Sharing

Most of us are familiar with the Show and Tell activity that takes place routinely in many primary classrooms. Children are encouraged to bring objects to school that have some importance to them and to display the objects while they tell the class about them. A similar activity appears in middle- and upper-grade classrooms (dubbed Demonstrate and Evaluate by Dorothy Nelson, 1976), where students demonstrate (rather than simply display) the games, sporting equipment, materials for crafts, and other objects of interest.

A variation of Show and Tell is Sharing Time, in which the teacher gathers the children and asks who has something important, interesting, or special to share. Children are not required to bring an object to share; they may simply share an experience.

Chenfeld (1978) suggests several variations on the topic of sharing. For example, in "Sharing Partners" Mandy tells Adam what she has to share that day. Adam then introduces Mandy to the class: "I want to introduce Mandy. Mandy played one of the children in *Annie* at Central High School last week. She's got a picture of herself on stage and she's going to tell you how it felt. Here's Mandy."

An Idea Fair

Dorothy Hennings (1986) introduced what she calls an "Idea Fair." In her example, four teams, each composed of two sixth graders, prepared diagrams, models, props, time lines, and photographs to illustrate reports about topics related to machines and modern society. These student pairs set up tables, and the rest of the class divided into four listening-reacting groups. Each pair presented the information to one of the groups using materials they had prepared. During the presentation, members of the listening groups were encouraged to ask questions and manipulate the models. After a period of time, the groups rotated so that each presenting pair had a new audience. The cycle was repeated until each pair had presented to each of the four groups.

This activity has many strong points:

1. The presenters are well prepared, having examined many references using research and study skills (see chapter 7) under the guidance of the teacher.
2. They present orally in a relaxed, small-group atmosphere with a partner.
3. The atmosphere (small groups, visual aids, models) encourages children in the listening-reacting groups to participate and ask questions.
4. The use of the models, diagrams, and other visual aids helps the presenters experience the use of oral, written, and nonverbal channels of communication and to understand that all three channels convey information.
5. The interaction with four separate groups permits the presenters to revise and improve their presentation in light of questions and comments made by previous groups. Two valuable lessons might be learned from this experience:
   a. an audience might not understand what you think you have told them, and
   b. after negotiating meaning through interaction with an audience, you can express yourself more clearly the next time.
6. Children in the listening-reacting groups will take their turns as idea fair presenters. Their experience as listener-reactors teaches them how to be more effective speakers.

Anderson and others (1984) report an interesting experiment to bear out this last point. In this experiment two groups of students (speakers) were asked to give fairly complex instructions to other students (hearers). One group of speakers acted only as speakers. The second group of speakers acted as hearers one week and then, one week later, as speakers in giving a different version of the instructions. Speakers who acted only as speakers talked less, gave less information, and tended not to repeat information. Speakers who acted first as listeners talked more, gave more information, and repeated information more. The authors conclude that speakers who acted first as hearers

> ... understand their hearer's requirements and are striving to provide helpful and informative instructions in these tasks. The speaker realizes from his [or her] own experience of trying to complete the task from a partner's less than adequate instructions, that in these tasks the hearer requires fully explicit information and that only the speaker can provide such information. Thus in his [or her] own subsequent spoken performances a speaker with this experience really understands what is needed and tries to provide the required information in his [or her] instructions. (p. 119)

Making Announcements

Children can make school and class announcements. You can either brief them orally or give them the announcement to read silently and then relay to the class. Children should be encouraged to add their own announcements regarding activities that are known to them and may be interesting to the class. These might include an impending school basketball game, a movie at the local library, and an upcoming television program about a topic of interest to the class.

Addressing Audiences

By the middle grades, children should be helped to reflect on how effectively they communicate in situations where they are presenting to an audience. This can be done through a simple self-evaluation checklist, such as the one below, that students can help develop themselves.

1. Could everyone hear me?
2. Did I look at the people I was talking to?
3. Did I make it interesting?
4. Did everyone understand?
5. Could everyone see what I was showing them?

A more formal and analytic rating scale was developed for middle-school listeners by communication specialists Bock and Bock (1981) (see Box 3.8).

Such scales may be used sparingly in upper-grade classrooms for giving students feedback; they are probably more useful as vehicles for discussion of points to consider in addressing an audience. From such discussion, a simpler self-evaluation checklist, like the one below, might emerge; this checklist would be useful in developing speaking skills as well as evaluating them.

1. Did I have a good introduction?
2. Were my main points clear?
3. Did I have a good conclusion?
4. Did I speak clearly?
5. Did I say *and* and *ah* too much?
6. Did I understand what I was trying to say?
7. Did the audience seem interested?
8. Did everyone see what I was showing them (objects, maps, and so on)?
9. Was my voice natural?
10. Did everyone hear me?

Additional speaking and listening activities can be found in chapter 10, which discusses the imaginative use of language (including storytelling and drama).

Name _____ Date _____
Subject of the Speech _____ Teacher _____

After you listen to each of the speakers, answer the following questions with a yes or a no. These questions will be used to help us decide which areas are important to us when preparing to give a speech, and how we may improve our speeches in the future.

Organization—how the speech is put together or arranged.
1. Could you easily pick out the main ideas of the speech?_____
2. Did the speech have an introduction?_____
3. Did the speech have a body?_____
4. Did the speech have a conclusion or a summary?_____
5. Was the speech developed or put together in a way that made it easy for the audience to understand?_____

Language—the sentence structure of the speech.
1. Were the explanations clear?_____
2. Was the language easy to understand?_____
3. Did the speaker make use of pauses to separate ideas from one another?_____
4. Were there too many and's or uh's used?_____
5. Was it easy to tell where one sentence stopped and the next one began?_____

Material—what the speech was actually about.
1. Was the subject interesting to you?_____
2. Was the speech easy for you to understand?_____
3. Did the speaker seem really to know the subject matter?_____
4. Did the speaker seem comfortable and at ease while giving the speech?_____
5. Was there eye contact with the audience?_____
6. Was the speaker aware of how the audience was reacting to the speech?_____
7. Did the speaker make good use of gestures and body language?_____
8. Did the main ideas stand out above the other ideas?_____
9. Were the other ideas less important but still necessary in the development of the speech?_____

Voice—how the speaker sounded.
1. Was the speaker's voice pleasing to the ear?_____
2. Was the pitch varied—that is, did it go up and down?_____
3. Was the speaker loud enough?_____
4. Did the speaker talk too fast?_____
5. Did the speaker use good expression?_____

Total Score _____ (add the number of "yes" responses)
Grade _____

BOX 3.8 Speech Rating Blank

Summary

Effective oral language communication requires that speakers understand what is required by the communicative setting and that they be able to produce communication that fits the setting. This involves listening as well as speaking.

Communicative stress describes factors that make a speaker's performance difficult, such as the information gap and characteristics of the listener (age, status, number, and behavior), the topic (difficult, complicated, poorly understood), the context (familiar, foreign), and the format (conversation, discussion, or lecture).

Teaching receptive communication skills (listening) is as important as teaching expressive communication skills (speaking). Demands made on listeners in school differ from the demands made at home. The question-answer-evaluate format is much more typical of the teacher-student register than of the parent-child register. Teachers ask more display questions, and they control the topic more. In school, the topic is more likely to be abstract or outside the immediate context than topics at home.

Communicative stress for listeners involves the level of complexity and vocabulary of the speaker's language; the speaker's ability to supply the listener with information necessary to understand what is said; and feelings the speaker may evoke in the listener. Other factors include the topic and who controls it and the amount of support provided by the context in which the message is conveyed.

Certain characteristics of the listeners themselves are also important. Support from previous knowledge can help the listener understand the message, or it can interfere by establishing expectations as to the message's meaning. Lack of knowledge can also make understanding difficult. The listener needs to know what questions to ask and what information is lacking. Finally, the listener must be willing to put forth effort and to suspend judgments and preconceived notions.

Teaching effective listening means providing activities that require direct focused involvement in the act of listening itself. Teachers can model good listening and offer opportunities for students to practice good listening throughout the school day. Each component of listening can be related to the functions of language and practiced along with exercises that focus on the specific functions of informing, persuading, expressing feelings, imaging, and ritualizing.

Conversations and discussions are forms of spoken discourse that have similar rules, such as turn-taking, cohesion, the given-new contract, and the cooperative principle. Discussions, however, have stricter rules about adhering to a particular topic.

Turn-taking assures that orderly exchange of speaker and listener roles occur. Cohesion assures that the topic is adhered to, that all the parts of the conversation relate to one another and result in a whole discourse. The given-new contract means that when new information is introduced, it is assumed to be related to the previously given information. The cooperative principle requires participants to try to be as informative, truthful, relevant, and clear as possible.

Teachers need to be aware of their own oral communication behavior, that is, their tendency to be too talkative or too inclined to silence. Middle- and upper-grade students can also benefit from learning about their inclinations to talkativeness or silence. Rules for good conversations such as described above can be established for the classroom and a checklist can be used to evaluate conversations in various contexts. Opportunities should be provided to practice good conversations between the teacher and students and among students.

Discussions are a more formal kind of discourse than conversations. In discussion a particular topic is set and more than one point of view is expressed. The purpose is to improve knowledge, understanding, or judgment regarding the topic. Participants respond to one another and are willing to be convinced by others' statements and reasons.

Discussions usually develop through certain stages. First the topic or problem is identified; then alternative responses are stated and argued; finally a decision or conclusion is reached. Procedural questions that need to be addressed include who will set the topic and purpose; who will regulate who speaks, when, and for how long; how will progress be facilitated and monitored; and how will the discussion be appropriately closed at an appropriate time?

Bridges refers to the attitudes and values necessary for a good discussion as the "moral disposition or principles" to which all participants must subscribe. These include reasonableness, peaceableness and orderliness, truthfulness, freedom, equality, and respect for persons. Establishing this moral culture for discussions is essential to growth in oral language communication.

Good discussion is helpful in clarifying one's thoughts. Sharing one's tentative, incomplete thoughts requires courage, and the skill to state ideas in a way that allows others to respond honestly without hurting the speaker's feelings. The teacher needs to establish an atmosphere of trust and security so that optimal learning can occur in discussing settings.

Stanford suggests the following techniques for fostering good discussions: arrange chairs so students can see, hear, and address one another; redirect students' questions instead of answering them; use redirection to keep students' attention; refrain from echoing students' responses; insist that contributions be responses to previous contributions and on the topic; make linking statements; and model good listening behaviors such as focusing on the speaker, encouraging the speaker to expand on ideas, and refraining from filling every silence with a response.

It is important to remember that a teacher-led discussion is different from a teacher-directed lesson or recitation. In the teacher-directed lesson a more clearly "correct" answer is being sought than in a teacher-led discussion. When teachers state opinions in a discussion, it can unduly influence the students who may think the teacher's views are the correct ones. To avoid stifling students' development of their own thoughts, teachers should probably refrain from expressing their opinions and views in discussions.

Reflecting on and evaluating the teacher-led discussion can become part of the aim of the discussion. Checklists can be used by students and/or teachers to assess the extent to which the characteristics of good discussion were in evidence. Students can be taught to take responsibility for conducting and evaluating their own discussion in small groups, which is the topic of chapter 4.

Other, more formal speaking and listening activities in the classroom include: sharing research projects and reports (better done in small rather than large groups), show and tell or demonstrate and evaluate, introducing partners, an idea fair, making class and school announcements, and addressing audiences.

For Review and Discussion

1. What factors make a speaker's performance difficult? Give examples from your experiences with different speaking situations.
2. How do typical teacher questions differ from typical parent questions? How might a child respond who has little previous experience with teacher-type questions?
3. Give examples of listening exercises that could be incorporated into lessons focusing on functions such as informing, persuading, expressing feelings, imaging, and ritualizing.
4. What are the rules of conversation? How are discussion rules similar to and different from conversation rules?
5. What are the stages of a discussion and what decisions must a teacher make to assure the discussion proceeds smoothly through these stages? What values and attitudes can affect these decisions?
6. How can redirection be used to foster good discussion behavior? Give examples.
7. What is your view of the proper role for the teacher in a discussion? Participant or nonparticipant?

For Further Reading

Beaver, J. M. (1982). Say it! over and over. *Language Arts, 59,* 143–148.

Camp, D. J., & Tompkins, G. E. (1990). Show-and-tell in middle school? *Middle School Journal, 21,* 18–20.

Devine, T. G. (1982). *Listening skills schoolwide: Activities and programs.* Urbana, IL: ERIC Clearinghouse on Reading and Communication Skills and the National Council of Teachers of English.

Erickson, A. (1985). Listening leads to reading. *Reading Today, 2,* 13.

Klein, M. L. (1979). Designing a talk environment for the classroom. *Language Arts, 56,* 647–656.

Putnam, L. (1991). Dramatizing nonfiction with emerging readers. *Language Arts, 68,* 463–469.

Roth, R. (1986). Practical use of language in school. *Language Arts, 63,* 134–142.

Tompkins, G. E., Friend, M., & Smith, P. L. (1987). Strategies for more effective listening. In C. R. Personke & D. D. Johnson (Eds.), *Language arts and the beginning teacher* (Chapter 3). Englewood Cliffs, NJ: Prentice-Hall.

CHAPTER 4

Oral Language: Small-Group Discussion, Cooperative Learning, and Conflict Resolution

Introduction
Small-Group Discussion
TO THINK ABOUT: Teacher Talk—Directive or Collaborative?
Lesson Plan: Disputes and Discussions
Lesson Plan: Potholes
Cooperative Learning
Conflict Resolution
Lesson Plan: Alliterative Name Games
Lesson Plan: Classroom Yellow Pages
Lesson Plan: Active Listening
Lesson Plan: The Description Game
Lesson Plan: Recognizing Methods of Decision Making
Activities
Summary
For Review and Discussion
For Further Reading

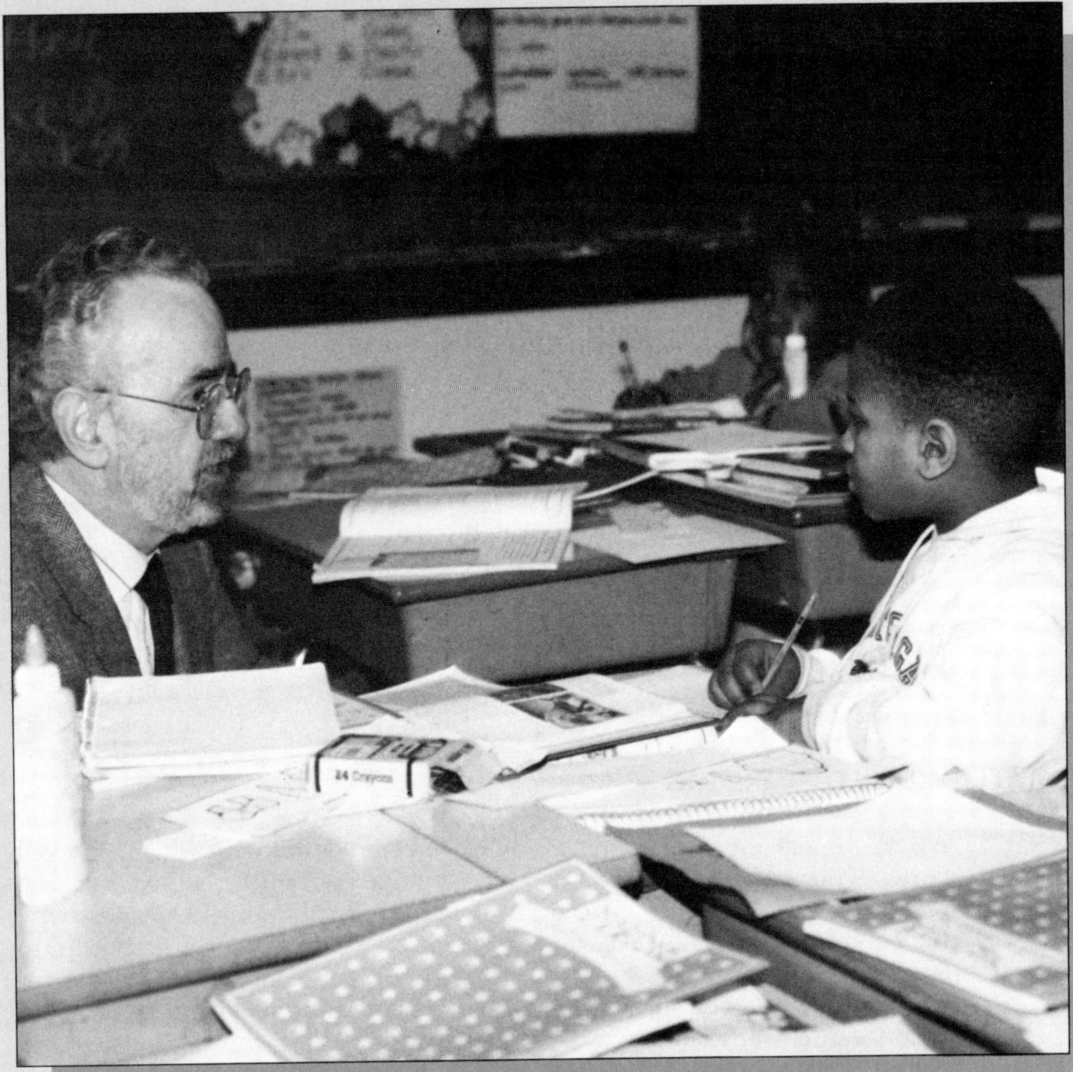
24 Crayons

INTRODUCTION

There has been great interest in recent years in the concept of cooperative learning. In this learning environment students work together in small groups to achieve a common learning objective. The situation is structured in such a way that students must depend on one another to accomplish the group goal, but each student is held individually accountable. A further essential characteristic of cooperative learning is that students reflect on the process they engaged in as each project is completed so as to increase their ability to make the process work in the future.

Teachers take an active part in teaching the language and social skills necessary to engage in cooperative learning. Since nearly every attempt at cooperation entails dealing with conflict, many of the language and social skills that must be addressed in cooperative learning come under the heading of conflict resolution.

The idea of students' learning from one another in small groups has a long history. Prior to the appearance of the cooperative learning concept, there was a long tradition of small-group discussion as a method of improving oral language facility, solving problems, and learning. Small-group discussion is a similar learning format, but it is not identical to cooperative learning.

This chapter addresses oral language development in the context of small-group discussion and cooperative learning. Since conflict resolution plays an important part in both these learning formats, it is treated as a separate topic.

SMALL-GROUP DISCUSSION

A seventh-grade teacher conducts a science demonstration in which a corked bottle is placed under a bell jar and air is pumped out of the bell jar until the cork pops out of the bottle. Students divide into small groups to discuss why the cork came out and what would happen to an astronaut who stepped into space without a space suit on. One group of boys has gone beyond the assignment and posed a new question: What would happen if the pressure inside the bottle were lower than the pressure around it? The following exchange takes place (Barnes & Todd, 1977, p. 34):

 44 Edward: If it'd been a plastic bottle it would have been erm, been erm, crushed in, wouldn't it?
 45 Philip: Yeah, but it'd have been if it were glass.
 46 Harold: Well, t'glass one would've probably cracked, wouldn't it?
 47 Edward: It, it wouldn't . . . If it was thick glass.
       If it was very very thin glass like slide glass . . .
 48 Harold: Or't cork would get sucked in.
 49 Edward: Or't cork, er. If it was thick glass . . .
 50 Philip: Yeah t'cork.
 51 Harold: Cork'd get pushed in though, wouldn't it?

52 Philip: Yeah cork'd also get pushed in then that'd mean that air would have got into the bottle, so it wouldn't have happened.
53 Harold: Most likely cork'd get pushed in, rather than t'jar smashed.
54 Edward: Yeah.

I presented earlier examples of talk involving Rosie and Elaine and Stuart (chapter 3) to suggest that collaborative talk often has advantages over directive talk between teachers and students, and that collaborative talk among students often has advantages over collaborative talk between teachers and students. The episode involving Edward, Philip, and Harold demonstrates some of the advantages of discussion over collaborative, informal conversation. These boys had a task set for them; they have had experience working in small groups. The talk is collaborative, interest is high, and the discussion is focused on a clear learning objective. In each of the conversations reported earlier involving Rosie and Stuart and Elaine, at least one of these characteristics was lacking.

❖ Some Basic Observations About Small Groups

Barnes and Todd (1977) studied small-group discussion of upper-grade children over a twelve-month period. Based on a total of eleven hours of taped discussion they made the following basic observations.

Group Size

The ideal size of a learning group is between two and four. Larger groups encourage some students to remain silent and introduce problems of deciding who talks and when; they also prevent close involvement of all members of the group where there is material present to be worked on.

The Degree of Familiarity Among Group Members

The aim of small-group discussion is to help students learn to state their views explicitly and to defend them and to evaluate the explicitly stated views of others. Familiarity and friendships encourage communication through allusion to shared and implicit beliefs. Therefore, the ultimate aim is to have students working in small groups of children with whom they are not particularly familiar or friendly so that they will need to be explicit to be understood. This also facilitates communication between children from different backgrounds and with different communication styles.

Barnes and Todd suggest that small groups begin with short tasks to be accomplished in groups of two where partners are self-selected. As the aims and process of small-group learning become established, tasks become more complex, time becomes extended, group size increases, and arbitrary assignment to groups replaces self-selections.

At times, a two-stage process may facilitate the aims of a lesson. A task is assigned to self-selected groups of two or three and then addressed by arbitrarily assigned groups of four.

Task Presentation

The way the task is presented may result in different kinds of discussion.

Tight Construction
Tightly constructed tasks often take the form of a series of questions or steps. For example:

1. Recall the demonstration from yesterday when we put a bottle with a cork in it inside a bell jar and pumped air out of the bell jar.
2. What happened?
3. Why?
4. If a piece of rock in space hit a spaceship and put a hole in it, what would happen to the air inside? Why?
5. What would happen if an astronaut stepped out into space without a space suit on? Why?

The purpose of tightly constructed tasks is to guide the group's thinking step by step so that conclusions from one step will be available for the next step. Such tasks tend to foster convergent thinking. There tends to be "correct" answers to earlier questions. The groups' task is to apply the facts established to a new situation introduced in the later question.

Loose Construction
Loosely constructed tasks often take the form of a statement and an invitation to agree or disagree, using evidence or giving reasons. For example, groups might be asked to decide whether they agree or disagree with the following statement and to state their reasons.

> When the classroom is set up in straight rows with everyone facing the front of the room, the room is quiet and everyone gets his or her work done. When desks are put in clusters, there is a lot of noise and no one does any work. It's always best to have the classroom in rows.

The purpose of loosely constructed tasks is to encourage a range of suggestions that pupils can evaluate. Such tasks do not lead to conclusions that are right or wrong. They encourage children to explore half-understood ideas and intuitions, work them out and make them explicit, and examine their probable consequences.

Neither tightly nor loosely constructed tasks have been shown to be superior, but the objectives and, therefore, the resulting discussion are clearly different. Students and teachers need to understand the probable results when they are constructing a task and when they are evaluating its results.

❖ Sources of Success and Failure in Small-Group Discussion

Barnes and Todd (1977) noted the following social skills in successful small-group discussion and sources of breakdown in unsuccessful small-group discussion.

Skills Contributing to Success

Ability to progress through the task
   Stating and interpreting the question, assignment, or problem
   Shifting the topic
   Ending the discussion
   Managing tasks that call for manipulation of materials
Ability to manage competition and conflict
   Competing for the floor
   Contradicting
   Joking
   Demanding participation of others
Ability to lend support
   Agreeing explicitly
   Referring to another participant by name
   Referring back to another's remarks
   Stating approval of others explicitly
   Stating shared feelings

Sources of Breakdown

- Conflict and rivalry which seemed to predate the discussion got in the way of sticking to the task, accepting one another's views, or working together.
- Conflict arising from the task itself sometimes got in the way. Assigning four students to do a manipulative task that could be done by only one might cause conflict over who would do the task. If the task was very difficult, criticism was sometimes directed at the doer, and irritation was directed at people making suggestions.
- Some conversations focused almost entirely on the difficulty of the task and worry about whether they were doing it right rather than focusing on the ideas the task was supposed to help them think about.
- Some groups suffered from failure to challenge views that were clearly incorrect.
- Some groups habitually agreed with the first view stated and discussion never developed.
- Reminiscences of experiences disintegrated into bull sessions. Students failed to apply the experiences to the problem at hand.
- Students sometimes engaged in mouthing platitudes without examining their meaning or stating their connection with the topic. In discussing

gang violence, for example, comments like "It's the television" and "You can't stop boys from fighting" were made but neither challenged nor developed.
- Students failed to apply to the tasks or problem. They simply ignored it, misunderstood it, or went off on a tangent.
- At times students did not seem to know when they had completed the task. After reaching a conclusion they reintroduced the problem or part of the problem and discussed it as if it were never talked about before.

❖ Five Kinds of Talk in Small Groups

While it is sometimes argued that all talk is beneficial to children learning to use language and using language to learn, analysis of the thinking associated with different kinds of talk suggests that not all talk is equally valuable in the classroom.

Phillips (1985) studied small-group discussion in middle grades and discovered five kinds of talk.

1. Hypothetical Talk

This kind of talk emerges in a brainstorming or think-tank phase of a discussion when children are throwing out ideas that might solve the problem assigned to the group. It is characterized by "Suppose we . . . ," "What if . . . ?," "Do you think . . . ?," and "What about . . . ?" Phrases like "a kind of a shovel," "a tunnel sort of thing," and "fairly heavy" are typical of hypothetical talk because they signify that the speaker has not formed this thought precisely and this is only a suggestion.

2. Experiential Talk

This kind of talk emerges when children are recalling personal experiences. It is characterized by "Once . . . ," "I remember when . . . ," and "That reminds me . . ."

Hypothetical and experiential talk encourage very desirable ways of thinking. Both kinds oblige the group members to continually review the conversation. In hypothetical talk, when children ask "What if we . . . ?" and use words like *could* and *might*, they are not seeking an immediate reply, but they are putting their ideas on the table alongside others for consideration. In experiential talk, children recount events in their past. They are asking their peers to contemplate this experience, relate it to the topic at hand, and relate it to their own experience. "Where hypothetical or experiential style talk is developed and sustained, a framework is provided which encourages children to turn away from the immediate and to reflect, hypothesize, evaluate, and order" (Phillips, 1985, p. 77). They are encouraged, in fact, to become involved in their own learning.

3. Argumentational Talk

This kind of talk emerges when children engage in dispute or argument. It is characterized by "Yes, but . . . " and "But, don't you think . . . ?" Although one would expect the language of logical argument to emerge, such as *because, if . . .*

then, and *on the other hand*, such language was rare in the discussion Phillips recorded.

Argumentational talk leads children to state their opinions and state reasons for them, but the benefits of argumentational talk are not automatic. Phillips notes that young children in small-group discussions tactfully put aside previous speaker's opinions and state their own. They sometimes give reasons for their own opinions, but not for rejecting the opinions of others. They do not compare ideas and come the a reasoned conclusion regarding them.

A typical exercise for promoting argumentational talk in small groups is called "Lost on the Moon" (Book & Galvin, 1975, pp. 24–26), presented in Box 4.1. Students are asked to do such exercises individually and then to do them again in small groups. Most children will find that the group response is more successful than their individual response. However, such assignments do not guarantee that the group response is the result of explicitly stated opinions and reasons for them.

You are part of a space crew originally scheduled to rendezvous with a mother ship on the lighted surface of the moon. Mechanical difficulties, however, have forced your ship to crash land at a spot some two hundred miles from the rendezvous point. The rough landing damaged much of the equipment aboard. Since survival depends on reaching the mother ship, the most critical items available must be chosen for the two-hundred-mile trip. Below are listed the fifteen items left intact after the landing.

Your task: Rank these items in terms of their importance to your crew in its attempt to reach the rendezvous point. Place number 1 by the most important item, number 2 by the second most important item, and so on through number 15, the least important.

- _____ Box of matches
- _____ Food concentrate
- _____ 50 feet of nylon rope
- _____ Parachute silk
- _____ Portable heating unit
- _____ Two 0.45-caliber pistols
- _____ One case of dehydrated milk
- _____ Two 100-pound tanks of oxygen
- _____ Stellar map of moon's constellation
- _____ Life raft
- _____ Magnetic compass
- _____ 5 gallons of water
- _____ Signal flares
- _____ First-aid kit containing injection needles
- _____ Solar-powered FM receiver-transmitter

BOX 4.1 Lost on the Moon

> **BOX 4.1** *(continued)*
> **SCORING KEY**
>
> (15) Box of matches—little or no use on moon
> (4) Food concentrate—supply daily food required
> (6) 50 feet of nylon rope—useful in tying injured; help in climbing
> (8) Parachute silk—shelter against sun's rays
> (13) Portable heating unit—useful only if party landed on dark side
> (11) Two 0.45-caliber pistols—self-propulsion devices could be made from them
> (12) One case of dehydrated milk—food, mixed with water for drinking
> (1) Two 100-pound tanks of oxygen—fills respiration requirement
> (3) Stellar map of moon's constellation—one of principal means of finding directions
> (9) Life raft—CO_2 bottle for self-propulsion across chasms, etc.
> (14) Magnetic compass—probably no magnetized pole; thus useless
> (2) 5 gallons of water—replenishes loss by sweating, etc.
> (10) Signal flares—distress call within line of sight
> (7) First-aid kit containing injection needles—oral pills or injection medicine valuable
> (5) Solar-powered FM receiver-transmitter—distress signal transmitter, possible communication with mother ship
>
> Two ways that "Lost on the Moon" can be altered to insure that children give reasons for their opinions and for rejecting others' opinions are:
>
> 1. a) Have each person in the group write down the two items he or she feels are most important, b) Have each person show his or her list to the others in the group, c) Have each person compare his or her list with an item suggested by someone else and explain why his or her item is a better choice.
> 2. a) Have each person list reasons why each item might be useful or useless. b) Have each person select the five *most* useful items and explain his or her choices. c) Have each person select the five *least* important items and explain his or her choices.

4. Operational Talk

This kind of talk emerges when children are working together on some physical object. It is characterized by "Push that down," "Take that off," "Wait a minute," and pronouns such as *this, that, these, those, it,* and *them.* The meaning of operational talk tends to be very context-dependent. A person cannot fully understand it unless he or she can see what is going on.

Operational talk leads to a kind of decision making in action. One child suggests "Push that down." Another child does the action. The rest watch. Another action is suggested: "Now hold it." Suggestions might even be challenged: "No! Let it go! Let it go!" However, only if the children are asked why they are doing what they are doing is there any opportunity for them to share their thoughts, and such questions rarely occur in operational talk. Language expressing long-term planning and reflection is absent.

In discussions employing the operational mode, it is a good idea to structure the discussion so that participants are encouraged to state the reasons for the actions they suggest. There can be a planning stage where children discuss what they might do but they are not allowed to touch the material until later. There might be a review period where children discuss ideas that were suggested but not tried or that were tried but did not work. Reasons why these ideas were rejected or did not work and the reasons why the successful suggestion did work could be made explicit. Children should learn that at any time during an activity it is possible, and often appropriate, to suspend the proceedings while they do some reviewing, thinking, and planning.

5. Expositional Talk

This kind of talk is characterized by wh- questions (who, what, when, where, how, and why) directed at a specific individual. Expositional talk is very directive because when such a question is addressed to an individual, it is difficult for the addressee to avoid answering it. This is a typical teacher mode. Expositional talk rarely emerged in the discussions Phillips observed. When it did appear it was never sustained. It may require an unequal distribution of power for this mode to be sustained, or else children may avoid it simply because they sense that it casts them into the role of teacher.

Phillips observed that the first four kinds of talk emerge in small groups of ten- to twelve-year-olds and that when one kind of talk is introduced, it is frequently picked up by others in the group. This results in cohesive discussion without one individual taking charge or directing the group. On the other hand, teachers rarely engage in the first four modes of discourse for any sustained period, and these modes of discourse tend to be absent from small groups when teachers are members of the group.

TO THINK ABOUT

Teacher Talk—Directive or Collaborative?

Reflect on the statement that teachers rarely engage in hypothetical, experiential, argumentational, or operational talk for any sustained period and such talk rarely occurs in small groups when teachers are a part of them. What is it about a traditional teacher's role in the classroom that makes this statement true (presuming the statement is true)? (You might want to review the interviews with Michael and Laura in chapter 1 before continuing.)

Based on what you have read in this book so far, devise an argument for or against the following proposition:

Teachers like Michael, who are unabashedly directive, are not often inclined to state hypotheses; they are more inclined to state the correct answer. For similar reasons they do not engage in experiential, argumentational, or operational talk. When such teachers join a small group of students in a discussion, the discussion ends; it becomes a teacher talking to a small group of students.

Teachers like Laura, who strive to be collaborative, have many more opportunities to engage in hypothetical, experiential, argumentational, and operational talk. If they are successful, they should be able to join small groups of students in discussion without disrupting the nature of the discussion too much. The role they assume as teachers has many of the characteristics of a good member of a small-group discussion.

❖ Supporting Small-Group Discussion in the Classroom

Getting into Discussion

In primary grades discussion is introduced in class meetings or magic circles. The children gather into a large circle. The teacher asks a question such as "What would you do if you had three wishes?", "What is a promise?", or "How do you feel when someone breaks a promise?" The important objective is to help children talk in groups. Everyone is encouraged to talk. All feelings and opinions are held to be important. As students learn to contribute they are gently reminded to stay on the topic. "That's interesting about your dog; do you have anything to say about a promise someone broke?"

A way of introducing discussion into classrooms at all grade levels is to plan events that capture the interest of students and to gradually turn the planning over to them. For example, the teacher declares a special day each month—Friday, September 30, is declared National Chocolate Day. There is math bingo with M & M markers. Children bring in recipes for chocolate-chip cookies, compare them, choose one, and make cookies. A list of words associated with chocolate, such as cocoa, fudge, vanilla, and confectionery, are used for vocabulary and spelling activities. Children research the countries that produce cocoa, how cocoa is grown, and the history of companies such as Hershey and Cadbury.

The third Friday of October might be declared National Peanut Day or National TV Sitcom Day. As students take over planning special days they will discover the characteristics of discussion. The teachers should be alert for opportunities to point out these characteristics when they appear and when they are lacking.

Teaching the Discussion Process

Two approaches have been suggested for teaching the process of small-group discussion (Barnes & Todd, 1977). One approach is to facilitate competence on the part of students while they are engaged in the process, and the second is to make the process the topic of study.

Facilitating Competence During the Process

Teachers can facilitate competence on the part of students by making sure that students understand the task, that they have something to say, and that they understand the process. One way of doing this is to base small-group discussions on teacher-led presentations and large-group discussions. This ensures that students will understand the material and enables the teacher to demonstrate that students' comments will be taken seriously, and that the problem presented can be solved through discussion.

A second way of facilitating competence while students are engaged in the process is to provide materials for students to refer to during the discussion. This increases students' understanding of the problem and helps them to focus on the task rather than on recall of previously learned material. In science, apparatus is often available for consultation. In history, a fact sheet might be supplied.

A third suggestion is to help students monitor their own progress while engaged in the process. For example, after about five minutes the teacher might interrupt the discussion and ask students to consider how the process is going. How far have they gotten in the questions? Have they stayed on the topic? What should they do next? After half a minute or so, ask the groups to return to the discussion of the task. When time is nearly up, ask the students to come to a rapid conclusion and then take a minute or two to decide the main points they have arrived at.

For older children such progress-monitoring procedures can be included on the written statement of the problem, list of questions, or data sheet.

Making the Process the Topic of Study

Teachers can record (audio or video) student discussion and make the recordings the topic of study. Teachers point out the unfinished character of the language of spoken discussion—the *ah*s, the silences, the sentences broken off in the middle—and reassure the children that the unfinished, fluid character of talk in discussion is what makes it suitable for the job it is performing. This is an opportunity to reassure students that using speech in the process of shaping meaning is as important a part of school work as producing completed, polished written language. We will see in chapter 8 that this kind of thinking and talking is, in fact, an essential part of the writing process.

Other ways of studying recorded small-group discussions are

- to look for examples of social skills necessary for successful small-group discussion and reflect on the purposes these skills serve (see Skills Contributing to Success in this chapter).
- to identify breakdowns in discussion and suggest ways they might have been avoided or repaired (see Sources of Breakdown in this chapter).
- to find examples of hypothetical, experiential, argumentational, operational, and expositional talk and reflect on how the discussion goals were furthered or impeded by these categories of talk.

| Date _____ | Group _____ |
| Time _____ | Observer _____ |

Participants' Names

Behavioral Functions						
1. Initiating and orienting						
2. Information giving						
3. Information seeking						
4. Opinion giving						
5. Opinion seeking						
6. Clarifying and elaborating						
7. Evaluating						
8. Summarizing						
9. Recording						
10. Suggesting procedure						
11. Supporting						
12. Tension relieving						

BOX 4.2 Behavioral Functions of Discussants

Participant _____ Date _____
Observer _____ Time _____

The checkmark on each scale indicates my best judgment of the degree of assertiveness of the participant in the discussion.

Behavior	*Nonassertive*	*Assertive*	*Aggressive*
Getting and holding the floor	yielded easily	usually refused to let other take over or dominate	interrupted and cut others off

Box 4.3 Assertiveness Rating Scale

BOX 4.3 *(continued)*

Behavior	*Nonassertive*	*Assertive*	*Aggressive*
Expressing opinions	never expressed personal opinion	stated opinions, but open to others' opinions	insisted others should agree with you
Sharing information	none, or only if asked to do so	whenever info was relevant, concisely	whether relevant or not; long-winded, rambling

Personal Manner			
Voice	weak, unduly soft	strong and clear	loud, strident
Posture and movements	withdrawn, restricted	animated, often leaning forward	unduly forceful, table pounding
Eye contact	rare, even when speaking	direct but not staring or glaring	stared others down
Overall manner	nonassertive	assertive	aggressive

The performance of individuals in a videotaped small group can be analyzed and evaluated through rating scales such as those suggested by Brilhart in *Effective Group Discussion* (1986). The rating scales in Boxes 4.2 and 4.3 are adapted from two of the seventeen scales Brilhart suggests for rating whole groups, individuals, and group leaders.

Some Specific Suggestions for Lessons

Behaviors that negatively effect discussion can be addressed explicitly, as in the following two activities.

LESSON PLAN: Disputes and Discussions

Procedure

1. Ask students, "What is the difference between a dispute and a discussion?" Note their ideas on the board. If they get stuck, ask "What about tone of voice, body language, choice of words?" The chart may end up looking something like this:

Dispute	**Discussion**
Loud, angry, harsh tone of voice	Quiet, calm, even tone of voice
Interrupting	Letting other person finish a point before you start
Insults, put-downs, sarcasm	Respectfulness, friendliness
Exaggerations (terrible, evil, never, everybody, always)	Careful, exact words
Goal is to win	Goal is to find truth

2. Put practice topics on the board and ask for two volunteers to enter into a dispute and then a discussion about one of the topics on which they disagree.

How does a dispute make you feel? A discussion?
Can you still be angry and have a discussion?
What are the benefits of discussions over disputes? (Kreidler, 1984, p. 96)

LESSON PLAN: Potholes

Procedure

1. On the board list communication potholes, that is, ways of acting that make the communication process more difficult. For example, you might note behavior that is bossy, superior, interrupting, putting down, absolutely sure, threatening, or sneaky.

2. Have students role play or give examples of these ways of behaving.
3. Have students rank the list from most annoying to least annoying.

Discussion

Why is _____ a communication pothole?
If you were in a conflict and someone started being _____ , how would you feel?
What could you do to counteract it?
Which of these potholes annoys you the most?
What potholes did we forget? (Kreidler, 1984, p. 97)

In recent years two teaching approaches have evolved, somewhat independently, which share many of the objectives and techniques of small-group discussion. They are cooperative learning and conflict resolution.

COOPERATIVE LEARNING

Johnson and Johnson (1984) discuss three kinds of learning, each of which is useful in teaching language arts. They define these in terms of "goal structures." The difference between goal structures is in the way an individual student's goals relate to the goals of his or her classmates. The Johnsons contrast the cooperative goal structure with two others: the competitive and the individual goal structures.

✤ Contrasting Goal Structures

Competitive Goal Structure

In a competitive goal structure a student's attaining his or her goal depends on other students' failing to attain their goal. When one student will be called on to give the correct answer, getting called on is a "win." When another student is called on and has the wrong answer, it is another form of win for the competing students. When students are marked on the curve they are deemed successful in comparison to others' behavior. In a spelling bee, or any kind of academic competition, a student's performance alone does not lead to success. Other students must fail. Much of the school day is conducted in a competitive goal structure. The competitive goal structure has a gamelike quality and is especially good for atomistic, rote learning of such things as spelling and list learning.

Individual Goal Structure

In an individual goal structure the achievement of a goal by one student is unrelated to the goal achievement of others. Individualized instruction programs that were prevalent in the 1960s and 1970s are based on this structure. Bright, hardworking students went through the ordered exercises quickly. Slower, less motivated students and students who were not familiar with the school agenda went through the exercises less quickly. What one student did had no bearing on the achievement of another student. Like the competitive goal structure, this structure often appears in circumstances where goals are set that all students are expected to achieve. For example, learning to spell a weekly list of words, or learning arithmetic facts (two plus two is four), or memorizing lists of inventors and inventions. Of course teachers often introduce competition into such learning, but an individual goal structure can be, and often is, adopted in these circumstances.

Cooperative Goal Structure

In a cooperative goal structure a student's achieving his or her goal depends on others achieving their goals. I will further explain this goal structure and lessons based on it.

Research by the Johnsons and others shows that while some memorization learning tasks are achieved best by competitive goal structures and some, such as mechanical skills, are achieved best by individual goal structures, most higher-order cognitive skills such as problem solving and mastery of concepts and principles, are best achieved through cooperatively structured learning. Affective kinds of learning, such as valuing diversity and democracy, enjoyment of learning, and positive self-attitudes, are also more effectively developed with cooperative goal structures (Schniedewind & Davidson, 1987).

❖ Two Cooperative-Learning Lessons

The following lesson is based on suggestion made by Schniedewind and Davidson (1987). Helen Milliken divides her fourth-grade class into six groups of four, making sure that each group contains a mixture of children in terms of ability. She tells each group that they are to write a set of three practice sentences for punctuation like the ones they find in some textbooks and standardized texts. For example:

Jody yelled can someone grab the other end of this shelf.

Helen suggests that the students remember what punctuation they are working on in their writing folders and what punctuation skills she has covered in minilessons recently (see chapter 8 for a discussion of writing folders and minilessons). Practice sentences are then circulated from group to group and children collaborate in rewriting them with conventional punctuation. The rewritten sentences are then returned to the originating groups and evaluated.

While the groups are working, Helen circulates, listens in, explains the task to groups that are off target, and encourages productive small-group behavior.

After each group has rewritten the sentences for every other group, Helen collects the practice sentences from each group and dictates six of them for each student to write and punctuate correctly. Each student's paper is graded individually. Members of groups that receive an average score of over 90 percent earn bonus points.

After this activity the group processes the experience by discussing these questions:

- In what ways was making up the sentences (or rewriting the sentences) with a group easy? Difficult? Satisfying? Frustrating?
- How was it different to make up examples (or rewrite the sentences) when people were cooperating?
- How did it help to have a group making up the examples (or writing the sentences) rather than doing it yourself?
- Were there any ways the group made it harder? If so, what could you do about that next time?

Robert Beardsley's seventh-grade class is learning about the civil rights movement of the 1950s and 1960s. He divides his class into groups of five. The groups are heterogeneous in terms of ability and (because he feels it is relevant in this case) ethnicity. These groups are labeled home groups. Students discuss what they know about the civil rights movement in their home groups for five minutes.

Robert then tells them to count off within their groups from one to five, and he regroups them into five "expert" groups. All the "ones" go to Expert Group One, all the "twos" go to Expert Group Two, and so on.

Robert has prepared the following instructions for each expert group.

Today we are going to watch a video entitled "Eyes on the Prize," which is a documentary about the civil rights movement.
Group 1 pay special attention to the role the courts, lawyers, and judges played in this drama.
Group 2 pay special attention to the role the churches, ministers, and churchgoers played in this drama.
Group 3 pay special attention to the role the schools, teachers, and school children played in this drama.
Group 4 pay special attention to the role the newspapers, television, and reporters played in this drama.
Group 5 pay special attention to the role the president and members of Congress played in this drama.

After students read their instructions, discuss them, and agree that they understand them, the class views the video, and members of each expert group work together to write statements about the role the institution and people assigned to them played in the movement.

Now students return to their home group, and each student reports the findings of his or her expert committee. After this discussion each child writes a first-person account of an incident in the documentary from the point of view of one of the participants, but it must be a category of person other than one studied in his or her expert group. The teacher reads these accounts and evaluates them. Each child receives a separate grade.

After the expert group activity the groups process the experience by discussing these questions:

Did I contribute?
Did I speak up when someone said something I disagreed with?
Did our group come to agree on our statements?

After the home group activity the students process the experience by discussing the following questions:

Did each member bring clear statements from her or his expert group?
Did she or he make us understand them?
Did I ask questions when I didn't understand?
Did I disagree civilly?
Did we all come to an understanding?

While the groups are working, Robert circulates, listens in, discusses the task with groups that are off target, and encourages productive small-group behaviors.

❖ Characteristics of Cooperative Learning

The two preceding activities illustrate the characteristics of all cooperative learning.

1. Students work together to achieve a common goal.
2. There is positive interdependence. If each member does not do his or her part the group effort suffers. This is more apparent in Robert's activity than in Helen's. However, through processing (helping students to reflect on the success and failure of their group) positive interdependence can be encouraged and made apparent in all cooperative-learning activities.
3. There is individual accountability. Helen holds each student accountable by a quiz. Robert holds each student accountable through individually written papers.
4. Students process their experience. Each activity provides training for making cooperative learning more effective by making successes and failures explicit and requiring thinking about remedies for failures.
5. The teacher observes, teaches, and intervenes during the process. Social skills such as communicating clearly and affirming others are taught directly.

Three Models of Cooperative Learning

Schniedewind and Davidson (1987) describe three models of cooperative learning proposed by Johnson and Johnson (1984), Slavin (1983), and Aaronson (1978).

Johnson and Johnson

In the Johnsons' model students work together in cooperative groups toward a common academic goal. They are positively interdependent because they have a common goal. Each completes a part of the task, and they are rewarded as a group. Students are individually accountable for mastering the materials. The teacher intervenes as needed, to teach or reinforce cooperative skills.

Establishing a common or mutual goal means all students must learn the material and make certain other group members learn it. One way of accomplishing this is to give group or joint rewards. For example, bonus points may be given to each student if all group members achieve above a certain percentage on a test.

Individual accountability can be stressed by giving each group member an individual exam or by randomly selecting one member to give an answer for the entire group. Students who need additional help from the group may be so identified.

The Johnsons' focus on group process requires instruction in social skills, especially conflict resolution skills, to enable students to work together cooperatively. Time must be set aside for the group to analyze how well they are functioning and using the necessary social skills.

Slavin

Slavin and his colleagues developed the student team model of cooperative learning, which involves students tutoring each other. One version of this model is known as STAD—Student Teams-Achievement Divisions. STAD has five components: (1) class presentations by the teacher of the material to be learned; (2) teams composed of four to five students heterogeneously selected to work together to master the material; (3) quizzes given as individual evaluations of student achievement on the material presented to the class and practiced in the team; (4) individual improvement scores allowing students to earn points for their teams based on improvement over a running average of past scores; and (5) team recognition using newsletters, bulletin boards, or other forms of recognition for the team with higher weekly performance or cumulative standing.

Aaronson

Elliot Aaronson and his colleagues developed the Jigsaw Classroom where each student in a heterogeneous group learns certain information that is essential to completing the group task. Each student is assigned to an expert group composed of members of other teams who have been assigned the same material to learn. Students meet in expert groups to exchange information and master the material each student is to present to his or her team. Students take individual tests or quizzes covering all the material of the learning unit; there is no group reward. While each group member has one piece of the jigsaw puzzle, each student must learn the material from every piece of the puzzle to complete the task and do well on the test. Students are thus highly interdependent.

You will notice that Helen's lesson followed the Johnsons' model and Robert's lesson followed the jigsaw classroom. Slavin's model focuses on competitiveness and tends to be more appropriate for the kind of learning for which the competitive goal structure is appropriate, such as the memorization of discrete facts. The Johnson and Aaronson models are much more compatible with a holistic, collaborative, integrated approach to teaching language arts. In other words, Laura would undoubtedly adopt the Johnson or Aaronson model, while Michael would be very much at home with Slavin's model.

✤ Cooperative Learning and Small Groups

Although it is a good idea to begin work using partners or triads, it is desirable to eventually assign students to groups of five or six. Remember that researchers studying small groups recommended groups of four. Perhaps cooperative-learning experts recommend larger groups because in this technique teachers intervene and teach effective group participation, thus overcoming the problems of nonparticipation by some students in larger groups. Cooperative learning is different in other ways from the small-group discussion technique that teachers have employed over the years.

- In small-group discussion students are not necessarily accountable to one another for what is learned. In cooperative learning the task is structured so that the students are required to work together and learn from one another.
- In cooperative learning groups are heterogeneous, that is, they are made up of students with varying abilities, interests, and characteristics. In small-group discussion, groups may be homogeneous. At least there is not usually a conscious effort to ensure that groups are heterogeneous.
- In cooperative learning students are taught the affirmation, communication, cooperation, and problem-solving skills they need to work together. Frequently, these skills are not taught explicitly in small-group discussion.

✤ Effective Cooperative-Learning Assignments

Cooperative groups provide the best opportunity for practicing "learning to learn and think" strategies. But the teacher must set assignments and tasks that challenge the group to the higher-order processes. Bellanca and Fogarty (1990) use what they call the "Three-Story Intellect Model" based on the following quotation that they attribute to Oliver Wendell Holmes.

"There are one-story intellects, two-story intellects and three-story intellects with skylights. All fact collectors who have no aim beyond their facts are one-story men [or women]. Two-story men [or women] compare, reason, generalize, using the labor of fact collectors as their own. Three-story men [or women] idealize, imagine, predict—their best illumination comes from above the skylight."

The first level of cognitive functioning engages the learners in typically schoolish tasks that direct them to list, name, locate, and describe facts and information. The second-story intellectual tasks engage students in comparing and contrasting, classifying, determining cause and effect, prioritizing, and analyzing. Here students manipulate the new information, trying to make connections to prior knowledge, previous experience, and/or developing concepts. This is where students make sense of what they have learned. In third-story thinking, students synthesize, predict, imagine, idealize, and begin to use the new ideas in meaningful ways. Here students begin to tackle "what if . . . ?" questions (see Box 4.4).

THIRD STORY: APPLYING

Evaluate	Predict	Forecast
Imagine	Apply a principle	Synthesize
Judge	Ask "What if . . . ?"	Idealize

SECOND STORY: PROCESSING

Compare	Distinguish	Classify
Contrast	Explain	Analyze
Sort	Generalize	Give examples

FIRST STORY: GATHERING

Count	Recite	Tell
Describe	Select	Enumerate
Name	Recall	List

Box 4.4 The Three-Story Intellect Model

Gathering (first-story) assignments might be:

- Looking at a map of the United States, list the capitals of all the states west of the Mississippi.
- After listening to the teacher read *Peter Rabbit*, re-create the scene where Mrs. Rabbit gives Peter instructions about Mr. McGregor's garden.

Processing (second-story) assignments might be:

- Looking at a map of the United States that shows density of population, list the states that would be most affected by laws regulating densely populated cities.

- After listening to the teacher read *Peter Rabbit,* compare Peter's experiences in the woods and in Mr. McGregor's garden. Which is a safe and natural place for Peter?

Applying (third-story) assignments might be:

- Looking at a map of the United States that shows density of population, which states do you think would have more members elected to the House of Representatives? How many senators does each state have? Which seems like a fairer form of representation—the Senate or the House? Why do you think our government has both a House of Representatives and a Senate?
- After listening to the teacher read *Peter Rabbit,* decide whether Mrs. Rabbit did the right thing by putting Peter to bed without supper. What might she have done if Peter was not ill when he got home? What should she do if Peter goes into the garden again?

Bellanca and Fogarty (1990) believe that gathering (first-story) assignments are inappropriate for cooperative-learning groups. Such assignments undermine the value of groups in doing complex and challenging tasks. Processing (second-story) and especially applying (third-story) assignments engage students in tasks that turn the groups into "corporate think tanks." Highly challenging tasks create the need for and appreciation for each group member's contributions.

❖ The Elements of an Effective Cooperative-Learning Lesson

Each lesson the teacher designs must cover the following five elements which can be remembered by the acronym BUILD.

B—Build in higher-order thinking with assignments that challenge the group's need to help each other complete the task. Assignments that are too easy make students feel they could do it quicker, easier, and better by themselves.
U—Unite teams by tailoring the task so that all sink or swim together—tasks that require each student's input for success.
I—Insure individual learning by holding each student accountable for his or her own learning through quizzes, assigned roles, random responses, homework.
L—Look over and discuss what the group has done with both the academic task and the cooperative task. Give students time to monitor and evaluate their work. Reflecting on where they are and how they got there will help them transfer these skills to new learning assignments.

D—Develop social skills needed for communicating, building trust, promoting leadership, and resolving conflict. Explicitly addressing these skill areas will give students a common vocabulary and set of social behaviors that facilitate collaborative efforts at all levels of the social spectrum. (Bellanca & Fogarty, 1990)

CONFLICT RESOLUTION

A third area of education—conflict resolution—developed rapidly in the 1980s. For decades the topic of conflict resolution has appeared in the literature of social studies, business management, and communication. By the early 1970s, elementary schools began to introduce conflict resolution, both in the curriculum and as part of classroom management. Conflict resolution has developed into a separate field of study in teacher education because it is believed to enhance the linguistic and cognitive skills that underlie all academic achievement, to give students the skills they need to engage in cooperative-learning groups, to improve the learning atmosphere of the classroom, and to reduce the time spent on discipline.

Conflict resolution programs usually treat four elements: affirmation, communication, decision making, and cooperation. I treated cooperation extensively under the topic of cooperative learning. In this section I will treat the remaining three elements: affirmation, communication, and decision making.

❖ Affirmation

Affirmation activities are essential to set the classroom atmosphere of trust and caring. Each student's self-worth and self-esteem must be valued and affirmed. Experts agree that the following norms or standards of classroom behavior are essential to insure that all members of the classroom community will feel self-esteem.

- No put-downs
- Listen
- Don't interrupt
- Everyone gets a turn, including the leader
- Equal time
- Everyone has the right to pass

Affirmation activities often take the form of finding and appreciating similarities and differences in one another. The following activities are designed to introduce the class to the importance of affirming strengths in themselves and others through celebrating their uniqueness as well as their commonalities.

LESSON PLAN: Alliterative Name Games

1. Have everyone sit in one large circle.
2. Ask the first person to give a positive adjective and his or her name, for example, "I'm Terrific Todd."
3. Ask the second person to say the first person's name and then his or her own. "You're Terrific Todd; I'm Super Scott."
4. The third person repeats the sequence. "You're Terrific Todd; you're Super Scott; I'm Caring Karen."
5. Continue this process around the circle until everyone has participated. The last person says everyone's name.

Variations could include favorite foods ("Ice Cream Todd"), activities ("Football Todd"), or something nobody here knows about me ("My name is Todd and once I shook hands with the president.") (Gibbs, 1987)

LESSON PLAN: Classroom Yellow Pages

Tell students that within the class there are many skills that are known and acknowledged and others which perhaps have not yet been shown. They will make Yellow Pages to share this information so that students can take advantage of one another's skills.

Start out with each student suggesting one skill she or he can teach the others. Stress that students need not be expert at something; they simply have to know how to do it well enough to teach someone who knows it less well. If students have trouble, prompt them; don't overlook some common but still appreciated skills, such as arranging flowers, tying knots in blown-up balloons, teaching Frisbee, doing headstands, naming bugs, baking ethnic specialties, teaching popular dances.

Write each skill separately on a piece of construction paper, one skill per page. Draw several boxes on each page. First have each student draw him/herself doing the skill they suggested in one box on the appropriate page. Then circulate those pages, having other students draw themselves doing any skill they think they fit appropriately. As students think of skills not yet listed, they can create new pages. If enough pages are moving around the room, and if some students spend more time on drawing than others, it will not be obvious how many times each student is including him/herself.

Have the students alphabetize the pages, make a cover, and bind them into a book. Place it in an accessible location and encourage students to use it when they want to learn something or when you want a skill taught. (Schniedewind & Davidson, 1987)

♣ Communication

One of the most important lessons to impart in conflict resolution education is the necessity of confronting conflict before it escalates to violence. Oral communication skills need to be practiced and the feelings or emotions that can cause or contribute to conflict need to be recognized. Feelings of conflict are natural and good if they are responded to appropriately. This section presents activities for acknowledging emotions and exercises which give practice in oral communication.

Expressing Feelings

An important part of conflict resolution is to learn that it is better to express our feelings than to accuse or criticize others. In the parlance of conflict resolution, it is more effective to send "I" messages than to send "You" messages. The formula for constructing "I" messages is

> I feel _____ (state feelings)
> when you _____ (state behavior)
> because _____ (state consequences).

For example: I feel angry when you don't listen because what I'm saying is important and I want you to hear it.

Design an "I" message for each of the following using the formula above:

1. You loaned your new bike to a friend. When he or she returns it, it has a flat tire.
2. You're standing in the water fountain line. All of a sudden, two students push right in front of you.
3. When you walk past Willie at recess, he calls you a name under his breath.
4. When you get home from school, you go to the kitchen to get a piece of pie. It turns out your sister just ate the last two pieces. (Foresta et al., 1987)

Reflective Listening

In addition to speaking it is desirable to give students practice in listening, especially active or reflective listening. The techniques of active listening, according to Stanford (1977), are:

- Look directly at the speaker.
- Give nonverbal signals that show you are listening (for example, nod head to show you understand).
- Do not initially express agreement or disagreement. Simply show that you have understood.
- Do not be afraid of silences. Say, "Can you tell me more about that?" if the silences become too long.

- Show you have understood by summarizing or restating the speaker's remarks from time to time.
- Respond to "feeling" messages as well as verbal messages. Ask yourself, "How is this person feeling?" "How would I feel if I were saying that?"
- Show that you recognize and accept the feelings being expressed. Say, "You seem to feel . . ." (pp. 125–132)

Other behaviors that encourage listening are:

- Think about what the speaker is saying rather than the ideas in your own head.
- Let the speaker finish before you talk.
- Comment on what the speaker said to show you understand.
- Ask questions if you don't understand something the speaker said. (Schniedewind & Davidson, 1987, p. 67)

LESSON PLAN: Active Listening

Divide the group into pairs. Each person talks to his or her partner for two minutes on "What I like about myself." The only rule is, you may not say anything negative or bad about yourself, including any negative limitations on good things about yourself. For example, you cannot say that you are a good cook but you can't make gravy.

After each partner in the pair has talked for two minutes, each pair introduces his or her partner to another pair using what they have learned.

The role of the listeners is to pay close attention to what is being said, using body language to show they are listening. The listeners should not talk except to remind the speakers if they say anything negative about themselves or put limits on their good points. If the speaker runs out of ideas before the two minutes are up, both parties remain silent unless the speaker gets some more ideas. No chatting is allowed.

Partners introduce each other to another pair of partners who introduce themselves in turn.

Process the experience after members of every pair have introduced themselves and have been introduced to the members of another pair. Ask "How did it go?" to invite expressions of feelings about being listened to and saying good things about ourselves.

Using Explicit Language

The activities above contribute to producing and receiving explicit language, the key to developing school discourse practices described in chapter 3. Additional practice in explicit communication can be gained with the following game.

> **LESSON PLAN: The Description Game**
>
> This game encourages people to listen and to observe carefully what others are describing.
>
> - Select a fairly complex object in the room that is visible to everyone.
> - Select three volunteers and ask them to describe the object to the class one at a time out of earshot of one another.
> - Ask the class to compare the three descriptions with what they see.
> - Discuss how people see and hear things differently. (Stern, 1987)

❖ Decision Making

Methods of Decision Making

There are essentially three ways a group reaches a decision: authority, voting, and consensus.

Authority

Authority is a method of decision making where a designated individual who is in charge decides what to do. This individual may be elected, appointed, or hired and must have some means of enforcing his or her decisions. A sizable percentage of the group must willingly accept this person's authority in order for him or her to remain in charge.

Voting

Voting has the advantage of encouraging more group members to participate in the decision and to share information and opinions, especially as individuals try to convince others to vote with them on an issue. Voting has several disadvantages, however. It polarizes the group by setting up a win-lose atmosphere; losers may not support the decision arrived at by the majority. This may be a significant problem if the opposing minority is large.

Consensus

Consensus is a third method of group decision making. Consensus requires the group to look for a solution with which all can agree. All viewpoints must be listened to and considered. While consensus may not be the best method for every decision, it is a method of which students should be aware and one for where they should have the necessary skills when its use is appropriate.

Consensus does not mean that everyone is in total agreement with the group's decision, only that in coming to the decision, no one felt his or her position on the question was misunderstood or that it wasn't given a fair hearing. It often happens that the group decision is a better one than any individual would have made alone; all of us together are smarter than any of us alone.

Consensus takes longer than voting or authority. However, the consensus decision-making process creates more commitment to the decision than either voting or authority because during the discussion period the different points of view are articulated to everyone's satisfaction and those who have trouble with a proposal have the responsibility of suggesting alternatives.

LESSON PLAN: Recognizing Methods of Decision Making

Write the words **Authority, Voting,** and **Consensus** on the board and help students define them. Have each student make a sign for each word. Read the following problems and after each reading have the students raise the card which they think is the appropriate decision-making method. You will be able to tell very quickly by glancing around the room if there are any differences of opinion. Ask students why they chose the method they did.

- Your school receives a telephone call saying that there is a bomb in one of the classrooms. A decision must be made about whether to evacuate the building. Who should make the decision and what method should be used?
- Your class is deciding whether to play soccer or kickball at recess. Who should decide and what method should be used?
- The people in New York are deciding who the next governor is going to be. Who should decide and what method should be used?
- You are at the zoo with three of your friends. You are going to spend the whole day but need to decide whether to start with the Lion House or the Bird House. Who decides? How?
- A police officer has stopped a car for exceeding the 55 MPH speed limit. It must be decided whether to issue a warning or a ticket. Who decides? How? (Mondschein, undated, p. 67)

ACTIVITY

Try this activity with your classmates or in an elementary-school classroom if you have the opportunity.

Button Battle

This game involves four players, eight large buttons, and a rectangular area six feet by ten feet on the classroom floor marked with masking tape. The rest of the class play the part of social scientists and observe the behavior of the players.

The four players line up on their hands and knees at the starting line, each with two buttons. At the teacher's direction each player in turn uses one button to snap his or her other button toward the finish line (ten feet away). If one player snaps her button so that it lands on an opponent's button, the covered button is captured and the

CONFLICT RESOLUTION

> **ACTIVITY (continued)**
>
> opponent is knocked out of the battle. If a player snaps his other button out of the arena before reaching the finish line, that player is out of the battle. The player who first reaches the finish line is the winner.
>
> Ask the social scientists these questions:
> Dr._____, were there enough buttons to play the game?
> Dr._____, were the players given rules to play by?
> Dr._____, could you observe that the players enjoyed the game? How?
>
> Choose four different students with good verbal ability to participate in a second round of the game. Retrieve the buttons and have the players wait while you talk to the social scientists in private.
>
> Inform the social scientists that they must carefully observe the behavior of the subjects to see how decisions are made when you change the rules slightly.
>
> Inform the players that once you place the buttons in the battle arena they cannot talk to you or the social scientists. They may talk only with one another. Now place only four buttons instead of eight in the arena. Remind the players that they may talk only with one another concerning the alternatives.
>
> After the players have reached a decision about how to use the four buttons and have begun to play the game, ask the social scientists to describe their observations about how the players decided who would use what buttons when and how.
>
> Review the concepts of authority, consensus, and voting and elicit from the group which method or methods were used in this game. (LaRaus & Remy, 1978)

Roles in Decision Making

Everyone has a part to play in a group decision-making or problem-solving session. The Alternatives to Violence program (Bickmore, 1984) has identified several different facilitating and blocking roles played by group members.

Facilitating roles that keep the group focused are

- The initiator—organizes the group, starts discussion, introduces ideas, and raises questions.
- The information seeker—clarifies issues and asks for information, definitions, and goals.
- The summarizer—listens, correlates ideas and suggestions, brings the group up-to-date by defining where the group stands, and indicates areas of agreement and disagreement.
- The evaluator—keeps the group aware of whether they are attaining their goals.

Facilitating roles that maintain group relations are

- The encourager—responds positively to others.
- The gatekeeper—makes it possible to hear from those who have not yet spoken.
- The compromiser—can admit error or ignorance on a point without surrendering his or her viewpoint.

The harmonizer—reduces tension using humor; keeps calm and reconciles differences by getting opponents to explore common ground rather than seeking surrender by one side.

Blocking roles are

The competer—criticizes, blames or puts others down; feels he or she has the best idea or has to be right.
The self-confessor—seeks sympathy for his or her point of view by telling personal problems.
The big talker—never listens to others.
The withdrawer—doodles, daydreams, talks to neighbors, and does not give the group the benefit of his or her ideas.
The clown—draws attention to her- or himself and away from the issue at hand. (Bickmore, 1984)

ACTIVITY

This activity gives the class an opportunity to role play the different facilitating and blocking group roles.

1. Brainstorm problems that the group is familiar with. Choose one on which the group has information and views or opinions.
2. Prepare a three-by-five card for each of the facilitating and blocking roles described above. Pass out the cards to students who will be the "fish." They are not to tell anyone what their card says.
3. Have the fish sit in the center of the room, the "fishbowl." The remaining students sit outside the fishbowl and observe. Each observer will need a chart naming and describing the roles to be played by the fish. The observers' job is to figure out which students are playing what roles and to fill in the chart with the appropriate students' names.
4. The fish are to discuss the problem that has been chosen and try to reach consensus on a solution.
5. After ten minutes freeze the discussion and ask the observers these questions:
   Did everyone talk?
   Did everyone listen?
   What happens when not enough people participate?
   What would make participation easier?
   Why is it hard to state areas of agreement?
   Would taking a vote be effective? Why? Why not?
   Who played what role?
6. Reverse the process and have the observers become the fish. After they try to reach consensus, repeat the discussion questions. (Bickmore, 1984, pp. 26–27)

❖ Beyond Language Arts Objectives

Conflict resolution can be considered part of the language arts curriculum because it facilitates effective discussion and cooperative learning, and because it results in cognitive and linguistic growth. It has also been shown to increase the efficiency of the classroom by reducing discipline problems.

Conflict-resolution programs have been shown to have other good effects. Research conducted on the Resolving Conflict Creatively Program (RCCP) in New York City indicated 70 percent of the teachers trained to teach the RCCP curriculum reported that children demonstrated less physical violence in the classroom; 63 percent observed less name-calling and verbal abuse; 77 percent saw more caring behavior among students; 69 percent observed increased willingness to cooperate among children; and 71 percent noticed that children had increased skills in understanding others' points of view (Metis Associates, 1990, pp. 6–7).

Many schools which teach conflict-resolution and negotiation skills also have peer-mediation programs. Selected students are trained in the same step-by-step mediation process that is used increasingly in divorces, consumer complaints, and labor disputes. Research in some of the 300 schools nationwide that had conflict-resolution and peer-mediation programs in place in 1990 indicates the following:

In five New York City high schools suspensions for fighting decreased by 46 percent, 45 percent, 70 percent, 60 percent, and 65 percent, respectively, during the first year of the program (Lam, 1988, p. 12).

In Ottawa, "in schools where mediation programs operate, there has been a decrease in the number of suspensions, expulsions, detentions and violent acts. Vandalism and chronic school absences have also decreased" (Picard, 1988, p. 7).

In San Francisco schools where the Conflict Manager Program is in place, records show discipline problems were reduced; Pennsylvania schools with the same program report a 75 percent drop in incidents that end up in the principal's office (Nancy & Ted Graves, 1988, p. 14).

There can be a mutually beneficial relationship between a conflict-resolution program and the language arts program. A conflict-resolution program teaches communication skills directly, as well as other skills that facilitate cooperative learning and small-group discussion. Meanwhile, cooperative learning and small-group discussion facilitate cognitive and language development which in turn enhance conflict-resolution skills.

Summary

Student-led small-group discussions have some advantages for learning over informal conversations and teacher-led discussions that were described in chapter 3. However, a clear task must be set on which the students need to collaborate, and students must be taught how to work productively in small groups.

Barnes and Todd have observed that the ideal size for small groups is two to four students; that the aim of small-group discussion is to help students learn to state their views explicitly and evaluate the explicitly stated views of others; and that it is best to assign short tasks in the beginning stages.

Tasks may be constructed tightly, that is, students may be assigned to follow a set series of steps or questions, or they may be constructed more loosely, that is, students may be given a statement with which to agree or disagree, using evidence or reasons.

Certain social skills must be learned for successful small-group discussion, such as the ability to progress through the task, to manage competition and conflict, and to lend support to fellow group members. Groups tend to break down under the following circumstances: when pre-existing conflicts or conflicts arising from the task itself are ignored or suppressed; when the focus is on the difficulty of the task; when incorrect views are not challenged; when everyone agrees with the first stated view; when socializing and reminiscences dominate the discussion; when underlying assumptions are not stated or challenged; when the task is misunderstood or ignored; or when students fail to recognize that they have completed the task and begin to discuss it anew. Phillips described five kinds of talk observed in small groups: hypothetical, experiential, argumentational, operational, and expositional. Expositional talk rarely occurs unless the teacher participates in the discussion, perhaps because this type of talk reflects an unequal distribution of power among the discussants. Interestingly, teachers in this study rarely engaged in the other four kinds of talk, all of which reflect the sort of collaborative teaching that this text recommends.

Tasks which can be set to promote small-group discussions include class meetings or magic circles in primary grades, or, for any grade, selecting a special events day and assigning the students to plan it. Whatever the task, students need to be taught the process of small-group discussion either directly, by facilitating their competence while engaged in the process, or by making the process the topic of study.

Cooperative learning, where achieving one's goal depends on others achieving their goals, is one of three **goal structures** described by Johnson and Johnson. The others are competition, where a student's attainment of his or her goal depends on others failing to achieve theirs, and individual goal structures, where the achievement of a goal by one student is unrelated to the goal achievement of others.

While competition and individual tasks are the best ways to achieve some types of learning (such as memorization or mechanical skills), research shows that cooperative learning is the best method to achieve most higher-order cognitive skills, such as problem solving and mastery of concepts and principles. Cooperative structures are also the best method for affective learning, such as valuing diversity and democracy, enjoyment of learning, and positive self-attitude.

SUMMARY

In all cooperative-learning lessons students work together to achieve a common goal, and there is positive interdependence, that is, each member's contribution is essential to the success of the whole group. There is, however, individual accountability through quizzes or individually written papers. Social skills such as communicating clearly and affirming others must be taught directly and time must be set aside to allow the groups to process their experience. The teacher observes, teaches, and intervenes when necessary in order to keep the learning process on track.

In order to assure that all students learn the material and take responsibility for seeing that others learn as well, the group can be awarded bonus points if everyone in the group reaches a certain percentage on the test.

Slavin and colleagues recommend the Student Team-Achievement Divisions (STAD) model where students work in teams and tutor other team members. Teams compete with one another for recognition or rewards based on the total achievement of individual team members.

Aaronson and colleagues developed the Jigsaw method where each student in a group learns certain information essential for the group's completion of a task. Students learn this information in expert groups where all are working on the same topic, then return to their home groups to relay what they have learned. Each student's grade depends on his or her score on a quiz; there is no group reward.

The STAD model is less compatible with the holistic, collaborative, integrated approach to language arts instruction than the Jigsaw and the Johnsons' models.

Cooperative learning differs from small groups in several ways: Group size is larger in cooperative learning, and students are required to learn from one another. Cooperative-learning groups are heterogeneous, and social skills such as affirmation, communication, cooperation, and problem solving are taught explicitly.

Cooperative-learning activities can promote higher-order thinking. In the "Three-Story Intellect Model," students must reach the third story in order to make sense of what they learn, that is, to synthesize, predict, imagine, idealize, and begin to use new ideas in meaningful ways. To provide students the opportunity to practice this higher-order thinking by applying what they learn, assignments must be given that turn groups into "think tanks" (in Bellanca and Fogarty's term) by creating the need for and appreciation of each member's contribution.

Characteristics of effective cooperative-learning lessons can be remembered through the acronym BUILD: Build in higher-order thinking; Unite groups by assuring all sink or swim together; Insure learning by holding each individual accountable; Look over and discuss both the assignment and the cooperation skills the group used to complete it; and Develop the social skills necessary to communicate, built trust, promote leadership, and resolve conflict.

Conflict-resolution education teaches the social skills which are a necessary element in small-group and cooperative learning. Affirmation activities such as name games and getting acquainted exercises can help establish a classroom atmosphere where each individual's self-worth and self-esteem is valued and strengthened. Oral communication skills such as sending "I" messages give practice in explicitly communicating feelings and views and can help students resolve conflicts before they escalate to violence.

Consensus decision making helps students solve problems and achieve goals by finding solutions with which all can agree. Without winners and losers there is greater likelihood of compliance with the decision and the decision is likely to be a better one.

The fishbowl activity makes it clear that the roles group members play in reaching a decision can either be facilitative or blocking roles.

Conflict-resolution programs can include peer mediation, which has been shown to reduce school violence and improve the learning atmosphere of the school. Incorporating conflict-resolution education can improve language arts instruction by teaching communication and problem-solving skills that facilitate cooperative learning and small-group discussions.

For Review and Discussion

1. What can heterogeneous student-led group discussions contribute to development of explicit language use that other teaching methods cannot?
2. What social skills must be learned for student-led discussion groups to be productive? Give examples of ways in which these skills can be taught.
3. Give examples of the five kinds of talk Phillips observed in small groups. Which contribute best to student learning? Why?
4. What are the three goal structures described by Johnson and Johnson? For what type of learning is each most efficient?
5. Give examples of how you might structure a cooperative-learning task to assure both positive interdependence and individual responsibility.
6. What problems might group grades present for student motivation? How can such problems be overcome? What are the advantages of group grades?
7. In what ways does the introduction of competition among teams in the STAD method of cooperative learning negate the benefits? How does the Jigsaw method work? What are the benefits and problems?
8. Describe the "Three-Story Intellect Model." How can cooperative learning help students reach the third story?
9. What social skills are taught in conflict-resolution education? How can conflict-resolution education be incorporated in the language arts classroom? Give examples.
10. What is peer mediation? What role might peer mediation play in improving the learning atmosphere of schools with which you are familiar?
11. How significant is conflict and violence in schools? In society? Is this a topic schools should include in the curriculum? If so, how?

For Further Reading

Anzul, M., & Ely, M. (1988). Halls of mirrors: The introduction of the reflective mode. *Language Arts, 65,* 675–687.

Bellanca, J., & Fogerty, R. (1990). *Blueprints for thinking in the cooperative classroom.* Palatine, IL: Skylight Publishing.

Bickmore, K. (1984). *Alternatives to violence.* Akron, OH: Peace Grows.

Kreidler, W. J. (1984). *Creative conflict resolution.* Glenview, IL: Scott, Foresman.

O'Neill, C. (1989). Dialogue and drama: The transformation of events, ideas, and teachers. *Language Arts, 66,* 528–540.

Schniedewind, N., & Davidson, E. (1987). *Cooperative learning, cooperative lives.* Dubuque, IA: William C. Brown.

Uttero, D. A. (1988). Activating comprehension through cooperative lives. *The Reading Teacher, 41,* 390–395.

Watson, K., & Young, B. (1986). Discourse for learning in the classroom. *Language Arts, 63,* 126–133.

Yanushefski, J. (1988). Group authorship in the language arts classroom. *Language Arts, 65,* 279–287.

CHAPTER 5

Oral Language: Focus on Function

Introduction
The Informative Use of Language
Lesson Plan: Photographic Field Trip
Lesson Plan: Listening to Directions
Lesson Plan: An Interview
Lesson Plan: Meeting Martians
Persuasive Language
Lesson Plan: Responding to Commercials
Lesson Plan: Scarce Resources
Lesson Plan: Problem Puppets
Lesson Plan: Frames of Reference
Lesson Plan: My Bike
Communicating Emotions, Feelings, and Attitudes: The Affective Function of Language
Lesson Plan: "Getting Into" a Part
Lesson Plan: Stereotypes
Lesson Plan: More Stereotypes
Lesson Plan: Mixed Signals
Lesson Plan: Reading Signals
Lesson Plan: Put-Downs
Lesson Plan: Affirming Statements
Creating with Language: The Imaginative Function of Language
Engaging in Social Transactions: The Ritualistic and Transactional Functions of Speaking and Listening
Lesson Plan: Folk Gestures
Lesson Plan: Manners
Lesson Plan: What Do You Say, Dear? What Do You Do, Dear?
Lesson Plan: Changing Times
Combining Functions
Lesson Plan: Create Checklists
Summary
For Review and Discussion
For Further Reading

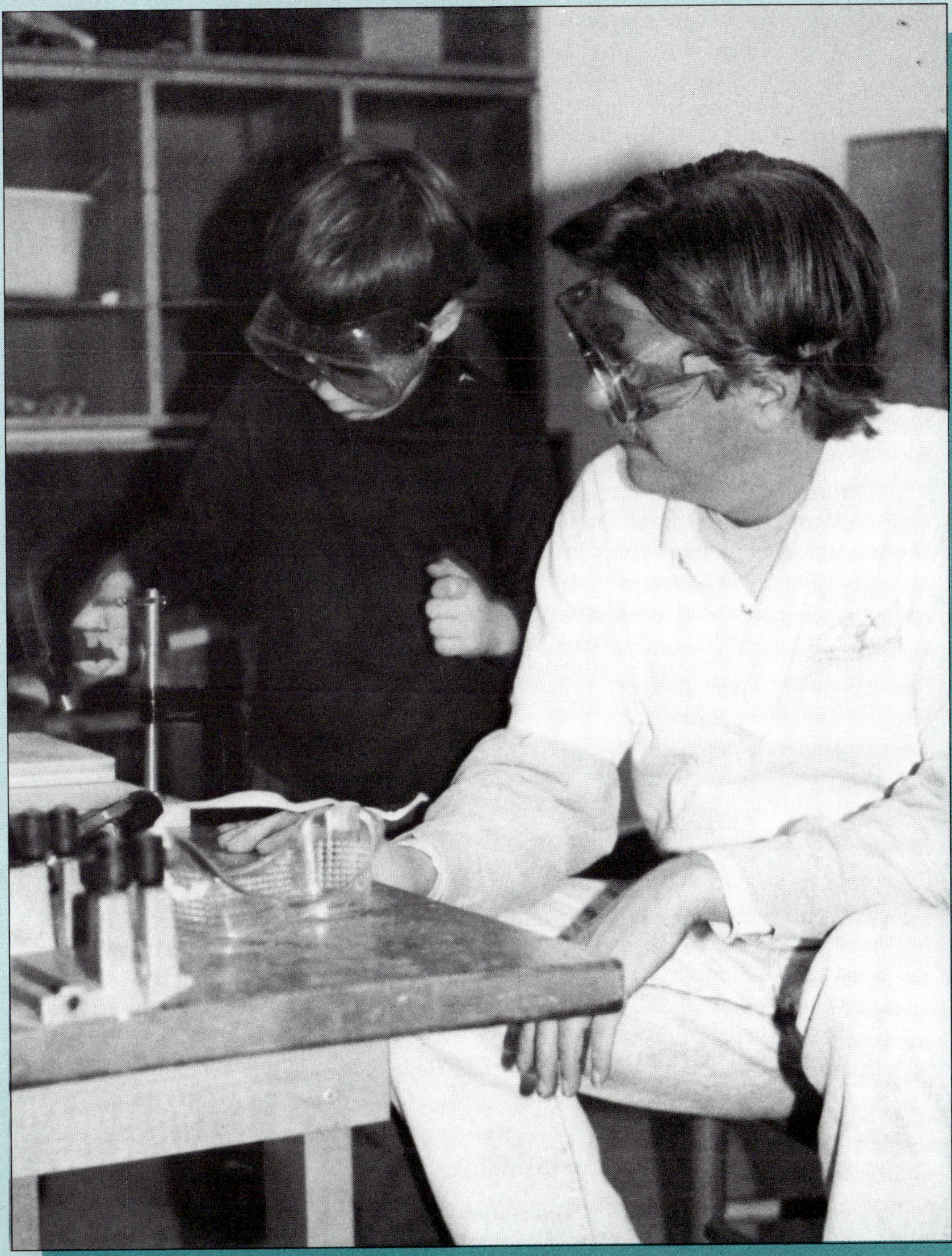

INTRODUCTION

This chapter will explore oral language and oral language learning in terms of the uses of language—to inform, persuade, express emotions, imagine, and engage in transactions and rituals. Each of these uses has its own special problems, skills, and demands. The following discussion presents these problems, skills, and demands, as well as examples of lessons to deal with them.

THE INFORMATIVE USE OF LANGUAGE

The informative use of language includes giving and receiving directions, descriptions, and explanations. Informative language appears in all the language formats discussed. Informative language may be directive or collaborative.

Directive informative language occurs when the speaker feels confident about the topic and the information needs of his or her audience. Directive informative language often arises in formal situations where the speaker has prepared a report, an announcement, or a book review. Such language may also arise spontaneously in conversation and discussion. Spontaneous directive informative language also arises in a speaker-audience format when a speaker is asked a question and his or her response is not prepared.

Collaborative informative language occurs when people work together to master information or to solve a problem. Conversation and discussion give rise to collaborative informing language.

❖ The Informative Function and Speaking

In early grades the skills related to a speaker's informative use of language include overcoming communication stress in conversation, teacher-led discussion, and small-group interactions. This includes speaking in an emotionally less supportive environment (compared with the home), addressing less familiar listeners, assessing their informative needs, and treating topics that are not supported by the immediate environment. As more formal informational presentations become more frequent in the middle and upper grades, specific attention may be directed to skills associated with directive informative language, such as choosing and narrowing a topic, finding information, analyzing the informational needs of an audience, organizing content, summarizing, and responding to questions.

❖ The Informative Function and Listening

All the sources of support and sources of difficulty for listening (chapter 3) can be applied to the informative use of language. Listening skills that are particularly associated with the informative function of language are these:

1. Taking in information (directions, descriptions, facts, explanations) while suspending judgment.
2. Aiding the speaker to communicate.
   Responding overtly to the speaker. Asking questions and making comments in conversation or discussion. Taking notes, looking alert, responding to humor, and showing agreement or disagreement nonverbally in a presentational (speaker/audience) format.
3. Thinking.
   Learning to understand language that is not supported by the immediate context or that is abstract rather than concrete. Learning to recognize when not enough information is given. Responding covertly to the speaker by raising questions, agreeing, or disagreeing mentally or on a notepad. Avoiding daydreaming or becoming overpowered by one's own questions.
4. Listening critically.
   Evaluating without rejecting the information out of hand, without being dogmatic, and without engaging in "group think"—that is, without being unduly influenced by the evaluations of others in a small-group discussion. Identifying the speaker's biases.
5. Aiding memory.
   Taking notes (in both discussion and speaker/audience format). Outlining. Making up questions for main points. Listing main ideas. Summarizing.

Teachers can facilitate the informative function of listening in students by paying attention to their own roles as speakers. Before beginning a presentation, teachers can explain the importance of the information they are about to convey and suggest how it will be used in the future. They can also use "advanced organizers," that is, present a broad outline of what will be said and suggest questions that might be answered by the presentation.

During a presentation teachers can enhance listening success of students by using pictures, props, and other audiovisual aids. They can intersperse questions within their presentation and ask students to predict what is coming.

After a presentation, understanding and memory can be aided by asking questions, asking for summaries, and discussing the new information presented, and then the new information can be related to information that the students already possess.

Such careful presentations create good listeners and function as models for students as speakers.

❖ Supporting the Informative Use of Language in the Classroom

Here are some activities designed to deal with some of the demands associated with the informative use of language. You will notice that each activity or lesson has a title followed by four descriptors indicating the use, channel, format, and grade level.

LESSON PLAN: Photographic Field Trip

Use: INFORMATIVE
Channel: SPEAKING
Format: SPEAKER/AUDIENCE
Grade level: PRIMARY

(1) Have some of the students in the class take photographs on a field trip to the fire station, the zoo, or just around the neighborhood. (2) Have them show the photographs and talk about them to the students who did not go on the field trip. Listeners can ask questions about the pictures. (3) Have the whole group discuss step 2. What questions were asked? (4) The speakers then repeat step 2 with different listeners. Speakers should be more explicit and informative in succeeding efforts.

LESSON PLAN: Listening to Directions

Use: INFORMATIVE
Channel: LISTENING
Format: SPEAKER/AUDIENCE
Grade level: PRIMARY/INTERMEDIATE

Give students blank papers. Tell them to follow directions like the following, using rulers and pencils. "Put a small pencil mark on the left edge of the paper two inches from the top. Draw to the right of the mark a line three inches long. Draw a line down from the right end of that line four inches...."

Make your directions as elaborate or as simple as necessary. When you have finished, have students compare their papers with the master (the one the teacher has done) to see if they are alike. Repeat the process using different (and eventually more difficult) directions.

LESSON PLAN: An Interview

Use: INFORMATIVE
Channel: NONVERBAL EXPRESSIVE AND RECEPTIVE
Format: CONVERSATION
Grade level: UPPER

THE INFORMATIVE USE OF LANGUAGE

Ask student A to interview student B about B's hobby. Have them leave the room to prepare. Place two chairs side by side touching each other in front of the classroom. Tell the class to observe how the two students arrange the chairs and what other nonverbal communication takes place between them.

When the two return, tell them to take the two chairs in front of the room and conduct the interview. Follow up with a class discussion:

1. How did they arrange the chairs and what effect did this have on communication?
2. What nonverbal communication was used and how was it used (a) to open the interview; (b) to explain the interviewee's hobby; (c) to show interest, understanding, and puzzlement on the part of the interviewer; (d) to close the interview.

LESSON PLAN: Meeting Martians

Use: INFORMATIVE
Channel: SPEAKING
Format: CONVERSATION
Grade level: UPPER

Divide the class into groups of three of four students. Explain that a family of Martians has come to visit Earth. They have studied English and know it well. They are peace loving and are visiting to learn about Earthly inventions and customs.

Each group will act as tutors to one member of the family. The groups draw cards describing the Martian they are to instruct. For example:

Teenager
Older Martian with an eighth-grade education
Seven-year-old in second grade
Fifty-year-old doctor

Then each group selects two cards naming the invention they are told to describe, such as a light bulb, a video game, or eyeglasses.

Give each group about ten minutes to prepare a two-minute explanation. Groups select one of their members to describe their Martian and to present the explanation.

The class then discusses the explanation, perhaps using a checklist similar to the one in Box 5.1 (Christenbury, 1985, pp. 9–11).

	Strongly Agree	Agree	Disagree
Explanation was clear.			
Martian would understand the invention.			
The Martian could easily explain the invention to others.			

BOX 5.1

PERSUASIVE LANGUAGE

✤ The Persuasive Function and Speaking

Language used to influence the beliefs, opinions, and behaviors of others is language used for persuasion. Children engage in persuasive language on the playground when they try to get friends to play a game or trade treats from their lunch boxes.

As children grow older the demands on them in terms of using persuasive language grow along two dimensions: (a) They direct their persuasive messages to people who are less and less familiar; and (b) the messages become more complex and harder to sell. A two-year-old tries to persuade his mother to pick him up, something the mother is likely to do in most circumstances. A five-year-old tries to persuade a new friend to run on the sand instead of playing in the water. He has no assurance that he will succeed. A thirteen-year-old goes door-to-door asking people to sign up as a sponsor for a bicycle ride for cancer research. She knows that more people will say no (possibly because they do not understand instantly what is being asked of them) than will say yes.

Knowledge and skills that are particularly related to using language for persuasion are taking the listener's point of view and using arguments.

Taking the Listener's Point of View

One of the most influential psychologists in early childhood education is Piaget. One of Piaget's best-known concepts is that young children are egocentric; that is, they have a difficult time separating what they know and how they feel from what others know and how others feel. An eight-year-old may make his request for extra pocket money when his mother is in a good mood. Three-year-olds make requests when needs arise and seem not to be aware that the mother's mood is relevant.

Using primitive strategies of persuasion, children simply state what they want their listener to believe or do. Using sophisticated strategies, children state reasons why the listener should believe them or do what they suggest. One mark of sophistication of persuasive language is that the speaker takes the listener's point of view into account when choosing his reasons.

Delia, Kline, and Burleson (1979) studied the development of persuasive communication in children from kindergarten through twelfth grade and identified three stages in taking the listener's point of view into consideration.

> Stage 1. The child does not recognize or adapt to the listener's perspective.
> "Could you keep this puppy?"
> "I want you to keep this puppy. Won't you, please?"
> Stage 2. The child implicitly recognizes and adapts to the listener's perspective.
> "This dog is really skinny, and he doesn't have any place to go."
> "This is a lost puppy. Could you keep it a day or two 'cause I can't keep it at my house?"
> "The dog is big enough to stay outside, and you only have to feed him and water him, and that doesn't take all day."
> Stage 3. The child explicitly recognizes and adapts to the listener's perspective.
> "You know, a dog's a good playmate for kids."
> "You look kind of lonely. This dog would be a good companion, somebody to talk to and everything."
> "If I were you and I lived alone, I'd like a good watchdog like this one."

Using Arguments

A second mark of sophistication in the use of persuasive language is to support reasons with arguments. Arguments may take the following form: (a) drawing conclusions from accepted facts; (b) drawing principles from examples; (c) using analogies; and (d) citing opinions or beliefs of credible witnesses or experts.

❖ Being Persuaded or Remaining Unpersuaded: The Persuasive Function and Listening

There are two categories of listening skills that are particularly related to the use of persuasive language: responding appropriately to the emotional aspects of the communication and recognizing the elements of the message.

Making Appropriate Emotional Responses

Since the listener's susceptibility or resistance to the persuasive message is likely to be influenced by the listener's subjective feelings toward the speaker, one category of skills consists of those which enable the listener to formulate appropriate emotional responses, feelings, and attitudes toward the speaker.

Recognizing the Elements of the Message

Russell and Russell (1979) suggest that listeners should learn to recognize the elements of persuasive messages in order to evaluate them and to decide whether to accept or reject them. The elements of a persuasive message are as follows:

1. The persuasive intent of the communication. What is the speaker trying to persuade the listener to believe or to do?
2. The reasons.
3. The underlying assumptions.
4. Irrational strategies (testimonials from film stars, celebrities, and the like).
5. Power strategies (I am stronger than you, so I can make you do it, or I am weaker than you, so you will look bad if you do not do it.).
6. The speaker's biases.

❖ Supporting the Use of Persuasive Language in the Classroom

Role playing and discussion are both useful ways of helping children learn to use language effectively for persuasion, as both speakers and listeners. Role playing and discussion are well suited to developing the ability to consider the point of view of other people. Discussion is also well suited to developing skill in argument.

Here are some lesson plans designed to deal with some of the demands with persuasive use of language.

LESSON PLAN: Responding to Commercials

Use: PERSUASIVE
Channel: LISTENING
Format: SPEAKER/AUDIENCE
Grade level: INTERMEDIATE/UPPER

Videotape commercials directed at children. Show the videotape and discuss the persuasive strategies used. What reasons were given? What evidence was used? What strategies were used?

Have students write their own commercials, present them to the class, and discuss them as above.

LESSON PLAN: Scarce Resources

Use: PERSUASIVE
Channel: SPEAKING
Format: SMALL GROUP
Grade level: PRIMARY

Divide the class into groups of five children. Tell each group to make one collage. Give each group a stack of pictures from magazines, one large piece of poster board, two crayons, one scissors, and one bottle of glue.

The point of this lesson is to present a situation where five children will need to share scarce resources in accomplishing a single task.

After each group has finished, gather them into one large group and discuss questions like the following:

1. When you wanted the scissors (crayons, glue) and someone else had them, what did you say?
2. What worked most often; that is, what did you say that worked best?
3. Did you usually get what you needed?
4. What would you do next time? (Wood, 1977)

LESSON PLAN: Problem Puppets

Use: PERSUASIVE
Channel: SPEAKING/LISTENING
Format: DRAMATIC FORM/CLASS DISCUSSION
Grade level: PRIMARY

William Kreidler (1984) keeps special puppets with large "P" monograms on their shirts in a special box marked "Problem Puppets." When children get into disputes that they cannot seem to resolve, Kreidler re-enacts the situation with the puppets, speaking for both "characters." He freezes the action at the point of conflict and asks the children to suggest how the dispute might be resolved.

Kreidler cites an example where two children were bickering about who would save a place on the rug for their kindergarten teacher to sit. Their teacher re-enacted the dispute using the problem puppets and asking for solutions. Unfortunately no solution was found at first, but on a later re-enactment of the same situation a student suggested that saving a seat for the teacher should be a job on the classroom job chart. One of the puppets was able to point out that some problems take a while to solve.

Acting out implausible or unworkable solutions suggested by the class helps students think through the consequences of their suggestions. When a satisfactory solution is suggested, the teacher models the persuasive language used in negotiating resolutions to conflict.

LESSON PLAN: Frames of Reference

Use:	PERSUASIVE
Channel:	SPEAKING/LISTENING
Format:	CLASS DISCUSSION
Grade level:	INTERMEDIATE

Ask students to agree or disagree with statements like the following:

> Main Central is the best school in town.
> Illinois is the best state to live in.
> The Angels are the best baseball team.
> The test we had in history (or whatever) was easy.

Explain that their answers are in part a result of their frames of reference, which reflect their beliefs, experiences, and upbringing.

Go back over the statements and ask how students' frames of reference influenced their beliefs. Ask what experiences, beliefs, or upbringing might have caused them to have different opinions.

Have students pair off and list three things that contribute to their sharing a frame of reference and three things that cause them to have different frames of reference. (Kreidler, 1984)

LESSON PLAN: My Bike

Use:	PERSUASIVE
Channel:	LISTENING (RESPONDING TO PERSUASIVE LANGUAGE)
Format:	TEACHER-LED DISCUSSION
Grade level:	INTERMEDIATE

Present a situation to students where they would refuse someone's request. For example, "Suppose someone asked to use your bike and you didn't want to let him or her use it. What would you say?" List the ways of refusing that students suggest.

Write a list of individuals who might have made the request, such as a younger sister, a best friend, a child of the same age whose family is visiting

> the student's family, and a neighborhood bully. Discuss which way of refusing would work best with each individual. Discuss what each individual might say or do in response to each refusal to ask for reasons. (Kreidler, 1984)

COMMUNICATING EMOTIONS, FEELINGS, AND ATTITUDES: THE AFFECTIVE FUNCTION OF LANGUAGE

❖ The Affective Function and Speaking

The use of language for expressing feelings includes the expression of feelings about oneself and others and expressing opinions.

The structure (one teacher–many students) and the cognitive bias of the schoolroom militate somewhat against the use of language for expressing feelings. One study found that only about one in twenty of children's utterances in first grade are used to express feelings (Pinnell, 1975).

Expressing feelings is an important use of language in maintaining relationships with others, both in and out of school. It also has an important cognitive function since much of our knowledge of the world begins with feelings and opinions. Inability to cope constructively with feelings can also make learning difficult. For example, in order for discussion to be a profitable source of learning, conflicts between people must be put aside or worked through to the point they do not interfere.

Encouraging the Use of Expressive Language

Teachers can encourage the use of language for expressing feelings by becoming alert to the facial expressions and body language of students and by asking questions. "You don't seem to like practicing for assembly, Jim. Why don't you like it?" or "You seem quite cheerful today. What's up?" Such invitations to express feelings not only give students the opportunity to talk about themselves, but also give teachers the opportunity to collaborate in helping students to express their own meanings.

The purpose of classroom discussion is often to enable students to (a) clarify their opinions and make them explicit, (b) discover the reasons that give rise to their opinions and state the reasons explicitly, (c) evaluate the reasons, and (d) validate or modify their opinions.

Small-group discussion also affords children the opportunity to experience the positive effects of expressing feelings about others. When children express encouragement and support or approval of others, it can have a very positive effect on the workings of the group.

Activities designed to help children to deal with interpersonal conflict may arise out of classroom incidents, or they may be planned as part of the ongoing curriculum. The purpose of such activities is to instill the following principles in students:

1. Negative feelings are natural and sometimes appropriate.
2. Making the reasons for negative feelings explicit enables one to examine the reasons and their validity.
3. Negative feelings that arise from valid reasons can be channeled into constructive action.

Classroom Goals for the Affective Function of Language

Successful use of language for expressing feelings depends on achieving the following goals:

1. Overcoming reluctance to talk about oneself and to reveal one's feelings.
2. Choosing words for their denotative meaning as well as their connotative meaning. "A rat's nest" and "an untidy room" may describe the same room, but they convey different feelings about the room and its inhabitants.
3. Choosing words that express feelings precisely. "He's a louse" is rather imprecise. "He's a bully" is a little more precise. "He thinks because he's bigger than me he can get ahead of me in line and that makes me mad" is beginning to state the problem explicitly.
4. Overcoming shyness about complimenting or praising others.
5. Becoming willing to acknowledge negative feelings toward others.
6. Learning to express negative feelings in a productive rather than destructive manner. Friedman (1986) suggests nine ways to "enhance the receptivity" of critical comments:
   a. focus on fact—not motivation
   b. describe rather than judge
   c. statements of "more or less" not "either/or"
   d. concentrate on recent events, not dim memories
   e. present alternatives, not one solution, one answer
   f. share information and ideas, do not give advice
   g. focus on value to recipient, not on "release" for yourself
   h. focus on amount recipient can use, not amount you have to offer
   i. set limits on time and place, do not disregard social norms and situation
7. Learning to make reasons for opinions and feelings explicit so the reasons can be examined.

✤ The Affective Function and Listening

Effective communication depends on the listener's ability to take note of and respond appropriately to the speaker's emotions, feelings, and attitudes. The speaker's language nearly always conveys affective messages. It expresses aspects of the speaker's condition, such as discomfort, pleasure, ease, tenseness, anger, and anxiety. It conveys information about the kind of person the speaker is—knowledgeable, fair-minded, stable, confident, and so on.

The listener must note and interpret such language-conveyed messages, and, furthermore, she or he must evaluate such communication appropriately. This requires that listeners guard against such pitfalls as stereotyping and ascribing positive traits to people who are similar to them (or whom they find attractive) and ascribing negative traits to people who are dissimilar (or whom they find unattractive).

A further part of the listener's task to assure successful communication is to interact with the speaker on an affective plane by being confirming and reassuring. Some ways of doing this are to make relevant responses, to paraphrase what has been said (demonstrating interest and understanding), and to make sympathetic comments (Right! I see. Isn't that terrible?).

In responding to negative messages or criticisms, the listener can timidly accommodate, deny, compromise, or engage in "creative collaboration" (Friedman, 1986).

❖ The Affective Function and Nonverbal Communication

Oral communication rarely relies on the language channel alone. Whether one intends it or not, such things as appearance, posture, tone of voice, and willingness to make eye contact send messages that affect all functions of language—informative, persuasive, and so on. However, nonverbal channels of communication are particularly associated with emotions, feelings, and attitudes. The major channels of nonverbal communication are grooming, apparel, gestures, body movements, posture, facial expressions, eye contact, touch, and the use of space and symbols.

Skills associated with nonverbal communication involve social awareness and the ability to size up a social situation (the context in the communication model presented in chapter 3) and to understand the meanings conveyed by nonverbal behavior. From a speaker's (expressive) point of view this means monitoring the appropriateness of one's own behavior considering the meanings one wants to convey. From a listener's (receptive) point of view, this means observing others' behaviors and taking them into consideration when attempting to comprehend the total communication.

❖ Supporting the Affective Function of Speaking, Listening, and Nonverbal Communication in the Classroom

Here are some lessons designed to deal with some of the demands associated with the affective use of language.

LESSON PLAN: "Getting Into" a Part

Use: AFFECTIVE/IMAGINATIVE/INFORMATIVE
Channel: NONVERBAL/EXPRESSIVE
Format: CONVERSATION/SPEAKER-AUDIENCE
Grade level: INTERMEDIATE/UPPER

In a teacher-led large group or in small-group discussion, treat the following question: When delivering the following messages, how would you expect the speaker to act?

a. stand tall or slouch?
b. smile or look serious?
c. stand near or far from the audience?
d. keep hands still or move them (how?).

A. Telling people swimming in the ocean that a shark has been sighted.
B. Teaching water skiing at summer camp.
C. Giving a school visitor directions for finding the principal's office.
D. Telling your father that you lost the twenty-dollar bill that he had given you to buy groceries.

Discuss the meaning of the behaviors and how they carry part of the message.

LESSON PLAN: Stereotypes

Use: AFFECTIVE
Channel: LISTENING/SPEAKING
Grade level: INTERMEDIATE/UPPER

Ask students to say what comes to mind as you say the following words: **game, bowl, corn, envelope.**
Jot key words and phrases on the board.
Now say the following words and phrases: **gym teacher, farmer, rock-music star, race-car driver.**
Jot key words and phrases on the board.
Of course the second list is meant to provoke stereotyped responses, while the first list will elicit different responses depending on the listeners' unique experiences.
Ask which list of words provoked responses that differed from one another. Which list of words provoked responses that were similar?
Ask how stereotypes interfere with communication; how they make communication easier.

LESSON PLAN: More Stereotypes

Use: AFFECTIVE
Channel: ORAL LANGUAGE/NONVERBAL EXPRESSIVE AND RECEPTIVE
Format: CONVERSATION
Grade level: INTERMEDIATE/UPPER

On small cards write names of roles people assume: movie star, mother, enemy, physically handicapped person, elderly woman, and so on.

Affix these names to students' foreheads with headbands or adhesive. Students should not know what is on the card they are wearing. Students circulate, speak, and interact verbally and nonverbally with individuals in response to the role written on each person's card.

Students then guess what role is written on their own card from the communicative behavior of others toward them.

Ask them what behaviors or what things said told them what role they were in. Were these behaviors fair toward people in that role? How do stereotypes interfere with communication?

LESSON PLAN: Mixed Signals

Use: AFFECTIVE/INFORMATIVE
Channel: SPEAKING/NONVERBAL EXPRESSIVE
Format: SPEAKER/AUDIENCE
Grade level: UPPER GRADE

Have students prepare a two-minute talk relating a happy, sad, frightening, or boring experience. Have them deliver the talk to the class, but attempt to send nonverbal messages that are the opposite of the verbal message.

Discuss the function of the nonverbal channel of communication as they are highlighted by being misapplied in this exercise.

LESSON PLAN: Reading Signals

Use: AFFECTIVE
Channel: LISTENING/NONVERBAL RECEPTIVE
Format: SPEAKER/AUDIENCE
Grade level: PRIMARY/INTERMEDIATE/UPPER

Take advantage of a school event, such as a talent show, a basketball game, an awards assembly, or a student's appearance on a local television show.

Talk about the event. Ask how the people involved must have felt—proud, frightened, angry, happy, and so on. How did they show their feelings, both verbally and nonverbally? What feelings may they have had that they did not show, or tried not to show? How did their verbal and nonverbal behavior hide feelings? How did their nonverbal behavior betray feelings they were trying to hide?

LESSON PLAN: Put-Downs

Use:	AFFECTIVE
Channel:	SPEAKING/LISTENING
Format:	CONVERSATION/DISCUSSION
Grade level:	INTERMEDIATE

Brainstorm for all the things one can say to put others down: name-calling, sarcasm, and so on. Write contributions on the board. Ask where we learn put-downs, how they make people feel, why we say them, and how the class would be if everyone always put everyone else down.

Have students close their eyes and think about how it would feel to have someone say these things to them. Read each example, pausing after each one.

Follow this lesson with the next lesson. (Kreidler, 1984)

LESSON PLAN: Affirming Statements

Use:	AFFECTIVE
Channel:	SPEAKING/LISTENING
Format:	CONVERSATION/DISCUSSION
Grade level:	INTERMEDIATE

Brainstorm for all the things one can say to make people feel good about themselves: friendly names, compliments, affirming humor, and so on. Write contributions on the board and ask how they make people feel and how the class would be if everyone said these kinds of things to others, rather than put-downs.

> Have students close their eyes and think how they would feel if someone said these things to them. Read each example, pausing after each one.
> Make a bulletin board of affirming statements and refer to it in preparing for and evaluating discussions. (Kreidler, 1984)

CREATING WITH LANGUAGE: THE IMAGINATIVE FUNCTION OF LANGUAGE

Imaginative language serves many purposes:

1. It enables children to try out roles. It sensitizes the child to the rules of the culture.
2. It enables children to establish the limits of sense by talking nonsense.
3. It enables children to establish the line between fact and fiction by identifying fiction while engaging in it.
4. It permits children to live vicariously, to experience adventures and new situations through identification with heroes and heroines.
5. It permits children to rehearse unfamiliar roles and situations. A little boy pretends to be the daddy. A kindergartner pretends to be the customer at a store. A fifth grader role plays his duties as a patrol boy with a child who will not stay on the curb.
6. It facilitates learning and memory. Children who create and enact a play about Columbus's seeking financial backing from the Court of Spain will probably learn and remember more about the event than if they had just read about it in a book.

✤ Classroom Characteristics

A good language arts classroom is one where language used for imagining is provoked, encouraged, approved of, and supported. In a successful language arts classroom:

- Space and materials are allotted for puppet shows, dramatizations, storytelling, role playing, and wordplay.
- Teacher-directed activities often involve the use of language for imagining, during language arts and other subjects.
- Student-initiated activities that promote language for imagining are fostered and encouraged during language arts and all through the school day.
- Language used for imagining is treated with as much attention and respect as language used for informing or persuading. Teachers listen attentively to children's language used for imagining; they respond to it, ask questions about it, and refer to it in later discussions where appropriate.

❖ **Skills**

Skills that are particularly related to using language for imagining include:

1. The ability to disorganize and reorganize reality.
   a. Imagine a world with different rules (People grow younger as time passes; plants can move about; animals can talk.).
   b. Pretend to be someone or something else (a parent, an astronaut, a spider, a frying pan).
   c. Pretend to live at another time or in another place (a child factory worker in nineteenth-century England, a circus clown, a nurse in an earthquake disaster).
2. Storytelling skills developed through listening to stories, re-telling stories, and creating stories.
3. The ability to gain control of forms associated with language used for imagining: stories, poems, and plays.

You will find many activities designed to deal with some of the demands associated with the imaginative use of language in chapter 10: Language as Magic.

ENGAGING IN SOCIAL TRANSACTIONS: THE RITUALISTIC AND TRANSACTIONAL FUNCTIONS OF SPEAKING AND LISTENING

Societies function smoothly by observing rituals and conventions. Entering school in the morning, a teacher may nod and smile as he passes the principal, say "Hello, Janet" in greeting the school secretary, and announce "O.K., class. It's nine o'clock. Get into your seats while I take attendance" to get the day started in his classroom. These uses of language are not primarily to inform, persuade, express feelings, or imagine. They are essentially rituals and transactions. They are ways of acknowledging that we are aware of another person's presence and that we are ready to continue, for another day, whatever relationship we have with that person. They are ways of transacting life's business and of marking the beginnings and endings of events.

Rituals are often used to mark changes in social relationships. The more drastic the change, the more dramatic the ritual. Rituals surround birth, death, marriage, becoming employed, retiring, acquiring credentials (degrees, licenses), being convicted of a crime, and so on.

Rituals are used to express and demonstrate solidarity. "Hi, how are you?" is more of an expression of friendship than a request for information. Cheering the home team, singing the "old" songs together, and reciting group prayers are ways of expressing our membership in a group and acknowledging the membership of others. Kidding, joking, and teasing are ways of expressing and acknowledging intimacy.

Rituals supply the glue for holding social events together and the oil that keeps events running smoothly. "Mother, I'd like you to meet my friend Larry Tompkins. Larry lived down the hall from me at school last year." This is an informative statement, but it is also highly stylized. It is part of the introducing ritual of society. "I like your tie," "Thanks" are informing and expressing feelings, but are also ritual.

❖ Classroom Characteristics

Children use language for ritual from their first "hi" and "thank you." Ritualistic use of language is necessary for much of the functioning of the classroom. The social skills developed in small-group discussion (chapter 4) involve much ritualistic use of language. Role playing affords children practice for using language in rituals they do not usually engage in, such as job interviews, conducting business on the telephone, and greeting hosts at a formal reception.

❖ Skills

Knowledge and skills that are particularly associated with ritual and transactions are

1. Knowledge of nonverbal communication regarding
   a. appropriate grooming and apparel.
   b. appropriate use of touch: shaking hands; kissing; hugging; backslapping; touching someone's arm to get his or her attention; putting one's arm around someone; holding hands; engaging in "insider" variations on hand shakes, such as "Give me five, Brother!"
   c. appropriate posture and body language: standing and sitting at attention, relaxed standing and sitting posture, facing others, turning away from others, leaning forward, maintaining distance from others, moving close to others, sitting back, sitting on the edge of the chair.
   d. use of facial expression: looking serious at a graduation, solemn at a funeral, happy at a party, enthusiastic at a basketball game.
   e. use of eye contact: looking at people we are speaking to, not staring at people, averting one's glance.
   f. use of the voice to express appropriate seriousness, sadness, enthusiasm, sincerity, happiness, respect.
2. Knowledge of appropriate verbal formulas for greeting, engaging in business, introducing, getting service, making complaints, being a guest, being a host or hostess.

❖ Supporting the Ritualistic and Transactional Functions of Language in the Classroom

Here are some activities designed to deal with some of the demands associated with the ritualistic use of language.

LESSON PLAN: Folk Gestures

Use:	TRANSACTIONAL/RITUAL
Channel:	NONVERBAL RECEPTIVE AND EXPRESSIVE
Grade level:	PRIMARY/INTERMEDIATE/UPPER

To make students aware of the rich gestural vocabulary they possess, give them a few examples: thumb a ride, smack lips (tasty!), thumbs up, stamp foot. For older children divide the class into teams to compile a list of their own gestures. Have groups demonstrate gestures and other groups express the meanings. For younger children, suggest gestures to teams and have them demonstrate gestures to be explained by other members of the team as in charades. An exhaustive list of such gestures can be found in Morain (1978, p. 22).

Discuss the fact that such gestures are not understood to mean the same thing in all cultures.

LESSON PLAN: Manners

Use:	TRANSACTIONAL/RITUAL
Channel:	SPEAKING/LISTENING
Format:	CONVERSATION/DISCUSSION
Grade level:	PRIMARY/INTERMEDIATE

Discuss the importance of saying "please," "thank you," and "excuse me."

Ask when we use words like "please" and "thank you." Why do we use them? How do we feel when people do (or do not) use these words when talking to us? What would our class be like if everyone used these words? If no one used them?

Make a bulletin board of courteous phrases and refer to it in preparing for and evaluating classroom projects. (Kreidler, 1984)

LESSON PLAN: What Do You Say, Dear? What Do You Do, Dear?

Use: TRANSACTIONAL/RITUAL
Channel: SPEAKING
Format: CONVERSATION
Grade level: PRIMARY

Share Sesyle Joslin's two children picture books, **What Do You Say, Dear?** and **What Do You Do, Dear?**, with the class. Have students draw pictures showing themselves engaged in a situation where social etiquette is used.

Similar activities can be developed from other books on etiquette, courtesy, and good manners such as Marc Brown and Stephen Krensky's **Perfect Pigs: An Introduction to Manners**; Geiett Burgess's **Goops and How to Be Them**; Jo McCormick's **Etti-Cat, The Courtesy Cat**; and Louis Slobodkin's **Thank You, You're Welcome**.

LESSON PLAN: Changing Times

Amy Vanderbilt's original **Book of Etiquette** was published in 1952. Recent books of etiquette can be found in the library, and many newspapers carry columns such as "Miss Manners." Upper-grade children might want to compare changes in etiquette over time, especially as they relate to girls and women. This could be part of a social studies project related to women's suffrage and the changing role of women in society.

COMBINING FUNCTIONS

Halliday (1975), one of the earliest writers, and perhaps the most influential on the concept of classifying communicative acts on the basis of the use they are intended to perform, noted that by the time his child was three years old, it was nearly impossible to specify a *single* use for a communicative act. Beyond infancy it is common for communicative acts to have more than one intended use. "Hello, how are you?" is clearly ritualizing, but in many cases it is also a sincere request for information. "If you keep teasing me, I'll go home" is intended to persuade and to express feelings simultaneously.

✤ Supporting the Combined Functions of Language in the Classroom

In the course of a discussion all functions of language are likely to emerge. The following exercise incorporates awareness of the functions of language into activities designed for self-study of the small-group process. It also aims to improve the use of oral language in small groups.

LESSON PLAN: Create Checklists

Use:	INFORMATIVE/PERSUASIVE/TRANSACTIONAL
Channel:	SPEAKING/LISTENING
Format:	SMALL GROUP
Grade level:	INTERMEDIATE/UPPER

Give simple small-group assignments such as those suggested in chapter 4. When time is up, ask individuals to tell the class who introduced the problem in their groups. How did they do it? What problems did they have? Did others help?

Make a list of positive initiating behaviors (Transactional), such as

1. State the problem or assignment in your own words. (Informative)
2. Ask questions of others in the group if you don't understand the problem or assignment. (Informative)
3. If you don't agree with the way the problem or assignment is stated, explain what you think the problem or assignment is. (Persuasive)

Ask for examples of how the discussion progressed. Who suggested solutions? What did they say? Who asked for further information from others? Who expressed agreement? Give examples.

Make a list of positive eliciting behaviors (Transactional), such as

1. Suggest solutions. (Informative, Persuasive)
2. Offer information. (Informative)
3. Express feelings. (Affective)
4. Ask others how they feel. (Affective)
5. Add to what others have said. (Informational)

Ask individuals to tell the class who stated to solution that the group decided upon. Did everyone have a chance to state agreement or disagreement? How were differences of opinion settled? Give examples.

Make a list of concluding behaviors (Transactional), such as

1. State the solution the group seems to have agreed on. (Informational)
2. If you don't agree with the solution, speak up. (Persuasive)

3. State the solution most people agree on, but note other opinions if differences still exist. (Informational, Persuasive)

Repeat this exercise, adding to the checklist and revising it. The checklist can then be used to evaluate groups and individuals, to monitor progress, and to discover areas where explicit teaching or coaching may be indicated.

Depending on the age and experience of the students, the exercise can address other communication behaviors, such as these:

Social Skills

Stating where the group is (initiating, eliciting, or concluding) and reminding others who seem to be out of step (Transactional)
Supporting, adding to, defending, and challenging others' opinions and ideas (Persuasive, Affective)
Dealing with conflict and competition among group members (Affective)

Cognitive Skills

Constructing or formulating the problem, question, or assignment (Informational)
Raising new questions (Informational, Persuasive)
Suggesting solutions (Informational, Persuasive)
Using evidence (Persuasive)
Expressing feelings (Affective)
Sharing experiences (Informational, Imaginative, Persuasive)
Changing one's opinion (Persuasive)
Learning from others (Informational)
Being persuaded (Persuasive)
Evaluating others' opinions, evidence, statements (Persuasive)
Arriving at understandings jointly with others (Informational, Persuasive)
Being aware of one's own learning (Informational)
Being aware of changing one's opinions (Persuasive)

Summary

Each use of language—to inform, persuade, express emotion, imagine, and engage in transactions and rituals—presents its own problems, skills, and demands.

Informing language can be directive, when the speaker feels confident about the topic and the information needs of his or her audience, or collaborative, when people work together to master information or solve a problem. Listening skills associated with informative language include suspending judgment, encouraging the speaker, thinking, listening critically, and aiding memory. Good listening habits are encouraged in students when teachers are good speakers.

Language used to influence the beliefs, opinions, and behaviors of others is persuasive language. Knowledge and skills that are particularly related to using language for persuading include taking the listener's point of view and using arguments. Two listening skills needed in listening to persuasive language are responding to the emotional aspects of communication and recognizing the elements of the message: the persuasive intent, reasons, underlying assumptions, irrational strategies, power strategies, and bias.

A third function of language is to express emotion. This is also known as the affective function. Although the structure and cognitive bias of the classroom militate against it, the expressive use of language is important for maintaining relationships in and out of school. The affective use of language is particularly important in collaborative-learning settings (such as discussion and cooperative learning) since interaction between students may become the occasion for conflict as well as cooperation.

Nonverbal channels of communication are particularly associated with the affective use of language.

The imaginative function of language enables children to try out roles, to establish sense by talking nonsense, to identify the line between fact and fiction, to live vicariously, to rehearse unfamiliar roles, and to facilitate learning and memory. In a good language arts classroom, language used for imagining is provoked, encouraged, and supported. Skills associated with the imaginative use of language are the ability to disorganize and reorganize reality; storytelling skills; and control of forms of language associated with imagination: stories, poems, and plays.

The transactional use of language holds society together and keeps things running smoothly. When transactions are highly routinized they become rituals. Facility with nonverbal communication conveyed through grooming and apparel, touch, posture, body language, facial expression, eye contact, and tone of voice are particularly important to the transactional use of language. Knowledge of verbal formulas for transactions such as greetings and introductions is also necessary.

Although it is useful to think about functions of language separately, nearly every discourse contains examples of language used for more than one function. Frequently, a single utterance has two or more uses simultaneously.

For Review and Discussion

1. Recall lessons suggested in this chapter and relate them to the function they are intended to focus on.

2. Find examples of language arts lessons involving speaking and listening and discuss the functions of language involved.

3. Think of examples of classroom activities, such as conducting science experiments, planning a field trip, and doing library research. What functions of language are involved?

For Further Reading

Allen, R., Brown, K., & Yatvin, J. (1986). *Learning languages through communication: A functional perspective.* Belmont, CA: Wadsworth.

Burgoon, J. (1981). Nonverbal communication. In M. Ruffner & M. Burgoon (Eds.), *Interpersonal communication.* New York: Holt, Rinehart & Winston.

Delia, J., Kline, S., & Burleson, B. (1979). The development of persuasive communication strategies in kindergartners through twelfth-graders. *Communication Monographs, 46,* 255.

Halliday, M. A. K. (1973). *Explorations in the functions of language.* London: Edward Arnold.

Halliday, M. A. K. (1975). *Learning how to mean: Explorations in the development of language.* London: Edward Arnold.

Knapp, M. (1978). *Social intercourse: From greeting to goodbye.* Boston: Allyn & Bacon.

Shafer, R., Staab, C., & Smith, K. (1983). *Language functions and school success.* Glenview, IL: Scott, Foresman.

Wood, B. S. (1977). *Development of functional communication competencies: Pre-K–grade 6.* Urbana, IL: ERIC Clearinghouse on Reading and Communication Skills.

Zajonic, R. (1980). Feeling and thinking: Preferences need no inferences. *American Psychologist, 35,* 154.

CHAPTER 6

Approaches to Teaching Reading

Introduction
The Concept of Emergent
   Literacy
TO THINK ABOUT: Underlying
   Assumptions in Emergent
   Literacy
TO THINK ABOUT: Reflections
   on the Writing Process
   Approach
TO THINK ABOUT: Reflections
   on the Language
   Experience Approach
TO THINK ABOUT: Reflections
   on the Individual Reading
   Program Approach
   Activity
TO THINK ABOUT: Reflections
   on Hansen's Reading
   Conferences

TO THINK ABOUT: Reflections
   on Atwell's Reading
   Workshop
The Traditional Concept of
   Reading Readiness
TO THINK ABOUT: Underlying
   Assumptions—Reading
   Readiness versus Emergent
   Literacy
TO THINK ABOUT: Underlying
   Assumptions—The Phonics
   Approach
Basal Reading Programs
   Activity
Summary
For Review and Discussion
For Further Reading

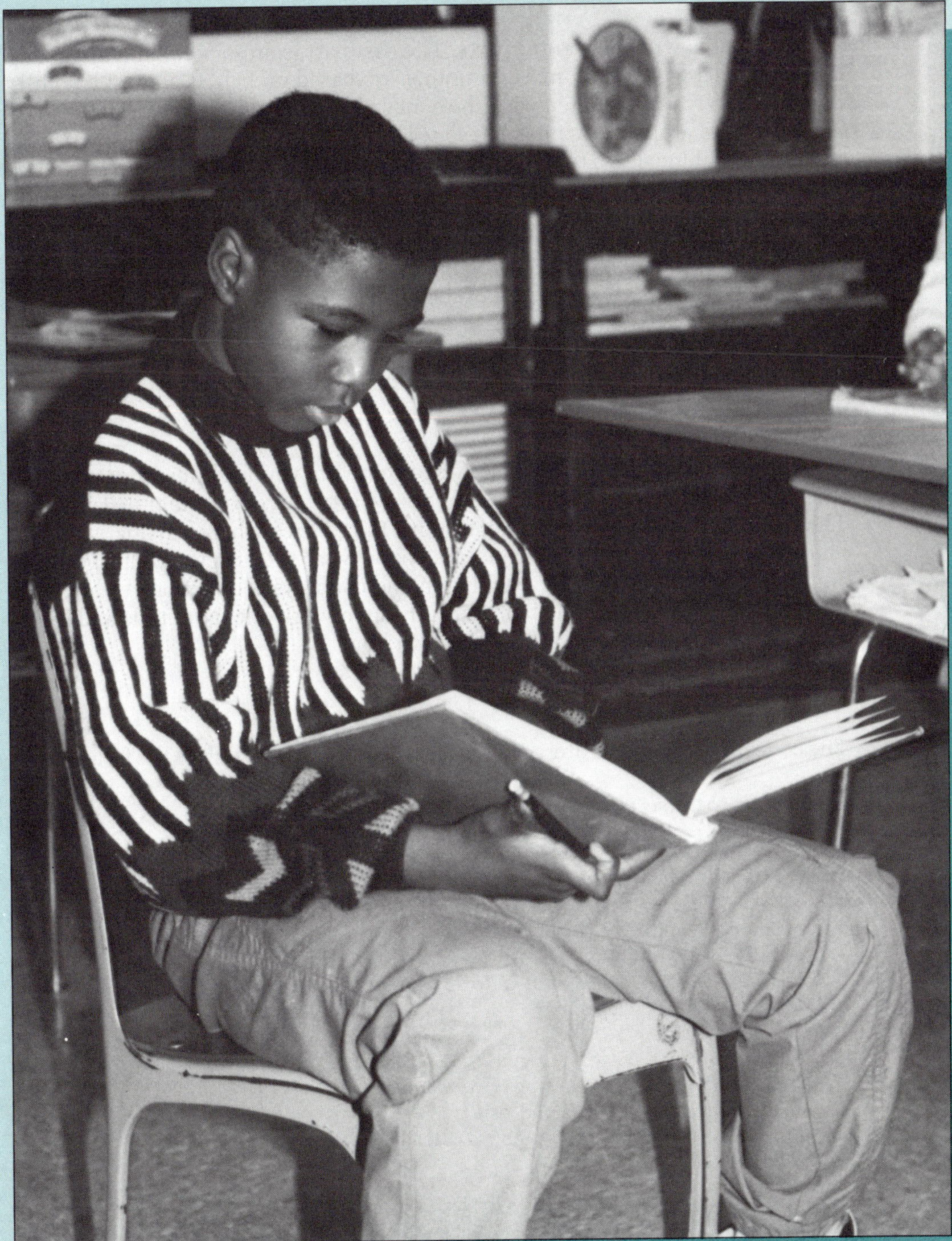

INTRODUCTION

This chapter is written in three parts. The first part examines collaborative, holistic approaches to teaching reading that are based on beliefs about how children learn to read associated with the concept of emergent literacy. The second part examines atomistic approaches to teaching reading that are based on beliefs about how children learn to read associated with the concept of reading readiness.

The third part of this chapter deals with basal reading programs. Basal reading programs do not fit neatly into the two categories—directive, atomistic versus collaborative, holistic. However, since basal reading programs have been and still are the most commonly used methods of teaching reading in the elementary schools, any discussion of approaches to teaching reading would be incomplete without discussing them.

THE CONCEPT OF EMERGENT LITERACY

In recent years educators have discovered that very young children learn many things about written language that cannot be attributed to formal instruction. The results are interesting and consistent. In cultures where writing is prevalent children start with broad concepts about what they can do with speaking and listening. Similarly, they establish broad concepts about what reading and writing are used for. If permitted, many children work out the details and learn the conventions while *using* reading and writing.

❖ Observing Children Using Language

The concept of emergent literacy is based on observations such as the following.

Catching on to Books and Stories

While sharing the book *Rosie's Walk*, two-and-a-half-year-old Emily and her mother have the following exchange:

> Mother: *Rosie's Walk* by Pat Hutchins.
>   Emily: Pat Hutchins.
> (Mother reads that a hen named Rosie went walking in the yard.)
> Mother: What's happening?
>   Emily: What?
> Mother: What's the fox doing?
> (Picture shows the fox jumping toward a rake.)
>   Emily: He's trying to catch Rosie.
> Mother: Do you think he's going to catch her?
>   Emily: No.
> (Mother turns page.)
> Mother: What happened?
> (Picture shows the fox hit by the rake.)
>   Emily: He banged his nose.
> (Mother reads that Rosie walked toward a pond.)

Emily: Uhmm.
Mother: What will happen next?
(Picture shows the fox falling in the pond.)
Emily: He's gonna splash!
(Mother reads that Rosie walked by a haystack.)
Emily: Uhmm.
Mother: What happened?
(Picture shows the fox covered by hay.)
Emily: He fell in a "stick" of hay.
Mother: And Rosie kept right on walking. (King, 1989, p. 14)

This exchange continues in like manner as the book describes Rosie's walk by a flour mill, under a fence, and past a beehive. As soon as the book is finished Emily asks for more and chooses another book.

Emily: This one.
Mother: Which one? This one? *Good Night Owl!* [In a formal reading tone] *Good Night Owl* by Pat Hutchins. This one's by Pat Hutchins, too. She wrote *Rosie's Walk.*
Emily: She wrote it by Pat Hutchins! (p. 15)

This conversation has many of the characteristics of the conversations involving Mark and Nigel and their parents in chapter 2, but there is an important new element. Emily and her mother are actively involved in constructing a text around a book. (Compare this with Mark and his mother constructing a text around the neighbor's imagined trip to the store and to Nigel and his parents constructing a text around the incident at the zoo.)

Mother and Emily take turns, but the mother structures the exchange and keeps the focus on the text. Unlike the conversations of Mark and Nigel, this is not Emily's topic. She has learned to collaborate with her mother and the book in creating text.

Focusing on the book, Mother helps Emily to interpret the pictures and to integrate them into a unified text. Each thing that happens is a result of a common thread. The fox is trying to catch Rosie.

Mother encourages Emily to anticipate and predict, underscoring the relatedness of what is happening, what has happened, and what will happen in the text.

Mother introduces a third person into this meaning-making event—Pat Hutchins, the author-illustrator. From Emily's response, "She wrote it by Pat Hutchins!" my guess is that Rosie doesn't understand authorship (a finding consistent with Applebee's 1977 study), but it is through such experiences that Emily will learn that reading is creating texts in collaboration with authors in the same way as she is now learning to create texts orally in collaboration with her mother focusing on books.

Catching On to Writing and Reading

When "writing" their names and "signing" their papers and artwork, some three-year-olds produced linear arrangements of marks. They produced the same linear arrangement of marks when writing their names on different occasions.

Joshua	
Curtis	
Allison	
Laura	

Figure 6.1 "Signatures" of three-year-olds. *(Sources:* "Joshua" by Joshua Foels. Reproduced by permission of Beth Foels. "Curtis" by Curtis Woodward. Reproduced by permission of Celia Woodward. "Allison" by Allison Glenn. Reproduced by permission of Karen A. Glenn. "Laura" by Laura Robinson. Reproduced by permission of Nancy Robinson.)

Examples can be found in Figure 6.1. These three-year-olds demonstrate that they know what writing is for and that they have discovered some of the characteristics of writing (Harste, Woodward, & Burke, 1984).

When shown a Crest toothpaste box and asked to read what was written on the box, three-year-olds responded with appropriate language such as "Brush your teeth," "Cavities," and "It's called Aim." Some of them even answered "Toothpaste" or "Crest." These three-year-olds demonstrate that they recognize writing and know what it is used for (Harste, Woodward, & Burke, 1984).

Catching On to Composition and Story Form

Five-year-old Ashley wrote the "story" found in Figure 6.2. When Kris Scrimshaw, Ashley's kindergarten teacher, asked her to read the story, her intonation and delivery conveyed the idea that the letters at the top of the page are the title and the drawing is the story itself. Ashley read the story as follows:

The Runaway Elephant

The elephant squirted her and the girl couldn't find the elephant. But she finally found the elephant and they were friends again.

THE CONCEPT OF EMERGENT LITERACY

Figure 6.2 Five-year-old Ashley's story. (Source: *The Runaway Elephant,* by Ashley Hatfield. Reproduced by permission of Joyce Hatfield.)

It can be assumed from her performance that Ashley's concept of "story" includes introducing characters and narrating some action. She has even introduced a problem and a resolution. Her concept of writing a story is to make marks on paper that represent the story she has created. She has shown an understanding of conventions—the title comes first at the top of the page followed by the story itself. Ashley has many details to control, but for a child who can't write, she shows a remarkable understanding of the imaginative use of language, of story form, of literary conventions, and of the function of writing. Similar examples can be found in Harste, Woodward, and Burke (1984).

When Sulzby and her colleagues (1989) asked 123 kindergartners to write stories "the way kindergartners write," they found numerous categories of responses, including drawings, scribbles, letter-like figures, letters, invented spellings (where there was a discernable relationship between the letters and the pronunciation of the chosen words), and finally, conventionally spelled words. When they asked these children to read back what they had written, they observed a wide range of responses, including these:

- "It doesn't say anything."
- Oral monologue where the child recites a story in a tone that is "entertaining and flowing, like that expected in oral storytelling."

- Written monologue where the child recites a story that is worded like written language and sounds like written language in tone. As in Ashley's case, this reading is unrelated in a conventional sense to the writing on the page.

One of the many fascinating findings of the study is that the sophistication of the stories the children produced when asked to reread their writing was not related to how conventional the writing was.

An observation confirmed by Dobson (1989) was that many children do not look at the page while rereading their own writing or in "reading" storybooks. Some attend to the pictures and even point to the pictures while reading. One sign of awareness of the relationship between print and talk is what Dobson calls the **time-space match.** Children begin to track the print with their gaze (and sometimes by pointing), and they make the amount said match the amount of print by hurrying or slowing their talk or their tracking so that they come to the end of the print when they finish talking.

Dobson (1989) observed eighteen children learning to write and read in an environment where they were encouraged to write and read in the fashion described thus far in this chapter. She reported that children first made discoveries about the way print related to language in their attempts to write. For example, their first awareness of letter-sound relationships became evident while they were writing or rereading their own writing. On the other hand, they composed more sophisticated and more conventional stories while reading storybooks than when rereading their own writing. Since we usually think of knowledge of letter-sound relationships in relation to reading, and of composition in relation to writing, this is an idea that you might want to stop and reflect upon: Children discover the letter-sound relationships that underlie reading by writing, and children learn to compose conventional written texts by reading.

Catching On to Formal Aspects of Writing: Handwriting, Spelling, and Punctuation

The story in Figure 6.3 was written by a first grader (Cazden, Cordeiro, & Giacobbe, 1985). Roy has demonstrated in this story that he has certain broad concepts about written language. He has written a story with characters, conflict, a problem, and a solution. Although his printing is barely legible, and he does not employ standard spelling or standard punctuation, he has a concept of letter-sound relationships. He has a concept of what a period is used for—it comes at the end. He also has a strong sense of clauses and phrases. Each line ends at the end of a phrase or clause.

Commenting on Roy's apparent sense of where phrases and clauses end, Roy's teacher and her fellow researchers write of Roy and his classmates, "They have somehow learned more than we might have thought possible about . . . 'the structure of meaning' that punctuation indexes, and more than we could have explained even if we had tried" (p. 120).

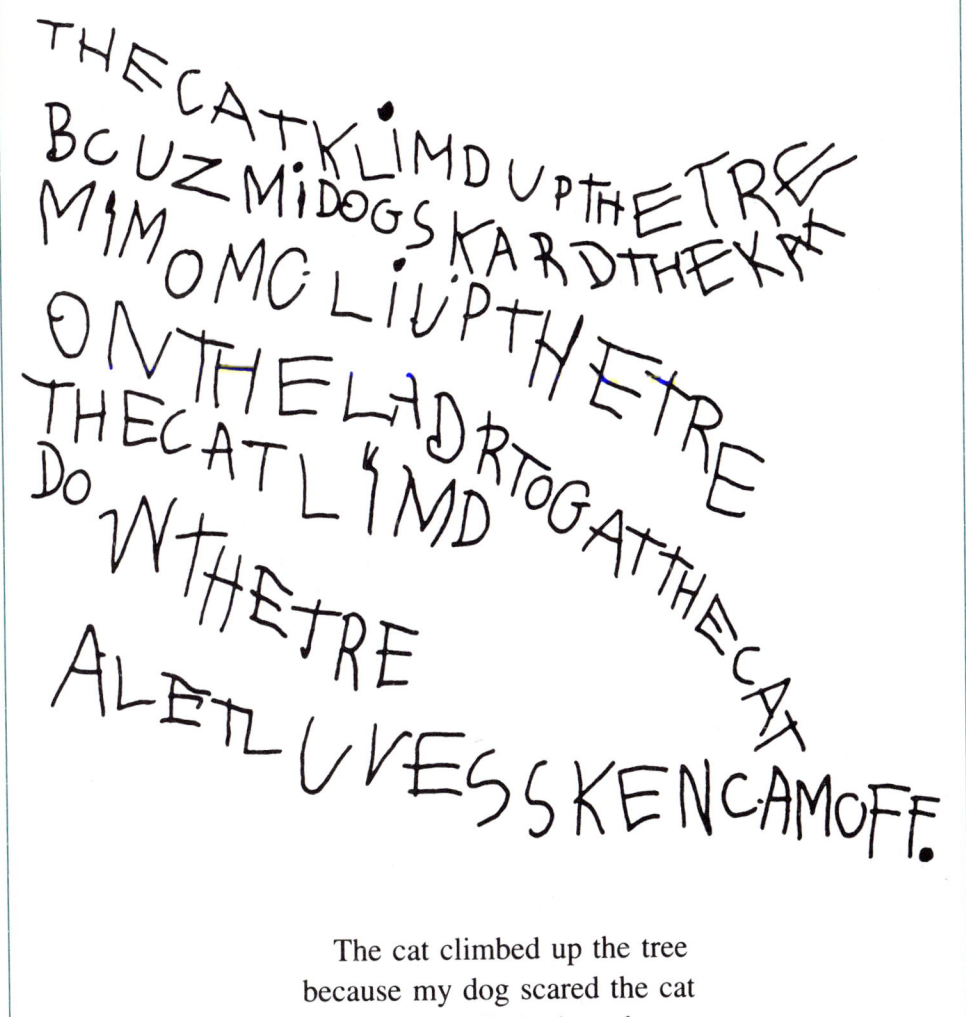

> THECATKLIMDUPTHETREE
> BCUZMIDOGSKARDTHEKAT
> MIMOMCLIVPTHETRE
> ONTHELADRTOGATTHECAT
> THECATLIMD
> DOWNTHETRE
> ALETLUVESSKENCAMOFF.

> The cat climbed up the tree
> because my dog scared the cat
> My mom climbed up the tree
> on the ladder to get the cat
> The cat climbed
> down the tree
> A little of its skin came off.

Figure 6.3 Story written by a first grader. (*Source:* C. B. Cazden, P. Cordiero, and M. E. Giacobbe, "Spontaneous and scientific concepts; Young children's learning of punctuation," in G. Wells and J. Nicholls, eds., Language learning: An interactional perspective [Philadelphia: The Falmer Press, 1985], pp. 119–120.)

❖ Assumptions That Underlie the Concept of Emergent Literacy

In summary, here are five assumptions that underlie the concept of emergent literacy. They are similar to the conclusions stated by Teale and Sulzby (1986, p. xvii).

1. Children exhibit reading and writing behaviors in the informal settings of home and community long before they start formal instruction.
2. Literacy develops in real-life settings and is used for real-life activities in order to get things done.
3. Children learn written language through active engagement with their world. They interact socially with adults in writing and reading situations; they explore print on their own; and they profit from being presented with models of literate behavior by significant adults, particularly their parents. At a later stage children profit from similar social interactions with their peers.
4. The child develops as a writer/reader. The notion of reading preceding writing, or vice versa, is a misconception. Listening, speaking, reading, and writing abilities (as both oral and written aspects of language) develop concurrently and interrelatedly, rather than sequentially.
5. Although children's learning about literacy can be described in terms of generalized stages, they can pass through these stages in a variety of ways and at different ages.

TO THINK ABOUT

Underlying Assumptions in Emergent Literacy

A. Compare the five assumptions that underlie the concept of emergent literacy with the following characteristics of the holistic, collaborative, integrated approach to teaching language arts developed in chapter 1.
   1. Collaborative rather than directive.
   2. Views the learner as active rather than passive.
   3. Focuses on functions of language rather than form.
   4. Views language learning holistically rather than atomistically.
   5. Approaches language learning from the top-down rather than from the bottom-up.
B. Compare the five assumptions that underlie the concept of emergent literacy with the five characteristics of parent-child interactions that facilitate development, which were covered in chapter 2.
   1. Intentionality
   2. Proximal development
   3. Collaboration
   4. Internalization
   5. Continuous development

Approaches to Teaching Reading That Are Consistent with the Concept of Emergent Literacy: Supporting Emergent Literacy in the Classroom

The Writing Process Approach in Primary Grades

The process approach is associated with Donald Graves (1983) and is frequently considered a method of teaching writing. But because it is a holistic, collaborative, integrated approach it is as much a method of teaching reading as it is of teaching writing. Therefore, I will describe one teacher's experiences using this approach here, and I will discuss the process approach again in greater detail in chapters 8 and 9, which focus on writing.

Marla McCurdy (1984) began experimenting with this approach by gathering her first graders around her one day and asking them how they would spell some words. Soon she had the sentence "The dog chased the cat" written on the board in the following way:

a dg sd a ct

After writing a few such sentences as a class project, Marla suggested to the children that in the future, when they were writing, they should try to write their own words without asking her how to spell them. She reminded them to put a space or dash between words and to write from left to right.

At first she was a little discouraged, but soon found that if she got to the children as soon as they had finished, many of them could read back what they had written. For example, a nonreader wrote what you see in Figure 6.4 and read back to her, "This is my imaginary friend, Bgooga." The writing of other children was more easily understood (see Figure 6.5).

Figure 6.4

Figure 6.5

Encouraged by these results, Marla continued her experiment. By the end of the year, her writing program incorporated the following features:

A Storybook Corner

Blank books made from lined paper and with construction-paper covers are always available in the storybook corner. Children's works-in-progress also are kept here. Children are expected to write every day.

Conferencing

Marla talks individually with the children on a regular basis. She helps them decide what to write about. She listens as they read their books to her. She reads their books as they listen and then asks them questions. For the following story,

> When I go home, I play with my dog,

she might ask, "What kind of dog is it? What color? What games do you play? How old is the dog? How is the dog special?" Sometimes, as a result of these conferences, the children add to their stories or revise them.

Publishing

When children are satisfied that their stories are finished, Marla or an aide types them, using conventional spelling, punctuation, and capitalization. Covers are made and books are created which are added to the classroom library of children's works.

A Literate Community

Children often read works-in-progress and borrow ideas from one another. They read one another's published books from the library, and show a great deal of interest in stories that are published.

Teaching and Learning Language Arts Is Integrated

Learning to read and write occur simultaneously. It is often impossible to say whether children are engaged in reading or writing, and the whole process is buoyed up on a sea of talk—speaking and listening.

TO THINK ABOUT

Reflections on the Writing Process Approach

A. Reflect on the writing process approach as a holistic, collaborative, integrated approach to teaching language arts. The following characteristics of this approach were developed in chapter 1.
   1. Collaborative rather than directive.

THE CONCEPT OF EMERGENT LITERACY   163

2. Views the learner as active rather than passive.
3. Views language learning as an interactional group process rather than as a teacher-to-students process.
4. Views language learning holistically rather than atomistically.
5. Views integrating teaching language arts from the top-down rather than the bottom-up.

Discuss your thoughts with a classmate.

B. Reflect on the writing process approach in terms of the five characteristics of parent-child interactions that facilitate development, which were covered in chapter 2.
   1. Intentionality
   2. Proximal development
   3. Collaboration
   4. Internalization
   5. Continuous development

Discuss your thoughts with a classmate.

C. Reflect on the writing process approach in terms of the five assumptions that underlie the concept of emergent literacy, which were given in this chapter. Discuss your thoughts with a classmate.

The Language Experience Approach

A typical beginning lesson using the language experience approach is as follows: Mary Weiss gathers her first graders around a table and uncovers a cage containing a white mouse. She opens the cage and soon the mouse ventures onto the table. She asks, "What do you think we should call her?" Billy suggests, "Whitey," and Mary prints *WHITEY* on the top of a large sheet of lined paper on an easel where all the children can see. She asks the children to tell something about Whitey and says she will print what they say on the paper. Soon the paper contains the following story.

WHITEY

Patrick said, "Whitey sniffs on the table."
Molly said, "He looked at me."
Amy said, "Whitey has a long tail."
Ralph said, "I think she is a girl."

Mary then reads the story, pointing to each word as she says it. Next she asks the children to read with her as she points to the words and says them. Finally she asks each child to draw a picture of Whitey, and she prints *WHITEY* at the top of each child's paper as he or she works.

The next day Mary reviews the story and asks the children to point to any words they know. Ralph points to his own name and the word WHITEY on the top line. Mickey recognizes Patrick's name and the word WHITEY at the top of the sheet. When asked if he sees the word *Whitey* anywhere else in the story, Mickey finds it in the third line. Lavonne appears to be able to read the entire story, relying somewhat on her memory of who said what, but relying also on her ability to recognize printed words.

Mary has engaged the students in an interesting and lively activity. She is not only teaching but also observing what the children know. She is encouraging those who know things to share what they know with others.

As days and weeks pass, Mary continues to write stories with the children, to read the stories with the class and to review them, and to encourage individuals to identify words they recognize from day to day. Soon she begins to print the words each child recognizes by sight on small cards and to give these words to the child for his or her word bank. After a few weeks of collecting words, Ada has twenty-five words in her word bank. Mary asks her to look at her words and to find two words that begin with the same sound as *bake* (one of Ada's words). Mary points out that the two words *ball* and *best* begin with the same letter as well as with the same sound. Ada is ready to begin to learn about sound-letter correspondences and about the names of letters (if she does not know these things already).

In the language experience approach children are encouraged to discover principles governing communication and language (including written language) through experience with language. Their discoveries are recognized, encouraged, and built upon. One of the great advantages of these programs is that children are given control over the language that will become their reading test. This retains some of the characteristics of the ideal home where parents follow the child's interest and lead from behind.

Word-recognition skills are an important part of the program. Skills are taught on an individual or small-group basis as children appear to need them. They may not be taught explicitly to children who catch on to them through experience with reading. They are not taught systematically since each child has difficulty with different skills; and even children who have difficulty with the same skills are likely to encounter them in a different order. To repeat, since this is a point that is often misunderstood, word-recognition skills are an important part of the language experience approach.

Dozens of experiences and activities with written language, such as the following, go on every day in Mary's classroom. They reassure children that writing makes sense, that it means something, that it gets jobs done, and that it communicates in the same way that spoken language does.

- Children dictate stories to teachers and older students who write them down.
- Teachers read storybooks to children.
- Children invent stories while turning pages of wordless picture books.
- Children write stories, journal entries, and news items.

Of course, you have recognized that Mary's language experience approach rests on a holistic, collaborative, integrated approach to teaching language arts.

TO THINK ABOUT

Reflections on the Language Experience Approach

A. Reflect on the language experience approach as a holistic, collaborative, integrated approach to teaching language arts. Discuss your thoughts with a classmate.

B. Reflect on the language experience approach in terms of the five characteristics of parent-child interactions that facilitate development. Discuss your thoughts with a classmate.

C. Reflect on the language experience approach in terms of the five assumptions that underlie the concept of emergent literacy in this chapter. Discuss your thoughts with a classmate.

Some books that describe the language experience approach are *Language Experiences in Communication* by Roach Van Allen (1976); *The Language Experience Approach to the Teaching of Reading, Revised Edition* by R. G. Stauffer (1980); and *Teaching Reading as a Language Experience* by MaryAnn Hall (1981).

The Individualized Reading Program

The individualized reading program was articulated by Veatch (1978). Children are encouraged to investigate books and to choose books to read. The teacher meets with children individually to see what progress they are making and where they are encountering difficulties.

The teacher then plans and carries out instruction. If more than one child is having the same problems, the instruction is carried out in groups. Some groups meet regularly with the teacher for direct instruction. Other groups work independently. The nature of what needs to be learned determines whether the children receive direct instruction or work independently. A regular time for sharing enables children to come together as a whole class. A six-step plan for an individualized reading program follows.

I. Selecting
   Child chooses materials based on two criteria
   A. He likes it
      and
   B. He can read it.
II. Planning. Child decides
   A. To read the book for himself. When finished he goes back to step 1.
      or
   B. To prepare this book for an individual conference with the teacher.

III. Independent work
   A. Reads.
   B. Proceeds with preparation for individual conference such as
      1. Intensive study to retell story to teacher.
      2. Develop a report to share with class.
      3. Polish a skill from another curriculum area, such as writing a composition based on the story.
IV. Individual conference: an intensive, individual session on a one-to-one basis with the teacher. Teacher keeps detailed records of each conference. Instruction is based on these records.
V. Organization of groups. Teacher forms groups based on observations made in individual conferences.
   A. Groups for instructional purposes are based on specific clear-cut needs that require continuing direct instruction from the teacher.
   B. Groups for independent work are based on specific clear-cut needs that do not require continuing direct instructions from the teacher.
VI. Sharing follow-up and evaluation
   A. Children tell about the book they read—preferably during time allotted in addition to the regular reading period.
   B. Children complete workbook pages and similar materials chosen by the teacher to meet the needs of individuals and groups.
   C. During individual conferences, children receive immediate evaluation of their progress. Reports to parents of student progress are based on records kept by the teacher.

As each child completes the six-step plan, he or she returns to step 1 to begin the cycle anew.

The individualized reading program rests on the following assumptions:

- Reading must be taught as part of all of the other language arts.
- Children learn to read better and faster when they are free to pace their own growth, seeking help when necessary.
- The act of reading must center on the child, with the materials used being of secondary importance.
- Children's own language is a valuable source material for reading instruction.
- Classroom efficiency is enhanced when groups are organized upon an identified need, problem, difficulty, or interest.
- There is no established rank order of reading materials.
- Reading growth results when a pupil commits himself or herself to a piece of material.
- As reading is a personal act, the choice of material is an expression of self.
- Personal commitment by the pupil will enhance reading growth when matched by the ability of the teacher to change and adapt procedures on the spot.

THE CONCEPT OF EMERGENT LITERACY 167

- Not all skills need be taught to every child, nor in identical sequence to more than one child.
- Progress may be steadily cumulative, but it may also be apparent in great leaps and bounds.
- Skills are gained during the act of reading and not before it.
- There is no clearly established sequence of skills for all children.
- There is no single piece of material that meets the needs of every pupil in any given class.
- The love of books and reading is encouraged when beloved books are read.

TO THINK ABOUT

Reflections on the Individual Reading Program Approach

A. Reflect on the individual reading program as a holistic, collaborative, integrated approach to teaching language arts. Discuss your thoughts with a classmate.

B. Reflect on the individual reading program in terms of the five characteristics of parent-child interactions that facilitate development. Discuss your thoughts with a classmate.

C. Reflect on the individual reading program in terms of the five assumptions that underlie the concept of emergent literacy, which were explained in this chapter. Discuss your thoughts with a classmate.

Although Veatch's individual reading program was recognized as an important alternative to more traditional methods, it was not widely adopted as the sole approach to teaching reading. Since the concept of emergent literacy was not widely recognized before the 1980s, the individual reading program was probably an idea that was ahead of its time.

Reading Conferences in Primary Grades

In her book *When Writers Read,* Hansen (1987) develops the concept of the response and the way responses operate in achieving reading comprehension. Children respond to texts (books, stories, essays, and so on). Teachers respond to students, affirming what students know, answering their questions, clarifying misunderstandings, and negotiating a shared meaning based on the text.

Teachers approach reading conferences with these principles in mind. Rather than explain these principles to students, teachers behave in accordance with them. After repeated experiences, the students understand how the reading conference works.

A conference between a teacher and child in the early stages of the process might go as follows:

> The teacher might stop beside Jeremy, for example, and say, "Oh, you're reading *Corduroy*. I've read it, too. What do you think of it?"
> Jeremy, when this response system is new to him, may say, "It's OK."

The teacher has yet to find out what Jeremy knows, so she pursues, "Show me a part you think is OK."

Jeremy shows the page where Corduroy emerges, shrunk, but doesn't say a word.

The teacher still hasn't found out much about what he knows, so she continues, "Yes, he shrank. Tell me about that."

Jeremy simply says, "The dryer was too hot."

The teacher starts to get excited, "You know heat can cause things to shrink. That's important. Do you have anything else to tell me?"

The child may or may not answer, but before the teacher leaves the child, she refocuses him, "Where were you when I came. . . . Please read just a bit to me."

When Jeremy is on track, the teacher moves on.

Over time, the student contributes more and more to the conference, usually starting to talk the moment the teacher pulls a chair up beside him. He knows she wants him to tell her about his book. Her goal is to find out one thing the student knows and restate it in specific terms. Often, when we respond to a student, he comes to understand his book better as he tells us about it. (Hansen, 1987, p. 184)

Students learn that the teacher wants to hear what they know from reading the text. Students learn that they are to re-create the meaning, to compose what they have comprehended. In such conferences, misunderstandings are revealed that questioning by the teacher might never have uncovered.

One day when researcher Tom Romano met with Matt and Randy, they talked about *Soup* by Robert Peck. The boys thought Rob had hit a nurse with a ball because they thought that "throwing the ball" back to the other person in conversation meant throwing a real ball. Romano didn't come to this session with a list of questions to ask the boys. He came to find out what they knew. They talked and he listened. When he realized that they misunderstood the words, he explained. He taught. (Hansen, 1987, pp. 41–42)

Teachers Ask "Real" Questions

In such conferences teachers ask real questions, that is, questions to which they do not know the answers. A teacher who has not read a story a child is reading might say, "You said the boy didn't like his father. Why didn't he like him?" This is not a comprehension question that can be classified as factual or inferential, and to which the teacher expects one right answer. The teacher really wants to know why the student thinks the boy in the story didn't like his father. The child may explain, "Well, when he didn't want to play football his father made fun of him in front of his friends, and things like that." The teacher might respond, "I see. That's a pretty good reason not to like someone."

The student may reformulate his or her understanding. "Well, he always was in trouble with his father. His father was always mad at him. I guess he liked him, but he was kind of afraid of him."

Students Ask Real Questions

When students become accustomed to answering real questions and having their answers listened to, responded to, and validated, they stop trying to hide what they don't know and ask real questions themselves. When teachers know the answers to real questions, they simply answer them. When they do not, they must find out the answers or encourage students to seek answers elsewhere. For example:

> One day first-grader Amanda came to me with a question: "I know the horse is friendly and the goat isn't but I don't understand why they become friends." I hadn't read the book, so I asked some questions. Amanda couldn't explain the story well enough for me to figure out why the two animals became friends. Amanda sat. I suggested that she read the book to someone. Amanda continued to sit. Finally she said, "I'll read the whole book to Stephanie. Then me and her can talk about it." (Hansen, 1987, p. 42)

Students Are Encouraged to Tell What They Know

Earlier in this chapter, I discussed the astonishing discoveries preschool children make about reading, writing, story form, and aspects of writing such as punctuation. This emergent knowledge becomes apparent when we permit children to display what they know. Similar discoveries have been made when children are empowered to express their opinions about such high levels of comprehension as imputing motives to story characters. For example:

> In October, Barry, a child in Pat McLure's first grade, shared *Tales of Oliver Pig*, by Jean VanLeeuwen (1979), in which Grandmother Pig comes to visit, and little Oliver Pig gets his monster books and toy elephant to put in Grandmother's room (Hubbard, 1985). Barry requested comments and questions about his book, and Chris asked, "Why do you suppose he got monster books and a toy elephant for an adult?"
>
> "Maybe he was being sneaky," Barry suggested. "She wouldn't really care about that stuff, but Oliver could sneak right in with her and cuddle up and she'd read him the book."
>
> "I don't think so," Roger stated. "Oliver's a nice pig. I think he gave her his favorite monster books to read; then he thought if she was scared, she could hug his elephant." (Hansen, 1987, p. 83).

The children attributed deeper motives to Oliver's actions than their teacher had considered.

ACTIVITY

A. Choose a reading selection and work with a partner. Plan a dialog between a teacher and student engaged in a conference like those described in this section. Decide on the following conditions before starting:
   1. The teacher has (or has not) read the story.
   2. The child is (or is not) used to these conferences and is (or is not) forthcoming.
B. Present a variety of these skits to the class where different conditions are evident. Comment on the teacher's performance and his or her fidelity to the principles of the holistic, integrated, collaborative approach as you understand them.

Students Help One Another

In a whole language classroom, students are encouraged to seek help from one another. When students read "books" written by fellow students, they go to the author for help with reading. When students read books that have been read by other students, they can seek out these others and ask for help in understanding what they are reading.

When students' interests become known to their classmates, individuals may be identified as knowledgeable on certain topics. Jenny is a good person to talk to about sport books because she loves sports and reads such books herself. Mark can probably answer questions about dogs because his mother is a veterinarian and he likes to read about dogs.

TO THINK ABOUT

Reflections on Hansen's Reading Conferences

A. Reflect on Hansen's reading conference as a holistic, collaborative, integrated approach to teaching language arts. Discuss your thoughts with a classmate.
B. Reflect on Hansen's reading conference in terms of the five characteristics of parent-child interactions that facilitate development. Discuss your thoughts with a classmate.
C. Reflect on Hansen's reading conference in terms of this chapter's five assumptions that underlie the concept of emergent literacy. Discuss your thoughts with a classmate.

Middle-School Reading Workshops

Nancie Atwell (1987) advocates a reading program for the upper grades, or middle school, that shares many of the assumptions of Veatch's individualized reading program. The reading workshop is based on the assumption that students need three basics in order to continue growing as readers: time, ownership, and response.

Time. Reading workshops begin with a ten- to fifteen-minute minilesson followed by thirty to sixty minutes of sustained silent reading. Sustained silent reading means that each student reads his or her own book without interruption in an atmosphere conducive to silent reading. For the first ten to fifteen minutes the teacher circulates, supervises, solves problems, and sees that everyone is on task. For the remaining twenty to forty minutes, the teacher silently reads a book of his or her own. These regular periods of sustained silent reading give the students one of the basics—*time*.

Ownership. Students choose their own reading material from the library (classroom, school, or public), bookstores, or home. The individual teacher may set limits. For example, a child who brings *Lady Chatterley's Lover* might be told to read that book at home if he or she wants to read it at all. But within a very broad range, the children are given genuine choice, which is the second basic—*ownership* over their reading material.

Response. Each student has a spiral-bound notebook called a "dialog journal" or "literature log." Students are required to write one letter a week to the teacher or to another student. These letters express the students' responses to the literature they are reading. They tell why the students chose a particular book and what they like or did not like and why. The person addressed responds to these letters in the student's journal, and the journals are returned. Dialog journals or literature logs provide the third basic—*response*.

Through the reading workshop, students read a great deal and learn from their experiences, from one another, and from their teacher. Through reading and responding to the students' literature logs, the teacher learns where students need guidance and exposure to new ideas. Minilessons that are taught at the beginning of each workshop session grow out of what the teacher learns from students' literature logs. Topics for minilessons range from how to choose a book to why authors sometimes use pseudonyms.

Rules are established for choosing books and stating exactly what behaviors are expected of students during reading workshops and what behaviors will not be tolerated. One-third of the student's grade is based on how well he or she observes these rules. Minimum requirements are set for entries into the literature logs, and the teacher's responses in the logs continually guide and evaluate the students' efforts in writing useful responses to the selections they read. Minilessons are often used to guide students toward making more useful responses to their reading. One-third of students' grades are based on their literature logs. One week in each term the teacher has individual conferences with students to set goals and to evaluate progress on previously set goals. One-third of students' grades are based on evaluation of progress toward goals that are set and evaluated during conferences.

TO THINK ABOUT

Reflections on Atwell's Reading Workshop

A. Reflect on Atwell's Reading Workshop as a holistic, collaborative, integrated approach to teaching language arts. Discuss your thoughts with a classmate.

B. Reflect on Atwell's Reading Workshop in terms of the five characteristics of parent-child interactions that facilitate development. Discuss your thoughts with a classmate.

C. Reflect on Atwell's Reading Workshop in terms of this chapter's five assumptions that underlie the concept of emergent literacy. Discuss your thoughts with a classmate.

❖ Structure and Holistic, Collaborative, Integrated Approaches to Teaching Reading

In describing teaching styles, Galton and Simon (1980) single out one teacher whom they obviously admire: "As pupils acquired the desired learning habits, the original formal structure was deliberately relaxed, with the pupils taking increased responsibility for planning their own work on an individualized basis" (p. 38). When teachers are new, one might apply the principle observed here to both teacher and students: As the pupils acquire the desired learning habits, and as the teacher acquires more knowledge of the reading process and the learning process and acquires the necessary organizational and managerial skills, the original formal structure is deliberately relaxed. Pupils take an increasing responsibility (in consultation with the teacher) for their own learning on an individualized basis.

This does not mean, however, that structure is abandoned. Hansen (1987) refers to structure, order, and routine repeatedly.

> Reading/writing classrooms are tightly structured. They must be. The classroom is full of decision makers, many of whom may be inexperienced and need guidelines. To complicate matters, many of us are new at this kind of teaching and don't know how to organize ourselves. We feel certain about only one thing: The classroom must be orderly.
>
> It bothers me when teachers say that basal-centered classrooms are more structured than those based on response. On the contrary, if children spend a lot of time reading and sharing books they have chosen, the classroom must be highly organized or it will be a mess. The structure is tight but in a different way than the basal classroom. In a response-based philosophy the teacher not only sets up the routine, she teaches the children to use it. This is probably what I found most difficult to understand and what many teachers find difficult to learn. Initially, when a few children meet to share their books, or a common book or story, the teacher establishes a structure. Every teacher's format will be different, but each teacher decides on a routine and initially adheres to it like Super Glue. (p. 49)

THE TRADITIONAL CONCEPT OF READING READINESS

In their excellent review of the history of the concept of reading readiness, Teale and Sulzby (1986) show that until the 1920s "the general belief was that literary development did not begin until the child encountered formal education in

THE TRADITIONAL CONCEPT OF READING READINESS

school" (p. viii). By the 1920s early childhood and kindergarten began to be viewed as a "period of preparation" and the concept of **reading readiness** took root.

The concept of reading readiness stands in sharp contrast to the concept of emergent literacy. Reading readiness is an older concept, and it is still very influential. While the concept of emergent literacy fosters collaborative, holistic approaches to teaching reading, the concept of reading readiness fosters directive, atomistic approaches to teaching reading.

From the start, reading readiness research was directed at identifying factors that "enabled children to be 'prepared mentally' for reading" (p. ix). The factors that researchers looked for were the kinds of knowledge and skills that were presumed to be necessary before a child could learn to read. Finding the presence or absence of these factors in children requires testing, and testing is an integral part of reading readiness and the approaches that grow out of it.

❖ Traditional Reading Readiness Skills

A typical task designed to determine whether a child is ready to learn to read is shown in Figure 6.6. This task is designed to test a child's ability to make judgments about visual similarities and differences in familiar geometric shapes. This ability is referred to as **visual discrimination.**

Auditory Discrimination

One way students can demonstrate **auditory discrimination** is to indicate that they hear the same sound at the beginning of *mat* and *mop* and different sounds at the beginning of *bet* and *set*.

Alphabet Knowledge

Ways children can demonstrate **alphabet knowledge** are

- to pick out instances of the same letter in a row such as the following:
  m r s m v

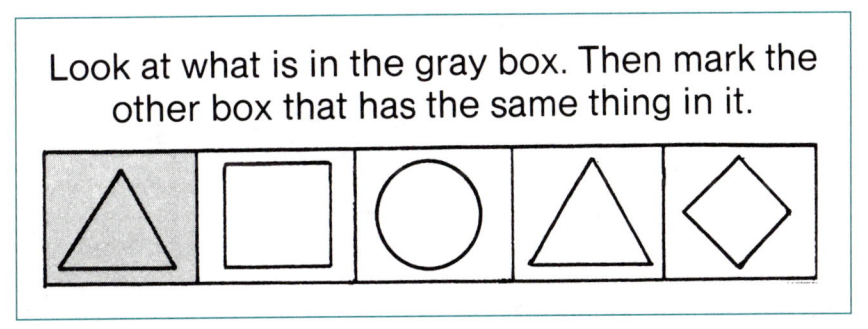

Look at what is in the gray box. Then mark the other box that has the same thing in it.

Figure 6.6

- to pick out the correct letter in the following row when the teacher says "Mark the letter *c*": a c o d r
- to pick out the fork from a group of pictures like those in Figure 6.7 when the teacher says, "Look at the cup, pin, and fork. Mark the picture that begins with the sound of the letter in the box."

Word-Learning Tasks

The following is an example of a word-learning task. Children are shown words such as *walk*, *fly*, and *swim* printed on the board. The children say the words as the teacher points to them. The words are presented on flash cards, and the children say them as the teacher presents each card and matches the word on the flash card to the word on the board. The words are used in several sentences by the teacher as the students look at the words: "Birds can fly. Airplanes can fly. You and I can't fly—except in an airplane." The teacher asks questions and holds up a card and the students must know the word on the card to answer: "Can fish do this? [holding up *swim*] Yes, fish can swim." Children are then tested on recognition of the words.

Vocabulary Knowledge

In an example of an item testing vocabulary knowledge the child might be shown a series of pictures as in Figure 6.8 and told to put a mark on the picture of the baby.

❖ Two Applications of the Readiness Concept

If They're Not Ready, Wait

Two reasons were generally put forward when the question "Why test readiness?" was asked. One was that by testing readiness the teacher could decide which children should begin to receive formal instruction in reading. That is, one tests readiness to select children for reading instruction. Most reading

> Look at the cup, pin, and fork. Mark the picture that begins with the sound of the letter in the box.

Figure 6.7

> Put a mark on the picture of the baby.

Figure 6.8

readiness research was done on a model that is very easy to understand. If you believe that a certain skill, such as naming letters, is a necessary prerequisite to learning to read, you can test children on letter names before reading instruction begins. If most of the children who know their letter names learn to read and most of the children who do not know their letter names do not learn to read, one would have strong evidence that learning letter names is an important prerequisite to learning to read. However, the studies are not that clear-cut. Success in learning to read is far from infallibly predicted by scores on letter-naming tests.

If They're Not Ready, Get Them Ready!

Another frequently cited reason for administering reading readiness tests is to identify necessary, prerequisite skills that are lacking in a child with whom reading instruction is about to begin. Its followers believe that a child who is not ready must be taught these skills before reading instruction begins. By the 1980s this version of reading readiness had become "firmly entrenched as the dominant approach" to beginning reading instruction (Teale & Sulzby, 1986).

❖ Assumptions That Underlie the Concept of Reading Readiness

Three assumptions that underlie the concept of reading readiness are these:

1. Early childhood behaviors involving "reading" and "writing" are distinct from "real" reading.
2. Only after the child has mastered the various subskills of reading readiness does the real part begin.
3. Readiness skills must be taught in school in a fixed order and by direct instruction. (Teale & Sulzby, 1987)

For better or for worse, the beliefs, concepts, and vocabulary of the reading readiness model of beginning reading permeate the methods and materials used in beginning reading instruction in American schools. Programs to teach reading readiness skills appear in many nursery schools and kindergartens. Visual and auditory discrimination, alphabet knowledge, word-learning tasks, and oral language comprehension are all incorporated into the initial stages of many published reading programs at the point where they appear to be relevant to reading instruction.

TO THINK ABOUT

Underlying Assumptions—Reading Readiness vs. Emergent Literacy

Compare the three assumptions that underlie the concept of reading readiness with the five assumptions that underlie the concept of emergent literacy.

❖ An Approach to Teaching Reading That is Consistent with the Reading Readiness Concept: The Phonics or Skills Emphasis Approach

Donald Vader is a first-grade teacher who uses a phonics or skills emphasis approach. He begins reading instruction by directing the children's attention to a page something like Figure 6.9 and saying:

"This is the letter *a*. *A* stands for the first sound in *airplane*.
A stands for the first sound in *an, ant, accident,* and *animal*."

He then introduces a variety of activities to give the children experience with identifying the form of the letter *a* and the sound /a/ and with associating the two. Over the next few days the class engages in activities like the following.

1. The children are each presented with a small card with the letter *a* printed on it, and they play a game. The children hold up their cards while Donald pronounces words such as *as, an, ant, be, afternoon*. The object of the game is for the children to quickly put their cards down when they hear a word that does not begin with /a/.
2. They are directed to use their fingers like a pencil and draw over the letters *a* and *A* as the teacher says words beginning with /a/.
3. They write upper- and lowercase *A*'s on the chalkboard.

The next lessons take up the letters *e, i, o, u, m, n, r,* and so on. At the point that *m* is introduced, children are taught that words are made of several sounds together and that by blending the sounds of the letters *a* and *m* a word is formed. Thereafter words are introduced made up of the letter-sound relationships that have been taught (*am, Nan, an, Ann, man, men, in, on, ran* . . .).
After the children have had repeated experiences in

- identifying sounds at the beginnings and endings of words,
- identifying letters at the beginnings and endings of words, and
- identifying words,

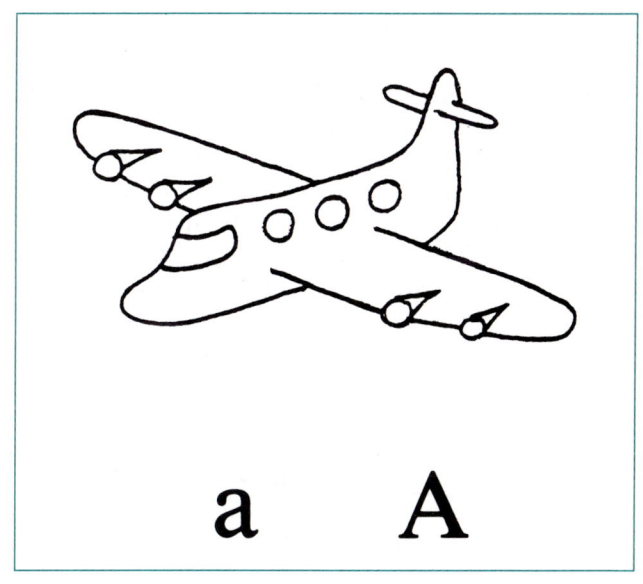

Figure 6.9 A typical first page in a phonics-emphasis basal reader.

poems and stories are introduced containing words that give students practice using the knowledge and skills they have been taught in these lessons.

Programs like the one Donald uses rigidly control the introduction of letters, speech sounds, and sound-spelling correspondences.

TO THINK ABOUT

Underlying Assumptions: The Phonics Approach

A. Contrast the phonics or skills emphasis approach with the holistic, collaborative, integrated approach to teaching language arts. (The characteristics of this approach are developed in chapter 1.)

B. Contrast the phonics or skills emphasis approach with the five characteristics of parent-child interactions that facilitate development (see chapter 2).

C. Contrast the phonics or skills emphasis approach with the five assumptions that underlie this chapter's concept of emergent literacy.

BASAL READING PROGRAMS

The most widely used materials for teaching reading in this country are referred to as basal reading programs. Basal readers are a series of textbooks for use in the elementary-school grades beginning with first grade. Preschool and kindergarten materials are also frequently included. Each set of students' books is accompanied by a teacher's guide or teacher's manual with page-by-page suggestions and instructions for teaching reading using the materials in the students' books. Other materials such as workbooks, audiovisual teaching aids, and software for computerized lessons are published to accompany basal readers. The teacher's guide or manual gives suggestions and directions for using these materials as well.

There are numerous basal reading series on the market. Greenlinger-Harless's (1987) index to "a number of popular basal reading series for the elementary school level" published between 1977 and 1987 lists seventeen publishers and forty different programs.

An important aspect of basal readers is that each book (ideally, each lesson) is created as part of a grand design. Decisions of what to teach, when to teach, and how to teach are guided by the authors' and editors' beliefs about the nature of reading, how one learns to read, in what order skills ought to be presented, and so on. Questions of content such as how minorities are portrayed, and whether once-taboo topics such as death, divorce, aging, or delinquency will be portrayed, are also answered in terms of a coherent policy. The most fundamental distinction among reading series is whether they are categorized as phonics or skills emphasis or eclectic.

❖ Phonics or Skills Emphasis Basal Reading Programs

Phonics emphasis readers are consistent with the concept of reading readiness. They rely heavily on atomistic, bottom-up assumptions about reading and learning to read. Although they pay attention to meaning and comprehending, they *begin* with attention to letter recognition and letter-sound relationships and continue to *emphasize* phonics and skills throughout the grades. Donald Vader's phonics emphasis beginning reading lesson described earlier in this chapter is typical of such programs.

The following programs are frequently identified as phonics emphasis basal reading series:

Economy Reading Series published by McGraw-Hill, 1986.
Lippincott Basic Reading published by Scribner, 1981.
The Headway Program published by Open Court, 1985.

Phonics emphasis basal reading programs grow out of an atomistic, bottom-up view of learning to read. Based on the literature and my own experience, I do not support this view.

❖ Eclectic Basal Reading Programs

The word *eclectic* means "selecting, choosing from various sources." In comparison to phonics or skills emphasis programs, eclectic basal reading programs rely more on holistic, top-down assumptions about reading and learning to read. However, you can easily find lessons on phonics generalizations and isolated skills throughout these programs, which will remind you that they are indeed *eclectic*.

The following programs are frequently identified as eclectic basal reading series:

The Ginn Reading Program published by Silver Burdett and Ginn, 1985–1987.
HBJ Basic Reading published by Holt, Rinehart and Winston, 1980 and 1986.
Houghton Mifflin Reading published by Houghton Mifflin, 1986.
Series r: Macmillan Reading published by Macmillan, 1980, 1983, and 1986.
Scott, Foresman Reading: An American Tradition published by Scott, Foresman, 1987.

In recent years publishers of eclectic basal reading programs have produced programs that incorporate the traditional features of basal readers with the addition of libraries of titles chosen for literary merit. These programs enable the teacher to move further toward the holistic, collaborative, integrated approach to teaching—an approach consistent with the concept of emergent literacy reading while continuing to use a basal reading series.

Four such programs are the following:

Heath Reading published by D. C. Heath, 1989.
Impressions published by Holt, Rinehart and Winston, 1988.
World of Reading published by Silver Burdett and Ginn, 1988.
Collections published by Scott, Foresman, 1989.

ACTIVITY

Go to a local school, university, or college and get materials from one of the phonics or skills emphasis basal reading series, one of the eclectic basal reading series, and one of the basal reading series that incorporates libraries of titles chosen for literary merit.

Work through one or two lessons at the beginning first-grade level from a series in each category. Choose two higher levels, say, fourth and seventh grades, and work through a couple of lessons from each category.
A. Demonstrate some of these lessons for your classmates.
B. Discuss whether these series and the differences between them have been described and compared accurately and fairly in this book.

Many seasoned teachers who employ holistic, collaborative approaches to teaching reading (reading conferences and reading workshops) began teaching by using eclectic basal reading series. Because of the flexibility of the programs and these teachers' inclinations, the progression from more traditional approaches to more holistic, collaborative, integrated approaches evolved gradually and seemingly naturally.

Teaching in Groups Using Eclectic Basal Reading Programs

When using eclectic basal reading programs, it is customary to teach reading in three groups. The following lists represent a three-group plan for teaching reading in the first grade and a three-group plan for teaching reading in the fifth grade.

Three-Group Plan for Second Half of First Grade

	Preprimer Group	*Primer Group*	*First Reader Group*
9:10–9:40	Work independently on teacher-made letter and word discrimination practice.	*Teacher conducts* lesson preparing for new story. Follows suggestions in teacher's guide for basal reader.	Silent reading of materials selected by pupils.
9:40–10:10	*Teacher conducts* lesson preparing for a new story. Follows suggestions in teacher's guide for basal reader.	Nonreading activity. (Work independently on addition facts.)	Nonreading activity. (Work independently on addition facts.)
10:10–10:40	Cut pictures from magazines for an initial consonant sound word file.	Work independently on duplicated worksheets, using letter-sound associations and context clues to recognize words.	*Teacher directs* lesson to check comprehension of last story. Selected oral reading.
10:40–11:10		Recess	
11:10–11:40	*Teacher directs* the whole class in developing an experience story about the school bake sale. Students practice reading the experience story.		

Three-Group Plan for Fifth Grade

	Red Book Group	*Blue Book Group*	*Green Book Group*
9:55–10:15	*Teacher conducts* discussion and oral reading of story read on previous day.	Silent reading of story introduced on previous day.	Silent reading and written comprehension check of materials from supplementary program (self-corrected).
10:15–10:35	Workbook exercises related to story.	*Teacher conducts* discussion and oral reading of story.	Plan dramatization of story with group chairperson or teacher aide.

10:35– Independent reading period.
10:55 *Teacher conducts* individual conferences and works with a group of students who have a common oral reading problem.

Grouping by Achievement

These plans are based on the assumptions that different achievement levels exist in classrooms, and that by grouping children by achievement levels one minimizes the risk that children will be asked to perform tasks that are too difficult for them and therefore impossible, or too easy for them and therefore a waste of time and effort.

Initially, groups are formed on the best information available, such as test scores or the teacher's evaluation of one or two oral reading performances. Long-term observation of a child in learning situations is a more valid measure of achievement than test scores, and teachers should not hesitate to move students from group to group as a result of such observations.

Temporary Groups Formed Around Needs

There are numerous reasons to form special-purpose groups that will last for a short duration. In a fifth grade, for example, two children from the middle group and one child from the high group may have similar oral reading problems. This group of three might meet with the teacher or with an aide to practice oral reading for meaning, reading with expression, or becoming aware of the role of context in word recognition. As soon as children accomplish the goal for which such a group is created, they are no longer a part of that group. When all the children in the group have accomplished the goal of the group, the group no longer exists.

Temporary Groups Formed Around Interests

Children with different levels of achievement and different skills strengths can comprise groups based on common interest. For example, as a result of a social studies unit some children in the class might become interested in finding out what it must have been like to be a child in colonial America. Children with varying levels of reading achievement might read from biographies of people who lived in colonial America and construct a list of differences under these headings: clothing, food, education, work, and so on.

Whole-Class Reading Lessons

One reason for regular whole-class reading lessons is that one does not want to lose sight of the value of a learning community. Separating children who know more from children who know less, and separating children who lack a skill from children who have that skill, prevents children from learning from one another.

Another reason is that some activities will benefit everyone in the class. There is nothing to be gained by repeating the activity two or three times in small groups. In a seventh-grade class, for example, students might read and discuss a weekly current events magazine as an entire class. A first-grade teacher might conduct a whole-class lesson on telling when word pairs begin with the same or different sounds. A teacher may read passages from books to the entire class in preparation for selecting books for individual reading.

Children Work Independently

When teachers group children for reading instruction, children are expected to work independently of the teacher more times than when they are engaged in a lesson conducted by the teacher. This kind of independent activity takes two forms: children work together as a group on some project or lesson, or they work individually at silent reading, computer programs, writing assignments, and so on.

Summary

In a literate society, children begin to develop concepts about written language and its function during infancy. For example, while two-and-a-half-year-old Emily and her mother engage in talk around a picture book, Emily gains experience with books, print, illustrations, and stories. Research shows that many preschoolers develop concepts about writing, reading, and story form. Given the opportunity and encouragement to "write" many children reveal that without formal instruction they can make discoveries about the formal aspects of written language—handwriting, spelling, and punctuating. This phenomenon is referred to as emergent literacy. The concept of emergent literacy rests on five assumptions: (1) Children may exhibit reading and writing behaviors without formal instruction, (2) literacy develops in real-life settings, (3) children learn to deal with written language through active engagement with their world, (4) children develop as readers and writers simultaneously, and (5) children pass through literacy stages in a variety of ways.

An approach to teaching writing and reading that is consistent with the concept of emergent literacy is known as the writing process approach. Features of this approach include a storybook corner; conferencing; publishing; fostering a literate community; and integrating learning of writing, reading, speaking, and listening.

The language experience approach to beginning reading includes a teacher's printing stories dictated by students followed by teacher-led choral reading of the text while the teacher points to words as they are read. Children begin to recognize individual words through exercises like this. These words are kept by individuals as word banks and word-recognition lessons begin based on individual student's known words.

The individualized reading program is a literature-based approach where students choose their own reading materials. Reading instruction is carried out using a six-step plan that includes individual instruction, small-group instruction, and whole-class sharing based on the students' self-selected books and stories.

More recent advocates of literature-based approaches to teaching reading highlight the ideas of response, teacher-student conferences, and students learning from one another. Atwell (1987) asserts that the reading workshop gives the student the three basics needed to grow as readers: time, ownership, and response.

In contrast to the concept of emergent literacy is the traditional concept of reading readiness. According to the reading readiness concept there are certain skills and understandings, such as visual and auditory discrimination and alphabet and vocabulary knowledge, that a child must have before formal instruction in reading begins. These assumptions underlie the concept of reading readiness: (1) Early childhood behaviors involving "reading" and "writing" are distinct from real reading, (2) only after the child has mastered the various subskills of reading readiness does real reading instruction begin, and (3) readiness skills must be taught in school in a fixed order and by direct instruction. The phonics emphasis or skills emphasis approach to beginning reading instruction is consistent with the concept of reading readiness. Although the concept of emergent literacy is more current, the concept of reading readiness is very widespread in American schools.

Basal reading programs are widely used for teaching reading. Basal reading programs can be classified as phonics or skill emphasis programs or eclectic programs. Recently, basal reading series have been published that incorporate traditional features of basal readers with the addition of libraries of titles chosen for literary merit. These series permit teachers to move further toward a holistic, collaborative, integrated approach to teaching reading while continuing to use a basal reading series.

When using a basal series it is customary to divide the class into groups for instruction. Students are grouped according to their reading achievement, and instruction is based on the level of the basal reader appropriate for the achievement level of each group. Ideally, temporary groups are formed around particular needs and interest of children regardless of their general level of achievement. Reading lessons that involve the whole class are also regularly conducted. Finally, students are regularly assigned work to be done individually and independently.

For Review and Discussion

1. Recall examples from the chapter that illustrate the assumptions that underlie the concept of emergent literacy. If you have had the opportunity to observe young children recall examples of your own.

2. Which approach to language arts is more consistent with the concept of emergent literacy—the holistic, collaborative, integrated approach or the skills emphasis approach? Why? Which approach is more consistent with the reading readiness concept? Why?

3. Consider each of the following approaches to teaching reading:
   the writing process approach
   the language experience approach
   the individualized reading program
   reading conferences and workshops
   the phonics or skills emphasis approach
   Answer the following questions about them:
   a. Is it a holistic, collaborative, integrated approach?
   b. Is it consistent with characteristics of parent-child interactions that facilitate language development as discussed in chapter 2?
   c. Is it more consistent with the concept of emergent literacy or with the concept of reading readiness?
4. How do eclectic basal reading programs differ from skills emphasis basal reading programs?
5. How do basal reading series that include libraries of titles chosen for literary merit differ from the reading workshop approach?

For Further Reading

Cianciolo, P. (1989). No small challenge: Literature for the transitional readers. *Language Arts, 66,* 72–81.

Golden, J. M. (1984). Children's concept of story in reading and writing. *The Reading Teacher, 37,* 578–584.

Heller, M. F. (1988). Comprehending and composing through language experience. *The Reading Teacher, 42,* 130–135.

Johnston, P. (1989). A scenic view of reading. *Language Arts, 66,* 160–170.

Lindquist, D. B. (1988). Joining the literacy club. *The Reading Teacher, 41,* 676–681.

McWhirter, A. (1990). Whole language in the middle school. *The Reading Teacher, 43,* 562–567.

Murphy, S. (1991). The code, connectionism, and basals. *Language Arts, 68,* 199–205.

Spencer, M. (1986). Emergent literacies: A site for analysis. *Language Arts, 63,* 442–453.

Strickland, D. S., & Morrow, L. M. (1988a). Emerging readers and writers: Creating a print-rich environment. *The Reading Teacher, 42,* 156–157.

Strickland, D. S., & Morrow, L. M. (1988b). Emerging readers and writers: Reading, writing and language. *The Reading Teacher, 42,* 240–241.

Strickland, D. S., & Morrow, L. M. (1988c). Emerging readers and writers: Interactive experiences with storybook reading. *The Reading Teacher, 42,* 302–309.

Trelease, J. (1989). Jim Trelease speaks on reading aloud to children. *The Reading Teacher, 43,* 200–206.

Veatch, J. (1987). Individualized reading: A personal memoir. *Language Arts, 63,* 586–593.

Whole literacy: Possibilities and challenges. (1990, April). *The Reading Teacher, 43* (8) (whole issue).

Wollman-Bonilla, J. (1989). Reading journals: Invitations to participate in literature. *The Reading Teacher, 43,* 112–120.

CHAPTER 7

Methods, Lessons, and Strategies in Teaching Reading

Introduction
Concepts Related to Print
The Vocabulary of Reading
   Instruction
   Activity
Concepts Related to Storybooks
   Activity
Word Recognition
   Activities
Metalinguistic Awareness
   Activities
Metacomprehension
   Activities
Comprehension
   Activities
Summary
For Review and Discussion
For Further Reading

rhinoceros shoulders crumbs
manners folds tough
ripple-soled sneakers
rhino
glimmer finally disgrace
frowned ashamed confused
woe
POETRY
IS

INTRODUCTION

Chapter 6 described three approaches to teaching reading. The approach associated with reading readiness and phonics emphasis basal readers rests on atomistic, bottom-up assumptions about language and literacy acquisition. The approaches associated with emergent literacy, Veatch's individual reading program, Hansen's reading conferences, and Atwell's reading workshop rest on holistic, top-down assumptions about language and literacy acquisition. The eclectic basal reader approach presumes that both atomistic, bottom-up and holistic, top-down assumptions have some validity. However, teachers who choose eclectic basal readers tend to lean toward holistic, top-down assumptions. They tend to emphasize lessons growing out of that tradition and often supplement the program with activities like the individual reading program, reading conferences, and reading workshops. As a result, eclectic basal reading programs in practice tend to rest more on holistic, top-down assumptions although they make certain compromises in implementing this approach.

In this chapter I will present numerous methods, lessons, and strategies for teaching reading that might arise in any one of the three approaches described in the last chapter. The difference would be in what precipitates the introduction of the method, lesson, or strategy. In a skills emphasis program these lessons would be presented only after other carefully enumerated skills had been presented, and they would be taught to all students. In an eclectic program, they would be suggested at particular places in the program where they seemed to make sense, but there would be some latitude regarding when they were introduced and even if they would be used in teaching every student. In a rather more purist holistic, collaborative, integrated approach they would be introduced only when the students' need for them becomes apparent.

CONCEPTS RELATED TO PRINT

The following concepts are taught in many preschool and kindergarten programs:

1. Understanding that printing represents spoken language.
2. Proceeding from left to right on a page.
3. Proceeding from top to bottom on a page.
4. Proceeding from page to page.

Practice in proceeding from left to right and from top to bottom is worked into numerous activities in preschool programs. In reviewing the names of shapes, the teacher might hold up a triangle, and when the children name it she puts it on the chalkboard ledge or an easel and holds up a square. When the children name the square, she puts it to the right of the triangle. Soon several

Figure 7.1

shapes are lined up, and the teacher reviews asking the children to name the shapes as she points to them from left to right.

On activity sheets as in Figure 7.1 children are directed to put a cross on the pictures that are of animals. They start at the top on the left side of the sheet and work across the sheet to the right and then to the next row. This might be a lesson in following directions, but practice with left-to-right and top-to-bottom processing is incorporated into the lesson, as it is in other lessons having diverse objectives.

Children's artwork may be captioned and stapled into "books," that the children may go through, page by page, "reading" captions.

Teachers frequently read to children in preschool programs. Teachers may point to words as they read, holding the book up, and proceeding from page to page. Teachers sometimes create "big books" by copying illustrations and texts onto large chart paper so the children can see the text more clearly as the teacher reads and points (Slaughter, 1983). Commercial versions of such big books are also on the market.

THE VOCABULARY OF READING INSTRUCTION

Preschool and kindergarten programs include activities to teach children the meanings of terms that will be used early in nearly every approach to beginning reading instruction. A list of such terms is as follows:

above	last	word	in front of
after	letter	alphabet	looks like
before	line	beginning sound	next to
below	next	begins with	rhymes with
beside	page	different from	same as
end	number	ends with	sounds like
first	under	first letter	

Preschool teachers take advantage of many opportunities to use these terms in situations where the children will learn their meanings or get a wider understanding of their meanings. When the children are in line the teacher may ask, "Who is first in line? Who is last? Who is standing next to Ann?" In more formal lessons the teacher may ask the children to "find the one that's different from the others" in a row with three oranges and a banana.

However, all children have not had such experiences or have not benefited fully from such experiences. Some children may experience difficulty in reading lessons because they do not know the meaning of terms like those listed above. When children are not performing as expected during reading instruction, the teacher must be alert to the possibility that it is a lack of understanding or a misunderstanding of the terms used in the instructions.

A formal procedure for discovering a child's knowledge of some of the concepts related to print and some of the vocabulary of reading instruction was developed by Clay (1972). Her Concepts About Print Test begins with the item "Show me the front of this book" and proceeds to test the child's knowledge of left-to-right progression, letters, words, punctuation marks, and so on.

ACTIVITY

A. The full details for administration of the Concepts About Print Test are given in **The Early Detection of Reading Difficulties: A Diagnostic Survey with Recovery Procedures,** 2nd edition by Marie Clay (1979).

   Obtain a copy of this test and administer it to several kindergartners and first graders. It will heighten your awareness of the conventions and vocabulary connected with reading—conventions and vocabulary to which accomplished readers respond unconsciously, but which beginning readers must know or be taught.

B. Creating a survey of your own to explore beginning readers' knowledge of the conventions of print and the vocabulary of reading instruction will heighten your awareness of these conventions that accomplished readers respond to unconsciously, but which beginning readers must be taught.
   1. Take a children's picture book and develop a list of questions about it to determine whether or not a child knows
      - how to open a book
      - when a book is right-side up or upside down
      - that when reading, people look at the print and not at the picture
      - what words, letters, spaces, capitals, and punctuation marks are

ACTIVITY (continued)

- that when reading people go from left to right and top to bottom
- what is meant by phrases such as
  the words under the picture
  the beginning of the line
  the end of the line

Add to these phrases by consulting "The Vocabulary of Reading Instruction" in this chapter.

2. Administer your survey to several kindergartners and first graders.

CONCEPTS RELATED TO STORYBOOKS

The following skills are taught in many preschool and kindergarten programs:

1. Following the sequence of events in a story.
2. Recalling details to tell a story.
3. Interpreting pictures.
4. Making inferences.

Preschool and kindergarten curricula are replete with opportunities to learn, recite, recall, and listen to songs, poems, and stories. For example, teachers may teach songs like "There Was an Old Woman Who Swallowed a Fly" with the aid of cutout creatures. With each new verse the appropriate cutout is added to the flannelboard or easel. After the cutouts are scrambled, children are encouraged to recall in what order the old woman swallowed the creatures. The same technique may be used with such poems as "The House That Jack Built" or stories like *Jenny's Hat* (Keats, 1966). In this picture storybook, Jenny thinks her hat is too plain so on each page she adds a new decoration, including flowers, birds' nests, and feathers. Some teachers bring in props to tell such stories and then leave them on a table where the children can come back to them and play teacher by telling the story to others using the props.

Children are also given experiences with interpreting pictures of happy faces, sad faces, and angry faces. Pictures such as Figure 7.2 are used to give students opportunities to make up stories, to retell stories presented by others, and to make inferences (Why is the girl sad?).

Such activities frequently appear in preschool and kindergarten. Although such experiences are obviously beneficial to children, reading instruction can begin with pupils who have not had them. Once reading instruction begins there is no reason for these experiences to stop. Such experiences should continue through the primary grades, and the skills used should be employed in relation to reading as the opportunities arise.

Figure 7.2 Telling stories and making inferences from pictures.

ACTIVITY

Visit a nursery school or kindergarten or view a televised educational show aimed at preschoolers. Record instances of attention to the following:

1. Traditional reading readiness skills (see chapter 6)
2. Concepts related to print and reading
3. Understanding the vocabulary of reading instruction
4. Concepts related to storybooks

WORD RECOGNITION

Word-recognition methods are traditionally classified by:

a. the unit of analysis
   —whole words
   —letter-sound correspondences (phonics)
   —meaningful word parts (prefixes, suffixes, and roots), and
b. the role of context in word recognition.

❖ The Whole Word Method

The objective of the whole word method is to have children see a printed word and identify it immediately without thinking about it, puzzling over it, or analyzing it. Instant recognition is the *ultimate* objective of *all* word-recognition skills. There is something more separating the whole word method from other methods. The whole word method can be classified by what the teacher does *not* do—he or she does not refer to letters, to sounds of letters, to syllables, to prefixes, to suffixes, or to roots when teaching children to recognize words.

The Language Experience Approach

The initial stages of the language experience approach described in chapter 6 is a whole word approach. Children tell the teacher which words they recognize from the previous day's story, and the teacher copies them down for each child's own word bank. Over several weeks, if things go well, each child has his or her own bank of many words that have been learned as whole words.

Eclectic Basal Readers

Perhaps the most widespread use of the whole word approach is with eclectic basal readers. Many eclectic basal reading series begin by helping students learn words as whole words through activities such as those illustrated in Figure 7.3. Students are helped to learn these words as whole words. These words are then repeated in new stories, and words are gradually added until longer stories with more complex sentences appear.

❖ Phonics

The question of whether or not one should teach phonics is often raised in shrill tones. Critics of programs that do not emphasize phonics charge that children do not read as well today as children did in the past and claim that this is true because phonics (which was the proven method of the past) has recently been abandoned for approaches where no phonics principles are ever taught. Critics charge that the aim of phonics emphasis programs is to teach word calling rather than understanding, and that in such programs children do not learn that language has meaning.

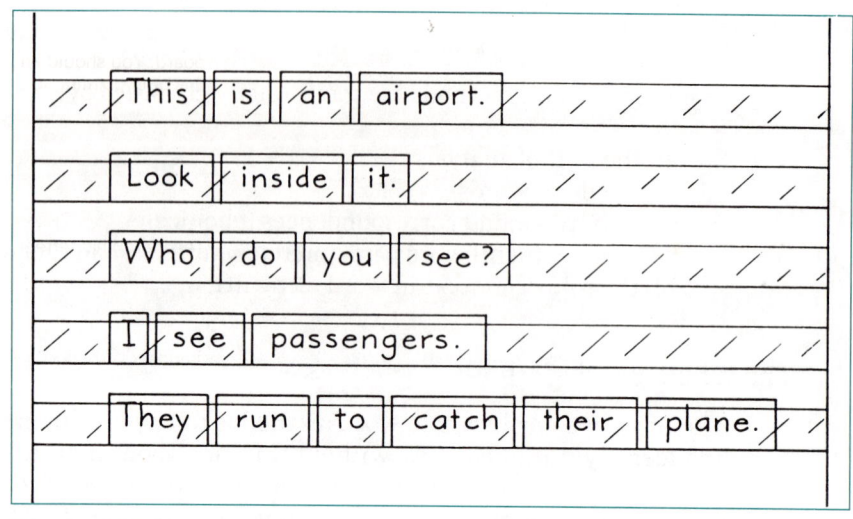

This is an airport.
Look inside it.
Who do you see?
I see passengers.
They run to catch their plane.

Figure 7.3 A whole word learning activity from an eclectic basal reader. (Source: *The Mouse in the House,* teacher's ed. [Lexington, MA: D. C. Heath, 1989], p. 118.)

Attacks from both sides contain false assumptions. Although historical trends toward more phonics and less phonics have been observed in America, the level of literacy among children who attend school in America has remained fairly constant (Matthews, 1966). More recent studies (Farr et al., 1978) have shown that reading test scores have not declined over the recent decades but have improved slightly.

Also, among programs that are designed to be used as *the* major approach to reading instruction (basal reading programs, individual reading programs, and so on; see chapter 6), none teaches all phonics and no comprehension or all comprehension and no phonics. Programs do differ, however, in terms of when and how many phonics generalizations are introduced, and the extent to which they are taught in isolation as distinct lessons.

A word-recognition lesson that would typically be suggested by a first-grade eclectic basal reading program appears in Figure 7.4. Notice that phonics and comprehension are considered simultaneously in this word-recognition lesson.

❖ **Analysis of Word Structure**

For the purpose of word recognition, the study of word structure has much in common with the whole word technique of word recognition. The point is to help students recognize word parts (prefixes, suffixes, and roots) on sight and to know how they are usually pronounced. Children who see *nonreturnable* may not recognize it immediately; if they recognize *non-* and *-able* as affixes, they

step 1	It is not a lion. It is a cat.	Teacher: Let's look at the sentences on the board. You should know all the words except this one (pointing to cat).
step 2	cat.	Teacher: What letter does this word begin with? Students: "C" Teacher: What letter does the word end with? Students: "T" Teacher: Think of the sound that c usually stands for. Think of the sound that t usually stands for.
step 3	cat.	Teacher: George, will you read aloud except for the last word? George: It is not a lion. It is a . . . Teacher: What is the last word, George? George: Cat.
step 4		Teacher: How do you know it isn't cut? George: Cut would not make sense.
step 5	cat.	Teacher: How do you know it isn't tiger? George: Tiger begins with /t/. Teacher: Yes and we want a word that begins with /k/ and ends with /t/.
	Get, Stop, and help are introduced in the same manner using the remaining sentences.	

Figure 7.4 Typical word recognition lesson from a first-grade eclectic basal reader.

are left with *return*. They may recognize *re-* as another affix and *turn* as an English root. If through this process they recognize a word they know and that makes sense in the context, they have used structural analysis for word recognition.

Notice that nothing has been mentioned here about the *meanings* of *non-*, *re-*, and *-able*. It is presumed that the reader knows the meaning of the word *nonreturnable*, but did not recognize it. Consideration of the meanings of *re-* and *turn* would only cause confusion in this case, but recognizing *re-* and *turn* as familiar word parts would be using word structure as a word-recognition technique. Figures 7.5 and 7.6 show materials that are typically used to make readers sensitive to word structure for the purpose of word recognition.

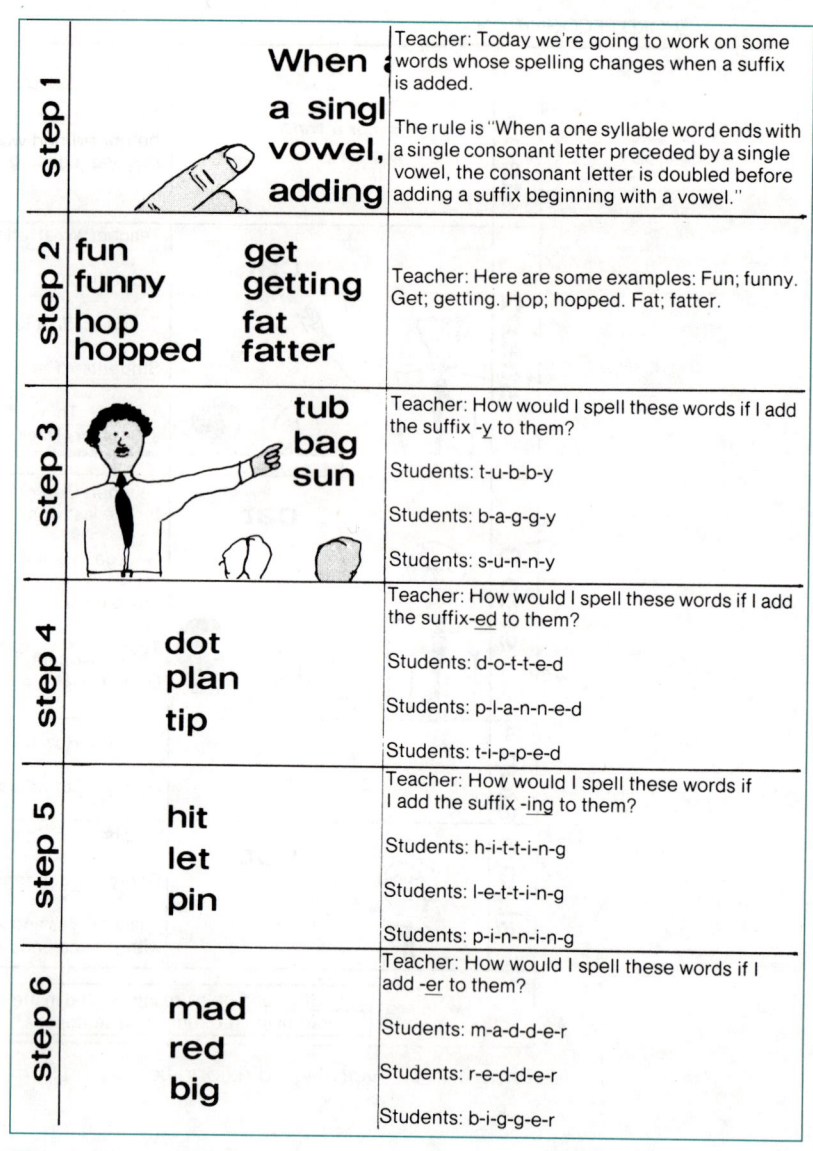

step 1	When a singl vowel, adding	Teacher: Today we're going to work on some words whose spelling changes when a suffix is added. The rule is "When a one syllable word ends with a single consonant letter preceded by a single vowel, the consonant letter is doubled before adding a suffix beginning with a vowel."
step 2	fun get funny getting hop fat hopped fatter	Teacher: Here are some examples: Fun; funny. Get; getting. Hop; hopped. Fat; fatter.
step 3	tub bag sun	Teacher: How would I spell these words if I add the suffix -y to them? Students: t-u-b-b-y Students: b-a-g-g-y Students: s-u-n-n-y
step 4	dot plan tip	Teacher: How would I spell these words if I add the suffix -ed to them? Students: d-o-t-t-e-d Students: p-l-a-n-n-e-d Students: t-i-p-p-e-d
step 5	hit let pin	Teacher: How would I spell these words if I add the suffix -ing to them? Students: h-i-t-t-i-n-g Students: l-e-t-t-i-n-g Students: p-i-n-n-i-n-g
step 6	mad red big	Teacher: How would I spell these words if I add -er to them? Students: m-a-d-d-e-r Students: r-e-d-d-e-r Students: b-i-g-g-e-r

Figure 7.5 A lesson in word structure taught by the deductive method.

ACTIVITY

A. Work in pairs and role play a teacher-student reading conference where the child is struggling with a word such as **musical**, **shortest**, or **disfigure** because he or she is failing to use knowledge of word structure.

B. Plan the students' "struggle" and the teacher's on-the-spot lesson. Present your dialog to the class.

WORD RECOGNITION

step 1	I like fun. Pam is funny. Here is a bag. His shirt is baggy.	Teacher: Let's read these sentences and look at the underlined words. How is the word fun like funny and the word bag like baggy.
step 2	(fun)ny (bagg)y	Students: Fun is the root word fun plus the suffix y. Teacher: Let's circle the root words and suffixes. What is left over in each word? Where did the extra letter come from?
step 3	 *(classroom illustration)*	Students: You double the last letter when you add y. Teacher: Yes. Sometimes, when we add the suffix y to some words, we double the last letter. But not always. Let's look at these word pairs. Let's see what the difference is.
step 4	fun fruit funny fruity bag tear baggy teary sun rain sunny rainy	Teacher: Fun, bag and sun are one syllable words. Fruit, tear and rain are one syllable words. Fun, bag and sun end in single consonant letters. Fruit, tear and rain end in single consonant letters. What is the difference? Students: Fun, bag and sun are spelled with a single vowel letter but fruit, tear and rain are spelled with two vowel letters.
step 5	fun sand funny sandy bag string baggy stringy sun mess sunny messy	Teacher: Good! Let's look at the next list and see what the rule is. Students are led to discover that the root word must end in a single consonant letter.

> In like manner the rule is derived for the suffixes -ed, -ing, and -er and finally the generalization is drawn that the rule works for suffixes beginning with a vowel letter.

Figure 7.6 *A lesson in word structure taught by the inductive method.*

❖ Using Context for Word Recognition

From their first encounter with print, children should be reminded as often as possible and in as many ways as possible that reading makes sense—that it fits in with what we know of the world and what we recognize as sensible language.

For example, when looking at yesterday's language experience story (see chapter 6), the children are reminded that the word centered at the top of the sheet is the title of yesterday's story.

Teacher: What is this word?
Student: Whitey.
Teacher: Yes. Let's see who can find that word later on in the story.

The words on the attendance board are children's names.

Teacher: Who can find his or her own name?
Teacher: Who can find Jim's name and put it in the "Absent" column?

As children progress in reading, there are more and more occasions where readers have to rely on the language of the text to help identify words they do not immediately recognize. However, the principle remains the same. The unrecognized word cannot be just any word because not just any word would make sense, and context may suggest only a few words that would make sense in this place.

Teachers should always be alert for opportunities to suggest the use of context for clues to word recognition. When a child does not know a word when reading orally, or when a child asks the teacher what a word is when reading silently, the teacher can often help the child through questioning or by modeling. If, for example, the child does not recognize the word *vehicles* in the passage below, the scenarios that follow may take place.

> Automobiles played a large part in our family life. My father owned a drugstore in 1912, but he decided to become an Oldsmobile dealer on the side to make some easy money. To get the dealership he had to buy two cars, a blue sedan and a somewhat sportier red one. He had no showroom so he parked both vehicles in front of his store.

Teacher: Read the whole sentence and just say "mmm" for the word you don't know.
Child: "He had no showroom so he parked both 'mmms' in front of his store."
Teacher: What did the father have that he parked in front of the store? What do you *park* on a street?
Child: Cars.
Teacher: The word must mean . . . ?
Child: Cars.
Teacher: Divide the word into syllables. What do you think the first syllable is?
Child: Vee-hi-kels. Oh! It's *vehicles!*

Teacher: Let's see. He parked both "mmm" in front of his store. The father has two cars in this story, so it probably says he parked both cars. Let's see. I would divide that word—v-e, h-i, c-l-e-s. That's "vee-hi-kels." Oh! Of course! It's *vehicles!*

> **ACTIVITY**
>
> Find passages that are typical of elementary-school reading material. Find words in these passages that are clearly supported by context. Since this is a demonstration, rewrite the passages to meet your needs if necessary.
> A. Work in pairs and role play a child failing to recognize a word and a teacher using a questioning technique to lead the child to use the word-recognition skills (particularly context) that apply.
> B. Repeat this exercise having the teacher use a modeling technique.
> C. Present your dialogues to the class.

METALINGUISTIC AWARENESS

As children begin to read, a new kind of knowledge related to language emerges. This kind of knowledge can be demonstrated through the following example:

Teacher: I'm going to read this sentence [pointing to a page in a book]: "The cups are on the counter." Now, tell me what are on the counter?
Student: Cups.

The child has demonstrated that he or she understands the sentence. Now consider a second exchange:

Teacher: I'm going to read this sentence [pointing to a page in a book]: "The cups are on the counter." Now, tell me how many words are in that sentence?
Student: Six.
Teacher: Is one or more than one cup on the counter?
Student: More than one.
Teacher: How do you know?
Student: *Cup* has an *s* on it.
Teacher: Good.

Here the child has demonstrated the ability to do something more than understand the sentence; he or she can talk about the language, reflect on it, and make statements about how it works. This kind of knowledge is referred to as **metalinguistic awareness.**

Metalinguistic awareness is an important component of learning to read. Students need to have the concept of word before they can recognize written words. Phonics generalizations, word structure generalizations, and the ability to reflect on context clues to word recognition all rely on

---

> *Directions:* The following passage was taken from a book and some of the words were replaced by blanks. Write the word in each blank that you think was in the original passage.
>
> ```
>            Raccoons can live in cities too. They go into cities
>            _____ for food. They often take
> treats _____ leave for birds. Tipping
>            _____ trash cans racoons find
>            _____ to eat. A chimney _____
> hole in a tree _____ be their home.
> ```

Figure 7.7 *A passage made into a cloze exercise.*

metalinguistic awareness. Much of our comprehension curriculum is composed of attempts to help children reflect on and state explicitly what they know about language.

Two methods for encouraging children to reflect on what they know about language have received considerable attention in recent years. One is the cloze technique with discussion and the other is sentence combining with discussion.

❖ The Cloze Technique

When using the **cloze technique,** the teacher deletes words from a printed passage and replaces the words with blank lines as in Figure 7.7. Students using the cloze technique write the words that they think were deleted into the blank lines. There are many ways to vary this technique. Teachers can delete every fifth word, tenth word, or whatever other numbered interval they wish. They can choose to delete only nouns, or nouns and verbs, or any words except function words. Another variation is to supply multiple-choice responses for the student to choose from when filling the blanks, as in Figure 7.8. This is sometimes referred to as a maze.

The cloze technique can be valuable when it is used to promote discussion of language. After students complete a cloze exercise the teacher asks why they chose those words and which of the various words chosen by different students is best, and why. Such discussion enables students to reflect upon and make explicit what they know about how language works—that is, it promotes metalinguistic awareness. Simply performing cloze tasks without the additional discussion and reflection on the exercise has no benefit (Jongsma, 1971; Bortnick & Lopardo, 1973).

ACTIVITY

A. Take three or four paragraphs from this book and make a cloze or maze passage from them.
  1. Do the cloze tasks as individuals.

> **ACTIVITY (continued)**
>
>   2. Discuss your responses. Are some better than others? Why?
>   3. Compare your responses to the actual words deleted. Do some of the actual deleted words fit better than yours? Why?
> B. Monitor your discussion. Tape-record it and replay it, or have one student observe and make notes.
>   1. What part did your knowledge of language play in your discussion?
>   2. What part did your knowledge of the topic play in your discussion?
>
> This might be a good small-group activity. Summaries of the activities can be shared with the class.

❖ Sentence Combining

The example sentence-combining lesson below demonstrates the basic idea of sentence combining. At least two sentences and a relation between them are presented, and the student writes (or recites) the sentence that results from combining them.

Every sentence-combining problem has a **matrix sentence** and one or more **insert sentences.** The way to solve the problem is to combine all the insert sentences with the matrix sentence.

The insert sentence will be indented underneath the matrix sentence, like this (Greenberg, McAndrews, & Meterski, 1975, pp. 2–3):

The zebra ate the grass.
    The zebra is *striped*.

Directions: Circle the word under each blank that you think makes the best sense for that sentence.

Raccoons can live in cities too. They go into cities
_____ for food. They often take
(searching, wanting, rest)
treats _____ leave for birds. Tipping
   (they, people, shall)
_____ trash cans racoons find
(on, hat, over)
_____ to eat. A chimney _____
(garbage, paper, small)   (the, or, wall)
hole in a tree _____ be their home.
    (stump, can, make)

Figure 7.8 *A passage made into a multiple-choice cloze exercise or maze.*

The answer to this sample problem would be:

The striped zebra ate the grass.

There might be more than one insert sentence, like this:

The zebra ate the grass.
    The zebra is *striped*.
    The grass is *green*.

The answer would be:

The striped zebra ate the green grass.

Here are two more examples of sentence-combining lessons. Look at this sample (Greenberg, McAndrews, & Meterski, 1975, pp. 9–12):

The dog ran down the street.
    The dog *had lost his master.* (who)

Here is the answer:

The dog who had lost his master ran down the street.

Notice the word *who* in parentheses next to the insert sentence. This is a clue word that must also be added to the matrix sentence.

Here is a more complex example (Greenberg, McAndrews, & Meterski, 1975, pp. 29–32):

The king wanted SOMETHING.
    The king was lonely.
    The king had never had a wife. (who)
    He married the Princess Guinevere. (to marry)
    Guinevere was beautiful.

The answer is:

The lonely king who had never had a wife wanted to marry the beautiful Princess Guinevere.

Doing sentence-combining exercises in groups or doing them individually and comparing and discussing the results are ways to facilitate discussion of how language words (Pearson & Camperell, 1981). William Strong (1986) presents numerous activities in *Creative Approaches to Sentence Combining* that will encourage students to reflect upon and state explicitly what they know about language.

> **ACTIVITY**
>
> A. Following the model presented in the preceding lessons, create several sentence-combining problems.
>   1. Write solutions to the problems as individuals.
>   2. Compare your solutions and discuss the differences.
> B. Monitor your discussion. Tape-record it and replay it, or have one student observe and make notes.
>   1. What part did your knowledge of language play in your discussion?
>   2. Did people use words like **adjective, adverb, clause**, and **conjunction**? These are words to describe the way language works.
>
>   This might be a good small-group activity. Summaries of the activities can be shared with the class.
> C. William Strong (1986) presents numerous sentence-combining activities in **Creative Approaches to Sentence Combining.** Obtain a copy of this booklet and report to the class on the various ways the idea of sentence combining can be used to promote metalinguistic awareness.

METACOMPREHENSION

Proficient readers display a kind of knowledge that poor readers seem to lack. Proficient readers can think about or talk about their own comprehension processes. This kind of knowledge is referred to as **metacomprehension.** It can be demonstrated through the following example:

A teacher gives the following written instructions to students for playing a card game and tells them that they will be asked how to play the game after they have read the instructions.

> We each put our cards in a pile. We both turn over the top card in our pile. We look at the cards to see who has the special card. Then we turn over the next card in our pile to see who has the special card this time. In the end the person with the most cards wins the game. (Baker & Brown, 1980, p. 8)

Teacher: [After students have read the instructions] Could you play the game?
Angelo: No.
Ernest: Yes.

Angelo shows an important characteristic of a person with metacomprehension awareness. He knows when he *doesn't know* something.

Teacher: How many cards does each player start with?
Angelo: I don't know.

Ernest: Twenty cards.
Teacher: How does a player win?
Angelo: He gets the most cards.
Ernest: He wins the most cards.
Teacher: What is a special card?
Angelo: I don't know.
Ernest: A joker.

Angelo shows a second characteristic of metacomprehension awareness. He is aware of what he *knows* as well as what he *doesn't know*. Ernest is not clear on this point.

Teacher: What further information would you need to play the game?
Angelo: How many cards are dealt to each player? What is a special card? Does the player with the special card keep his card and the other player's card?
Ernest: I don't know.

Angelo shows the third characteristic of metacomprehension awareness. He knows what he *needs to know* to understand the text.

Teacher: What did you do when you finished reading these instructions and you knew I was going to ask you about them?
Angelo: I reread them to see if I missed something. I looked to see what a special card was because I thought I missed it.
Ernest: I waited for the questions.

Angelo shows the fourth characteristic of metacomprehension awareness. He tries *repair strategies* that have worked in the past when comprehension has failed. He rereads. He looks for specific information that he believes is crucial to understanding. Unfortunately, Ernest's answers show that he does not monitor his own comprehension.

ACTIVITY

A. 1. Using the card game instruction from Baker and Brown (1980), replicate the question-and-answer session reported with Angelo and Ernest. Act as the teacher and ask individuals not in your class to act as students.
   2. In the course of your discussion, classify information referred to as "known" and "needs to be known."
   3. Have students rewrite the instruction so that all the information is present.
B. Try this activity with younger students—fourth-, eighth-, and twelfth-graders, for example.

❖ Modeling Comprehension

Fitzgerald (1983) suggests a variety of ways to foster metacomprehension. Modeling comprehension is one. Teachers model comprehension by reading orally and thinking aloud the comprehension processes they engage in. For example, the teacher might take a text that begins with the words, "He jumped out of the seat," and carry on the following monologue:

> Teacher: [reading from text] "He jumped out of the seat."
> [looking up . . . thinking aloud] I'm wondering who he is. Where is he?
> [reading from text] "He tried to get her to sit down so he could push her, but she refused."
> [looking up . . . thinking aloud] Who is *she*? What does he want her to sit on "so he can push her"? Is it a wagon or a sled?
> [reading from text] "So the next time they were on the playground, he let her swing very high for a long time."
> [looking up . . . thinking aloud] Oh! It's a boy and girl playing on swings. She probably wouldn't play because he hadn't given her a long enough turn on the swings.

A monologue such as this is referred to as a "think aloud protocol."

ACTIVITY

Have one student act as teacher and several act as students. Engage in the following demonstration for the class:

Find a text, such as the example used in Modeling Comprehension above. Divide the chalkboard into two columns and label them Known and Don't Know. Read the text sentence by sentence. Write facts in the Known column and questions in the Don't Know column.

As each new sentence is read, facts may be added to the Known column and questions may be removed from the Don't Know column.

Experiences like this are designed to promote metacomprehension.

❖ Question-Answer Relationships (QARs)

Raphael (1982) proposed a questioning strategy to increase metacomprehension. She proposed that questions can be classified in terms of the source of the information required for the answer.

Raphael's three question classifications are illustrated and defined below using her example text and questions.

Text: Ralph sat on an old wooden rocking chair. He rocked harder and harder. Suddenly he found himself on the floor.
Question: What kind of chair was Ralph sitting in?
Type: Right There
Definition: Right There questions can be answered with words from one sentence.
Question: What did Ralph do while sitting in the chair?
Type: Think and Search
Definition: Think and Search questions require information from more than one sentence.

In this example, readers need only to find the antecedent of *He,* but since they must look across sentence boundaries, this is a Think and Search question.

Question: Why did Ralph find himself sitting on the floor?
Possible answers: The chair broke. The chair tipped over.
Type: On My Own
Definition: On My Own questions require prior knowledge on the part of the reader. The answer is not in the text. Readers need to reflect on their own experience and information to answer the question.

Raphael suggests that students learn these three categories of question-answer relationships (which she refers to as **QAR**s), and that identifying question types should become a routine part of answering comprehension questions. This method has been shown to improve comprehension question answering performance in fourth grade (Raphael & Wannacott, 1985). This finding supports the idea that attention to metacomprehension improves comprehension. An important aspect of the QAR concept is that it calls attention to the importance of the reader's prior knowledge and experience in comprehension.

As a further use of the QAR concept to promote metacomprehension, middle- and upper-grade teachers might ask students to write several questions of each variety (Right There, Think and Search, and On My Own) for selections they have read.

COMPREHENSION

Methods, lessons, and strategies for promoting effective comprehension in students usually focus on one of four areas:

1. Preparing readers to understand a text.
2. Helping readers monitor their comprehension processes (helping them engage in metacomprehension).
3. Helping readers check on their comprehension (usually through questioning and feedback).

4. Helping readers to organize what they have learned from a text in ways that help them understand better and recall what they have learned.

However, since these are highly interrelated activities, it is neither possible nor desirable to completely isolate them. In the methods, lessons, and strategies described below, you will notice that the focus changes from lesson to lesson, or from stage to stage as certain lessons progress, but that all four areas tend to be present to a greater or lesser degree at all times.

❖ Semantic Mapping

A group is about to read a selection entitled "The Raccoon." The teacher writes the word *Raccoon* on the chalkboard, draws a circle around it, and asks, "What do you know about raccoons?"

The children respond: "They have striped tails." "They come out at night." "They knock over garbage cans to get food at the campground."

The teacher responds: "Well, we've got one fact about what they look like. Let's call that *appearance* [writing the word *appearance* on the board]. We have two facts about what they do. Let's call that *behavior* [writing *behavior* on the board]."

As students volunteer more about the behavior and appearance of raccoons, the teacher adds words and phrases under these categories. As information that fits into new categories is suggested, the teacher creates new categories on the board. Soon a semantic map like the one in Figure 7.9 appears on the board.

This technique is referred to as **semantic mapping.** In this example it is used as a prereading activity to enable children to marshal their prior knowledge about a topic.

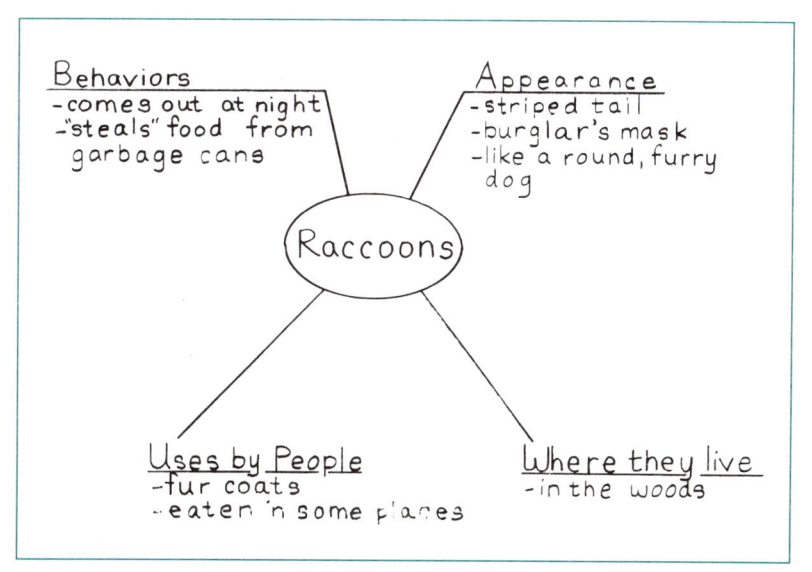

Figure 7.9 A semantic map of prior knowledge.

Teachers can work vocabulary development into semantic mapping by introducing words that will appear in the passage or supplying a word for a concept that students suggest. The teacher might write the word *nocturnal* after *comes out at night* and *habitat* after *where it lives*.

Semantic mapping can also be used as a postreading activity. In the case of "The Raccoon," the story offers a great deal of information about raccoon behavior, raccoon appearance, and a unique use of a raccoon by people—as a pet. After reading the story the class filled in more information on the semantic map (Figure 7.10) and made a new semantic map showing the main idea of the story—adopting wild animals as pets may create problems (Figure 7.11).

Semantic mapping is a useful strategy for activating prior knowledge, showing the relationship between prior knowledge and text information, and organizing and integrating information.

Semantic mapping (Heimlich & Pittelman, 1986) can be utilized as early as first grade to organize information in a text in a way that has characteristics of both outlining and summarizing. For example, a first-grade class has read a story about Kate's trip to the zoo. In a circle on the board they label five spokes extending from the center: "Things Kate sees at the zoo," "Things Kate does at the zoo," "Things Kate likes at the zoo," "How Kate looks," and "How Kate feels." Taking categories one at a time, the teacher elicits information from the students and produces the semantic map in Figure 7.12.

A fifth-grade teacher, using a similar technique, has students use the titles and section headings in a text to identify main ideas, secondary categories, and supporting details to create postreading study maps such as the one in Figure 7.13. Such maps can easily be turned into outlines and are a good first step to summarizing.

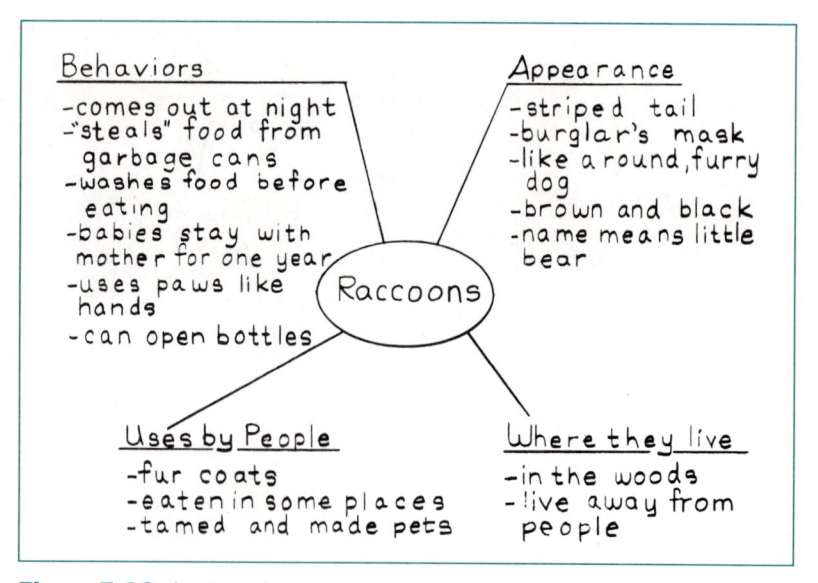

Figure 7.10 A semantic map as a postreading activity.

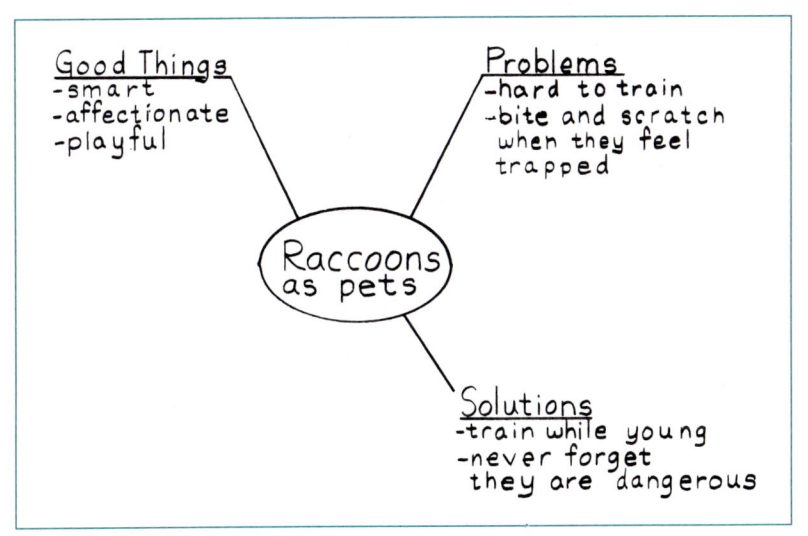

Figure 7.11 A semantic map for main ideas.

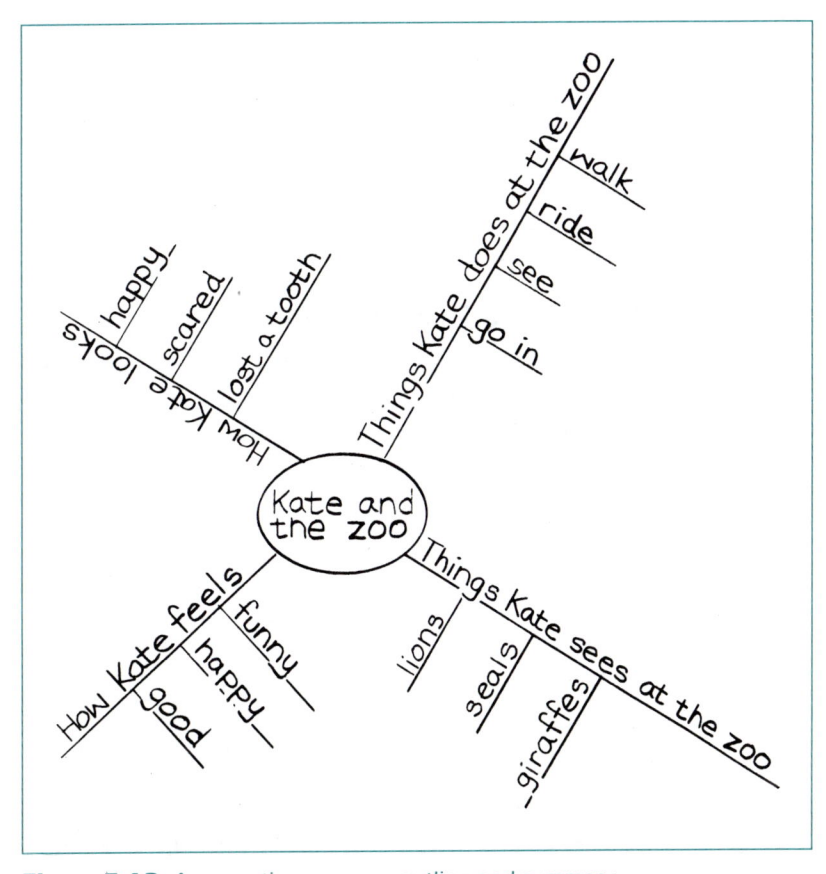

Figure 7.12 A semantic map as an outline and summary.

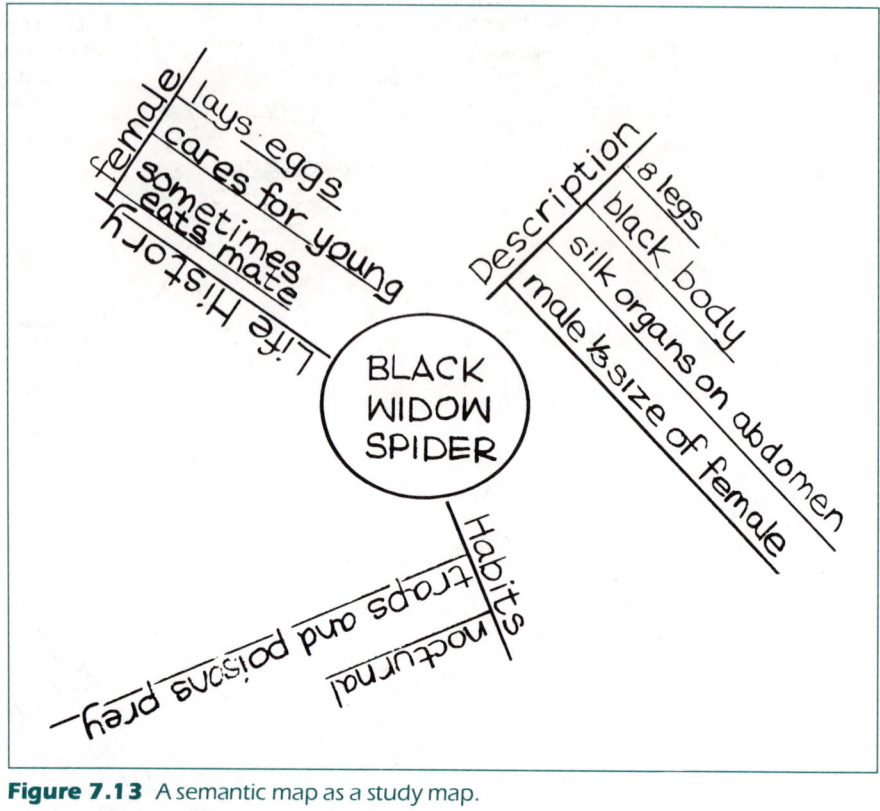

Figure 7.13 A semantic map as a study map.

❖ Directed Reading and Thinking Activity

In a directed reading and thinking activity the teacher helps students look for clues concerning what a text will reveal, make predictions, read, and check their predictions for accuracy. The procedure is applied to sections of a text in a cyclical manner as shown in the following example.

A reading group is preparing to read a short excerpt from a biography of Sammy Davis, Jr. The group looks at the title and two illustrations accompanying the text—a montage of photographs of Sammy Davis, Jr., appearing in nightclubs and on television shows, and a picture of Sammy, aged two, in a minstrel costume and blackface makeup.

Teacher: What will this story be about?
Andrea: About Sammy Davis, Jr.
Teacher: Right. What do you know about him? What will the story tell you about him?
Arthur: It will tell you how he got into show business.
Rebecca: It will tell you he got into show business when he was a little boy.

Teacher: What makes you think that?
Rebecca: There is a picture of him as a little boy in a costume.
Teacher: O.K. Read page 143 and the top two lines on page 144. When you've finished, stop reading and look up at me.

[The introduction to the selection states that Sammy Davis, Jr.'s parents were both dancers on the vaudeville circuit and his paternal grandmother raised Sammy because his parents were always traveling.]

Teacher: What do you think? Did our prediction come true?
Paul: Yes. It's about how Sammy Davis, Jr., got into show business.
Lillian: It is about Sammy Davis, Jr., but it doesn't tell us how he got into show business, *yet*.
Teacher: What do you think will happen in the next part?
Paul: It will probably tell us where he went to school.
Teacher: Why do you think that?
Paul: It's the story of a little boy.
Teacher: And little boys go to school. Do you think the next part will talk about school?
Rebecca: No. I think it will tell us about how he got into his first show. In the picture on page 146 he's in a show.
Teacher: Yes. And he still looks like almost a baby. Any other ideas about what the rest of the story will tell us?
Arthur: It will tell how he went back to live with his parents and got into their act.
Teacher: That's a pretty good prediction from what we know so far. Let's read the next two pages now. Stop and look up at the bottom of page 145.

An important point to underscore here is that the teacher does not tell any students that they are wrong. Predictions are evaluated, and corrective feedback is given in terms of how reasonable the prediction is in terms of what has been revealed so far in the text and in terms of the reader's prior knowledge. A second important function of teacher feedback is to encourage students to reflect on how they made their predictions, that is, to reflect on their thought processes.

Students who have had repeated practice with this procedure begin to make observations that are surprisingly insightful. Students begin to recognize stock characters and stock plots and base their predictions on them. They recognize genres such as mystery stories, adventure stories, expository passages in geography and history books, and so on and make predictions about what they will read based on their knowledge of these kinds of texts.

Directed reading and thinking activities foster comprehension in these important ways: (1) They activate prior knowledge; (2) they emphasize the importance of the relationship between text knowledge and prior knowledge; (3) they illustrate the concept that comprehension calls for activity rather than passivity on the part of the reader; and (4) they encourage readers to reflect on their own comprehension processes.

> **ACTIVITY**
>
> A. Have one student act as teacher and several act as students. Select a story or essay and conduct a directed reading and thinking activity.
>   Use selections designed for primary, middle, and upper grades. How does the activity change as the nature of the material changes? For example, pictures may be useful for making predictions in primary materials, but titles, subtitles, headings, diagrams and so on may be useful in upper-grade materials.
> B. Try this activity with younger students—second-, fifth-, and eighth-graders, for example.

❖ Directed Listening and Thinking Activity

A directed listening and thinking activity shares all the characteristics of a directed reading and thinking activity except that the teacher shows the book, pictures, and title to the students and then reads a segment of the selection and stops and asks for predictions of what will come later in the text. This activity is frequently used in primary grades and preschools. It has all the advantages of a directed reading and thinking activity, but it permits the teacher to use books that the children are not yet ready to read for themselves.

> **ACTIVITY**
>
> Have one student act as teacher and several act as students. Select a story from a book intended for primary grades and conduct a directed listening and thinking activity as described in this chapter.

❖ SQ3R

After a great deal of experience in guiding college students in formulating successful study habits, Robinson (1970, originally published in 1961) presented what he found to be a sound systematic approach to study. The approach involves five steps:

1. Survey. Read chapter title, subtitles, and headings; read topic and summary sentences and introductory and summary paragraphs.

2. Question. Formulate questions based on chapter titles, subtitles, paragraph headings, and main ideas discovered in step 1.
3. Read. Seek answers to the questions developed in step 2.
4. Recite. Answer questions orally or silently to check on recall of the content and one's ability to express the content.
5. Review. Go over material that presented difficulties in step 4.

Robinson (1961) originally referred to this process by the formula "Survey QRRR." It is currently referred to by the more abbreviated formula SQ3R.

ACTIVITY

A. Select a chapter from a middle- or upper-grade content area textbook, such as a science or history textbook. Have one student act as teacher and several act as students. Have the teacher model SQ3R for the students.
B. Work in small groups using a variety of textbooks. Have each group report a summary of its experience to the class and discuss differences in texts in terms of the appearance of titles, subtitles, headings, outlines or tables of contents, summaries, pictures, graphs, figures, and so on.

❖ The Guided Reading Procedure

The guided reading procedure (Manzo, 1975; Ankney & McClurg, 1981) is a group comprehension/study activity consisting of seven steps:

1. Preparation and reading. Students survey the text, predict its content, create several purpose-setting questions, and read.
2. Unaided recall. When they are finished reading, students close their books and volunteers give as much information as they can recall from the text. Without evaluation or comment, the teacher jots down all the information in the order it is volunteered. When complete, this list often contains inconsistencies and students will become aware of information in the text that cannot be recalled.
3. Aided recall. Students open their books and read to clarify inconsistencies and to look for unrecalled information. The teacher corrects the items and adds items of information as the students find the relevant text.
4. Organization. Teacher and students work together to organize the information on the board in the form of an outline, a diagram, or a semantic map.
5. Comprehension questioning. The teacher asks higher-level comprehension questions calling for synthesis, interpretation, inference, judgment, or application.

6. Comprehension testing. The teacher administers a quiz testing factual recall (steps 2 and 3), organization (step 4), and higher-level comprehension (step 5).
7. Application. An optional last step calls for applying the information in the text to a new problem or situation.

This procedure works best with texts containing a heavy load of factual material. It is suggested that texts be divided into sections of about 500 words and that the procedure be repeated to cover longer texts.

> **ACTIVITY**
>
> A. Select a chapter from a middle- or upper-grade content area textbook, such as a science or history textbook.
> B. Have one student act as teacher and several act as students. Apply the guided reading procedure.

❖ The Directed Reading Lesson

The directed reading lesson is particularly associated with basal reading programs. It involves four stages:

1. Preparation
2. Reading
3. Questions/discussion
4. Skills development

The Preparation or Prereading Stage

There are three kinds of activities during the preparation phase that are designed to facilitate comprehension: supplying knowledge that the author of the text presumes the reader to have, presenting vocabulary, and setting a purpose for reading.

Supplying Background Knowledge
A third-grade basal reader has a story about a village in China in 1913. An airplane lands near the village, and the people are very surprised. To mark this amazing event the village holds a kite-making contest. The story opens with the line, "In the Year of the Water Ox, a long time ago...."

The teacher's guide might simply suggest that the teacher tell the children that each year in the old Chinese calendar is named for an animal and that 1913 was the year of the Water Ox and that airplanes and automobiles were not commonly seen in China in 1913.

Innovative teachers might do more with these ideas; they might find out what animal the present year is named for on the old Chinese calendar and find pictures of 1913 airplanes, cars, or American street scenes to help the children understand how different the world was then. The important point in terms of a directed reading lesson is that reading selections are previewed to determine whether comprehension may be impeded because the students are unfamiliar with concepts that are necessary for understanding the story.

This is an example of an application of the very old idea that comprehension is relating information contained in a text to information already in the reader's possession. Some authorities believe that when students reach the point where they can read intermediate-level (grades four to six) materials, the major cause of reading comprehension failure is limitation of knowledge on the part of the readers. That is, when students fail to comprehend texts, it is because they do not have the necessary prior knowledge to which to relate the text information (Carver, 1981; Sticht et al., 1979).

Vocabulary

In the primary grades, care is taken to introduce only those words that are already in the students' speaking and listening vocabularies. The objective is not to teach students new words in reading but to teach them to recognize printed words whose meanings are familiar. In intermediate grades, words whose meanings may not be known begin to appear in texts.

Teachers' guides for basal readers supply lists of words whose meanings may be unknown to the students before each story. Teachers are urged to write the words on the chalkboard and use them in a strong oral context. Some teachers' guides supply sentences such as the following for "target" words:

> After days of climbing the party reached the *summit*, the highest point on the mountain.

At times the line between filling in background knowledge and teaching vocabulary becomes indistinct. For example, in a story about Harriet Tubman the following words might be identified for student attention before reading: *Quaker, Underground Railroad, free states, slave states, overseer, traders, bloodhounds, runaways,* and *patrol.* A discussion of the list of words would supply a great deal of necessary background information for this story.

Purpose Setting

Purpose setting usually consists of remarks by the teacher intended to (1) get the students thinking along the lines of the story they are about to read; and (2) identify particular information that the students should be alert for or questions that the students should keep in mind as they read the selection.

In beginning reading, the story is often divided into short segments and the preparation, reading, and questioning cycle is repeated several times during the course of a story. Purpose-setting questions tend to be concrete and designed to focus on one item of information that is explicitly stated in the text.

Beyond primary grades, good purpose-setting activities "should prepare children to construct the meaning of a text by evoking a network of relevant associations. . . . Direction setting activities should provide a framework for the organization of events and concepts in the text so that many aspects of the text become interrelated and thus memorable" (Beck et al., 1979, p. 87).

For example, in setting the purpose for reading a story about a girl who believes she can pursue any career goal regardless of her sex, the teacher might ask what jobs students want to have some day and follow up by asking girls if they would like to be pilots, police officers, or football coaches, and asking boys if they would like to be nurses, secretaries, or kindergarten teachers. After establishing that there are no valid reasons why a woman or man cannot perform nearly any job, the teacher might say, "In today's story we are going to read about a girl who is planning her future. You'll find out the problems she runs into and how she deals with them."

What recommends this purpose-setting activity is that it does not focus on some particular facts in the story the children are about to read. Instead it prompts the students to think along the lines of the story they are about to read; to identify the social issue this story relates to; to recall what they know about this issue; their attitudes toward it; and the attitudes they have heard expressed. This activity gives the readers an orientation that will enable them to recognize important elements in the story and to relate them to one another.

The Reading Stage

Students read the selection silently.

The Question/Discussion or Postreading Stage

Asking questions is the most common classroom practice that is identified as teaching comprehension. This is a curious fact as one would think that the reason a teacher asks questions is to *test* comprehension rather than teach it. There is, however, good reason to believe that questioning, *if done* properly, does teach comprehension.

Dewey (1933) described the "art of questioning" as the art of showing pupils how to "*direct their own inquiries* and so to form in them the *independent habit of inquiry*" (p. 266). Dewey offered five suggestions to accomplish this goal:

1. Questions should require students to *use* information rather than to produce it literally and directly.
2. Emphasis should be on developing the subject and not on getting the one correct answer.
3. Questions should keep subject matter developing; each question should add to a continuous discussion. Questions should not be asked as if each one were complete in itself so that when the question is answered, the matter is disposed of, and another topic can be taken up.
4. There should be periodic reviews of what has gone before in order to extract the net meaning, to focus on what is significant in prior discussion, and to put old material into the new perspective that later material has supplied.
5. At the end of a question/discussion session there should be a sense of accomplishment and an expectation and desire that more is to come. (p. 266)

A child acting alone may be able to read a story about Andrew Jackson and see it as a collection of facts about an American patriot, but fail to see that the story also tells how democratic ideas were especially useful for life on the frontier. A skillful teacher can elicit such understanding through questioning and, if this is done frequently enough, students will begin to ask themselves the kind of questions that the teacher asks and reach higher levels of comprehension when acting on their own.

The Skills Development Stage

The reading selection is often used as a springboard for the skills development lesson. For example, a lesson in Greek and Latin roots may start with several appropriate words from the reading selection and go on to consider the meanings of many other words that contain Greek and Latin roots. This, in turn, may lead to a computer software program that states the meanings of such roots as *auto, graph, micro, photo,* and *scope* and asks students to choose the correct meanings for words like *autograph, microscope,* and *photosensitive.*

The four-part directed reading lesson is a time-honored format for guiding students as they read selections from basal reading programs. Over the years variations on this procedure, or elaborations on one phase of the procedure, have been introduced. QARs is an example of such an elaboration of the question/discussion phase.

❖ Reciprocal Teaching

Palincsar (1984) has identified four activities that foster comprehension and metacomprehension. These four activities are self-questioning, summarizing, predicting, and clarifying. As in a directed reading and thinking lesson children engage in these activities not only before and after reading, but at intervals throughout the reading process.

Palincsar's teaching strategy is one of interactive dialogue. First, the teacher models a strategy. Second, students engage in the strategy while the teacher guides them through corrective feedback. This is called guided practice. Finally, students take over as teachers. Palincsar refers to this final phase as reciprocal teaching.

The Modeling Phase

The teacher and students have books open to a story entitled "A Meeting with Stone Age Eskimos." In the modeling phase, the teacher suggests that they all read the first paragraph silently. Then, when everyone has finished:

> Teacher: Let's see, how would I *summarize* this paragraph? Maybe I'd say: "The exploring party sets out on a 250-mile trip across frozen, unoccupied territory."
> Now what *questions* will probably be answered in this story?

How about: Why are they making this trip? The author talks about his food supplies in this paragraph. I wonder, will they run out of food?

What *predictions* might we make? Because of the title I think they will meet a group of Eskimos. I'll bet they'll run out of food and meet Eskimos who will help them.

Last, what is there in this paragraph that needs to be explained to me; what needs clarifying? Well, the author says they are heading east from Cape Perry. I wonder where that is exactly. We could look on a map, but maybe it won't be that important.

The teacher continues with this cycle—silent reading, summarizing, questioning, predicting, and clarifying. In each case the teacher further defines these concepts by thinking aloud as he or she does the tasks. For example, after reading a particular paragraph the teacher might say, "This section lists the hardships that the drop in temperature caused. I'll begin the summary with the words 'The sudden drop in temperature caused four problems. They were. . . .'" After reading another group of paragraphs the teacher might say, "This section talks about the author's Eskimo companion's fear of ghosts. I think they are going to meet an unfamiliar group of Eskimos and think they are ghosts. That's what I predict."

Teaching the *clarifying* concept presents a special problem. *Clarifying* may be called for when the meanings of words or phrases are unclear, but it is also called for when referents are unclear, when the text is disorganized, or when the reader lacks necessary prior knowledge or experience. In well-written texts that are appropriate for the reader's skill, the need to clarify should not occur in every paragraph. Encouraging children to find puzzles in every line is not constructive.

On the other hand, teachers should be alert to the need for clarification and bring examples to the attention of the class. Later in the passage about the Arctic journey is the sentence "We found footprints and sled tracks not more than three months old." It seems fair enough to wonder how three-month-old tracks would still be present. Citing such examples when they arise helps children to see that questions may arise because of problems in the text: The reader is not always at fault.

The Guided Practice Phase

If "A Meeting with Stone Age Eskimos" were a text used for the first time during the guided practice stage, the following dialog might occur. After modeling the comprehension fostering/monitoring activities, the teacher asks students to summarize, question, predict, and clarify.

Summarizing

Student: They left Cape Perry for Cape Krusenstern with a two-week supply of food. They had two hundred and fifty miles to go and they thought there were no animals to hunt and no people along the way and they went on dog sled.

Teacher: Yes. Well, that's quite a lot of detail for a summary. What are

they doing—in one or two words?
Student: Taking a trip.
Teacher: Good. What's special about the trip?
Student: It's a long way.
Teacher: Where is it? What's special about where it is?
Student: It's in the Arctic.
Teacher: Good. Now put those three facts into a sentence.
Student: They started a long trip in the Arctic.
Teacher: Good.

Questioning

Student: How many people are on the trip? Will they make it?
Teacher: Those are both good questions. What does he say about hunting?
Student: There are no bears or seals to hunt on the way.
Teacher: Does that give you any ideas about what might happen?
Student: Yes. I think they'll meet a bear and they won't be ready.
Teacher: Turn that into a question.
Student: Will they meet any bears on the way?
Teacher: Good.

Predicting

This phase is identical to the directed reading and thinking activity.

Clarifying

As stated above, teachers should not overdo this activity because students might become too mistrustful of the text. In asking students for points that need clarification, teachers should imply that clarifying may not always be necessary—for example, "Does anyone need anything cleared up at this point?"

The Reciprocal Teaching Phase

When students are familiar with the concepts of summarizing, questioning, predicting, and clarifying, and when they can perform these activities reasonably well, the teacher begins to turn the teaching job over to the students. For example, the adult teacher might introduce a text and act as teacher for the first silent reading segment and then say, "All right. Let's read the next three paragraphs down to the bottom of page 221 and Donnell will be the teacher. Donnell will summarize, question, predict, and clarify—if any clarifying is necessary."

At this stage the adult teacher continues to give the "teacher" feedback through questioning, making suggestions, and asking students for suggestions.

Palincsar and Brown (1986) suggest that each of the techniques be taught separately through explaining, modeling, and guided practice before the four techniques are put together.

Palincsar and Brown (1986) make the following observation about reciprocal or interactive teaching:

1. Reciprocal teaching promotes comprehension and comprehension monitoring (metacomprehension).

2. The summarizing component teaches students to integrate information from the text.
3. The questioning and predicting components link prior knowledge to text information and encourage students to make use of text structure by reflecting on what usually comes next in a text of this type.
4. The clarifying component helps children become aware of what they *don't* know. Making this explicit leads to discussions of what to do when clarification is necessary—reread, ask for help, look ahead.
5. Reciprocal teaching has been shown to have a good effect, especially on students whose comprehension lags behind their word recognition skill.
6. Reciprocal teaching has been used in peer tutoring. Students with better comprehension have been paired with students with poorer comprehension, and both tutor and tutoree have profited. This is a superb application of the zone of proximal development concept. Students are encouraged to engage in comprehension in collaboration with others who are more proficient.

The interaction between teacher and student during guided practice and between the adult teacher and student teacher in reciprocal teaching is similar to the scaffolding (chapter 2) that parents supply for children in their fledgling attempts at language use.

ACTIVITY

A. 1. Form two small groups.
   2. Find a selection from a basal or another source that would typically be used in the middle grades.
      Group 1: Prepare a directed reading lesson for the selected passage.
      Group 2: Prepare a reciprocal teaching lesson for the selected passage.
   3. Groups 1 and 2 present your lessons to other students in the class.
B. Class discussion: Referring to specific instances in the two lessons, discuss the following points:
   1. A directed reading lesson is highly directive; a reciprocal teaching lesson gives the students more initiative.
   2. In a directed reading lesson, the teacher decides what knowledge is important; in a reciprocal teaching lesson, students have more opportunity to identify knowledge that they feel is important.
   3. In a directed reading lesson, the teacher decides on correctness; in a reciprocal teaching lesson, there is greater opportunity for correctness to be negotiated.
   4. In a directed reading lesson, there is a great effort to foster comprehension, but practically no effort to teach metacomprehension; in a reciprocal teaching lesson, there is a great effort to foster comprehension and to teach metacomprehension.

Summary

Regardless of what approach a teacher takes to teaching reading, the same concepts, understandings, and skills are likely to be covered. Skills emphasis programs teach them in a fixed order to all students, while holistic, collaborative teachers teach skills to individuals when they seem to be appropriate.

Young children must acquire basic concepts related to print, such as that print represents spoken language and that readers follow print from left to right, from top to bottom, and from page to page. Children need to understand the meaning of words like *letter, line,* and *page,* and even words like *above* and *next* as they relate to print in order to profit from nearly any instruction in reading.

Following sequence, recalling details, interpreting pictures, and making inferences are all concepts related to storybooks that young readers must master.

One method of teaching word recognition is to simply help children recognize whole words without analysis. This method is used in the initial stages of the language experience approach and in many basal reading series.

Phonics refers to the relationship between language sounds and spelling. How much phonics is enough and how much is too much is a controversial issue. Phonics emphasis programs begin with phonics and emphasize word-recognition skills throughout, but all widely used programs address comprehension early and consistently. More holistic approaches begin with meaning and de-emphasize isolated skills, but all widely recognized holistic, collaborative approaches address phonics early and as long as students need it. Analysis of word structure is a third widely taught method of assisting in word recognition. Helping student recognize common prefixes and suffixes helps them recognize words that seem unfamiliar at first.

Context is the final clue to word recognition. Where a word appears is often a clue to its identity. Part of processing text is to be able to predict what is coming. This knowledge gives clues to the identity of words that seem unfamiliar at first.

Through questioning and modeling, teachers help children recognize words that seem unfamiliar at first by using phonics, structure, and context simultaneously.

Metalinguistic awareness is demonstrated by the ability to talk about language, reflect on it, and make statements about how it works. The ability to use phonics, structure, and context in word recognition depends on metalinguistic awareness. Many lessons designed to facilitate comprehension are attempts to help children reflect on how language works. These are lessons in metalinguistic awareness.

Cloze techniques and sentence combining are two methods of encouraging children to reflect on what they know about language. Both techniques are effective if they are used in combination with discussion. Merely completing cloze and sentence-combining exercises alone is not effective.

The ability to think and talk about one's own comprehension is referred to as metacomprehension. One way to foster metacomprehension is to have students read directions that are not complete and discuss what one knows and what one needs to know in order to carry out the directions. Think-aloud monologues and the question-answer relationship strategy are other methods of facilitating metacomprehension.

Methods, lessons, and strategies for promoting comprehension focus on one of four areas: (1) preparation, (2) monitoring comprehension (engaging in metacomprehension), (3) checking comprehension, and (4) organizing information presented in the text.

One activity designed to facilitate comprehension is semantic mapping. It is sometimes used before reading to recall and organize prior knowledge on a topic and to introduce vocabulary. It is used after reading to recall and organize material presented in the text and to relate prior knowledge to information presented in the text.

The directed reading and thinking activity is another method of promoting comprehension. In this activity the students survey the text they are about to read and make predictions about what they will learn in the first part of the text. They then read to a predetermined point, check on the accuracy of their predictions, and make predictions about the next part. This activates prior knowledge, emphasizes the importance of the relationship between prior knowledge and text knowledge, illustrates the fact that comprehension calls for activity, and encourages readers to reflect on their own comprehension processes.

The directed listening and thinking activity shares the characteristics and benefits of the directed reading and thinking activity except that the teacher shares the books with the students and reads it to them following a cycle of predicting, reading, checking predictions, and making new predictions. This is often done in primary grades.

SQ3R (study, question, read, recite, and review) is a comprehension study technique that is often suggest for older students. The guided reading procedure is a seven-step group comprehension-study activity: (1) prepare to read and then read, (2) unaided recall, (3) aided recall, (4) organization, (5) comprehension questioning, (6) comprehension testing, and (7) application.

The directed reading lesson is associated with basal reading programs. It consists of four stages: (1) preparation—consisting of supplying or recalling prior knowledge necessary to comprehend the text, presenting vocabulary, and setting a purpose for reading; (2) reading silently; (3) question/discussion; and (4) skills development.

Questions should require students to use information. Emphasis should be on developing the subject rather than on getting one correct answer. Each question should add to a continuing discussion. There should be periodic review. At the end of a question/discussion session there should be a sense of accomplishment and a desire for what is to come.

Reciprocal teaching is a method of teaching comprehension through four activities: self-questioning, summarizing, predicting, and clarifying. First the teacher models the strategy. Then the students engage in the strategy with teacher guidance and feedback. Finally, students take over as teachers.

For Review and Discussion

1. Identify the concepts related to print, vocabulary of reading instruction, and concepts related to storybooks. How would these concepts be taught in a skills emphasis program? In a holistic, collaborative program?
2. Identify and explain the four methods of word recognition. How would these concepts be treated in a skills emphasis program? In a holistic, collaborative program?
3. Define metalinguistic awareness and describe two activities suggested to teach it.
4. Define metacomprehension and describe two activities suggested to teach it.
5. There are seven methods or strategies suggested for teaching reading comprehension: semantic mapping, the directed reading and thinking activity, the directed listening and thinking activity, the guided reading procedure, the directed reading lesson, and reciprocal teaching. Describe each.

For Further Reading

Blanton, W., Wood, K., & Moorman, G. (1990). The role of purpose in reading instruction. *The Reading Teacher, 43,* 486–493.

Carr, E., Dewitz, P., & Pathberg, J. (1989). Using cloze for inference training with expository text. *The Reading Teacher, 42,* 380–385.

Clay, M. M. (1989). Concepts about print in English and other languages. *The Reading Teacher, 42,* 268–277.

Davis, Z., & McPherson, M. (1989). Storymap instruction: A road map for reading comprehension. *The Reading Teacher, 43,* 232–240.

Freppon, P., & Dahl, K. (1991). Learning about phonics in a whole language classroom. *Language Arts, 68,* 190–197.

Gaskins, R., Gaskins, J., & Gaskins, I. (1991). A decoding program for poor readers—And the rest of the class too! *Language Arts, 68,* 213–225.

Haggard, M. R. (1988). Developing critical thinking with the directed reading-thinking activity. *The Reading Teacher, 41,* 526–535.

Hess, M. (1991). Understanding nonfiction: Purpose, classification, response. *Language Arts, 68,* 228–232.

Lipson, M. Y. (1984). Some unexpected issues in prior knowledge and comprehension. *The Reading Teacher, 37,* 760–764.

McGee, L., & Richgels, D. (1989). "Kis Kristen's": Learning the alphabet from a child's perspective. *The Reading Teacher, 43,* 216–225.

Raphael, T. E. (1986). Teaching question answer relationships, revisited. *The Reading Teacher, 39,* 516–523.

Trachtenburg, P. (1990). Using children's literature to enhance phonics instruction. *The Reading Teacher, 43,* 648–655.

Weiss, M. J., & Ranoe, H. (1985). A key to literacy: Kindergartners' awareness of the functions of print. *The Reading Teacher, 41,* 574–579.

CHAPTER **8**

Approaches to Teaching Writing

Introduction
What We Know About Writers
 and Writing
Activity
TO THINK ABOUT: The
 Audience's Role in
 Communication
Activity
The Process Approach to
 Teaching Writing

Activity
Contrasting Modes of
 Instruction
Activities
Summary
For Review and Discussion
For Further Reading

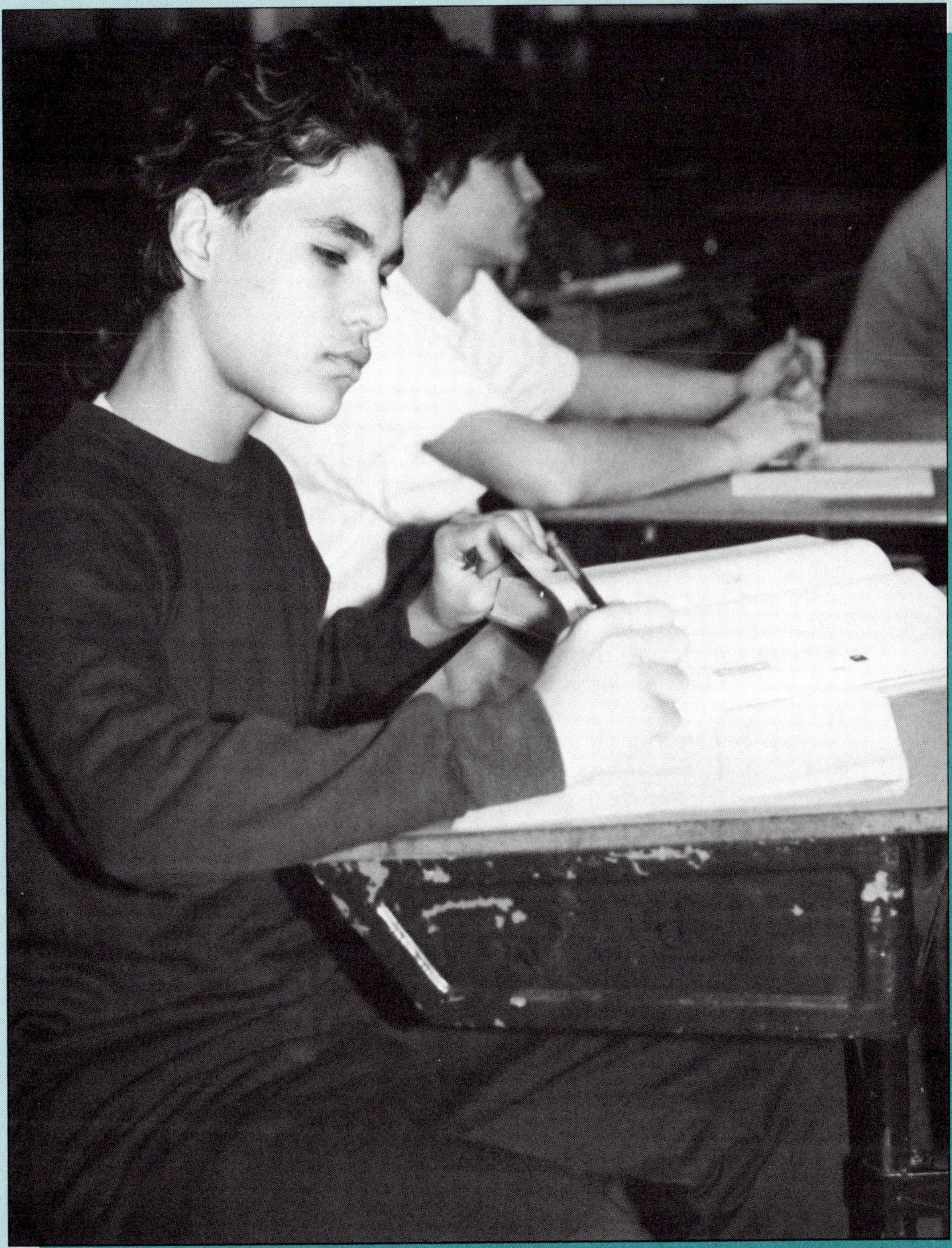

INTRODUCTION

In this introduction to the two chapters on writing I will discuss what is understood about the process of writing—what writers do when they write. I will then briefly review previous discussions in this book regarding the acquisition of language and the emergence of literacy. Finally I will describe the process approach to teaching writing—an approach that is consistent with what we know about the process of writing, the acquisition of language, and the emergence of literacy.

WHAT WE KNOW ABOUT WRITERS AND WRITING

✤ What Professionals Say

In an effort to understand what accomplished writers do when they write, Janet Emig (1971) reviewed four kinds of literature: (1) established writers' (such as James Joyce, D. H. Lawrence, and Thomas Wolfe) accounts of their own writing processes; (2) analysis of the writing process based on notebooks and drafts written by established writers; (3) rhetoric and composition texts and handbooks that offer advice on how to go about writing; and (4) books on theories of creative processes, such as *The Art of Thought* (Wallas, 1926), which proposes four stages in the creative thought process: preparation, incubation, illumination, and verification.

Emig found contradictions. A once widely used handbook of English grammar and composition, for example, states that there are three basic stages of composition (choosing a subject, preparing to write, and writing) and that writers proceed "according to certain definite steps" (choosing the subject, assembling materials, organizing materials, outlining, writing the first draft, revising, and writing the final draft). These steps present writing as a tidy process of elaborating a fully preconceived and formulated plan. Emig contrasts this with Gertrude Stein's view of writing. Stein states that one must

> . . . think of the writing in terms of discovery, which is to say the creation must take place between the pen and the paper, not before in a thought, or afterwards in a recasting. Yes, before in a thought, but not in careful thinking. It will come if it is there and if you let it come, and if you have anything, you will get a sudden creative recognition. (p. 22)

Many professional writers disagree with the generalization that is often implied in writers' manuals—that planning precedes writing and writing precedes revising. For Jerome Bruner, planning often takes the form of conversations with friends; however, he continues to plan and to revise previous plans as the writing evolves. John Ciardi is quoted as saying, "The writing and the thinking are inseparable. Any other assumption can only produce hack-work" (p. 25).

Professional writers also differ among themselves in matters such as outlining. B. F. Skinner is quoted as saying this:

> When I begin to think of a developed paper or a book, I turn almost immediately to outlines. These grow in detail, almost to the point of producing the final prose. (p. 23)

Poet Max Bluestone refers, not to an outline, but to a "map":

> The map is never precise, first because the territory has not been thoroughly explored and second because writing is in itself the discovery of new territory. I usually anticipate discovery in the act of composition. (p. 24)

Novelist Eileen Bassing states this:

> I always feel that my method can only be called "chaotic." The complete outline isn't for me.
>
> I do have a shadowy outline in my mind—as I did in *Home Before Dark*, for example. I knew what I wanted to say, and I knew a great deal about my central character. Once you have the character you're pretty well started.... (p. 24)

✣ Describing the Writing Cycle

Armed with this data Emig did case studies of eight twelfth-grade writers and identified "elements, moments, and stages" within the composing process which can be "distinguished and characterized in some detail" (p. 33). She described the writing process itself as:

> Prewriting
> Planning
> Starting
> Composing
> Reformulation (correcting, revising, rewriting)
> Stopping
> Contemplation of the product.

Numerous other writers and researchers have attempted to describe the writing process (Britton et al., 1975; Koch & Brazil, 1975; Murray, 1968 & 1985; Flower & Hayes, 1981). Graves (1981) defined the writing process as "a series of operations leading to the solution to a problem. The process begins when the writer consciously or unconsciously starts a topic and is finished when the written piece is published" (p. 4). Authors agree that there are behaviors that typically occur in four stages:

> Prewriting—finding a topic, sensing an audience, collecting ideas and facts, planning, rehearsing

Writing—creating a first draft
Rewriting—correcting, revising, editing, proofreading
Sharing—delivering the piece to the intended audience

All the cited authors express concern, however, that presenting the writing cycle as an ordered set of steps grossly misrepresents what actually occurs in the writing process. For example, as writers compose (the writing stage), they often revise their plans, stop to collect new facts, formulate new ideas, and even change their topics (activities supposedly occurring during the prewriting stage). Also, as they compose, they often reread, edit, revise, and correct (activities supposedly occurring in the rewriting stage). Betty Flowers (1981, p. 835) aptly described four roles the writer plays in the writing process:

> Madman: full of ideas, writing crazily and sloppily
> Architect: selecting, choosing chunks to rearrange in a plan
> Carpenter: stabilizing, fastening parts together firmly and effectively
> Judge: inspecting, examining

The writer continually shifts roles, functioning as architect, madman, carpenter, judge, madman, judge, carpenter, architect, and so on.

Sondra Perl (1980) observed college writers and reported that they wrote "by shuttling back and forth from the sense of what they wanted to say forward to the words on the page and back from the words on the page to the intended meaning." She suggests that writers in general develop meaning through construction and discovery: "Writers know more fully what they mean only after they have written it" (p. 26). After an exhaustive review of the literature Hillocks (1986) concluded:

> We do know, from a wide variety of studies, that composing is recursive, with writers moving back to what has been written and forward to what has not. Further, we can be fairly certain that the subprocesses of composing interrupt each other. The writer moves from high-level plans to the transcription of words and back to higher level planning, rereading what has been written, reconstructing plans already made, making new plans, generating new data, or performing editing of some kind. . . . Together, these recursive and bobbing actions present a far different notion of composing than there is to be found in composition texts which traditionally assume that all planning precedes all transcribing and that all editing follows. That, in itself, is a finding that could have important instructional value. (p. 60)

ACTIVITY

One of the data-gathering techniques used by Janet Emig was to have subjects "compose aloud." Emig asked the students she observed to say aloud what they were thinking as they wrote—including what went through their heads as they

ACTIVITY (continued)

decided what to write about. For example, in response to Emig's invitation to "write about a person, idea, or event that especially intrigues you," one twelfth grader began, "Is that such as say, I could talk about taking a bus ride downtown . . ."(p.46).

While planning a piece she said, ". . . this Snoopy [thing] might be interesting if I could think of enough examples" (p.54).

While writing she said, "Yeah, I can sort of wrap it up by saying like, 'throughout the interview which involved the math test blah, blah, blah—ah, he still remained sunny,' and then I can just say, 'after having worked there for two weeks, he's still smiling . . .'" (p.57).

A. Accept Emig's invitation. Write about a person, idea, or event that especially intrigues you. Speak into a tape recorder all the thoughts that occur to you as you undertake this project and as you begin to write. Play back the tape and classify your remarks as those typical of
   1. the prewriting, writing, or rewriting (perhaps even anticipating sharing)
   2. the role of madman, architect, carpenter, and judge.
B. Instead, you might form small groups in class and have one student compose aloud as others take notes. Classify the student writer's comments as above.

You will no doubt find that you can classify writers' processes in terms of stages or roles, but that these stages and roles are recursive and do not appear in an orderly and predictable sequence.

❖ Observing Writers

Emerging Writers

In chapter 6, I described five-year-old Ashley who produced a line of letterlike figures across the top of her paper and a drawing below it and "read" her story to her teacher: "The elephant squirted her. . . ." I described a first grader who wrote what are clearly letters grouped into what look like words and read this "text" as "This is my imaginary friend Bgooga." Although there is little about these texts that can be described as conventional, these children exhibit the beginnings of written composition.

Susan Sowers observed Sarah, a first grader in a classroom where emergent literacy was encouraged. Children wrote as well as they could on topics they chose. These are some of the observations Sowers made about Sarah (1979).

Prewriting
Before Sarah writes she draws a picture and talks about it to the teacher or other children. She then writes about the scene on the same page and begins the drawing, talking, and writing process over again for the next page. When she fills a six-page book she writes an elaborate "The End."

Planning
Sarah wrote two kinds of books. Sowers refers to one as an "attribute book" which lists enough of the hero's good qualities to fill six pages. For example, "I

like the sun. It feels good. The sun looks nice. It looks fun. I like the fun. It feels good"(p. 831). In writing an attribute book, Sarah works steadily, drawing, writing, turning the page, drawing, and so on.

Sarah also wrote "action-sequence books" that tell stories containing at least three events. When writing action-sequence books, she often leaves her desk to talk to friends, to eat a snack, or to get more paper.

Three months into the school year Sarah planned two episodes before beginning to draw. "Woody's [an owl who appears in other stories by Sarah] going to eat a poison egg, no a poison worm, and he's going to die. Poor Woody. He's going to eat the worm here [pointing to page 2 of her book] and he's going to die here [pointing to page 3]." Later she says to a classmate, "He's going to die—he's going to eat a poison worm and he's going to come to life again"(p. 832).

During this same composition Sarah composed aloud for the first time: "'Woody . . .' What should I say? 'Woody is . . .'" And two pages later she said: "Poor Woody. Woody died." And she wrote, "Woody dead"(p. 832).

The text Sarah produced read as follows: "Woody is cute. He took a worm. Woody dead. Woody wake. Woody good. Woody nice." Sower observed that this is the most "telegraphic" book Sarah had written. Often, when Sarah attempted something new the text suffered.

Revising
Sarah often reads her book to another child and if she notices an omission or an inconsistency in a drawing or in the text, she makes the appropriate changes.

Considering the Reader
Sometimes she writes nonsense or mixes up her syntax. If the meaning is clear to her and unclear to others, she refuses to make any changes. Sowers comments "Sarah is still too egocentric to let her audience spoil her play."

✤ An Accomplished Writer

Janet Emig (1971) devoted thirty pages to her description of the writing behaviors of Lynn, a twelfth-grade writer. The following observations and quotations from Lynn are particularly relevant to the present discussion.

Choosing a Topic
Lynn considers several topics. For example, an upcoming party where two boys she has been dating will both be present, or how she had noticed during a recent visit that her grandmother was aging. She decides not to write about her grandmother because it would be "hard to formulate the entire theme," and she decides not to write about the party because it would appeal to a limited audience.

Choosing a Form
Lynn decided to write a poem about a boyfriend—a poem rather than a story because "short stories involve a good plot and I find it hard to invent plots."

Planning and Revising Plans
A poem that was initially supposed to be about a boy does not mention the boy

until the last two lines of a five-stanza poem. Finally she cut the last stanza and the only reference to the boy.

Planning and Revising While Composing

In one piece after first mentioning her boss's smile, she says, ". . . and then I can say . . . for anyone to have a phoney smile for that long, he's either got terrific endurance or he's sincere. Then I could end it right there."

At the beginning of a second essay she refers to a motto she attributes to Snoopy: "To live is to dance, to dance is to live." The motto appears in the next-to-last sentence in the essay.

After a long oral discourse on her cat whom she had mentioned tangentially, she says, "That's an entirely different story. I think I'll just drop the cat."

At other places, while composing, Lynn makes comments like the following: "I want to read this part over again; I think I might start a new paragraph. . . . I'm reading over that last paragraph. I think I have a better ending. . . . This is sort of a digression, but I think it's okay because it brings in a sort of different point."

Reflecting on Her Own Thought Processes

Lynn is able to talk about her own thought processes. For example, while composing aloud she said, "Now I could lie a little and say 'It was a complicated mathematics test and Mr. H———'s smile remained constant.' I'll do that. It sounds better, even though it's not true."

Considering the Reader

"I don't know if everyone who reads this would get the implication."

Rewriting

"I never took it on myself to rewrite a composition. It seemed to be punishment work . . . if you have more than so many mistakes you have to rewrite your composition. . . . I never remember any suggestions [from the teacher] which inspired me to rewrite something . . . the only changes seemed to be technical ones." Lynn seems to have meant that her teachers were not really interested in any revision or reformulation she might attempt.

Nevertheless, Lynn was quite an accomplished writer. One of the papers she wrote for Emig's study began with this paragraph:

> After a few days of desperate searching, having just quit my job at Woolworth's sweat shop, I walked into a warm-looking yellow-and-orange dress shop on East Randolph. My anticipations of a cozy atmosphere were dispelled when I was greeted by a wall of frigid air from the hard-working air conditioner.

❖ Dimensions of Growth in Writing

As writers mature, their engagement in all the processes involved in the writing cycle becomes more apparent and the order in which they engage in these processes becomes more recursive and less predictable. Differences are also seen in the writing they produce: (1) Writing becomes less like spoken language.

(2) Writers overcome egocentricity, and their writing reveals more sensitivity to the reader's probable knowledge, attitude, and point of view. (3) Writers achieve critical detachment. They learn to view their audience, their text, and themselves from outside the process. (4) Writers engage in a greater variety of forms and modes of discourse. These four dimensions of growth in writing are discussed in the following sections.

Writing Becomes Less Like Spoken Language

In comparison with formal writing, informal spoken language is private, implicit, and redundant. There is greater tolerance for inaccuracy in spoken language than in written language. Formal writing (what I referred to as institutional writing in chapter 2) is public, explicit, concise, and accurate. As writers mature their writing exhibits less characteristics of spoken language and more characteristics of formal writing.

Children's earliest writing has many characteristics of informal spoken language. The writing processes of very young writers appear to be closely associated with conversation. Texts are brief—about the same number of words as a turn in conversation. When children begin to write, most of their activity is external. They often speak aloud as they write, tell other children what they are writing, and tell the teacher what they have written before the teacher has a chance to read it. Gradually, children's talk that accompanies writing diminishes. During this stage children often exhibit a pattern of writing, holding a conversation, and continuing to write "suggestive of switching [that is, turn-taking] in conversation" (Graves, 1981, p. 22).

Although Hidi and Hillyard (1983) found that as late as fifth grade, written and spoken compositions are similar in length, O'Donnell, Griffin, and Norris (1967) found that in fifth grade the syntax of many children's writing becomes more complex than the syntax of their speech.

The process by which children's writing becomes clearly distinct from their spoken language and takes on the characteristics of institutional writing is a lengthy one. The writing of Lynn, Emig's twelfth grader, is clearly distinguishable from speech and has the characteristics of institutional writing.

Children's earliest awareness of differences between written and spoken language can be seen in the early stages of emergent literacy. Sulzby, Barnhart, and Hieshima (1989) encouraged kindergartners to write "the way kindergartners write" (whether it be scribbles, drawing, letters, or conventional writing) and asked them to reread what they had written. The responses of many kindergarten children showed that they understood many characteristics that distinguish written language for spoken language. They often began with a title, specified who the people in the story were, and ended with "The End." Their "readings" often sounded like expressive oral reading done by an accomplished reader—the listener would almost think the child was reading from print. In short, their stories were worded like and sounded like written stories.

Writers Overcome Egocentricity

Over a two-year period Graves (1981) observed sixteen youngsters who exhibited low, middle, and high levels of writing ability. He followed eight children from the beginning of first grade to the end of second grade and eight youngsters from the beginning of third grade to the end of fourth grade.

According to Graves, early writing resembles play. Writers write down what they want without fear of mistakes or failure. During this period, children learn how to control pens, pencils, and crayons. At first, writers sequence letters on a page in a variety of ways: horizontally, vertically, and indiscriminately. As young writers begin to see the need for communicating a message, they adopt more conventional left-to-right and top-to-bottom sequences. They learn to separate words that flow together in speech. They become more concerned with the cosmetic appearance of their writing.

In the beginning, children are confident that what they write, regardless of its form, will be meaningful to others. If necessary, they can simply explain the context and the intended meaning to the audience around them. Ashley and Bgooga's friend "read" their stories to their teachers. Sarah told her story twice and wrote it in an abbreviated form.

Eventually, children discover that they and their teachers cannot decode their messages or that peers have many questions about what they write. Such discoveries make their writing less playful. They begin to see a need for their products to communicate beyond the context of the immediate writing situation. In Calkins's words, "Children no longer write solely for themselves. Writing is no longer all-process, all-present, all-personal. Children are concerned with product and with audience" (1980a, p. 213).

This is the beginning of a process that is referred to variously as "overcoming egocentricity," "decentering," and "achieving detachment." Growth in this area continues over many years. It is of the utmost importance in becoming a mature and proficient writer.

I discussed egocentricity in chapter 5 in connection with the persuasive function of language and speaking. The points made in that discussion are equally relevant to the present topic of egocentricism and writing.

Understanding the Concept of Egocentricity

Piaget is one of the most influential writers on the topic of children's development. Through his experiments, Piaget concluded that young children are unable to take the perspective of another person. They behave instead as if others see what they see, know what they know, are affected the way they are affected, and are thinking the same thing they are thinking. Piaget labeled this phenomenon egocentricism.

There are many examples of egocentrism. A four-year-old child begins to cry, and his mother calls from the next room, "What's wrong, Donny?" Donny responds, "I can't get this one in there." He fails to say what he is trying to put where. He seems to think his mother can see what he is doing despite the fact that she is in another room. In another example, a three-year-old child is singing but she doesn't want nearby strangers to hear her so she covers her own ears (Cazden, 1972).

On the other hand, there are many examples of young children who demonstrate that they are aware of others' points of view. Cazden (1972) describes a three-year-old who is trying to get her father's attention, which is riveted on the television screen. The child walks over and stands in front of the screen and faces her father. This child was apparently aware of her father's point of view (literally) and acted on this awareness to achieve her ends. Another three-year-old interrupts a story about "John" to insert "He's my friend"—information he apparently realizes his listener did not have.

Children between ages two and five ask many questions of adults and few questions of age-mates, and when interacting with age-mates and an adult, they direct questions to the adult. This demonstrates some understanding of what others are likely know (Smith, 1933). Four-year-old children talk differently to two-year-old children than they do to other four-year-olds or adults. They give two-year-olds direct commands—"Give me that!"—but make requests of other four-year-olds and adults—"Can I have that?" (Shatz & Gelman, 1973). Schiff (1976) observed normal-hearing children of deaf mothers and discovered that by age two these children speak to hearing adults differently from the way they do to their deaf mothers. Three- and four-year-old children are more explicit in talking about toys to a blind adult than in talking about the same toys to seeing adults (Maratsos, 1973). Menig-Peterson (1975) asked three- and four-year-olds to talk about an experience to adults who had participated in the experience (knowledgeable listeners) and to adults who were not present during the experience (naïve listeners). The children made more references to, and introduced more information about, the earlier event to the naïve listeners than to the knowledgeable listeners.

Menig-Peterson concluded that children between three and four years of age can modify both the form and the content of their speech according to what they presume that their listeners know. However, children only gradually learn to make such judgments about the informational needs of the listener.

After reviewing the research, Menyuk (1988) concluded that Piaget overestimated the degree to which egocentricity governs children's perception and communication. However, the inability or disinclination to take the reader's point of view into consideration when writing is a widely recognized problem that remains well beyond early childhood and, for some, never disappears. Kantor and Rubin (1981) pointed out that "the transcription process itself poses an intellectual challenge for novice and basic writers, at times requiring such attention that writers lapse into egocentrism." Recall how Sarah wrote a particularly telegraphic text when she first attempted to write a story for which she had planned two incidents in advance.

Evidence of Egocentricity in Older Students

Flower (1979) called the writing of ineffectual college-aged writers "writer-based" prose. Such writing is written by writers for themselves and to themselves; they use "privately loaded terms and shifting but unexpressed contexts" for what is said. Effective writers turn writer-based prose into reader-based prose. The writer chooses words considering the meanings they will have for the reader, includes information that the reader will need but probably does not have, and states things explicitly so that meaning can be derived from the language rather than implied.

Berkenkotter (1981) classified the activities used by professional writers in considering their audience's needs. They all constructed a hypothetical audience and evaluated the content in relation to the audience reaction they anticipated. They planned ways to meet the audience's needs and interests. They asked themselves the questions their readers might be expected to ask and adjusted their writing so that they could supply the answers.

According to Hillocks, the shift from assuming that the whole world thinks as we do to accepting the responsibility for designing messages with meaning for many readers may not be completed before years of writing have been experienced. It is based on an increasing social awareness. As writers develop the ability to size up their audience's beliefs, interests, experiences, and language-processing abilities, they begin to supply their audiences with contexts, putting in details that they feel are needed and omitting those that they decide are unnecessary.

Writers Achieve Critical Detachment

Accomplished adult writers are able to step back from the writing transaction and ask how their text would affect them if they were the reader. They ask questions such as the following about the writer of the text (themselves): Is the writer naïve or experienced, meticulous or careless, humble or overbearing, an authority or a partner in the struggle to understand? Based on the effect they wish to have on the reader they adopt appropriate tone and produce a text accordingly. At the same time, mature writers view their text as a draft, one that is temporary, tentative, and exploratory.

While asking themselves "What do I want to say, and to whom, and what do I want the audience to think about me?" accomplished adult writers reread the text to see whether or not it will accomplish their purpose. If it probably will not, they revise.

This is not a mechanical process. Which of these questions will be given precedence at any moment is highly unpredictable and the answers to one question may change as the writer gains clarity on the answer to others. What a writer wants to say may change as his or her audience comes into focus. How a writer wants the audience to feel about the writer may change as what he or she wants to say becomes clearer.

This is not merely becoming aware of the reader's point of view. It is the ability to view the reader, the message, the text, and the writer from outside the process. It is achieving what Moffett (1968) terms "critical detachment."

---TO THINK ABOUT---

The Audience's Role in Communication

Think about your ideal date. How would you describe this for a local newspaper column? How would you describe it in a letter to a friend? How does the identity of the audience change what you want to say? What you want your audience to think of you? How does the answer to the second question affect your answer to the first?

Writers Engage in a Greater Variety of Modes of Discourse

Mature writers exhibit greater versatility than beginners in the sense that they are able to produce many different kinds of writing—writing for different purposes and in different forms. By first grade Sarah already writes two kinds of books—attribute books and action-sequence books. Twelfth grader Lynn produced poetry, narratives, and descriptions in Emig's study, and judging from the maturity of her writing, she is probably capable of producing other forms.

Numerous scholars have attempted to trace the development of writers in terms of the "modes of discourse" they successfully engage in. Halliday (1975) applied this same framework to describing the functions of *oral* language that infants discover and attempt to engage in (see chapter 2).

Classical Modes of Discourse: Narrative, Descriptive, Expository, and Persuasive

One of the oldest classification systems for written discourse is ascribed to Samuel P. Newman of Bowdoin College in 1827 (Haley-James, 1981).

This system identifies four modes of written discourse as defined below:

The Narrative Mode
Writing that tells a story with characters, a setting, and episodes.

The Descriptive Mode
Writing that creates a verbal portrait. It tells what the readers' senses would tell them if they were present in the setting or enables readers to experience feelings or live an event.

The Expository Mode
Writing that explains. It tells readers how to do something, or how things are, or why things are the way they are.

The Persuasive Mode
Writing that attempts to convince readers to take some action or accept some belief.

Britton's Functions: Expressive, Transactional, and Poetic

Britton (1970) and Burgess and colleagues (1973) describe children's early writing as serving "the expressive function." Expressive language is intimate and unrehearsed; it is free to follow the speaker's or writer's shifting focus of atten-

> ### EXPRESSIVE FUNCTION OF LANGUAGE
>
> Intimate
> Unrehearsed
> Follows speaker or writer shifting-focus of attention
> Reveals speaker's preoccupations
> Takes audience interest for granted
>
> ### POETIC FUNCTION OF LANGUAGE
>
> Emerges from the expressive function
>   Focuses on formal properties of the text (stories, poems, and plays, for example)
>   Focuses on creating a text as a work of art
>
> ### TRANSACTIONAL FUNCTION OF LANGUAGE
>
> Emerges from the expressive function
>   Deals with facts, information, and theory
>   Focuses on topic
>   Attempts to engage an audience

BOX 8.1 Britton's (1975) scheme to describe children's development as writers in terms of functions of discourse.

tion. It is thought to reveal the speaker's preoccupations; it takes for granted the audience's readiness to be interested in the writer and his or her message.

As children develop, they begin to modify expressive language in two directions. On the one hand, they begin to deal with facts, information, and theory. They use language, not merely to reveal their consciousness, but to engage a topic and an audience. Britton refers to this as "the transactional function" of language. This is the language of science and philosophy. On the other hand, children exhibit an awareness of the form of language. They modify their expressive language to reflect an awareness of the formal properties of stories, poems, and plays. They use language not merely to reveal their consciousness but to create verbal objects, works of art. Britton refers to this as "the poetic function" of language (see Box 8.1).

Kinneavy's Modes of Discourse: Expressive, Persuasive, Referential, and Literary

Kinneavy (1971) classified discourse in terms of four components—the encoder, the decoder, the referent, and the text itself (see Figure 8.1).

> Expressive discourse results when the emphasis is on self-expression and the encoder. (Compare with Britton's expressive function.)

Persuasive discourse results when the emphasis is on persuasion and the decoder. (Compare with Britton's transactional function.)

Referential discourse results when the emphasis is on the referent and conveying reality. (Compare with Britton's transactional function.)

Literary discourse results when the emphasis is on the text and its formal characteristics. (Compare with Britton's poetic function.)

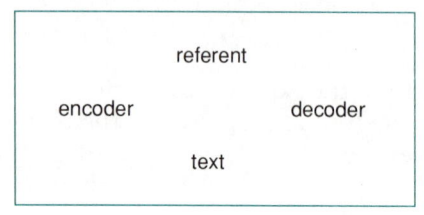

```
                    referent

       encoder                 decoder

                      text
```

Figure 8.1 Kinneavy's (1971) four components of discourse.

ACTIVITY

I. Divide the class into groups.

Group A: Each student brings three written texts that clearly exemplify three of the four classic modes of written discourse: narrative, descriptive, expository, and persuasive.

Group B: Each student brings three written texts that clearly exemplify three different functions as described by Britton: the expressive function, the transactional function, and the poetic function.

Group C: Each student brings three written texts that clearly exemplify three of Kinneavy's four categories of discourse: expressive, persuasive, referential, and literary.

1. Ask other members in your group to categorize your examples by the system assigned to your group.
2. Classify the same samples of writing assembled by your group by the two remaining systems (those assigned to other groups).
3. Decide which system you feel is the easiest to work with and which is most useful in describing the functions (or modes) of written discourse. If possible, it would be instructive to do this exercise using elementary-school children's writing.

II. Repeat this activity but rather than finding written texts that exemplify categories, write texts that exemplify the categories assigned to your group.

You will probably notice that it is easier to create texts to exemplify categories than to find them because written language is really too organic to find pure examples. Writing teachers find these categories useful, however, in thinking about the challenges that face students.

In chapter 2, I reported Halliday's findings concerning infants' discovery and use of the functions of oral language. One of his findings was that soon after the onset of language it is almost impossible to classify an utterance as an example of *one* function. Every utterance appears to serve more than one function. Since written discourse is usually longer than spoken utterances, it is even more difficult to find texts that exemplify only one mode or function of discourse. For example, description appears in narrative, expository, and persuasive texts (using the classic four modes of classification), and both transactional and poetic writing is often expressive (using Britton's functions for classification). Nevertheless these classification systems are useful.

Without such a classification system, a fifth-grade teacher might notice that Rodney writes in a very narrow range, but he or she may be unable to articulate the problem. Such systems enable teachers to identify the problem of limited versatility and to remedy the problem within a coherent framework. They also enable us to describe a dimension of growth in students' writing. Proficient adults are capable of engaging competently in a wide variety of modes or functions of written discourse. Children and nonproficient adults engage competently in a narrower range of modes.

In summary, as students mature and gain in writing skill the following changes occur:

1. Their engagement in each of the behaviors involved in the writing cycle (finding a topic, sensing an audience, collecting ideas and facts, planning, rehearsing, writing a draft, correcting, revising, editing, proofreading, and sharing) becomes more apparent.
2. The order in which they engage in these behaviors becomes more recursive and unpredictable.
3. Their writing becomes less like spoken language and takes on the characteristics of institutional writing. It becomes public rather than private, more accurate, explicit, and concise.
4. They overcome egocentricity. Their writing reveals a sensitivity to the reader's probable knowledge, attitudes, and point of view.
5. They achieve critical detachment.
6. They engage in greater varieties of modes of discourse.

Each of these signs of maturity interacts with and facilitates the others.

THE PROCESS APPROACH TO TEACHING WRITING

Over the last several decades, an approach to teaching writing has evolved which has come to be known as the "writing process approach" or the "process approach to teaching writing." This approach is based on an understanding of:

1. The writing process as described earlier in this chapter.
2. The dimensions of growth in writing as described earlier in this chapter.

3. The validity of the holistic, collaborative approach to teaching language arts as described in chapter 1.
4. The concept of language acquisition as described in chapter 2.
5. The concept of emergent literacy as described in chapter 6.

Hillocks refers to the writing process approach as "the natural process mode of teaching writing," and points out that it has antecedents in Rousseau (1712–1778) and Dewey (1859–1952). Hillocks traces its more recent roots to the 1966 Dartmouth Conference (Dixon, 1967), where leading authorities on teaching writing met to discuss the state of their craft and its future, and to Emig's (1971) study described at length earlier in this chapter. Donald Graves (1975) observed the processes of primary-school writers and developed the writing process approach in primary grades. It is Graves most people think of in connection with the writing process approach in the elementary school.

In the process approach, writing is taught in a workshop format. In the typical adult writer's workshop, people bring writing they have produced elsewhere. Several people may be working on poems or short stories. One may be writing a family history. Another may be working on a walking tour of the town for the garden club, and another may be working on a script for a television situation comedy. They come to the workshop to talk about their writing, to explain what they are trying to do, to ask others for suggestions, to get new ideas, to talk about the writing process, to be among writers, and to get and give support. Sometimes members ask for help with editing their work for publication. "I'm really terrible at [spelling, punctuation, grammar, . . .], so please don't be shy about telling me when I've got something wrong."

There may be a leader—a person hired by the community center or night school to run the workshop, or simply the person who has the key to the church basement—but successful leaders are writers themselves, and they become members of the workshop. Members consult one another as well as the nominal leader. If this is not true at the beginning, it becomes true in successful workshops.

Most people attend writing workshops with the hope that their writing will be published. Some send a poem to a newspaper or magazine and hope. Others submit their stories or scripts to a Los Angeles or New York agent and pray. Others may be confident that their guide for the garden club's walking tour will be used; they just want to make it as good as they can. Workshops often result in a collection of work published by the workshop itself.

In elementary-school workshops the teacher retains more of the role of leader and teacher. There are short teacher-directed lessons and the teacher retains responsibility for keeping students on task. However, the process approach to teaching writing shares many of the characteristics of the adult writers workshop.

❖ Observing the Process Approach in Grade Four

Irene Silo-Miller (1984), a fourth-grade teacher, uses the process approach to teaching writing. Since she does not assign topics, she uses a number of techniques to help children find topics and get started writing. She visits children individually as they begin to write and expresses interest in their topics. She asks children who have begun to write to read aloud what they have written so far. This often gives ideas to those who have not started. She encourages children to draw, and she has brief conferences with the artists, asking questions about the pictures and developing a topic for a story. She encourages children to speak their stories into tape recorders and insists that a written product follow. She points out good examples of story openers in books the children read and in those she reads to them.

Silo-Miller teaches the children how to participate in a conference. She first holds a writing conference with an individual child in front of the class. The child reads his or her story slowly and clearly. She asks questions to help the author expand and clarify the story. This process is then incorporated into individual student-teacher conferences, group student-teacher conferences, conferences between two students, and group conferences among students. Silo-Miller teaches students how to function in conferences both as authors and as responders and supplies guidelines like the following for responding to writing:

1. Say something positive about the story.
2. If the story does not have a title, ask what a good title might be.
3. Comment on the lead. Is it interesting?
4. Ask what the author's favorite part of the story is. Is it explained clearly so you can picture what is happening? Ask what more you would like to know to make that part clear.

Silo-Miller could tell students what to write about and how to revise it to make their writing acceptable to her, but she feels the children need to feel a sense of responsibility for their writing and to retain decision-making power in revising their own writing.

After two conferences on the story itself, the author and teacher have a proofreading session. In discussion with each child, Silo-Miller identifies one or two problems that the child agrees to work on, such as capitalizing first words in sentences or indenting paragraphs.

After proofreading, the student can decide to publish, which means binding the neatly and correctly recopied story into a decorated cover, putting the copyright date inside, making a card for the classroom library card catalog, and placing the book on the library shelf.

Children often sit with one another during free time and read one another's books. They also share their books with children from different grade levels. Authors from different classes sometimes come in and read their stories to Silo-Miller's class, and authors from Silo-Miller's class go to other classes and read their stories.

❖ Observing the Process Approach in the Middle Schools

Nancie Atwell is a middle-school teacher. Her classroom writing workshop is described in her widely read book *In the Middle: Writing, Reading and Learning with Adolescents* (1987).

Atwell's workshop consists of four routines: the minilesson, status of the class conference, workshop proper, and group share. Publishing is an integral part of the approach.

The Minilesson

Atwell begins each writing class with a five-minute lesson. These lessons introduce concepts and techniques as students in the class appear to need them. Minilessons fall into the following three categories:

> Lessons on what is expected of students in a writing workshop: where to put pieces for teacher editing or how and where to engage in conferences with other students.
>
> Lessons on the craft of writing: how to use proofreader's marks that are useful for revising papers (such as carets [^] for inserting words in lines and arrows to show where to insert added text written in margins) or how to find new topics.
>
> Lessons on conventions of writing: how to format letters, résumés, and poems or how to divide words between syllables.

Atwell keeps minilessons short (five minutes maximum) and reminds herself that they are not the most important part of the workshop. The most important teaching comes in her personal responses to students' writing—"conversations in which kids begin to discover what they passionately desire to say" (p. 148).

Status of the Class Conference

Each day Atwell begins writing class with a status of the class conference. When class begins and for a brief period before students begin to work, she calls each student's name and asks what he or she will be working on that day and where the student is in the process. Students respond with "A story, I'm writing the first draft," "Editing a poem," "Working on the letter I started yesterday." She notes each student's response in the appropriate place on her Status of the Class Chart, where each student's name is followed by spaces in five columns labeled Monday through Friday.

The status of the class conference lasts no more than three minutes. Through it, Atwell accomplishes four objectives:

1. Students commit themselves each day to specific tasks.
2. Students get ideas from one another through this brief public reporting of work in progress.
3. Atwell can see at a glance what each student has been doing and satisfy herself that each student is using his or her time productively. For example, Rachel worked on a yearbook poem and the first draft of an essay on Monday, finished the poem on Tuesday, finished the first draft of her

essay on Wednesday, and revised the essay on Thursday and Friday. Darren worked on a résumé on Monday, self-edited the résumé on Tuesday, was scheduled for an editing conference with the teacher on Wednesday, and so on.
4. When, for one reason or another, students are not producing, Atwell addresses herself to setting goals with the students and notes on the chart the date on which they have agreed a piece will be ready for editing.

Content Conferences

Once every student has committed himself or herself to the day's work the workshop begins. Atwell takes a primary-grade chair and carries it to the side of the desk of a working child and asks "How is it going?" This signals the beginning of a brief teacher-student conference. During these conferences Atwell responds to the students' writing. She listens, tells what she hears, summarizes, paraphrases, restates, asks questions about things she does not understand or would like to know more about, and asks what the writer might do next. She suggests things they might do next, but she does not write her suggestions down or in any way indicate that they are more than suggestions.

Some noteworthy aspects of these conferences are the following:

1. The teacher goes to the students' desks. This enables her to determine when the conference is over—she simply gets up and leaves. Keeping conferences short enables her to conference with every student nearly every day. Going to the students also enables her to monitor classroom behavior in general. A student who appears to be doing something other than what she or he stated in the status of the class conference is likely to be her next conferee.
2. The teacher sits on a primary-sized chair next to the students' desks so that she looks into their faces—not at their papers. She finds that if she looks at their papers, she begins to read and edit, to focus on mistakes, spelling, and punctuation, the very things she insists they not worry about while drafting. Most English teachers recognize this failing in themselves; too few of us resist succumbing to it.
3. She never reads students' writing; she listens as they read parts of it to her.
4. She never writes on their papers except when editing—and then she edits without adding comments.

Peer Conferences

The four corners of the room are designated conference areas. When students need a response to something they have written or to an idea, they are free to ask one or two other students to join them in a conference area where they consult in quiet voices.

Editing Conferences

When a student is satisfied that his or her paper is finished—it says what he or she wants to say, the way he or she wants to say it—the student takes a pen or pencil of a different color from the one in which the paper is written and edits it; the writer corrects the spelling, writes out abbreviations, indicates paragraphs, supplies punctuation, and so on. The piece is then submitted to Atwell for final editing. She takes the piece home and in a third color of ink makes any editorial changes necessary to bring the piece up to minimal standards. She records the skills that the student seems to have mastered plus one or two skills that need attention.

The next day, during the status of the class conference, Atwell informs the student that she will be having an editorial conference with him or her during the class period. At this conference Atwell teaches the one or two skills she has identified and makes note of what she has taught. She will continue to monitor those skills in future editing conferences with the student.

Evaluation Conferences

Atwell evaluates students' progress during quarterly evaluation conferences. She asks the student what someone has to do to be a good writer; which is the student's best piece of writing from the last quarter and what makes it best; and what the student's goals are for the next quarter. Atwell comes to these conferences with goals she will suggest for the student. These goals are based on a review of the student's folder containing his or her writing—finished, in-progress, and abandoned—as well as lists of the student's accomplishments and items taught during editing conferences. Together, she and the student agree upon and write down two or three goals the student will pursue in the coming quarter.

Atwell assigns a letter grade on the basis of the progress the student has made in achieving the goals determined between them during the previous quarter's conference.

Group Share

Seven or eight minutes before the end of each workshop, Atwell tells students to stop what they are doing and to sit together in a circle on the floor. One or two writers read a paper or part of a paper. During her rounds, Atwell finds volunteers or suggests to writers that they share something that day. During group share, Atwell models productive ways of listening and responding, and the group discusses useful and not very useful responses. Calkins refers to this kind of meeting as a vehicle for helping children become good writing teachers. Group share also brings closure to each day's workshop and helps students stay apprised of what others are doing.

Publishing

Atwell views the writing workshop as a daily opportunity for students to discover what is appropriate for sharing and how it might be shared. She does not insist that every piece that goes through the editing process be published. Some pieces are not meant to be shared with classmates. However, Atwell believes that going public should be frequent and ongoing, not only for pieces the teacher judges to be good writing, but for all writing that children wish to share.

Sharing in conferences and during group share is the easiest and most frequently used form of going public. Photocopying papers to share with family and friends; posting writing on bulletin boards; submitting writing to contests, school newspapers, local newspapers, and magazines; tape-recording radio plays; and videotaping commercials are only a few of the numerous publication opportunities Atwell recommends to her students.

❖ Characteristics of the Process Approach to Teaching Writing

The process approach to teaching writing accommodates what is known about the process of writing (the writing cycle) and what is known about the way youngsters acquire language and literacy.

Ownership

In a process-approach classroom, topics are not assigned. Children are nearly always free to choose their own topics and forms of expression—stories, poems, descriptions, and so on. A great deal of instruction takes place during conferences when teachers respond to the students' writing. These practices are consistent with the characteristics of parent-child interactions that facilitate language development—intentionality, proximal development, collaboration, internalization, and continuous development (as discussed in chapter 2).

Intentionality is particularly important in regard to choosing a topic. When twenty-five-month-old Mark embarked on his first fanciful account regarding the disappearance of the man next door (chapter 2), his mother was able to recognize his intentions and help him. When twenty-month-old Nigel tried to report his experience at the zoo (chapter 2), his father and mother recognized his intentions and "scaffolded" his efforts until he was able to render a connected discourse.

As writers mature, freedom to choose their own topics continues to pay dividends. Graves compared ownership of one's writing to home ownership when he said, "When people own a place, they look after it. When it belongs to someone else, they couldn't care less" (quoted in Calkins, 1983, p. 23). Dyson put it this way: "Authentic writing is couched within ones own intentions. Inauthentic writing is done to fulfill the teacher's intentions" (1984, p. 623).

Giving students ownership of their topics is consistent with the writing processes of skilled adults. Donald Murray is a Pulitzer Prize–winning author and teacher of writing. In his books he describes at length ways of discovering topics. Asking his editor/publisher to assign a topic is not one of them. Although adult writers sometimes write on topics suggested by others or by external circumstances (the woman writing the walking-tour guide for the garden club may be an example), their motivation and involvement rest on real-life goals. Writing on teacher-assigned topics rarely satisfies real-life goals.

In the process approach children are given ownership of their writing in other ways. If they wish, they may work on the same piece day after day, for the first draft through publication. They may put one piece aside and work on another. They may abandon a piece entirely. When they receive feedback from peers, they may respond to suggestions in various ways or not at all. They may cross things out, draw arrows, cut and paste, and use colored pencils for revisions. The paper belongs to the writer.

When conferencing with students I do sometimes write comments on their papers (unlike Atwell), but I write the comments on "Post-Its" (small tabs of paper with adhesive that can be stuck on and removed from the papers) and paste them to the students' papers in the appropriate place. This underscores the message that the student owns the writing and the teacher has no right to mar it—or even to take up margin space that the student may need in revising. One of my most gratifying moments as a teacher was when I said to an eighth-grade student during a conference—"Do you mind if I write on your paper?" At first she didn't understand that I considered the page we were discussing to be her paper and that I, the teacher, should ask permission before putting pencil marks on it. In a moment she understood, said "Sure," and squared her shoulders and sat up straighter. I've had similar experiences since.

Writers' Folders

Students are not required to finish one piece before beginning another, nor are they required to complete every piece they begin. Each student keeps a folder in which all works-in-progress are kept. For the purpose of record keeping, lists like the following are kept on lined sheets of paper stapled to the covers of the folder: (1) ideas for writing, (2) titles of finished pieces of writing—with the date of completion; (3) writing skills the student has mastered or has been taught in an editing conference, and (4) goals for writing arrived at by the teacher and student in evaluation conferences.

❖ Conferencing

Conferences between teachers and students and among students (peer conferences) are two of the chief components of the process approach to teaching writing. Four benefits are like to accrue from conferences:

Writing Conferences Accommodate the Recursive and Unpredictable Nature of the Writing Cycle

Teachers and peers respond to the writer regarding the stage of writing that he or she is involved in at that time—finding a topic, making plans, rehearsing, writing, revising, editing, or publishing.

Writing Conferences Permit Teachers to Collaborate with Students

They permit teachers to engage in an activity with young writers that is similar to the scaffolding parents do with youngsters struggling toward new achievements in oral language. They permit the teacher to observe what the child is trying to do while he or she is trying to do it and to collaborate with the writer to achieve the writer's goals.

In conferences, teachers suggest ways of solving problems the writer is struggling with, but they remember who owns the piece. They do not tell students what to do or rewrite their papers for them. This, too, is reminiscent of scaffolding.

In editing conferences, teachers are a bit more directive. They teach one or two conventions that will help the student achieve his or her purpose in the piece of writing under consideration. Teachers make note of which conventions have been taught and expect the student to incorporate these conventions, when they are appropriate, in later papers. Even here, the spirit of collaboration is preserved. Students are consulted on which conventions they will address.

Writing Conferences Facilitate Growth Away from Egocentricity and toward Detachment Regarding the Writing Process

As stated earlier, many experts relate growth in writing ability to progress from egocentricity, to greater awareness of the reader's needs and attitudes, and finally to detachment where the writer can view the writer (herself or himself), the reader, the meaning, and the text as an outside observer would. Nothing facilitates this process like getting the honest response of others to one's writing. Bissex (1979) recorded a conference between five-year-olds Tiffany and Amy. After Tiffany read her story to Amy, Amy replied, "Why don't you tell what happened to the other mice? 'Cause how would I know that?"

Writers do not outgrow their need for readers' responses. Peter Elbow's principle thesis for *Writing Without Teachers* (1973)—an influential handbook for adult writers workshops—is that writers need to know how readers react to their writing. They need to know whether their writing makes readers feel confused, angry, amused, bored, sympathetic, or repelled.

Writing Conferences Make Writing Easier

According to Elbow, readers' honest responses during conferences make writing easier because they remedy the two principle phenomena that make writing hard.

First, writing is hard (compared with speaking) because writers do not know how their words will affect their audiences. Without knowing how the first paragraph will be received, they write the second paragraph, and the third, and so on. Writing conferences come as close as possible to giving writers feedback while in the process of writing and that, according to Elbow, makes writing easier.

Second, writing is hard because writers worry over whether their readers will like what they write. When writers get enough reactions from enough people, they learn not to care whether or not the reader liked their words, but to be interested instead in how the reader understood and responded to their words. A writer who has experienced a lot of honest reaction from readers is able to say, "George understood the paper and it made him mad. That's good because that's what I was trying for. He didn't like the paper, but that doesn't matter. I wasn't trying to write a paper George would like." When writers learn to write to accomplish their own goals and not to please readers, they are free to write. This too, according to Elbow, makes writing easier.

> **ACTIVITY**
>
> Divide the class into two groups. Discuss the characteristics of the process approach to teaching writing in terms of
>
> Group A: Issues that define approaches (chapter 1)
> 1. Teaching is directive/collaborative
> 2. Learners are viewed as passive/active
> 3. Language learning is viewed as teacher-to-student/an interactional group process
> 4. Atomistic/holistic
>
> Group B: Parent-child interactions that facilitate language development
> 1. Intentionality
> 2. Proximal development
> 3. Collaboration
> 4. Internalization
> 5. Continuous development
>
> Report summaries of your discussions to the class.

CONTRASTING MODES OF INSTRUCTION

✣ The Presentational Mode

Although the observations of the way children learn language and language arts have, for the past quarter-century, overwhelmingly supported the writing process approach, it is not the approach to teaching writing that is found in most classrooms. A more traditional and more widespread approach is referred to as the **presentational mode** of instruction (Hillocks, 1986).

A Typical Lesson

The following middle-school lesson is typical of the presentational mode. The objective of the lesson is to teach children to develop and use a thesis sentence in their writing. The teacher gives the students the following instructions:

- Choose a topic that you know a lot about and on which you have a strong opinion.

- Write your topic on the top line of your paper.
- Write down every idea, word, or thought you can think of that relates to your topic, no matter how farfetched. Write them in any order.
- Read your list and look for one group of related ideas. Put a one (1) in front of these related ideas. Reread your list for a second group of related ideas. Put a two (2) in front of these ideas. Continue this process until you have found all the groups of related ideas. You may discard ideas if you wish.
- Read your lists and write a sentence at the bottom of the page that states the main idea or main opinion expressed in the lists. This is your thesis sentence. It provides a focus for your writing.
- Write a rough draft that tells your ideas on your topic. The audience is your classmates. Write at least two pages.
- Edit your draft and write a final draft.
- Hand in your list, your rough draft, and your final draft.
- Your grade will be based on how well you combined your ideas on your list, how well your thesis sentence expresses the ideas in your lists, and how well your rough draft and final draft support your thesis sentence.

Good and poor examples of student work on this assignment may be presented to the class before students begin to write. Students may be given the opportunity to share their efforts at each stage and to discuss their success in carrying out the teacher's directions. This would typically take the form of a teacher-led class discussion.

Characteristics

The presentational mode of instruction has five characteristics:

1. Lessons have specific objectives that are clearly stated—writing a strong lead paragraph, using more descriptive adjectives, or learning the format and rhyme scheme of a limerick, for example.
2. Concepts to be learned and applied are presented in the form of lectures and/or teacher-led discussions.
3. Models and materials that illustrate or explain the concepts are presented for study.
4. Students are given specific assignments or exercises which generally involve imitating patterns or following rules presented in the lesson.
5. Teachers supply feedback on the written assignments, usually in the form of red-pencil corrections, marginal comments, and grades.

Assumptions

Hillocks lists four assumptions about teaching and learning in the presentational mode of instruction:

1. Teachers have useful knowledge about writing to convey to their students.
2. This knowledge is best conveyed directly in the form of verbal formulas, rules, examples, and admonitions.
3. The abstractions referred to by these formulas and rules that the teachers have in their heads are the same as those that the students have in their heads—or will get into their heads as a result of the lesson. That is, when the teacher says, "Write a lead that will grab the audience," students have the same concept of "audience" and of a "grabbing lead" as the teacher. To be fair to teachers who adopt this mode of instruction, much of the teacher-directed lesson, discussion, presentation of models, and so on is based on the premise that the students do not have these concepts in their heads. The whole point of the presentation is to get these concepts across.
4. Students will convert formulas, rules, and so on into their own writing.

Despite the fact that research shows it to be the least effective mode of instruction, the presentational mode is the predominant mode of instruction in many elementary-school classrooms.

ACTIVITY

Divide the class into two groups. Discuss the characteristics of the presentational mode in terms of

Group A: Issues that define approaches (chapter 1)
1. Teaching is directive/collaborative
2. Learners are viewed as passive/active
3. Language learning is viewed as teacher-to-student/an interactional group process
4. Atomistic/holistic

Group B: Parent-child interactions that facilitate language development
1. Intentionality
2. Proximal development
3. Collaboration
4. Internalization
5. Continuous development

Report to the class on which characteristics of the presentational mode appear to be in conflict with the criteria your group has examined.

Notice that some of the characteristics of the presentational mode and the assumptions upon which this mode rests are present in the minilesson and in teacher-student conferences in the process approach to teaching writing. There are three important differences:

1. The concepts treated in a minilesson and during conferences arise out of observations of what students appear to be trying to do with their writing. In the presentational mode, lessons are almost always presented in an easy-to-hard sequence (the teacher or curriculum expert's idea of what is easy and what is hard) and all students are presented with every lesson in the same order.
2. Minilessons and lessons taught in conference are brief. In the presentational mode the teacher-directed lesson usually takes up a major portion of class time.
3. There is not the expectation that every child will learn every concept on the day it is first presented, or even that every child will show much interest. In the presentational mode, the present-practice-evaluate paradigm reflects a much more directive notion of the teacher's role in the process of teaching writing.

❖ The Environmental Mode

A second widespread mode of writing instruction is referred to as the **environmental mode** of instruction. The following two lessons are examples of the environmental mode of instruction (Hillocks, 1986).

❖ Observing Teachers Teaching

The Environmental Mode I

A small group of students is presented with two seashells and is asked to write a description of one shell.

The shells and the writing are then passed to a second group. The second group decides which shell is described and picks out very useful details and those that were not useful or that were confusing in the task of choosing between the shells. The first group observes and listens as the second group evaluates the written description.

The two groups then discuss characteristics of details useful in describing objects.

All the students in both groups are then presented with two ears of corn. Each student is required to write an individual description of one ear of corn. These descriptions are collected and evaluated by the teacher in terms of how well the student used useful details as defined in the previous discussion.

Sounds, smells, conversations, scenes from movies, and so on are later used as data in this exercise.

The Environmental Mode II

Children plan to visit a site near their classroom—the school kitchen, the kindergarten room, or a nearby garden. In both whole-class and small-group discussion the students develop sets of questions they will want to answer in describing the site.

They discuss the way they will want to report specific details—not "a big room," but "a room twice as large as our classroom"; not "a messy table," but "a table with bits of old newspaper pasted to it, spattered with different-colored paint, and covered with scattered brushes, spilled sand, jars, and dishes."

After the visit, small groups write reports of their observations. The teacher presents each small-group report to the class on the overhead projector and leads a discussion of how well the group answered the questions that were developed before the visit and how well the group reported specific details such as those in the examples developed beforehand.

Characteristics

The environmental mode of instruction has six characteristics:
1. There are clear and specific objectives in the teacher's mind, but the objectives may not be clearly stated at the outset as is typical in the presentational mode.
2. Materials and problems are selected to engage students with one another in processes that are important in some forms of writing—for example, observing closely and supplying details in writing description.
3. Students engage in activities before writing, such as small-group, problem-solving discussions.
4. In contrast to the presentational mode, teacher lectures and teacher-led discussions are used minimally—usually only to introduce the problem or activity to the small groups and to summarize or draw generalizations after the groups have engaged in the activity or problem solving.
5. Principles and concepts are approached through concrete materials and problems. In working through these problems, the students are introduced to principles and concepts; they are engaged in using principles as they are introduced to them.
6. Students get feedback from peers as they use new principles and concepts in working through the assigned problem in small groups.

Assumptions

Hillocks lists five assumptions that underlie the environmental mode of instruction:

1. Teachers can and should actively seek to develop identifiable writing skills to learners.
2. Skills develop by using them orally before using them in writing.
3. A major function of prewriting activity is to teach identifiable skills.
4. Collaboration and feedback are beneficial, and perhaps necessary, to acquire many skills, concepts, and principles associated with writing.
5. Students acquire complex skills, concepts, and principles associated with writing through the collaboration and feedback inherent in solving carefully conceived problems with small groups of peers.

> **ACTIVITY**
>
> Divide the class into two groups. Discuss the characteristics of the environmental mode in terms of
>
> Group A: Issues that define approaches (chapter 1)
> 1. Teaching is directive/collaborative
> 2. Learners are viewed as passive/active
> 3. Language learning is viewed as teacher-to-student/an interactional group process
> 4. Atomistic/holistic
>
> Group B: Parent-child interactions that facilitate language development
> 1. Intentionality
> 2. Proximal development
> 3. Collaboration
> 4. Internalization
> 5. Continuous development
>
> Report to the class on which characteristics of the environmental mode appear to be in conflict with the criteria your group has examined.

The environmental mode of teaching writing has many things in common with small-group discussion and cooperative learning (chapter 4). It is unlike the process approach to teaching writing in that it is much more teacher directed. The teacher determines objectives, assigns tasks, and evaluates outcomes in terms of stated criteria.

The environmental mode is popular among upper-grade and high-school teachers because it is conducive to the demands of content area writing. This is because the teacher wants the students to learn to write through "doing" science, and to learn science through writing. The same is, of course, true for social studies, math, and so on. If students have complete ownership of their writing, the chances that they will choose topics that accomplish both these goals are very slim, particularly since the curriculum for content area subjects is somewhat inflexible.

For this reason a judicious blend of the writing process approach and the environmental mode is undoubtedly desirable in the middle and upper grades.

Summary

Although people who have studied writing have proposed different models of the process, researchers agree in general that the writing cycle consists of four stages: (1) prewriting, (2) writing, (3) rewriting, and (4) sharing. However, the writing cycle should not be viewed as an ordered set of steps. Composing is not a linear process. Writers often reread, edit, revise, stop to collect new facts, formulate new ideas, and even change their topics while they write.

Early experiences with writing reflects many characteristics of children's spoken language: brief texts, simple syntax, accompanying external activity, and the assumption that the audience shares the writer's knowledge. However, children are aware at an early age that there are differences between spoken and written language. Asked to read back their "writing" (scribbles, drawings, or letters), kindergartners intonate their stories as if they were reading published texts.

A conspicuous trait of young and inexperienced writers is egocentricity. They are confident that what they produce will be meaningful to others and assume that their readers share their experiences and knowledge. When classmates and teachers confer on writing, the audience asks questions about what is unclear, and young writers begin to recognize the readers' needs. This process is referred to as "overcoming egocentricity," "decentering," and "achieving detachment." Revision is an attempt to translate writer-based prose to reader-based prose in order to meet the needs of the audience while accomplishing communication goals.

Teachers need to create a variety of purposes for writing so that students will gain experiences in using the narrative, descriptive, expository, and persuasive modes of discourse.

Atwell's writing workshop is one examples of the writing process approach to teaching writing. It features minilessons, status of the class conferences, content conferences, peer conferences, editing conferences, evaluation conferences, group share, and publishing. Student ownership of writing, the use of writing folders, and conferencing are prominent features of the writing process approach to teaching writing.

The more traditional approach to teaching writing is referred to as the presentational mode of instruction. It is characterized by clearly stated specific objectives, lectures, teacher-led discussions, presentation of models, specific assignments, and corrected feedback. It is the least efficacious mode of teaching writing.

A third method of instruction is referred to as the environmental mode. It is characterized by guiding objectives (not always stated), materials that engage students in process, minimal lectures or teacher-led discussion, concepts approached through concrete problems, and feedback from peers throughout the process. The environmental mode of teaching writing is like cooperative learning in that it encourages students to collaborate but remains teacher-directed. For this reason it is associated with writing in the content areas. I recommend using it in addition to the writing process approach.

For Review and Discussion

1. Think back to your recent writing experiences. Describe your writing processes using the terminology and concepts introduced in this chapter.
2. Recall your history as a writer from your earliest memories to the pres-

ent. Describe your progress using the terminology and concepts used in this chapter.

3. Discuss the dimensions of growth in writing: (a) Writing becomes less like spoken language. (b) Writers overcome egocentricity. (c) Writers achieve critical detachment. (d) Writers engage in a greater variety of forms and modes of discourse.

4. Describe Atwell's three types of minilessons.

5. Describe the following types of conferences: state of the class, content, peer, editing, and evaluation. What purpose does each serve?

6. Discuss the concept of ownership in the presentational, environmental, and writing process modes of teaching writing.

7. Discuss the advantages to using conferences as a format for teaching writing.

8. Relate the presentational, environmental, and process approach modes of teaching writing to the two approaches to teaching language arts developed in chapter 1: the skills emphasis approach and the holistic, collaborative, integrated approach.

For Further Reading

Barrs, M. (1987). Voice and role in reading and writing. *Language Arts, 64,* 207–218.

Fox, M. (1988). Notes from the battlefield: Towards a theory of why people write. *Language Arts, 65,* 112–125.

Freeman, E. (1991). Informational books: Models for student report writing. *Language Arts, 68,* 470–473.

Guilbault, J. (1988). Between the lines: An affective look at real-life writing in the classroom. *Language Arts, 65,* 461–464.

Lendfors, J. (1988). From "talking together" to "being together in talk." *Language Arts, 65,* 135–141.

Peters, B. (1989). What sixth graders can teach us about form and competence. *Language Arts, 66,* 171–183.

Sanford, B. (1988). Writing reflectively. *Language Arts, 65,* 652–657.

Spaulding, C. (1989). Understanding ownership and the unmotivated writer. *Language Arts, 66,* 414–422.

Sudol, D., & Sudol, P. (1991). Another story: Putting Graves, Calkins and Atwell into practice and perspective. *Language Arts, 68,* 292–300.

Talbot, B. (1990). Writing for learning in school: Is it possible? *Language Arts, 67,* 47–56.

Voss, M. (1988). The light at the end of the journal: A teacher learns about learning. *Language Arts, 65,* 669–674.

CHAPTER 9

Methods, Lessons, and Strategies for Teaching Writing

Introduction
The Prewriting Stage
    Activity
TO THINK ABOUT: Conversation and Prewriting
    Activities
The Writing Stage
Lesson Plan: The Green Monster
The Rewriting Stage: Revising

TO THINK ABOUT: "Tidy" and "Messy" Writing—The Revision Process
    Activities
The Rewriting Stage: Editing
The Sharing/Publishing Stage
Summary
For Review and Discussion
For Further Reading

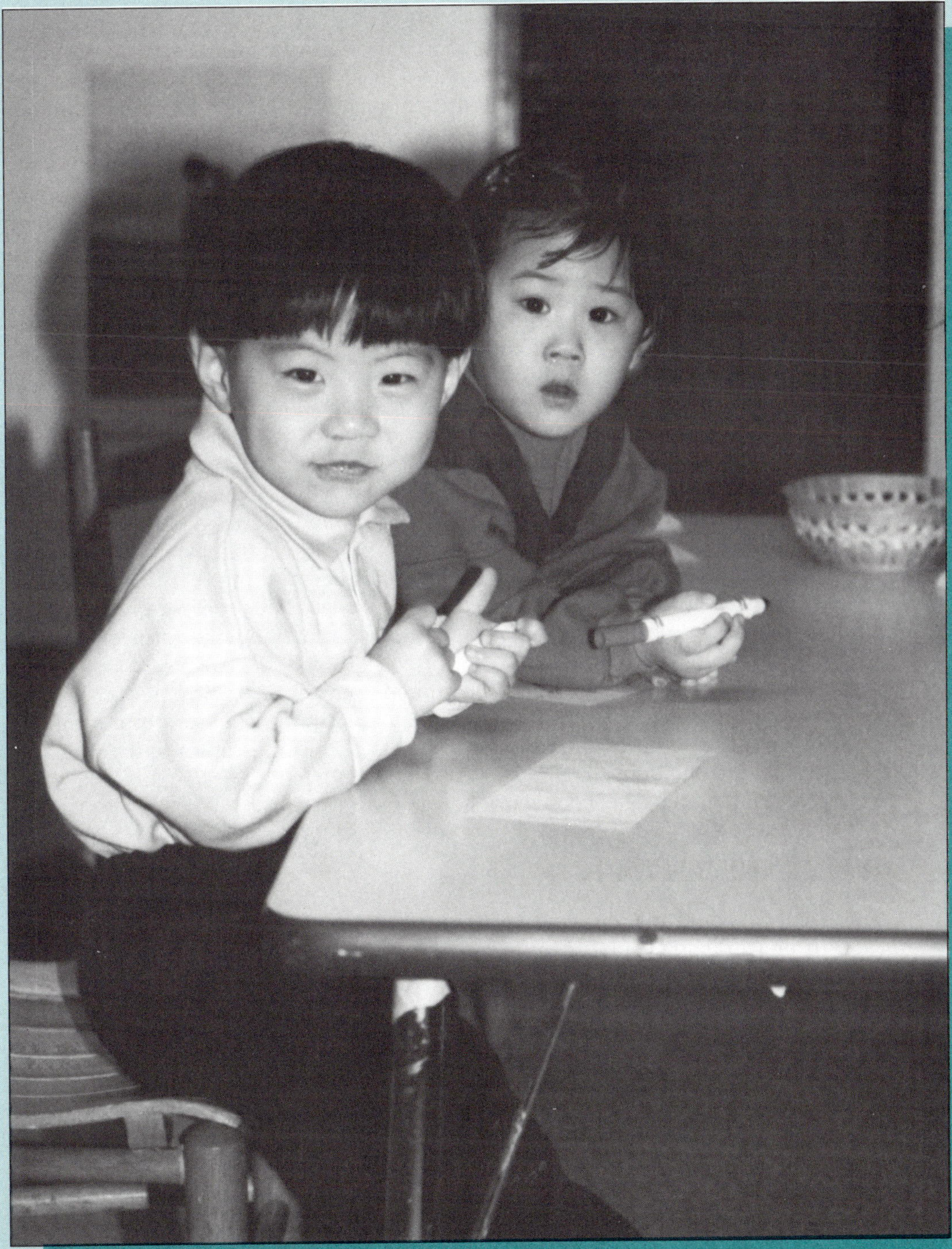

INTRODUCTION

Whether instruction occurs during conferences, during minilessons, or in small groups, there are things that developing writers need to learn and that teachers need to teach. In this chapter I will present teaching ideas and strategies related to the prewriting, writing, revising, editing, and publishing stages of the writing cycle.

THE PREWRITING STAGE

Hollman (1981) reports that professionals who regularly write as part of their work confirm "the existence and importance of the prewriting or incubation stage of the composing process" (p. 27). Some write out ideas to discover what they have to say. Some talk to colleagues. Almost all report that during this process they regularly discover things they knew or thought, but of which they were not conscious. Professional writers often look at a completed piece of writing and are able to recall thoughts, speculations, conversations, snatches of earlier writing, and things they have read (stretching back for years) that all might be considered as part of the prewriting process for that particular piece.

In school, prewriting may be considered as everything that happens up to the time the child writes the first word on the page. The process may differ as a function of the writer's personality, skill, and topic and the form of writing being considered.

The teacher's role in helping children gain facility with the prewriting stage of the writing process involves helping children choose a topic, collect their thoughts, and organize their thoughts. Choosing topics and collecting thoughts are open-ended, generative activities. Organizing thoughts takes discipline and knowledge of conventional forms of writing.

❖ **Modeling Choosing a Topic**

Teachers should model every stage of the writing process. Recently, as guest writing workshop leader in an inner-city eighth-grade class, I gathered the students into a circle and began:

> It's writing time, and the first thing I have to do is decide what I will write today. I thought about this as I was driving down here today. I could always write a letter to my daughter who is away at school. I'll jot that down on my pad. I'm also working on a story about something I did when I was about ten—a Halloween prank that resulted in a automobile accident—and how scared I was, first because I didn't know if anyone got hurt and then because they might find out I did it. I also have to write a report about a retreat that I was in charge of for my church. I guess those are enough ideas to choose from today.
>
> Now we are all going to be writing for the next twenty minutes. What ideas do you have that you might write about?

As volunteers offered suggestions I jotted them down on the board—letters to relatives (the influence of the teacher's suggestion was obvious), a story about the death of a dog, a description of a person that you'd pity (I suspected that this was an assignment given by the regular English teacher and commented that students were permitted to write on any topic—even topics assigned for other classes, if they chose).

After several suggestions were on the board I asked each student to write down at least three topics that he or she might write on.

> OK, now we have to decide what to write on today. I don't think I'll write a letter to my daughter in this class because everything we write in this class will go into our folders, and we'll share what's in our folders with one another. I want to be able to say things to my daughter that are none of your business. [Humor intended.] I may even be talking about you in letters by the time the semester is over. [More humor intended.] Then there's the report I have to write. I really should have my records of how many people were at the retreat and that sort of thing when I write that. Of course I could write the report and leave blanks where I don't have the exact facts.
>
> But I think what I would most enjoy writing about is the Halloween prank, so I'll work on that today. Chandra, could you read the topics you've written down and tell us which one you'll write about today?

I asked Chandra to give reasons why she chose the one topic and why she chose not to write on the other topics and engaged in a similar dialogue with several other students. After all students agreed that they had chosen topics, I continued:

> All right. Put your lists of topics into your folders. We'll be doing more with it later. Now, for the next twenty minutes, I'm going to be writing and I expect all of you to be writing. Well, that's not quite true; I'm going to begin writing now but in a few minutes I'm going to walk around and see how all of you are doing. Then I may come back to my writing.

❖ Planning

During the planning stage the writer gathers information relative to the topic and begins to organize it. This is what Murray (1980) refers to as collecting and connecting. Authorities dating back to 1917 (Leonard, 1917; Carlson, 1970; Murray 1973, 1978) have recommended that teachers encourage students to talk about their topics and what they might do with them before they begin to write and to confer with students while they are writing. The following activities have been shown to be beneficial to writers at the planning stage.

Brainstorming

A brainstorming session is designed to produce as many different ideas as possible. In an ideal brainstorming session there are about six people whose thinking is as unalike as possible. Ideas are not judged—they are accepted uncritically.

Far-out responses are encouraged since they widen the universe of possible responses. In warmup sessions, or in sessions to teach brainstorming, the questions are intended to allow for a wide variety of responses. How many things can you do with a paper clip? How could you make a homeless person a little better off? The teacher is not in the room when class starts; what could have happened to him?

The teacher acts as a scribe, writing ideas as quickly as possible on the chalkboard. Spontaneity and rapid-fire responses are encouraged. As the volume of responses diminishes, the teacher encourages one last outlandish round of responses.

As a prewriting activity, brainstorming may be used by the entire class to suggest topics for writing or to generate ideas for a topic that several members of the class are writing on. This technique is frequently used for teacher-assigned topics. Individuals might also ask a small group to brainstorm for ideas related to their individual topics. "In my story someone has laid a trap that several people might have fallen victim to—like putting poison in the milk dispenser in the lunch room or weakening the handrail on a staircase. My story takes place in a school. What might the trap be?"

Key Words

In listing key words the writer or a group of writers lists words that will almost certainly appear in writing about a particular topic, but will probably not appear in writing on other topics. In writing about newspapers, for example, the words *column* and *headline* will almost certainly appear, but so will the words *the* and *in*. On the other hand, the words *column* and *headline* are unlikely to appear in writing about other topics.

Free Association

In free association, the writer (or writing group) lists words or phrases that come to mind when key words related to topics are presented: *reporter, gossip column, headline, editorial, editor, publisher,* and so on. This technique is similar to semantic mapping.

Listing key words and free-associating are two ways of activating a writer's memory of words associated with a topic. They are different from brainstorming because there is some criteria for "correct" responses. However, associations are sometimes so idiosyncratic that they resemble brainstorming.

These are techniques that enable teachers to stimulate prewriting processes. Experimental studies verify that these techniques produce writing that is better by various measures of writing quality (Kock, 1972; Anderson, Bereiter, & Smart, 1980).

Brainwriting

In brainwriting, the class is divided into groups of three or four students. The topic is given as in brainstorming and students are instructed to write as many ideas as they can. After a brief time, the teacher calls time and students put their lists into the center of the table. Then each student takes another student's list. The students silently read the ideas on the paper they have and add new ideas, building on the ideas already listed. This process may be repeated. Finally, the group examines all the lists and develops one list, adding new ideas that may be generated in this group process. Each group reports its final list to the class. Once again, this activity resembles brainstorming, but it permits less spontaneity and encourages building on other ideas to a greater degree than brainstorming. Noyce and Christie (1989) suggest this activity, not to replace brainstorming, but as an alternative to enrich the brainstorming activity.

Free Writing

The directions for free writing are as follows: Start writing and keep writing. Follow your ideas wherever they lead you. Don't go back to revise or reword. Keep writing for a specified time—often ten minutes. If you cannot think of anything to say, write what you see in front of you, or repeat the last sentence you wrote until something else comes to you, or write "I cannot think of anything more to say" over and over until something else comes to you.

According to Elbow (1981), the benefits are these: (1) Free writing makes writing easier by helping you with the root psychological difficulty in writing—finding words in your head and putting them down on paper. (2) It helps students learn to write when they don't feel like writing. (3) It helps them produce written language in the way they produce spoken language—without thinking about it. (4) It helps them to get on paper those ideas and feelings that are blocking their attempts to write about their chosen topic. (5) It helps them find topics to write about. Myers (1983) claims that by simply filling pages with free writing, students learn that writing helps them discover what they know, what they don't know, and, in fact, what they want to write about.

Free writing is a little like brainstorming, except there is not even a question or topic constraining your output. You write whatever comes into your head.

Focused Free Writing

Focused free writing is a little more like solitary brainstorming. The directions for focused free writing are as follows: Keep X (an assigned topic) in mind. Start writing and continue writing. Follow digressions out, then return to X. Keep writing. Do not go back to reword or revise. After ten minutes, or any other specified time, reflect on what you have written and sum up the main point in an assertive statement. The writing step of focused free writing is a collecting step. The summing-up step is a connecting step.

Free writing has other advantages. It permits students to write a great deal without fear of criticism or grades; it stimulates fluency; it teaches students that they do have things to write about—that they are the source of writing. It demonstrates to students why Frank Smith's (1982) third myth is a myth: "Writing involves transferring thoughts from the mind to paper." Students learn instead that thoughts are created in the act of writing.

> **ACTIVITY**
>
> Divide the class into five groups. In each group assign appropriate roles and engage in the assigned technique(s) for three to five minutes. Prepare to do the following:
>
> 1. Do a two- or three-minute demonstration of the technique(s).
> 2. Report to the class any problems you encountered or insights you gained into the technique (if any)—particularly those not treated in the text.
> 3. Ask the class for feedback: Did your group understand the technique properly? Did it show how techniques differed from one another—particularly when the differences were subtle?
>
> Group A. Model Choosing a Topic
> Group B. Brainstorming, Key Words, Free Associations
> Group C. Brainwriting
> Group D. Free Writing
> Group E. Focused Free Writing

Discussion

One of the most widely used activities for collecting and connecting ideas during the prewriting stage of the writing cycle is discussion—both teacher-led class discussion and small-group discussion. Review the section on Discussion in chapter 3 and the section on Small-Group Discussion in chapter 4.

TO THINK ABOUT

Discussion and Prewriting

Review the material in chapters 3 and 4 on teacher-led discussion and small-group discussion. What concepts are relevant to collecting and connecting in the prewriting stage of the writing cycle? Consider "Using Discussion to Clarify Thoughts," "Conducting a **Teacher-led** Discussion," and "Teacher Neutrality in a **Teacher-led** Discussion" in chapter 3 and "Some Basic Observations about Small Groups" in chapter 4.

✣ Discovery Strategies

Prewriting activities help writers call on their own resources. Even very young writers know a vast amount, but in order to use it they have to retrieve what they know, combine old knowledge and experience in new ways, and fit new knowledge and experience with the old. Finding ways to retrieve what we already know and to decide what we need to find out has been called "invention" in classical rhetoric, "discovery" in modern rhetoric. Some contemporary experts on the writing process call this process "heuristics," a word that comes from the same root as *Eureka!* Using lists, questions, and "cubing" are three discovery strategies.

Lists

Lists are records of names, words, or concepts that are generated by some controlling concept, such as things needed for a picnic, ballplayers who batted over 300, Shakespeare's comedies, things found in a medicine cabinet, and things I know about giant turtles. Many professional writers use lists to generate ideas and organize their thoughts. After creating the list, writers begin to look for some way to group items.

The semantic mapping exercises described in chapter 7 are a form of list-making. Things known about raccoons are written on spokes emanating from the word that represents the controlling concept. Later, words belonging on the same spoke are gathered together, and the new map shows the relationships graphically. Similarly, lists can be turned into outlines.

In fact, many techniques for collecting and organizing what readers know about a subject in preparation for reading (see chapter 7) are very similar to techniques for collecting and organizing what writers know in preparation for writing. The purpose is the same as well—to retrieve what is known, to combine old knowledge and experience in new ways, and to fit new knowledge and experience with the old.

Questions

Teachers of college composition are familiar with "invention techniques" or "discovery procedures" that take the form of a list of questions. One that may be introduced to children as young as middle-graders is the conventional five *W*'s known to every journalism student—and which can be seen behind every story on television news: *who, what, when, where,* and *why?* I personally favor a slight variation on this, by adding *how.*

> Who did it?
> What did they do?
> When, where, how, and why did they do it?

Variations on these questions abound:

> Who did it/to whom was it done?
> What happened/to whom did it happen?
> When, where, how, and why did it happen?

Another variation is to have students simply write their titles or subjects on the top line of their papers and write twelve questions beginning with the words *who, what, when, where, how,* and *why,* and write the answers to their questions. As they write and answer questions other questions may present themselves. The next step is to put the answers into a good order for telling—collecting is followed by connecting.

Cubing

This discovery procedure is called cubing because it has six parts (as a cube has six sides) and it is a way of viewing a subject from different angles (as a cube can be turned over and viewed from different perspectives). The idea is to take a subject and examine it in six ways. Students are instructed to write their subjects on the top line of their papers and to write for two or three minutes in response to each of the following directions, skipping a line between responses.

1. Describe it. Name it. Give its size, color, shape, surroundings, origin, and anything else that will give the reader a mental picture or definition of the subject.
2. Compare it. Tell what it is like. Think of how you described the subject (size, color, and so on) and tell how those characteristics are similar to other things.
3. Associate it. Tell what the subject makes you think about. Where is it found? Where did you first hear about it? What people are associated with it? What jobs, activities, tools, or time of the year is associated with it?
4. Analyze it. What are its parts? How are they put together? What uses does it have? How are its uses related to one another?
5. Apply it. What do you usually do with the subject? What could you possibly do with it? What would you like to do with it?
6. Argue for or against it. Is it a good thing or a bad thing? Should it remain? Should there be more of them? Give your reasons.

The next step in this approach is for writers to choose the items they want to include in writing a paper and to put them in order; after collecting the writer begins connecting.

The way subjects are worded can make a big difference in the usefulness of this approach. "Should junk food be served in the school cafeteria?" would be a difficult topic to work with, but "junk food" would work very well.

Graser (1983) suggests producing a real cube with one of the six directions—describe it, compare it, and so on—printed on each side. Turning the cube over every two minutes as the new direction on the top surface is read to the class might be good way to symbolize the turning over of a subject in the mind as we collect and connect in the prewriting stage.

ACTIVITY

Divide the class into three groups. In each group assign appropriate roles and engage in the assigned strategy for three to five minutes. Prepare to do the following:

> **ACTIVITY (continued)**
>
> 1. Do a two- or three-minute demonstration of the strategy.
> 2. Report to the class any problems you encountered or insights you gained into the strategy (if any)—particularly those not treated in the text.
> 3. Ask the class for feedback: Did your group understand the strategy properly? Did it show how strategies differed from one another or from other prewriting techniques—particularly when the differences were subtle?
>
> Group A. Lists
> Group B. Questions
> Group C. Cubing

The prewriting techniques and discovery strategies described here are designed to help children in the prewriting stage to collect ideas and plan. They should not be taught to young writers as lists of steps to be memorized. They can be used as minilessons or suggested to individuals or groups in conferences. These techniques should be understood by and easily available to elementary-school writing teachers so that they can be suggested in response to individual writing problems. Teachers should be familiar enough with these ideas to be able to say, "Have you got a topic but can't get started? Why not try brainstorming or cubing with three or four other students? If one doesn't work, try the other, or how about...."

THE WRITING STAGE

Researchers and teachers who observe students in the process of producing a draft agree with Frank Smith (1982): Writing is not easy. Writers do not get it right the first time. The activity of writing is not sedentary, not silent, not solitary, not tidy. The process of writing is not the same for everyone.

Graves (1975) classified seven-year-old writers as reactive or reflective. Reactive writers need to rehearse before they write. They may draw, paint, build, or talk to others or themselves as a form of rehearsal for writing. They often talk or subvocalize while writing and therefore produce fewer words per minute while writing than reflective writers do. They write one sentence at a time, giving little evidence of planning beyond the next sentence or building on previous sentences. The sequence of ideas is apt to be jumbled. They are not interested in proofreading, revising, sharing, or publishing.

Seven-year-old reflective writers, according to Graves (1975), are constantly rehearsing as they read, watch TV, talk to others, daydream, and so on. They write rapidly and silently. Their ideas are connected and their writing moves toward a conclusion. They sometime rephrase what they have written.

They draw illustrations after they write. Graves believes that reflective writers possess more highly developed writing and problem-solving skills than reactive writers.

Studies of older writers have consistently shown that strong writers pay greater attention to matters of content and organization whereas weaker writers tend to be preoccupied with mechanics—particularly spelling (Bechtel, 1979; Metzger, 1977; Pianko, 1979; Sawkins, 1971; Stiles, 1977). This suggests, of course, that students be encouraged to concentrate on content and organization in the drafting stage of the process, and they must be reassured that these matters that concern them so greatly will be attended to at the appropriate time—during the editing stage.

Hillocks has suggested (1986, p. 28) that the reason strong writers are not concerned with mechanics and spelling is that they have mastered these skills, and that weak writers are concerned with mechanics and spelling because they have not mastered these skills. This interpretation cannot be ruled out, and it is a reminder that helping students achieve this mastery is an important responsibility of teachers. Nevertheless the same strategy (to encourage students to concentrate on content and organization while drafting and to reassure them that these matters will be attended to during the editing stage) appears to be appropriate.

An important message to get across to students is that a first draft is temporary, tentative, and exploratory. Writers write sentences out fully if that style is appropriate to the way the writing is going. If ideas are coming fast, they may use abbreviations, spell words as well as they can, jot notes to themselves about information that will need filling in (for example, "put names of three other players here" or "explain the rules of the game here"). They may even ignore punctuation and not bother about grammar and usage niceties at this point.

I once heard a political writer say that in first drafts he uses four-letter words and makes slanderous, outrageous, and insupportable charges. He cleans up his language and takes fair play and libel laws into consideration only after he has expressed in a loud, angry voice what he believes to be the facts and his opinion of them. Young writers should learn to do something comparable to this. Get it out and worry about conventions and even strict accuracy later.

The following strategies address student development in the writing stage of the writing cycle:

❖ Conferencing

Teaching done by conferencing during the writing phase of the writing cycle was discussed in chapter 8. Conferences permit teachers to engage in a process that facilitates progress in writing. This process is similar to scaffolding—the process described in chapter 2 that facilitates progress in spoken language. Teacher (and peer) responses during writing conferences help children overcome egocentricity and achieve detachment.

✣ Developing Fluency

Graves observed that when primary-aged children are encouraged to write—as Ashley was encouraged to write (see chapter 6)—writing resembles play. "Children are quite pleased with their own competence and they experiment fearlessly with the new medium, given a small amount of encouragement" (Graves, 1981, p. 179). Primary teachers capitalize on this fearlessness in ways like the following:

Playlike Writing

Teachers distribute pencils, felt-tip pens, crayons, lined and unlined paper, notebooks, and notepads around the room and encourage children to write during free-play time. Children are encouraged to write their names, letters of the alphabet, and captions for art work. They are encouraged to write "props" for their spontaneous dramatic play—"Mother" writes a grocery list, "the doctor" writes a prescription, and "the police officer" writes a traffic ticket. After group dictation of language-experience stories, teachers take individual dictation of experience stories from students. Some children who tire of waiting their turn write their own. All efforts at writing—scribbles, invented spellings, and so on—are praised and responded to as meaningful written language.

World-class musicians, athletes, artists, and scientists frequently report that their earliest experiences in their chosen fields were playful ones, free of the severe discipline that they eventually adopted. "The same may be true for writers—that positive play experiences in early attempts at writing are important to develop high-level commitment to the task" (Hillocks, 1986, p. 11).

Functional Writing

Starting in the primary grades children can be expected to sign in when they arrive at school and sign up for turns at the painting easel or for a teacher conference. Children are encouraged to write invitations to class plays and parties, notes to the custodian, and lists of supplies needed and make signs stating classroom rules.

Interactive Writing

Hall and Duffy (1987) suggest "dialogue journals" to help link writing with oral language and to promote spontaneity in writing. The teacher and child share a sheet of paper or page of a notebook (journal), taking turns and responding to one another's writing. These authors found that when children were asked questions, they gave brief, stilted replies. For example:

> Teacher: Did you do anything nice on Sunday?
> Child: No. (p. 526)

Personal declarative statements got better results:

Teacher: I am upset today.
  Child: What is the matr with you?
Teacher: My dog is sick. I took her to the vet and he gave her some medicine.
  Child: I hope she get betr sun did the medsn wok. (p. 527)

Dictation by Writers

Group and individual dictation of stories by beginning writers as in the language experience approach to beginning reading instruction (see chapter 6) enables them to compose without the onerous task of forming letters, spelling words, and so on. For older students dictation into tape recorders serves the same purpose.

Forms That Are Fun and Easy to Follow

Another way of helping writers attain fluency is to encourage them to engage in forms of writing that are fun—where form is amusing and simple and easy to follow. Numerous such forms of writing are described in chapter 11.

Temporary, Tentative, and Experimental First Drafts

Older writers find getting started difficult. They often believe their first draft is their only draft and they want it to be perfect. They worry about mechanics. They may have learned that they must write a strong lead and are overwhelmed by the task of writing a lead to a paper that is not clear in their minds. A major objective of the process approach to teaching writing (chapter 8) is to help children to see their first draft as temporary, tentative, and experimental. Accomplishing this goal brings a student a long way toward fluency.

Returning to the Prewriting Stage

A closely related objective of the process approach to teaching writing is to help students see the writing cycle as recursive. Writers "stuck" in the writing stage sometimes need only realize that they can return to the prewriting stage of collecting and connecting and that brainstorming, free writing, cubing, and other strategies appropriate during prewriting are appropriate even after writing the first draft has begun.

✤ Developing Criteria for Good Writing

A lesson like the following was developed by Sager (1973) for use with sixth graders and was used successfully with gifted second and third graders.

LESSON PLAN: The Green Monster

The class is divided into groups of five students and each group is given the following story to read.

THE REWRITING STAGE: REVISING 269

> The Green Monster came down to America. He didn't have a mouth. "Who goes?" they said. There was no answer. So they shot at him and he ran away.
>
> The class is told that on a scale of 0–3 this story scores 0 for elaboration or details. Student groups are instructed to do the following:
>
> 1. List all the places the Green Monster might have come from. All the reasons it might have come to America. All the possibilities of who "they" might be. All the thoughts "they" might have had when they saw the monster. All the places the monster might have run to.
> 2. When the groups have created their lists, the teacher says, "To be interesting and easy to understand, a story needs details such as you have written. Add some of these details to the story and take turns telling the story the way you would have written it."

Exercises like this one are designed to introduce qualities of good writing, such as *elaboration* in the case of The Green Monster. Once students understand the quality that is under consideration, the teacher presents stories that are rated 0, 1, 2, and 3 and leads a discussions of how these stories differ in terms of that quality. Finally, sets of stories are given to small groups for group evaluation.

Additional qualities of good writing such as effective word choice, organization, and good leads are introduced in this manner and criteria for judging writing on these qualities are developed.

The two examples of the environmental mode of teaching writing presented in the last chapter (describing seashells and visiting a local site) are also examples of developing criteria for good writing. The environmental mode often results in developing criteria for good writing.

THE REWRITING STAGE: REVISING

✣ The Revising Process

Writers identify a goal: They want to tell a story, describe a scene, express their feelings, impart information, and so on. They decide more or less what they want to say and begin a temporary, tentative, exploratory draft. As they write they discover what they really know and think about the topic, how it really fits together, and what they really want to say. As they write, they repeatedly ask themselves two questions:

1. Does it say what I want to say?
2. Will it say to the reader what I want it to say?

The first question is the basis for "internal revision"; the latter question is the basis for "external revision" (Graser, 1983).

Internal Revision

Revision is made possible when the writer is able to look at the text as something separate from his or her intended meaning. A writer can mean one thing but produce a text that fails to convey that meaning or that means something different. In the process of writing, knowledge and opinions that the writer was not fully conscious of at the outset often become apparent, and the writer's intended meaning changes, so the question needs to be repeated during the composing stage. Does the text say what I intend to say *now*? This private and introspective process depends on the writer's ability to view a draft as temporary, tentative, and exploratory. The text may be indecipherable to others but mean to the author what he or she wants to say. A list of words and phrases numbered in the right order or a paragraph full of abbreviations may convey to the writer exactly what he or she wants to say.

External Revision

To engage in external revision the writer must step back, reach for detachment, and consider the reader, the intended meaning, and the text, and ask him- or herself if the text will convey the intended meaning to the reader. Will the reader's attitude toward the writer be what the writer intends? External revision depends on the writer's ability to overcome egocentricity (in the Piagetian sense) and think about what the readers probably know, what they need to be told, what their attitudes are, and how such things as choice of words, poor spelling, and neatness will affect the readers' attitude toward the meaning and the writer.

Internal and external revision are two components of the revising process. A third component is to change the text—to manipulate the written language so that it will accomplish the writer's purposes. Teaching children the process of revision must address all three components of the process.

Boiarsky (1980) observed revising activities of professional writers—including herself. While revising, professional writers alter form, reorganize material, create transitions, delete material, expand information, emphasize ideas, subordinate ideas, create closer contact to the reader, improve syntactic structure, improve language use, and clean up!

❖ Observations of Students' Revising

The capacity to revise depends on the ability to step back from the process and view the writer (oneself), the reader, the message, and the text from outside the process. This is a very difficult task for young children. Chomsky (1981) observed that children "look through language to meaning, rather than at language" (p. 609). They have a difficult time understanding that what they write is a separate entity from what they mean.

Graves (1983) found that beginning writers tend to focus their revision efforts on mechanics of writing—spelling, handwriting, appearance, capitalization, and punctuation. As writers mature, revisions begin to involve addition, deletion, and reorganization of information, and refocusing of topic. However, some writers apparently never progress beyond revision of mechanics.

Calkins (1980a) observed seventeen third graders while they were revising their own work and when they were asked to add information to a composition written by Calkins. She classified four kinds of drafting behavior:

Random Drafting

These writers wrote successive drafts without looking back at earlier drafts. Changes seemed arbitrary. When asked to add information to the teacher-constructed composition, they added it at the end, instead of where it belonged.

Refining

These students recopied drafts making the handwriting neater, changing spelling, and occasionally adding a sentence. Aside from cosmetic changes, between 75 percent and 99 percent of their final drafts were identical to their first drafts. When asked to add information to the teacher-constructed composition, they appeared to struggle with where to put the new information, but finally wrote a new draft without consulting the prepared draft.

Transition

These students recopied as did refiners, but were not satisfied with the results. They often wrote new drafts that bore little resemblance to the original. When asked to add information to the teacher-constructed composition, they inserted it in the appropriate place.

Interacting

These writers allowed what they had written to prompt new ideas and used carets, arrows, and so on to indicate where new information and reformulated ideas should go. When asked to add information to the teacher-constructed composition, they asked if they could change other parts of the composition and did so, adding details and reformulations. According to Calkins, "For these children, revision results from interaction between writer and draft, between writer and internalized audience, between writer and evolving subject. Children reread to see what they have said and to discover what they want to say" (p. 340).

Only about one in ten of the third-grade children in Calkin's study were classified as random drafters, and nearly two out of ten were already at the interacting stage.

Bridwell (1980), who studied the revising behavior of twelfth graders, found that:

- overall, most revisions were of punctuation, spelling, and word choice
- some students wrote successful essays with little revision
- other high-rated essays showed revision in spelling, punctuation, word choice, and also at the phrase, clause, sentence, and multiple-sentence level
- poorly rated essays were simply recopied or revised only at the spelling, punctuation, and word choice level

Faigley and Witte (1986) found that only 12 percent of the changes made by poor college-aged writers affected meaning. Thirty-three percent of the changes made by good writers of college age and older affected meaning.

After reviewing the literature of student revising practices, Hillocks (1986) states:

> We know that younger children and even many college students confine their revisions to the cosmetic, lexical, and clause or phrase levels. We know that text level changes [refocusing of the topic, reorganizing information, and so on], at least after some written text is produced, appears to be practically nonexistent . . . [and] that addition is a prominent strategy. (p. 44)

Very young writers are capable of revising at the text level (Calkin's third graders), but revision for most writers never reaches the text level. Among older students, the presence of revision at the text level is associated with good writing and the absence of revision or revision only at the cosmetic level is associated with poor writing. We must remember, however, that some good writing is produced without much revising. This is a reminder that there is not only one way in which to produce good writing. It may also indicate that good writers are not encouraged to revise—like Emig's twelfth-grade student who apparently never had a teacher who seemed interested enough in her ideas to encourage her to revise them.

❖ Teaching Strategies Associated with Revising

Modeling Revision

Experts going back over fifty years (Graves, 1978; LaBrant, 1955; Murray, 1978; Smith, 1983) have observed that it is important for teachers of writing to be writers, to write with children, and to share their processes of writing with children. In this way, teachers convey to students that writing is an interesting and worthwhile activity. They show students that a first draft is temporary, tentative, and exploratory, and that drafting is a different process from revising or preparing a revised draft for publication (editing).

Teachers who write with their students demonstrate the revision process. The most casual student observer can see that the teacher crosses out words and sentences, writes things in margins and draws arrows to show where they go, cuts out portions of texts and pastes them elsewhere, and so on. In occasional minilessons, teachers can do a "think aloud" revision of their writing, making explicit their reasons for crossing out, writing in the margins, and so on. For example:

> I realized that the two reasons I had listed were really the same [I changed my thinking after I wrote out what I thought], so I crossed out "There are two reasons why" and wrote "The reason why . . . . ," and I reworded the rest of the sentence.
> In my first draft I put a blank for the name of a town that I couldn't remember. I remembered the name of the town later, so I went back and wrote it in.
> I realized that people wouldn't understand what happened if they didn't know that my washer and dryer are on the second floor of my house, so I went back and put that in.

I have a presentation that I have done in middle- and upper-grade classrooms. I bring in the physical specimens of stages of my published book.

- notes on cards and scraps of paper
- handwritten pencil drafts that are erased, crossed out, cut apart, and stapled together
- typewritten drafts that are crossed out, cut apart, and stapled together
- printer's galleys with numerous corrections, a few crossed-out lines, and a few added lines on yellow paper, taped in at the appropriate places
- page proofs with few corrections and rare deletions and additions
- and finally the book with no changes (I do, however, show the students the one or two mistakes that escaped detection or were introduced over the numerous revisions, editings, and proofreadings that a published book is subjected to.)

Students are always amazed at how much revising goes into writing, editing, and publishing a book—how many words, sentences, paragraphs, and passages are changed, added, moved, or eliminated in the process. The message is that writing-in-process is temporary, tentative, and exploratory.

Students are often particularly taken by the fact that I plan chapters by making lists and numbering the items in the order I want them—which is almost never the order in which I have written them down—or by sorting notes into piles and putting the piles in the order I want them. I make my first outline *after* I have produced a draft of the entire chapter. If I cannot outline it easily, it needs revising.

As I discuss each of these stages I put the specimens on a single pile so that at the end the note cards are at the bottom and the book is at the top. I then liken this stack to an archeologist's dig. Each level is built on the previous level. At the bottom, disorganization is at its greatest. At each level upward, order becomes more apparent. It calls to mind Betty Flowers's (1981) madman, architect, carpenter, and judge.

TO THINK ABOUT

"Tidy" and "Messy" Writing—The Revision Process

Look at a term paper you are currently writing. What does it suggest about the truth of Frank Smith's assertion that it is a myth that writing is tidy? What does it suggest about the notion that there is only one right way to write? (Remember the variation that Emig found when she studied the writing methods of professional writers.) What does the advent of word processors and computers do to the process of editing and revision—to the "tidiness" or "messiness" of writing?

Think about how you write. Talk to your classmates about how they write. Do your methods and approaches vary? What does this suggest about the aptness of the writing process as an approach to teaching writing?

Teaching Qualities Expected in Particular Modes of Discourse

Repeatedly, over several lessons, Cohen and Scardamalia (undated) asked sixth graders to write opinion themes in class and introduced one or two diagnostic statements when the students had finished. The statements were (1) too few ideas; (2) part of the essay does not belong here; (3) introduction does not explain what the essay is about; (4) idea said in a clumsy way; (5) conclusion does not explain ideas; (6) incomplete idea; (7) ignored a strong point on the other side; (8) weak reason; and (9) needs an example to explain the idea. These statements suggested criteria for judging qualities that are expected in opinion themes.

After the teacher led the class in a discussion applying the criteria to sample essays, the students applied the criteria to their own essays and revised them. The authors reported an increase in the amount of revision—especially in the area of "idea" revisions.

Checklists of criteria for good writing are often developed with student participation. An item on a second-grade checklist might be: "Does my story have a beginning, middle, and end?" An item on a seventh-grade checklist might be: "Did I use published expert opinion to back up my ideas?" These are further examples of teaching students the conventions of written discourse.

❖ Facilitating Revision through Content Conferences

At the emergent literacy stage children think their writing is great, and they have no doubt that the reader will understand and accept exactly what they intended to say. The teacher's objective at this stage is to help the child discover what can be done with writing. The teacher focuses on what the child is trying to accomplish and helps him or her to do it. Recall how Nigel's father's questions helped Nigel to remember parts of the report that he was leaving out (from the listener's point of view) and prompted the language that would remedy the situation. By bedtime, Nigel had a reasonably well formed story that could be understood by his listeners.

By talking to children about their writing, even when they are almost at the point of execution, parents and teachers can facilitate emergent literacy through a process similar to scaffolding. For example, Ashley and Bgooga's friend's teachers helped them establish the meaning they intended in their writing. As children grow older and their writing becomes more conventional this kind of support and teaching continues in conferences.

When Amy says to Tiffany, "Why didn't you tell what happened to the other mice? 'Cause how would I know that?" (Bissex, 1979) she is not only pointing out Tiffany's failure to appreciate her reader's point of view, but she is also suggesting a way to fix it—to manipulate the text by adding a sentence or two. This interaction is very similar to Nigel's father's saying, "Why did the man say, 'no'?" . . . implying " 'Cause how would Mommy [the intended audience] know that?"

Characteristics of parent-child interactions that facilitate development and the assumptions that underlie the concept of emergent literacy continue to apply throughout life as people gain facility with language and communication. Just the other day in a conference with an exceptionally able doctoral student, I made the following comment about her written dissertation proposal: "Oh, I see [in response to something she had just told me]. There are two kinds of magnet schools in Buffalo. I didn't know that, and that's why I didn't understand your selection procedure." I might have added, "Why didn't you tell me? 'Cause how would I know that?"

Conferences also give the teacher the opportunity to respond to other problems they detect in the writing—problems arising from the students' inexperience with the characteristics of written discourse. Atwell (1987, p. 96) suggests questions teachers might ask to help the writer become aware of these problems. For example:

- Do you have more than one story here? or What's the most important thing you're trying to say? (Written discourse is focused and topic-centered.)
- Where does your piece really begin? (In expository writing opening paragraphs introduce the topic, problem, or theme. They do not ramble.)
- Can you show how these people spoke? (In narratives, conversations are usually recorded as dialog with conventional form and punctuation.)
- What do you want the reader to know at the end of your piece? (Written discourse usually ends with a summary or explicitly stated conclusion.)

This can be compared to chapter 2 where I listed a similar series of questions that would help a student writer become aware that institutional writing is accurate, explicit, and not redundant.

Finally, conferences enable teachers to teach the meaning of terms such as "lead," "draft," and "tighten," and to teach children how to use revising devices such as carets, arrows, and cut-and-paste techniques. Krashen (1984) and Smith (1983) point out that these technical aspects of the writing and revising process cannot be learned through reading; they must be taught to students.

✤ Facilitating Revision through Peer Conferences

Teaching Students How to Function in Peer Conferences

Children need to be taught how to function profitably in peer conferences. The following two strategies have worked in helping children as young as second and third graders to function well in peer conferences.

In Group Paper Revision, the teacher writes a short paper on a topic that might have been chosen by members of the class. The paper has some obvious good qualities—it is funny or surprising, for example. It also has one or two obvious problems—it is confusing at one point, for example.

Using an overhead projector, the teacher projects the paper onto a screen and acts as the author. He reads the entire paper and asks for positive reactions. Children are encouraged to comment on the built-in good qualities—humor and surprise, in this case. They are then asked what questions they have about the paper. Where is it confusing? What might be done to remedy the confusion? Lists of questions such as those suggested in previous paragraphs can be made available and consulted for appropriate questions.

As a next step, teachers participate in small groups that engage in group paper revision of student papers. Student-authors read their papers and respond to positive reactions, questions, and suggestions. Teachers engage in such conferences with particularly able students while other students observe. Finally, true peer conferences without teacher participation commence.

Russell (1983) suggests questions that are a helpful guide for conferencing with sixth graders. For example:

1. What is your favorite part?
2. Which part are you having trouble with?
3. How did you feel?
4. Do you *show* feelings or events with examples, or do you only *tell* about them?
5. Does your lead sentence grab your audience?
6. What do you plan to do next with this piece of writing?

Group paper revision is a way of teaching children to respond to one another's papers, and it also makes them better readers of their own writing.

Another way to help children learn to function in peer conferences is known as the Circle Strategy. Crowhurst (1979) assigned third- and fifth-grade writers to small groups of three or four and provided them with forms on which to write (1) encouraging responses, (2) comments on content, and (3) suggestions for improvement. Students circulated papers so that each child's paper was read by the two or three other children in the group, and each reader attached his or her written encouraging responses, comments on content, and suggestions for improvement. Crowhurst found that written feedback lessens the likelihood of negative interactions between writers and readers, and that effective oral responses usually followed when groups had become comfortable with making and receiving written peer responses, comments, and suggestions.

Processing Peer Conferences

Follow-up evaluation of peer group sessions is essential. Older students can regularly use feedback forms such as the following:

> How well did the group listen to you as you read your paper?
> What good things did the group say about your paper?
> What questions did they ask?
> What suggestions did they make?
> Was the group extremely helpful, helpful, or somewhat helpful?

Whole-class discussion of the conference process can be based on such written conference evaluation forms. With younger students, teachers use similar questions in follow-up discussions in peer groups.

Teaching More Mature Responses to More Mature Students

Responses to the writing of older students should let the writer know (1) that the audience was listening attentively, (2) what the audience wants to know more about, and (3) how the writing affected the audience.

Summarizing, paraphrasing, and restating are ways of letting the writer know that the audience was listening or reading attentively. Elbow suggests simply repeating words or phrases from the writing that "stick out," that seem effective or noteworthy, as a way of letting the writer know that the reader (listener) was paying attention and giving the writer a sense of how his or her words affected the reader (listener).

As with younger writers, responses should let the writer know what was puzzling or what the reader (listener) wants to know more about. This enables the writer to determine whether the writing was understood.

In order to let the writer know how the writing affected the reader (listener), Elbow suggests that the reader (listener) gives "movies" of his or her mind. For example, "At first I was confused. . . . I wondered if that was supposed to be funny. . . . I didn't think that was true. . . . I was surprised. . . ." Readers (listeners) do not give their opinions of the writing. They tell what they are thinking as they read or listen.

Another of Elbow's techniques for letting the writer know how his or her words affect the reader (listener) is to invent similes and metaphors for how the writing "sounds." For example, "It sounds like angry shouting," or "At first it was giving facts like the evening news, but then it was whining."

Notice that these responses are not simple requests for more information like Amy's "Why didn't you tell . . . ? 'Cause how would I know that?" These responses tell the writer how the listener/reader *feels* about the writing. The writer might hear, "It sounded angry, but in a couple of places I wanted to laugh." The writer might have meant to sound angry, but want to know why the reader wanted to laugh, at what point, and for what reason.

Of course, these responses and the writer's responses to them reflect a great deal of maturity and understanding of the function of writing conferences.

Teachers should learn to make such responses and help children learn to profit from them. By the time students reach the upper grades, they should be able to deal with such responses and some students will be able to make such responses in peer conferences. In minilessons, conferences, and sharing groups, students should be learning to become good writers and good teachers of writing.

> **ACTIVITY**
>
> Divide the class into four groups. Each group should report on the relevance of the following topics (addressed in chapters 3 and 4) to facilitate revision through peer conferences.
>
> Group A. Attitudes and Values Necessary for Discussion (chapter 3)
>   Learning to Deal with Criticism (chapter 3)
> Group B. Sources of Success and Failure in Small-Group Discussion (chapter 4)
> Group C. Supporting Small-Group Discussion in the Classroom (chapter 4)
> Group D. Conflict Resolution (chapter 4)

Writers Conferring with Themselves

An important process that occurs when parents scaffold young children's attempts at language is internalization. Once the young learner masters a simple story outline, one can expect simple stories to begin to appear, and parents begin to scaffold new uses of language as they are attempted by the child. As writers mature, it is to be expected that they will internalize the benefits of conferencing and they will begin to attempt new things in their writing. Atwell (1987) formalized this expectation with her eighth-grade writers by developing a guide which she called "Having a Conference with Yourself." It is a list of about fifty questions such as "Have I told where, when and with whom this is happening?" and "Have I said something more than once?" These questions are listed under five categories: Questions about Information, Leads, Conclusions, Titles, and Style. Atwell uses these questions as the basis of minilessons. The students are taught to use these questions in conferences with other students and the teacher, and as a guide to revising their own work in "conferences with themselves" (Atwell, 1987, pp. 103–105).

THE REWRITING STAGE: EDITING

✣ The Importance of Teaching at the Editing Stage

Students edit their papers when they are satisfied that the text says what they want it to say and that the intended audience will understand it. At this point they turn their attention to matters of correct spelling and punctuation, standard usage, and so on. It is important that teachers do not focus on these matters before this stage, because that sends the message that observing conventions is all that good writing is about. However, it is equally important that teachers do not brush conventions aside or treat them as inconsequential. Writers who have mastered these aspects of writing do not fret over them because they do not need to. Writers who have not mastered them may fret over them because they have learned—quite rightly—that their writing fails to accomplish its intended purpose when readers are distracted by unconventional spelling, punctuation, and so on.

Writers must feel confident that they will get help on these important matters at the appropriate time, and they must feel confident that their teachers are willing to and interested in teaching them these troubling conventions. Graves (1982) observed that "the ideal is for conventions to be put behind the writer in order to focus on information and one's own intentions exclusively" (p. 178). A writer puts problems of conventions behind her or him when they no longer present problems—when they have been mastered.

❖ Teaching One or Two Conventions at a Time

Most teachers agree that they should address only one or two matters of convention at a time with individual students. In primary grades the writing conventions that are observed are kept simple, in keeping with the purposes children attempt to accomplish with written language. For example: (1) Begin each sentence with a capital letter. (2) End each sentence with a period or question mark. (3) Leave a space between each word. (4) Read stories aloud to be sure you have not left any words out.

Teachers teach these conventions in minilessons and reteach them in editing conferences if necessary. Once a convention has been taught in a conference, it is recorded in the student's folder under "Things I am working on." In future writing the teacher looks for mastery of these items and as mastery is demonstrated the item is moved to another column in the student's folder—"Things I can do." The principles of intentionality, collaboration, internalization, and continuous development apply at this stage of the writing process as well as at the earlier stages of language development.

Over the years, numerous conventions are taught in this fashion on such diverse matters as paragraphing, spelling, use of colons and semicolons, the correct spelling of *all right* (two words, not one), the use of single quotation marks within double quotation marks, the proper format of letters, use of apostrophes, *ad infinitum*.

It is important that teachers keep track of what conventions children have mastered and what they are working on. Parents and supervisors want this information and they have a right to it. Keeping careful track of such information sends a message to students, parents, and supervisors that writing teachers take teaching the conventions as a serious responsibility.

❖ What Teachers Need to Know

The open-endedness of this process frightens many teachers and prospective teachers. One thing I've learned over many years of experience as a teacher, a writer, and an editor is that many teachers, writers, and editors have surprising blind spots regarding conventions.

- I knew a staff writer/editor who worked for a major publisher and who was a graduate of an elite college. Although she had taught for several years in an elite private school and was an excellent writer, she did not know when to set off adjective clauses with commas—she didn't know what an adjective clause was.
- A second staff writer/editor at the same publisher tended to capitalize all nouns.
- I was raised in a neighborhood in Chicago where we did not distinguish between the verbs *lie* and *lay*. I did not make that distinction until I became an editor. I had a master's degree in English and had taught elementary school for eight years at that point in my career.
- When my last book was published, the final copy editor found several "split infinitives" and transposed words to correct them. I was well aware of the convention that forbids splitting infinitives, but I had stopped observing it because I thought—perhaps prematurely—that it was old-fashioned.

The point is that no one can be sure that he or she knows all the conventions. It is not probable that a college graduate's blind spots regarding conventions would make him or her unfit to teach writing in elementary school. When students' failures to observe the conventions limits the effectiveness of their writing, teachers must be ready to teach those that they know.

On the other hand, I believe writing teachers should love the study of language and never cease to be interested in learning more about the conventions of written English, but my writer/editor friend proved to be an exception to that rule. I am certain she was an excellent teacher of writing, but she was not at all interested in learning about punctuating adjective clauses.

❖ Teaching Strategies Associated with Editing

Daily Edits

Noyce and Christie suggest a daily edit. A short text containing a breech of convention that has been the topic of a minilesson is put on the board each day. Children are instructed to write the sentence in their journals in conventional form. Here are some sample sentences:

> I walked to school with larry.
> We had pancakes eggs and sausage for breakfast.
> After my dad got the fire started. He cooked the ribs.

Specialized Editing Committees

Cramer (1977) recommends setting up editing committees that specialize in one aspect of the editing process—a Spelling Committee, a Punctuation Committee, and a Sentence Committee, for example. After students have edited their own papers and believe they have them in as conventional a form as possible, they take them to each editing committee in turn. The spelling committee looks for words that are possibly misspelled; the punctuation committee edits for punctuation that has been introduced in minilessons—sentence-end punctuation, commas in series, commas and conjunctions joining compound sentences, and commas in dates, for example; and the sentence committee edits for sentence fragments and run-on sentences. Each group has a consulting editor who is proficient in the conventions under consideration and provides a model for less accomplished students. Students rotate from group to group, gaining experience with proofreading and becoming aware of the conventions of writing through editing experiences.

Editing Checklists

Before handing their papers to the teacher for final editing, students consult the list of conventions they have mastered or have been taught but not mastered. They read their papers carefully with these conventions in mind. Using a pen or pencil of a different color than the one the paper is written in, they make any corrections they find necessary. Proofreading charts listing the conventions that the entire class is expected to have mastered are often displayed in a prominent place for students to consult while proofreading.

❖ Teacher Editing

After a student has revised and edited a paper, it is handed to the teacher for final editing. The teacher's job is to mark the paper up the way a copy editor does. With a pen or pencil of a different color than was used by the student for writing or editing, the teacher adds and deletes punctuation, changes lowercase letters to capitals, or vice versa, circles misspelled words, indicates new paragraphs or combines paragraphs, and changes wording that grossly violates conventions of standard usage. The teacher does not rewrite or comment on the content of the paper at this point. She or he has already done that at the writing or revising stage. The teacher then prepares for an editing conference.

Consulting the student's folder or records of previous conferences, the teacher observes whether the student is committing breeches of convention in areas that have been taught or are believed to have been mastered. The teacher considers whether this paper is an especially good vehicle for addressing a convention that the student has never before addressed and whether or not the student is ready to address one or two new conventions.

The teacher-edited paper serves two purposes. First, it is the basis for the editing conference. The teacher reviews previously taught conventions and moves them from the "taught" to the "can do" category if appropriate. If the student is ready, one or two new conventions may be introduced. Teachers who observe that several students are addressing the same convention may make it the topic of one or more minilessons.

Second, the teacher-edited paper is recopied by the student for various forms of publication. Published student writing should be reasonably conventional, including being free of grossly nonstandard usage. Just as my writer/editor friend was unruffled if I set one of her nonrestrictive adjective clauses off by commas—but was not interested enough to want to discuss the principle involved, so, too, can students copy words altered to show agreement in number between subject and verb, or to reflect the correct case of a pronoun, but not be ready to learn the principles that govern these conventions. If they have a list of conventions they have mastered, they can feel confident that, in due time, they will be ready to address and master these conventions as well.

THE SHARING/PUBLISHING STAGE

✤ Publishing Books

A standard way of enabling students to publish and share their writing is by binding their completed, edited, and recopied writing into books and including them in the school library along with professionally published works. A card for each student book is placed in the card catalog along with the cards for the professionally published books.

✤ Author's Chair

The simplest form of sharing in a classroom is for children to read their work as others listen. Graves and Hansen (1984) elaborated on this simple notion and created the idea of the Author's Chair. A chair in the classroom is designated as the author's chair. The teacher sits in this chair and reads trade books to the class and gives the students biographical information about the author. The teacher sometimes reads books the children have written and treats them the same way as the trade books. Children also take turns reading from the author's chair. They read books they have written themselves, books others in the class have written, and trade books. The audience "receives" the story. The children make comments about it—their favorite part or their interpretation of what the story was about—and they ask questions of the author or reader.

The author's chair technique serves several purposes. It establishes a link between child authors and adult authors. The audience responds to their books (whether read by themselves, another student, or the teacher) in just the way that children respond to books by adult authors. When students read books written by others, it puts them into the author's shoes. They listen to comments and answer questions (as well as they can) about texts that they did not

THE SHARING/PUBLISHING STAGE 283

write, perhaps would not have written, or perhaps could not have written. The experience may prompt them to try to write something like what they have read from the author's chair. The children in the audience learn to associate adult published writers with themselves and their classmates. They perceive adult published writers as people like themselves and their texts as writing like their own writing.

❖ Other Ways to Publish

Numerous teachers have discovered scores of ways for children to share (or publish) their writing. Ten ways are listed below. You will find more ideas in chapter 10: Language as Magic.

1. Write and illustrate a book for a lower-grade level. Bind the book and present it to the lower-grade classroom for its library.
2. Compile a class notebook of short stories or poems. Illustrate each piece and decorate the cover.
3. Display student work on bulletin boards.
4. Publish a class newspaper.
5. Display examples of student writing on mobiles, attached to photos, on posters, covering boxes, attached to seasonal shapes.
6. Duplicate writing for classmates and families.
7. Bind books for the classroom library.
8. Tape-record books for a library of recorded literature.
9. Submit writing to magazines that publish children's writing.
10. Send letters to friends, pen pals, government officials, and so on.

❖ Technology in the Classroom

The increasing availability of microcomputers in the classroom adds new opportunities for enriching the literacy environment of the classroom. Published versions of student writing can be made to look very professional with the use of word processors designed especially for youngsters. Some excellent programs include Muppet Slate, Magic Slate II, Bank Street Writer III, and Discovery Writer. Projects of various kinds can be enhanced through the use of graphic software such as Print Shop, Designer Prints, and MacPrint. Desktop publishing programs such as Multiscribe, The Children's Writing and Publishing Center, and Pagemaker enable students to format text into columns with graphics.

There are two models for using these publishing aids. The teacher or professional support staff sometimes act as typesetter, taking the students' completed work, entering it into the computer, and producing printed copy with or without graphics. Alternatively, students learn to use the microcomputer themselves. Which model individual teachers follow will depend on their own familiarity with the computer and software, the availability of microcomputers, and the age of the students.

There are aids available to make word processors "friendly" to very young students. Muppet Learning Keys is a special keyboard which is designed in alphabetical order so that students can find the letters more easily. Microtype: The Wonderful World of Paws and I Can Type are the names of two software packages for teaching children keyboarding—the system of typing using all ten fingers without having to look at the keyboard.

Students who are able to use word processors find spelling checkers and thesauruses a great boon. Whether or not the use of these tools will enhance spelling and vocabulary knowledge remains to be seen.

For help in staying abreast of this rapidly expanding field teachers can turn to specialists in their schools, colleagues with like interests, teacher centers, local colleges and universities, and professional journals such as *The Computing Teacher, Computers in Education,* and *Teaching and Computers.*

Summary

This chapter is devoted to teaching strategies and aids related to the stages in the writing cycle. During the prewriting stage teachers might model choosing a topic—thinking aloud as they consider what they will write about during the writing class that day, asking students to go through a similar thought process, choosing a topic from the list (thinking aloud once again), and asking the students to choose from their lists.

Once the topic is chosen, planning begins. Seven activities are presented that are designed to help students gather information and begin to organize it: brainstorming, listing key words, free association, brainwriting, free writing, focused free writing, and discussion.

Writing lists, formulating questions, and cubing are three strategies that writers engage in to aid in recall of what they know about a topic under consideration. These are referred to as invention, discovery, or heuristic strategies.

Students should be introduced to planning and discovery strategies so that they will be able to use them when they are appropriate or so that a teacher can suggest them when a student needs help at the planning stage.

Developing fluency and developing criteria for good writing are two writing-stage concerns. Developing fluency, particularly among very young students, can be facilitated through playlike writing, functional writing, and interactive writing. Methods for developing and maintaining fluency among students of all ages can be facilitated by dictation and by writing forms that are fun and easy to follow. Viewing first drafts as temporary, tentative, and experimental and returning to the prewriting stage when the flow stops are other ways of promoting fluency.

Lessons may be designed to teach children criteria for good writing, such as effective details, word choice, organization, and leads.

Revising and editing are two activities that occur in the rewriting stage. In revising one responds to two questions: Does my writing say what I want to say? Will it say to the reader what I want it to say? The answer to the first question concerns internal revision and to the latter, external revision.

Revising is often a difficult process for writers, especially young writers. Calkins observed four kinds of revising among third graders: random drafting, refining, transition, and interacting. A review of the literature on revising reveals that many young writers are capable of revising, but revision for most writers never reaches the text level. Text-level revision is associated with good writing, while no revision and cosmetic revision are associated with poor writing. Nevertheless, good writing is sometimes produced without much revision.

Perhaps the most effective way to teach revising is by modeling the process. Teachers might save notes, drafts, outlines, and so on from their own writing and show students how a final draft comes together out of apparent disorder. Checklists of qualities expected in particular modes of discourse (narrative, persuasion, and so on) can be developed with student participation so that they have guides for revising their writing. Content conferences are also the basis for revision. The writer learns from the reader's response what has worked and where the reader is confused or misunderstands or is left wondering.

Group paper revision and the circle strategy are techniques for teaching students to function appropriately in peer conferences. It is necessary to process peer conferences so that students can evaluate success and learn to participate more effectively. More mature students need to learn ways of letting the writer know they are listening, what they want to know more about, and how the writing has affected them. Summarizing, paraphrasing, restating, or simply citing words and phrases that "stick out" are ways of letting a writer know one is listening. Giving the writer movies of one's mind and inventing similes and metaphors for how the writing sounds are two ways of letting a writer know how the writing affected the reader. As writers mature, they should be able to internalize the kind of affective responses they have had from teachers and peers in conferences and base their revisions on conferences with themselves. Teachers can compile lists of questions that students can use in such conferences.

In editing, writers turn their attention to matters of correct spelling, punctuation, standard usage, and so on. There are two reasons why it is important that these matters be given serious attention at the editing stage and that teachers give direct instruction at this point. First, writing fails to accomplish its intended purpose when readers are distracted by unconventional spelling, usage, and so on. Students who have not mastered these conventions will not put them aside during prewriting, writing, and revising unless they are confident they will be given serious attention during the editing stage. Second, teaching these conventions at the editing stage leads to mastery over them. Students who have mastered these conventions are free to concentrate on the essentials of composition.

Teachers should address only one or two matters of convention at a time with individual students. Teachers should keep track of what conventions each child has agreed to work on and which have been mastered. Keeping careful record of such information sends a message to students, parents, and supervisors that teaching conventions is seen as a serious responsibility.

Teaching conventions in the writing process approach is so open-ended that it may frighten teachers. I advise teachers to deal with the conventions they are familiar with and to maintain their interest in learning the conventions of written English.

Activities for teaching conventions associated with the editing stage of the writing process are daily edits, specialized editing committees, and editing checklists.

When the student is satisfied that her or his paper is finished, the teacher edits it in a pen or pencil of a different color from the student's. The teacher checks the student's folder to see which conventions have been taught and mastered, taught but still not mastered, and not taught. In the editing conference which follows, conventions are retaught if necessary or new conventions are chosen for attention. If the piece is to be published in some form, the student recopies it, incorporating all the teacher's editing changes.

A regular part of the writing process is to publish students' work. Binding stories into books that are added to the library is a favorite way of publishing. The author's chair is another way. A chair is designated from which teachers and students read trade books and books they have written or that others in the class have written. The class receives the story and asks questions of the author. This establishes the link between child and adult authors. Other methods of publishing include writing letters and submitting writing to magazines.

The introduction of microcomputers into the classroom has added new dimensions to publishing and to drafting. Word processing, graphics, and desktop publishing software make it possible to put student writing into very professional formats. Special programs are available to make keyboarding easier for children and to teach keyboarding. Spelling checkers and thesauruses are aids to drafting and editing. Since this is a fairly new and fast-developing area, teachers will need to keep abreast of developments through colleagues, professional organizations, teacher centers, and professional journals.

For Review and Discussion

1. Describe modeling choosing a topic.
2. Describe brainstorming, key words, free association, brain writing, free writing, focused free writing, and discussion as aids to planning.
3. Describe lists, questions, and cubing as discovery strategies.
4. How do reactive writers differ from reflective writers?
5. How do strong and weak writers differ in their attitudes toward mechanics and conventions during the writing stage? How should teachers respond to weak writers' concerns with mechanics and conventions during the writing stage?
6. Compare conferencing during the writing stage to scaffolding.
7. Describe the following methods of developing fluency: playlike writing, functional writing, interactive writing, dictation, and using forms that are fun and easy to follow.

8. Explain the difference between internal and external revision.

9. Describe these four forms of drafting behavior: random drafting, refining, transition, and interaction.

10. How is the level of revision related to the quality of writing? Is it true that all good writing is the result of extensive revision? Explain.

11. Describe the following methods and strategies associated with teaching students to revise their writing: modeling revision, teaching qualities expected in particular modes of discourse, and teacher-student conferencing.

12. Describe ways of teaching students to function effectively in peer conferences through group paper revision, the circle strategy, and processing peer conferences.

13. Describe ways of teaching more mature students to let the writer know they are listening and to let the writer know how the writing affects them.

14. Why is it important to teach mechanics and conventions at the editing stage?

15. Describe daily edits, specialized editing committees, and editing checklists.

16. What is the purpose of teacher-editing of students' papers?

17. Describe the author's chair as a method of publishing.

18. What publishing possibilities are made possible with the introduction of the computer into the classroom?

For Further Reading

Afflerbach, P., Bass, L., Hoo, D., Smith, S., Weiss, L., & Williams, L. (1988). Preservice teachers use think-aloud protocols to study writing. *Language Arts, 65,* 693–701.

Bromley, R. (1989). Buddy journals make the reading-writing connection. *The Reading Teacher, 43,* 122–129.

Daiute, C. (1989). Research currents: Play and learning to write. *Language Arts, 66,* 656–664.

DeGroff, L. (1990). Is there a place for computers in whole language classrooms? *The Reading Teacher, 43,* 568–573.

Fitzgerald, J. (1989). Enhancing two related thought processes: Revision in writing and critical reading. *The Reading Teacher, 43,* 42–48.

Hubbard, R. (1989). Inner designs. *Language Arts, 66,* 119–136.

Hauser, C. (1986). The writer's inside story. *Language Arts, 63,* 153–159.

McGinley, W., & Madigan, D. (1990). The research "story": A forum for integrating reading, writing and learning. *Language Arts, 67,* 474–483.

Samway, K. (1987). Formal evaluation of children's writing: An incomplete story. *Language Arts, 64,* 289–298.

CHAPTER 10

Language as Magic: The Language and Literacy-Rich Classroom Community

Introduction
The Imaginative and Affective Use of Language in Early Childhood
What Can Happen in the Classroom
Teaching the Spoken Arts and Creative Dramatics
Lesson Plan: Focusing on Storytelling
Lesson Plan: Criteria for Storytellers
Lesson Plan: Practicing Storytelling
   Activities
Lesson Plan: Suggestions to Facilitate Role Playing
Lesson Plan: Objects
Using Creative Dramatics to Teach
Children's Literature
   Activities
TO THINK ABOUT: Detachment and Communication
Language Across the Curriculum: Using Thematic Units
   Activities
Summary
For Review and Discussion
For Further Reading

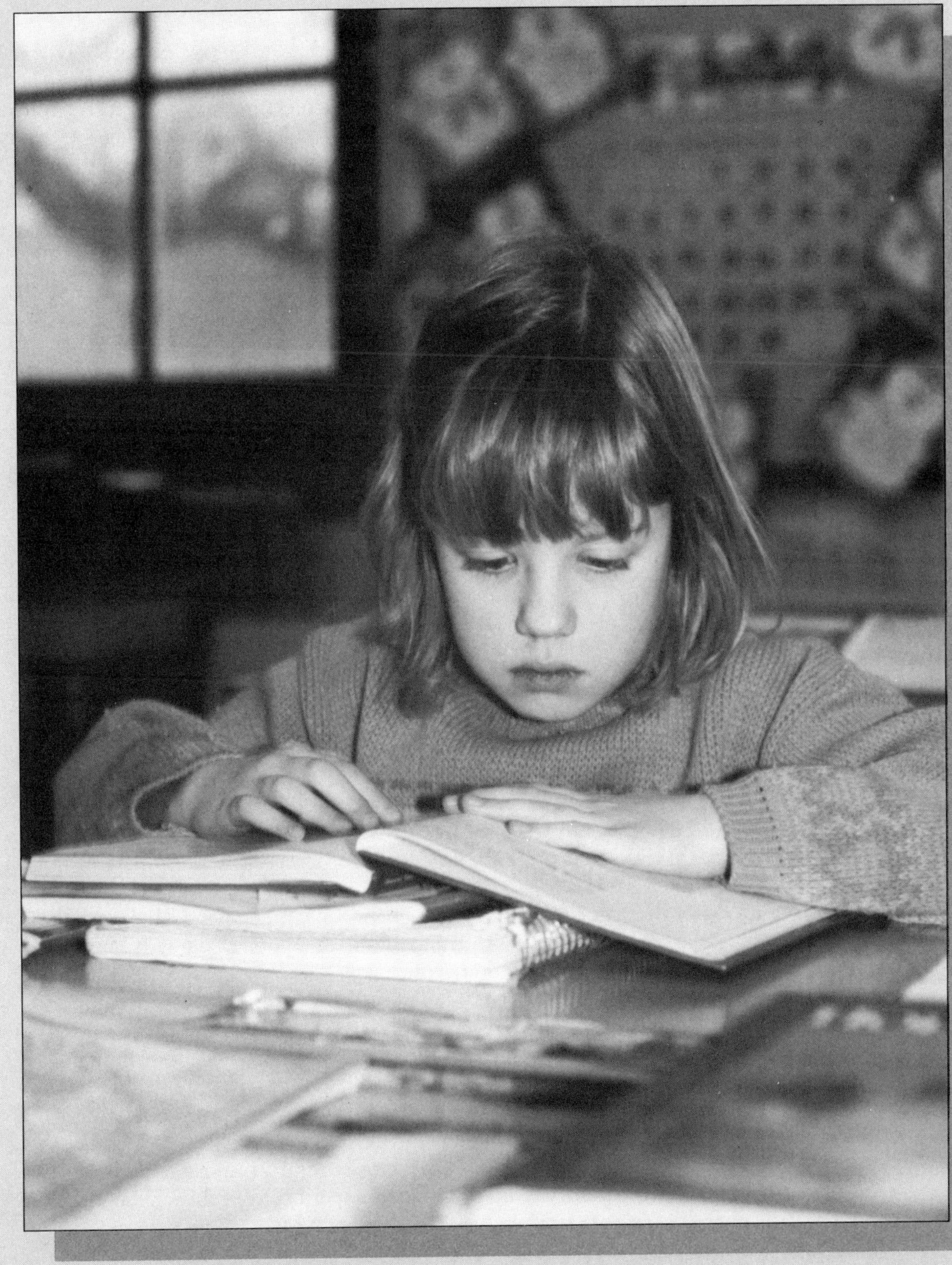

INTRODUCTION

In previous chapters I tried to show that nearly all children arrive in school with rich experiences in language use and that many children arrive at school with rich experiences with books and the language of literature. This chapter deals with the affective and imaginative functions of language. I will discuss the beginnings of the affective and imaginative uses of language, their development, and their potential for making children knowledgeable, productive, happy, and compassionate—in short, more fully human. The major theme of this chapter is that the work of the schools is not to *introduce* children to the magic of language, it is simply to keep the magic alive.

Children come to school knowing stories. Make them storytellers par excellence. Make them voracious consumers and interpreters of stories. Put them in touch with other great storytellers.

Children come to school doing poetry. Use poetry every day. Read it; speak it; write it; listen to it. Introduce them to other great poets.

Children come to school accomplished role players—mommies and daddies, Barbies and G.I. Joes. Encourage it; built on it; teach them through it; build their understanding of others through it. Introduce them to great performances and other great performers.

They come to school as dancers and melody makers, mimes and visual artists, mimics and creators of drama. Great teachers, especially great teachers of language arts, take this as a given.

THE IMAGINATIVE AND AFFECTIVE USE OF LANGUAGE IN EARLY CHILDHOOD

Long before the onset of language, infants convey delight, anger, and hurt feelings. Meek (1985) points out that "unlike other developmental processes, feelings in infants are full-sized, so that early communicative interactions are shot through with affect" (p. 43).

Infants put to bed for the night have been observed using language imaginatively, apparently for their own amusement. They practice newly acquired language forms; they greatly exaggerate tone, stress, and pitch beyond the range normally found in conversation. They laugh at their own jokes, invent dialogs, and play on variations of single phrases (Meek, 1985).

Examples of toddlers' imaginative, poetic, and dramatic use of language abound.

A two-and-a-half-year-old roared at a towel with his hands outstretched like claws and said, "I monstered that towel" (Meek, 1985, p. 45).

A two-and-a-half-year-old boy in a poverty-stricken minority community heard a distant bell. Apparently remembering his experiences in church, he uttered what can only be described as a poem (Heath, 1983, p. 170):

> Way
> Far
> Now
> It a church bell.
> Ringin'
> Dey singin'
> Ringin'
> You hear it?
> Far
> Now

The same child responded to an adult who, in exasperation with the child's behavior, had threatened to tie him to the railroad track (Heath, 1983, p. 110):

> Railroad track
> Train all big 'n black
> On dat track, on dat track, on dat track
> Ain't no way I can't get back
> Back from dat track
> Back from dat train
> Big 'n black, I be back

As soon as children begin to learn what goes together in the world and what does not, they begin to delight in poems of absurdity. A favorite from my childhood was a standard with my children by the time they were three:

> What's your name? Pudding and Tame.
> What's your number? Cucumber.
> What's your street? Pigs' feet.

Spencer (1976) observed two girls aged three and a half and four and a half for three months. They repeatedly reenacted the same drama—a game they called "going to the cemetery." The older girl was used to visiting the grave of a deceased brother with her family. This game involved dressing up, carrying a picnic basket and flowers, an imaginary journey on public transportation, a picnic lunch, and so on. It had endless variations but it had unity, conventions, and rules as does any drama. Through such playmaking, children process and reprocess their experience of the adult world.

Fox (1983) recorded eighty-six monologs from a boy between the ages of five and six in which he tells stories from books, recites original poems, and mimics newscasters and weather reporters. Observers could tell from conventions of form and oral delivery whether the boy was assuming the role of storyteller, reciter of poetry, newscaster, weather reporter, and so on.

The validity of these reports lies in the familiarity of these episodes to anyone who has ever been around infants and preschoolers. However, adults often fail to see the significance and profound accomplishment revealed by these examples of affective and imaginative uses of language in infants and toddlers. The real significance of these events is as follows:

- By age three, children are able to switch in and out of discourse styles and "real" versus "imaginary" activities.
- Children attempt in play what they dare not attempt in everyday activity—linguistically, emotionally, and even cognitively.
- Through play, children experience the "pervasive ritual" of language use, the styles of discourse, and the conventions of literary forms.
- Children are able to detach themselves from actual situations and envisage situations that are nonactual.

Eisner (1976) points out that the arts are "areas of human performance and experience that require a willingness to suspend the press of the practical, to venture into the world of the imagination." He urges teachers to give students the opportunity to "play with images, ideas, and feelings, to be able to recognize and be able to construct the multiple meanings of events, to perceive and conceive of things from various perspectives." Eisner urges school programs that emphasize flexibility of thought, acceptance of many answers, and divergent modes of thinking.

Preschoolers' use of language has these characteristics, but Meek (1985) argues that when "children learn the more conventional forms of language the 'firstness' of their feelings is edited out unless it is legitimized by authors of stories and poems and by good teachers who understand the role of the imagination in the development of talk and learning" (p. 46). As children grow older "experimentations are laced with risks of being misunderstood or thought to be senseless or stupid" (p. 48). The job of the schools is not to teach children to play with images, ideas, and feelings; to construct multiple meanings of events; and to see things from various perspectives. The job of the schools is to give students permission to continue to do these things rather than editing them out.

WHAT CAN HAPPEN IN THE CLASSROOM

Unfortunately, the culture of the home, which gives the child ownership and finds parents collaborating with the child's imaginative and affective use of language, comes into conflict with the culture of the school. Goodlad (1984) found that nearly all classroom instruction takes two forms. The teacher lectures to groups of students (on the teacher's topics) or students work individually on teacher-assigned tasks which are then evaluated by the teacher. Anderson and colleagues (1985) found that 70 percent of reading instruction is devoted to worksheets.

There is often even a further clash of culture between the home and the school when the teacher is from the American mainstream and the child is from a nonmainstream culture. For example, in chapter 3 I related the incident of the little girl who told a topic-associating story beginning with an episode where her father "hung her on a hook." The teacher, exasperated by the child who "doesn't make sense," tells the child to be seated without any comment on her story. Since it is the teacher's practice to make supportive, summarizing comments to children who tell topic-centered stories, this child soon learns that her way of making sense of her world and expressing it are unacceptable in the classroom. Fortunately, such children's affective and imaginative use of language continues to develop outside of school. Unfortunately, it is never tapped as a vehicle for developing their use of language to inform (and become informed) and to persuade (and be persuaded).

In this chapter I will discuss creative dramatics and literature in the classroom as ways of

- nurturing the affective and imaginative uses of language that most children bring to school.
- using children's facility with affective and imaginative use of language to teach them about the world and our shared cultures—that is, to teach the subject matter curriculum.
- enabling children to become familiar with the conventional forms of literature and drama—the two forms of language most closely associated with the affective and imaginative uses of language.

I will also focus on a second aspect of an effective language arts program—the classroom as a literacy-rich community. I will show that children's facility with all uses of language and their acquisition of knowledge prospers in a classroom where speaking, listening, writing, and reading are shared among children, among children and teachers, and among children and the larger community.

TEACHING THE SPOKEN ARTS AND CREATIVE DRAMATICS

✤ Storytelling

Storytelling is an ancient art that is practiced by a few professionals and millions of amateurs (nearly every mom and dad and five-year-old) despite the availability of entertainment via electronic and print media. The purpose of storytelling remains unchanged. Its goal is to share between the storyteller and listeners a heightened awareness that involves speech, wonder, mystery, and creativity. The most important factor in storytelling is the storyteller's sensitivity and enthusiasm.

The three historic purposes of storytelling are to entertain, to teach, and to transmit culture. Traditional storytellers do not memorize stories because they believe it leads to a stilted presentation. Instead they learn stories so well that they can tell them in their own words. They use words that suggested seeing, hearing, tasting, smelling, and touching to get their audience interested and involved. They impersonate characters to bring them to life. They give full reign to natural facial expression and gestures to add interest and spontaneity. To achieve fluency, they rehearse stories several times.

Techniques of storytelling have changed over the past several decades. Twenty-five years ago storytellers saw themselves as distinct from actors. They did not involve theatrical techniques or trappings in their art. Today many storytellers use costumes, props, make-up, movement, mime, vocal effects, and musical accompaniment. Some memorize their material.

Librarians and teachers tend to follow traditional rules. Their aim is not to give professional performances. They usually want to create a quiet atmosphere and to focus on the language of the story rather than to rely on costumes and props. One study (Kaiser, 1985) showed the wisdom of this belief. Children were more verbally and physically involved in a story that was told without props than in the same story told with props.

Encouraging children who are not yet able to read and write in their natural propensity to tell stories helps them gain facility with many skills and concepts (story sequence or schema and the use of dialogue in narrative) that are important in reading and writing.

In primary grades most children simply need to be permitted to tell their stories. Teachers encourage them, comment on interesting details, praise effective delivery, and help them to summarize. In middle and upper grades teachers begin to call attention to storytelling as a spoken art—a form of literature and performance through activities like the following.

LESSON PLAN: Focusing on Storytelling

Invite a fellow teacher or librarian into your room to tell a well-known fable or fairy tale.

Tell students to pay attention to the choice of words, intonation, gestures, and use of dialog that make the story interesting.

Discuss ways that this experience is different from reading a story, listening to a story read from a book, or watching a dramatization of the story.

> **LESSON PLAN: Criteria for Storytellers**
>
> Watch several storytellers on videotape and develop a checklist of things a good storyteller must do. The list might include the following:
>
> - know the story very well
> - understand the conflict in the story
> - visualize the characters and setting
> - know which sentences must be repeated exactly, such as familiar dialog
> - use facial expression and gestures to enhance the story

> **LESSON PLAN: Practicing Storytelling**
>
> Divide the class into small groups. Have students elect a story from a book or a personal story to tell their small group. Ask members of the group to comment on the storyteller's presentation of setting, characters, conflict, and plot; make suggestions for improvement; and finally retell the story.
>
> - Have each group present the most successful story to the class.
> - Have storytellers who are well prepared by this exercise present their stories to other classes—particularly classes with younger children.

❖ Choral Speaking

Choral reading or speaking is simply reading or reciting in unison under the direction of a leader. It was an important part of Greek theater, and it appears today in theater, church, and school. Like drama, its function in society is to be performed, and the emphasis is on the artistic product. However, in elementary school it is a teaching tool, and the emphasis is on the linguistic, emotional, and cognitive growth of the students (performers).

Choral speaking can be used as a vehicle for speech improvement. Today many teachers are rightly concerned about calling attention to individual children's pronunciation and diction. They do not want to embarrass children who may have a genuine speech handicap. When they suspect that this is the case, they refer the child to the school speech therapist. Teachers also worry that they may be dealing with dialect differences and that calling attention to speech patterns may be interpreted as devaluation of nonmainstream cultures.

In using choral speaking teachers can call attention to pitch, volume, rate, tonal quality, articulation (production of sounds), and diction (distinctness of sounds) in connection with an enjoyable activity and without focusing for more than brief moments on individual children.

Choral speaking is an activity where each individual contributes to a common goal. Children with strident voices learn to soften their voices and shy children work to speak a bit louder without feeling self-conscious.

In early infancy, many children engage in choral-speaking games like "patty-cake" where the child joins in with the rhythm and motion even before he or she can pronounce all the words. With younger children, choral speaking in school can spring from their enjoyment of poems and their desire to speak them aloud with the accompaniment of action.

For older children, opportunities for oral reading often arise from the study of literature—especially poetry. When a poem that particularly lends itself to oral recitation is read, the teacher may suggest that the class read it aloud together and suggest the following ways of introducing variety into choral reading.

Unison: The whole group reads together. This is particularly effective with some short poems.
Antiphonal: The group is divided into two groups with each group speaking certain parts.
Cumulative: One or a few voices begin; voices are added individually or in groups as the poem builds toward high points or a climax.
Solo: Individuals read a line or stanza.
Line-around: Solo reading of each individual line.

Once students are familiar with these techniques, choral reading can become a more cooperative, rather than a teacher-directed effort. When a poem is introduced, children discuss the meaning and ways of reading it to bring out the meaning. After one reading, children can discuss difficulties of phrasing and diction, consider further insights into meaning, and plan a second reading. This cycle can be repeated as many times as interest is maintained and it continues to be profitable.

McCaslin (1990) suggests the following seven reasons for including choral speaking in the language arts classroom:

1. It can be done with groups of any size and age.
2. It emphasizes group rather than individual effort.
3. It provides an opportunity to introduce poetry.
4. It offers the shy or handicapped child an opportunity to speak.
5. It promotes good habits of speech through enjoyable exercise, rather than drill.
6. It is a satisfying activity in itself.
7. It can be combined successfully with rhythmic movement and pantomime.

> **ACTIVITY**
>
> Experiment with choral speaking of the following poem or chose a poem of your own. Discuss McCaslin's reasons for including choral speaking in the language arts curriculum in connection with this experience.
>
> **A Sioux Indian Prayer**
>
> O' GREAT SPIRIT
> *Whose voice I hear in the winds,*
> *And whose breath gives life to all the world,*
> *hear me! I am small and weak, I need your*
> *strength and wisdom.*
> LET ME WALK IN BEAUTY, *and make my eyes*
> *ever behold the red and purple sunset.*
> MAKE MY HANDS *respect the things you have*
> *made and my ears sharp to hear your voice.*
> MAKE ME WISE *so that I may understand the*
> *things you have taught my people.*
> LET ME LEARN *the lessons you have hidden*
> *in every leaf and rock.*
> I SEEK STRENGTH, *not to be greater than my*
> *brother, but to fight my greatest*
> *enemy—myself.*
> MAKE ME ALWAYS READY *to come to you with*
> *clean hands and straight eyes.*
> SO WHEN LIFE FADES, *as the fading sunset,*
> *my spirit may come to you*
> *without shame.*

❖ Creative Drama

Creative drama has many attributes of preschoolers dramatic play—the "cemetery game," for example. It is improvised. It is not intended that a performance before an audience will occur. It may revolve around a story. The difference is that in creative drama participants are guided by a leader and it is engaged in for the purpose of imagining, enacting, and reflecting upon human experience.

Creative drama is different from theater in that lines are not usually written down or memorized. Scenes are replayed to enhance the details and organization of the story—not to produce a more polished performance. The leader's goal is to foster the growth and development of the children. Scenery, costumes, and props are out of place unless they serve to stimulate the children's imaginations.

Movement

Young children express through movement what adults state in words. Asked how a horse moves, a child is more likely to gallop than to describe a gallop. Asked how tall daddy is, a child will hold his hands above his head rather than respond "Five foot ten."

Preschoolers prefer running to walking. They gallop, skip, hop, jump, and roll. By allowing and encouraging such movement, teachers can help children gain confidence in their bodies and develop spatial awareness. It is easy to go from movement into dance and drama.

Rhythm classes for young children build on this natural impulse. In simple rhythm exercises, children simply walk, skip, hop, or crawl to the rhythm of tape-recorded music, a piano, or a drum. Other rhythmic activities include the following. These come from *Creative Drama in the Classroom* (McCaslin, 1990):

> Sitting in a circle on the floor, the group creates different rhythms and sounds. Clapping hands, snapping fingers, tapping knees, and brushing the floor softly with the hands are among the sounds that can be made in this position. Have each child put two and then three of these sounds together in a rhythmic sequence. The group listens carefully and tries to repeat the sequence. (p. 56)

> Rhythms can suggest people working or moving in unison. Try beats that describe the following: an assembly line, a marching band, robots, motorcycles, athletes warming up, workmen using picks, joggers, and so on. (p. 55)

> Not only young children but also adult actors enjoy suggesting different animals through rhythmic movement. Try to find rhythms for the following:

Horses	Chickens	Mice
Cats	Cranes	Frogs
Rabbits	Kangaroos	Sea gulls
Snakes	Monkeys	Pigeons (p. 55)

Nancy Larrick (1987) suggests using poetry to capitalize on children's natural delight in movement by asking them to move the way the poem tells them to move. Patricia Hubbell's poem "Bedtime" (Hubbell, 1965) begins

> Hop away
> Skip away
> Jump away
> Leap!

"The Prayer of the Butterfly" (de Gasztold, 1962) sets children darting and whirling, tilting and flitting in butterfly fashion. "The Prayer of the Ox" (de Gasztold, 1962) changes their pace to slow, heaving plodding. Through movement the children's bodies help them feel the mood and meaning of such poems.

Children's earliest efforts to try out roles of others and re-create life situations arise through dramatic play. Children first mimic the actions and behaviors of others. Words are scanty at first. It is for this reason that McCaslin suggests movement as an entree to drama at all grade levels. Here are some movement activities that verge on dramatic play:

- Move like a caterpillar, a high cloud, a person on stilts, a lion pacing in a cage.
- Do movements that are
  fast like an arrow or a racehorse,
  slow like a clock or a turtle,
  turning like curling smoke or a figure skater,
  strong and heavy like chopping wood or great waves,
  soft and light like a butterfly or kite,
  sharp like a cuckoo clock or woodpecker.
- Change movements like a candle standing tall, then melting into a pool of wax.
- Be rushing water, carry water, walk on water.
- Be a forest fire raging, put out the fire, choke on smoke from the fire.

Pantomime

Movement becomes dramatic play when participants make use of it to become someone or something other than themselves. Pantomime is the art of conveying ideas without words. Encouraging pantomime with younger children is a way of *not* editing out the child's ways of communicating and a way of not insisting on the school's way of communicating. Pantomime uses the child's inclinations to accomplish the school's objectives. For older children pantomime is used as a warm-up for class activities. It helps students to overcome self-consciousness and fosters involvement. It pays a special dividend in classrooms where there are children whose mother tongue is not English. Ideas are expressed across cultures and language barriers.

Fostering Imagination

The teacher calls six or seven children into a circle. (McCaslin suggests that pantomime be used in groups of less than twenty.) The teacher hands one child an object (a chalkboard eraser, for example) and tells the child that it is the most beautiful diamond bracelet in the world. The child is to look at it, react to it, handle it, and pass it on to the next student, who is to do the same. After the object is passed around, it becomes a soft, furry kitten, or a dirty, leather purse, and so on.

Observers are asked how they knew what each object was, whose actions were particularly useful in telling what it was as it changed from round to round. Players might be asked how the bracelet or purse (or whatever) looked, felt, smelled, and sounded as they handled it. How did they convey these attributes? How might they have conveyed these attributes?

The following suggestions for pantomime concentrate on the senses:

Seeing: Go into a dark closet and look for your sweater; watch a parade go down the street.
Hearing: Hear an explosion; listen to a band marching down the street.
Smell: Come home and smell cookies baking; try on different perfumes at a department store.
Taste: Eat a piece of delicious chocolate; try a food you have never had and decide you like it.
Touch: Touch velvet; hold a piece of ice.

The following suggestions add action: Play a video game; choose food in a cafeteria.

The following suggestion adds mood and feeling: Boys enter an abandoned house. They find a box of money and jewels. They hear someone coming. Two men enter and walk past the hiding boys and go into another room. The boys stuff their pockets and flee.

The following suggestion concentrates on characterization: A group of people are waiting for a bus. One is an old woman going to visit her grandchildren; another is a businesswoman late for an appointment; a third is a blind man who needs assistance; a fourth is a high-school boy. They wait, and finally the bus arrives and they get aboard.

Scenes from Literature

An upper-grade teacher asked several students who were reading *Johnny Tremain* to pantomime the scene where Johnny burns his hand. There was silence. She then asked three students to stand and, handing each an imaginary broom, she asked them to join her in sweeping water from a flood out the door. As soon as they were enthusiastically involved in sweeping the floor, she returned to the burned hand episode. After the first couple of mimes the group discussed the accuracy, reread the scene, and reenacted it in mime. The children were not only responding to literature, but also reading carefully for details to enhance their response (Sebesta, 1987).

Adding Music, Movement, and Sound (Middle Grades)

Read a story such as "The Wedding of the Hawk" (Courlander, 1962) and have students mime the story as it is read aloud. After a performance and discussion, the pantomime is repeated without words. A drum is then added. Appropriate rhythms for the various characterizations are worked out and movements become more exaggerated. Repetition is added. The story is told through words, pantomime, and finally dance.

Sebesta (1987) suggests these stories as a starting place for this activity:

Aardema, Verna. *Oh, Kojo! How Could You!* Illustrated by Marc Brown. Dial, 1984.

Courlander, Harold. "The Wedding of the Hawk." *The King's Drum and Other African Stories.* Harcourt Brace Jovanovich, 1962.

Dayrell, Elphinstone. *Why the Sun and the Moon Live in the sky.* Illustrated by Blair Lent. Houghton Mifflin, 1968.

Moss, Anita, and John C. Stott (Eds.). *The Family of Stories: An Anthology of Children's Literature.* Holt, Rinehart and Winston, 1986.

Uchida, Yoshiko. "Momotaro: Boy-of-the-Peach." *The Dancing Kettle and Other Japanese Folk Tales.* Harcourt Brace Jovanovich, 1949. (Also in *The Arbuthnot Anthology of Children's Literature,* fourth edition, revised by Zena Sutherland. Scott, Foresman, 1976.)

Story Theater

Several authors use the term "story theater" to describe an activity where one person reads a story or poem while others pantomime the words. Tiedt (1989) suggests using two groups of students—readers and actors. Using Maurice Sendak's *Where the Wild Things Are,* Tiedt leads the readers in reading the text in unison and later assigns parts to different readers. Meanwhile the actors work out their pantomimes of the action, each taking a part. Repeated performances give students a chance to read and pantomime different parts. For variety, she suggests having all the actors play all the parts. When Max acts, all the actors simultaneously pantomime his part. When Wild Thing acts, all the actors simultaneously pantomime his part, and so on. It sounds like great fun.

Other stories suggested for this activity are these:

The Elephant's Child by Rudyard Kipling
Chicken Little by Steven Kellog (Reteller)
The Funny Little Woman by Arlene Mosel, illustrated by Blair Lent
Ol' Paul, The Mighty Logger by Glen Rounds
John Henry, An American Legend by Ezra Jack Keats

Some poems suggested for this activity are these:

"The Elf and the Dormouse" by Oliver Hereford
"A Visit from St. Nicholas" by Clement Moore
"Lewis and Clark" by Rosemary and Stephen Benet
"The Owl and the Pussycat" by Edward Lear
"You Are Old, Father William" by Lewis Carroll
"The Walrus and the Carpenter" by Lewis Carroll

Role Playing or Improvisation

Role playing and improvisation are two different names for the same activity. The different terms are used in different settings. In early childhood and and in psychological counseling and therapy the term "role playing" is used. In high school and college, particularly when it is used as an exercise for theater students, the term "improvisation" is used. In the following discussion the words *role play* and *improvise* are used interchangeably.

In one sense, role playing is pantomime plus speech. The pantomime exercises presented above might be used to introduce role playing. After the scenes are pantomimed, they are replayed with speech added. Students often find it difficult to use no speech in pantomime so relaxing the prohibition on speech can naturally facilitate the introduction of role playing.

LESSON PLAN: Suggestions to Facilitate Role Playing

Your parents are angry because you came home from school an hour late—for the third time this week. Assign roles and act out the scene in small groups. Present the scene to the class and discuss alternate solutions to the same problem. Then invent variations on the same problem. For example, your father is late picking you and your friends up from an after-school activity—for the third time in a row.

Use listings and summaries of shows from **TV Guide** to generate conflict situations that could be used for role playing.

You and your friends pass the home of an elderly woman every day on the way to school. She is very unfriendly and chases you away if you come near her fence or pause as you pass her house. One day you see that someone has trampled her flower garden and you feel sorry for her. What do you do? How does she react? Do all the children feel the same toward her? Does her attitude toward you change?

LESSON PLAN: Objects

The class is divided into groups. An object (a velvet jewelry case, a foreign coin, a wooden spoon) is placed in the center of each group, and they are asked to look at it silently for three or four minutes and try to invent a story about it. Where is it? Where did it come from? How did it get there? The children then tell their stories and decide which one to present in an improvisation.

Story Drama

When a group has had experience with pantomime and improvisation they are ready to attempt dramatic presentations of stories—what Noyce and Christie

(1989) refer to as Story Drama. Story drama can involve five steps: (1) Presentation of material; (2) Organization; (3) Dramatization; (4) Evaluation; and (5) Replaying.

Presentation of Material
Stories to be dramatized may be read by the students, read to the students, or told to the students. Whatever the method of presentation, the important thing is that the students are able to become thoroughly familiar with the story. When the story is told, the storyteller should be thoroughly prepared so that he or she brings the story to life and introduces as much detail as the audience can handle. Students are given the opportunity to ask questions and get clarification from the storyteller. The story may be read several times, students may pick favorite parts to be reread, or students may retell (or read) favorite parts to the class.

Organization
First, focus on characters. Who are the people? How would they look, talk, move, and walk? Use a semantic mapping strategy to find words that describe the characters. Have volunteers pantomime characters and let others guess who they are. Discuss each presentation. What were good clues (gestures, expression, actions)? How could the pantomime have been improved?

Next, focus on plot. Discuss and decide how to divide the story into scenes. Decide who will be in each scene. Review character traits and improvise each scene. Appoint someone to call out each scene number at the beginning and "curtain" at the end of each scene. The older the children are, the more preliminary planning must go into creative dramatics. Young children move quickly to action.

Dramatization
Ask for volunteers at first, but encourage many children to take many parts. Remember that what is important is the involvement of students in the process. Choosing the best actors to produce the best performance is not.

Evaluation
Discuss what helped the audience to understand the characters and the plot. What parts were interesting, funny, or sad? What could be added, subtracted, or changed?

Replaying
Evaluation should lead to replaying with new depth and richer detail. It is not necessary to change every actor every time, but each child should get a chance to play the part he or she chooses.

When the evaluate and replay cycle has gone as far as possible, one final playing gives the process closure.

Reader's Theater

This is a relatively new form which involves reading the original material, writing a dramatic (play) version of the material, and reading the script with expression suitable to drama. It is unlike other forms of creative dramatics because the script is actually written out and because the emphasis is on reading with expression suitable to drama. However, its form and purpose are enough like those of creative dramatics to include it in this discussion.

Noyce and Christie (1989) suggest five stages of reader's theater:

1. Select material.
2. Create a script.
   a. List title, time, setting, and characters. There is usually a narrator as well.
   b. Discuss important events that will be portrayed.
   c. Decide what each character will say to portray events.
   d. Decide what the narrator will say to set the stage and connect the events.
   e. Produce a written script.
3. Assign parts and have players *read* their lines. They should understand that their *expression* as they read is important in portraying the material.
4. Discuss the performance. How might the oral interpretation be improved?
5. Reread the script with the same players or assign new players.

Steps 4 and 5 are repeated for as long as interest is maintained and for as long as it remains profitable. Improvisation might be incorporated into step 2 by having students improvise/discuss and improve in preparation to writing each scene.

❖ Teachers "In Role"

Teachers sometimes assume roles in order to teach. I once watched a first-grade teacher don a costume and assume the role of Beatrix Potter. She introduced a signal to the class. While she was wearing her bonnet she was Beatrix Potter. When she removed her bonnet she was herself, Mrs. Sconiers. In twenty minutes she told her rapt audience a good deal about the life of the author of the Peter Rabbit books, which she had read to them.

Teachers occasionally assume a role in an improvisation. They explain that they are to be Galileo and several students are to play fellow scientists who believe the sun travels around the earth. These teachers step in and out of character. When a fellow scientist says to them that the sun moves across the sky, Galileo answers that it only seems to because the earth is rotating on its axis. When a fellow scientist says she is going to send up a spaceship to see if the earth is turning, the teacher steps out of character, explains that there were no spaceships in the seventeenth century, and reassumes the role for the next exchange.

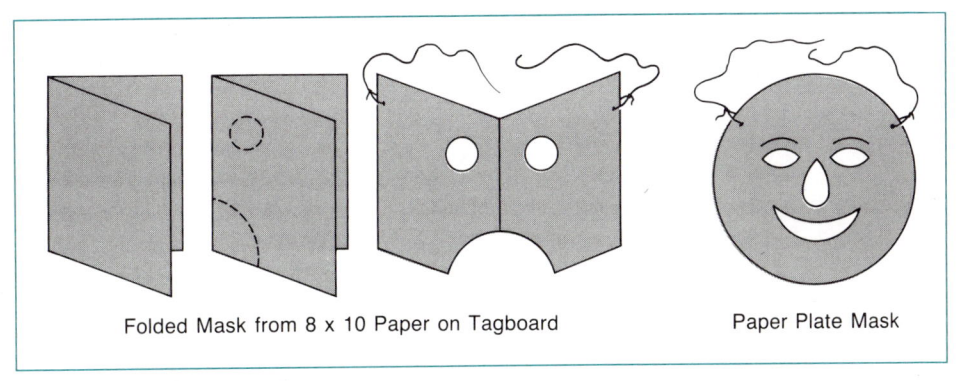

Folded Mask from 8 x 10 Paper on Tagboard   Paper Plate Mask

Figure 10.1 Simple masks

❖ Puppets and Masks

Twenty-five years ago puppets were thought of as doll-like objects that were manipulated from above by strings (marionettes) or that fit over the puppeteer's hand (hand puppets). Since then we have all come to know the Muppets—hand-held puppets, puppets manipulated with sticks from below, life-sized puppets with people inside. Many people have seen a form of Japanese theater where life-sized puppets are manipulated by black-clad puppeteers moving alongside them on stage. We have seen Gumby and other plastic creatures that are manipulated and photographed frame by frame to create animated movies. Now, more than ever, we can appreciate McCaslin's (1990) definition: "Puppets are actors who come to life with the help of a puppeteer" (pp. 123–124).

Puppetry starts when young children play with dolls and toys, manipulating them to perform roles and actions. Most children are introduced to masks at age three or four as part of Halloween costumes worn by themselves and others. Children see numerous puppets on television and may have owned them.

Puppets and masks appear in the language arts classroom in two guises: as a vehicle for encouraging expression and as a tool for teaching. Since creative dramatics frequently requires a child to perform in front of a group, it presents a special challenge to shy or troubled children who find it difficult to express themselves or who are particularly stressed by the idea of being the center of attention. Authorities uniformly assert that such children are encouraged to participate if they are able to speak for a puppet rather than perform themselves. The novelty and fun associated with puppetry motivates most children to greater involvement in creative dramatics and to greater attention when the teacher assumes a puppet character as a teaching device.

Puppets and masks can be made in many ways. Figure 10.1 shows two kinds of masks. Figure 10.2 shows five kinds of puppets, and Figure 10.3 shows three kinds of puppet stages. The creation of masks, puppets, and puppet stages may be considered an art or a craft. Although such activity no doubt has a place

Figure 10.2 Types of puppets

in a well-rounded elementary-school classroom, teachers should keep their objectives clearly in mind. If language development is the objective, simple masks and puppets are preferable to elaborate ones.

The objective of all creative dramatics in the classroom is for children to engage in the process and learn from the process. Elaborate costumes, sets, props, and rehearsals are out of place. However, drama is a performance art and it is natural for students to want to do an occasional performance for the class or as a class project to be performed for another class. Teachers must remember

Figure 10.3 Types of puppet stages

that this is not the reason for creative dramatics in the classroom, and the time and energy devoted to performances should be carefully evaluated.

USING CREATIVE DRAMATICS TO TEACH

Any area can become the basis for creative drama. Are you studying Columbus in social studies? Improvise a scene between Columbus and Queen Isabella and King Ferdinand. Are you studying space travel? Improvise a scene between a prospective astronaut and the person in charge of a flight to Mars. Are you studying the industrial revolution? Improvise a scene in a family when the father explains why he must leave the house and farm to work in a factory or when they discuss whether to send their twelve-year-old to the mines to work. Are you studying the geography of Africa? Improvise a scene where a group is putting together gear to cross the Sahara or to travel up the Congo River. Students will need to find information on these topics in order to improvise their scene. Many educators believe that this gives children personal identification with learning that not only motivates them to seek out knowledge but also enables them to remember and integrate new information into their previous knowledge.

♣ Creative Dramatics and Oral Language

McCaslin (1990) points out that drama demands that speakers stay in their roles, elaborate appropriately, be relevant, be coherent, choose words precisely, and craft discourse for a desired rhetorical effect. This encompasses all the desired attributes for speakers in conversation, discussion, and addressing audiences. Creative drama has also been shown to improve students' vocabulary.

♣ Creative Dramatics and Writing

Creative drama facilitates growth in writing on several levels. At the more obvious level, it often involves writing (as in reader's theater) or it may be seen as a prewriting activity. An improvisation of a scene where a group gathers equipment to cross the Sahara can easily motivate narrative or expository writing.

On a less obvious but perhaps more important level, creative drama gives students practice in simultaneous engagement in communication, contemplation of the meaning intended, and the form of the message. Cecily O'Neill, quoted in McCaslin (1990), speaks of successful creative drama exercises as heightening the participants sense of "seeing" while still demanding participation. The plan-attempt-evaluate-plan sequence of creative drama helps students to (nearly simultaneously) contemplate meaning, convey meaning, and think about the way meaning is being conveyed. This is very similar to the critical detachment that is necessary for later stages of development in writing.

The repeated cycle of plan-attempt-evaluate-plan that has appeared in this chapter regarding storytelling, choral reading, and creative dramatics is reminiscent of the writing cycle (prewriting, writing, conferencing, and rewriting). With creative dramatics, however, the process is usually much more observable, shareable, and discussable at every stage. In the planning stages of creative dramatics, different participants offer ideas, plans, and insights, whereas in the writing process, ideas, plans, and insights appear in the writer's mind. The process is not as observable because ideas, plans, and insights are not as clearly distinct, nor are their sources as identifiable. In the attempt stage of creative dramatics, one can observe the process as it unfolds. It is the most observable stage of the process, whereas its counterpart, writing, is the most covert stage of the writing process. In the evaluation stage of creative drama, all participants have shared in the planning and have observed the unfolding of the text. In the reattempt stage the extent to which the text improves in response to the evaluation is observable and discussable. This is somewhat true of the writing process in that changes in the text resulting from rewriting after a conference can be similarly observed. However, because one writer usually confers with one other person, there may be a great deal more subjectivity in this matter than when numerous participants share in the planning, observe (or participate in) the attempt, discuss and evaluate it, and observe the results.

Skills and concepts learned through creative dramatics may carry over directly into the writing process. Teachers can certainly refer to planning, attempting, evaluating, planning, and attempting in creative dramatics when urging students to engage in the roughly equivalent activities of prewriting, writing, conferencing, and rewriting.

✤ Creative Dramatics and Reading

Kukla (1987) found that improvising a drama after reading a story improved the comprehension of poor readers. He believes that the creative dramatics cycle causes children to explore deeper meanings of stories and to clarify concepts. Knowing they will be involved in creative dramatics after reading may also motivate children to put more effort and attention into their reading. Cunningham (1981) believes that creative dramatics motivates readers to strive for higher levels of comprehension: "The main idea and supporting details must be clear in your mind. Events must be remembered in proper sequence. Inferences must be made about characters, motivation, and intention" (p. 468). Cunningham maintains that story drama is a "natural vehicle for improving speaking skills and listening/reading comprehension and fostering that love of stories which separates 'readers' from those who can but don't" (p. 468). I believe Cunningham refers here to the magic of drama and literature in the classroom that I hope this chapter conveys.

CHILDREN'S LITERATURE

Purves and Monson (1984) use the poem "Who Killed Cock Robin?" to illustrate several qualities of literature and the story of Peter Rabbit to illustrate several elements of literature.

✤ Qualities of Literature

The centuries-old poem "Who Killed Cock Robin?" begins

> Who killed Cock Robin?
> "I" said the sparrow,

"With my bow and arrow
And I killed Cock Robin."

In the next twelve verses various animals lament Cock Robin's death and plan his funeral. The final verse is

And all the birds in the air
Fell to sighing and sobbing
When they heard the bell toll
For poor Cock Robin.

What makes this poem literature? Purves and Monson use the following criteria:

1. It uses language—words, sentences, sounds, images, and metaphors.
2. It does more than merely say something. It portrays emotion, suggests pictures, and gives pleasure.
3. It is organized. It has a beginning and an end. It has repetition, pattern, and rhyme.
4. It speaks to us in a voice—many voices in the case of Cock Robin.
5. It conveys experience. It has no specific purpose beyond getting the reader to think about experience—life and death in the case of Cock Robin—and to experience pleasure in the way thoughts are expressed.
6. It invites us to think about other works of literature that are like it—other stories or poems about death, other stories about animals, other nursery rhymes.

Notice that these qualities can be found in a wide spectrum of writing—current novels and poems, contemporary drama, and even television situation comedies. Teachers should choose stories they read to children or stories, poems, and plays they suggest for children's reading from the best literature, but they should be very tolerant of the literature children choose to read for themselves. The very best literature includes current books like *Where the Wild Things Are* or *The One in the Middle Is the Green Kangaroo*. On the other hand, teachers' individual as well as community standards may rule out *Tobacco Road* or books by Stephen King as classroom fare. Children may be advised to read certain books at home if their parents approve, but that they may not read them in school for reasons of propriety.

❖ Elements of Literature

Characters

Peter, his mother, Mr. McGregor, Peter's sisters, and various minor players make up the characters in *Peter Rabbit*.

Setting(s)

Peter's home, the woods, and the garden are the settings where the story unfolds.

Action or Plot

Peter ignores his mother's warning and enters Mr. McGregor's garden to steal vegetables. Mr. McGregor nearly catches him, but Peter escapes and returns home. His mother puts him to bed without supper because he is ill.

Conflict

Peter is warned to stay out of the garden, but he goes in to steal. Peter's natural inclination is to eat vegetables; Mr. McGregor wants to protect his vegetables.

Contrast

Peter's home and the woods are simple, safe places. The garden is complex, threatening, and dangerous. Peter has human characteristics—he wears clothes and talks. His rabbit nature is to eat vegetables wherever he finds them. As the story unfolds, he loses his clothing as he acts more like a rabbit.

Structure

Readers may notice that a plot has a structure that they have seen before. A youngster begins safe at home, ventures out into a hostile world, and returns to the safety of home just as in *The Wizard of Oz, Hansel and Gretel,* and countless other stories. Recognizing the structure of a story and relating it to other stories with the same structure may help the reader discover the theme.

Tone of Voice

Peter Rabbit is a tale of lawbreaking and a near scrape with death, but the reader perceives it as light entertainment. The reason for this is that the reader responds to the author's tone of voice. In the opening, Mrs. Rabbit says, "You may go into the fields or down the lane, but don't go into Mr. McGregor's garden: your father had an accident there; he was put in a pie by Mrs. McGregor." What is revealed in these lines is quite horrifying. It is the author's tone of voice that tells the reader that this story is intended as light entertainment addressing themes of childhood.

Content: Subject and Theme

When asked what *Peter Rabbit* is about, a person may respond, "It is about a young rabbit named Peter and his mother and sisters and a farmer. Peter goes into Mr. McGregor's garden, and Mr. McGregor nearly kills him, but he escapes."

In the vocabulary of those who study literature, this response refers to the content of the book. Content is often divided into subject and theme.

Subject
The subject is what the book is about—a rabbit who escapes danger in a garden.

Theme
The theme is the underlying generalization readers may infer from the subject—children face danger when they leave the safety of their homes or children who disobey their mothers face risks. Most readers agree on the subject of a story, but readers often see different themes in the same story depending, perhaps, on their emotional needs or the kinds of challenges they are facing in their lives.

> **ACTIVITY**
>
> In small groups choose a work of literature that is familiar to all students and identify the characters, setting(s), action or plot, conflict, contrast, structure, tone of voice, and content (both subject and theme).
>
> You may choose a classic familiar to all of you like **Huckleberry Finn** or a recent movie or television drama you have all seen. Choosing the latter will remind you of two important ideas: (1) The definition of literature as applied to the elementary-school program is a liberal one. It may include current writing as well as classics. (2) Literature includes drama and poetry as well as prose.

❖ A Transactional View of Literature

Louise Rosenblatt (1978) describes experiencing literature as a transaction. For her a poem (story, novel, or play) is not an object, but an event. It happens during the coming together of a reader and a text. The reader's experiences, personality, and memories are drawn upon and combine with the poem to create a new experience which becomes part of the ongoing stream of experience.

The reader decides what is written and how it is written. Decisions about what is written concern the subject, characters, setting, plot, conflict, contrasts, and identification. Decisions about how it is written concern structure and tone of voice. On another level the reader must decide what the book means. He or she must infer the theme. Relating the book to other works of literature through subject, characters, setting, action, conflict, structure, and tone of voice often influences the reader's decision about what the book means (theme).

Each reader enters into his or her own transaction with what is read, so for each reader the transaction with a given text is somewhat different. On the other hand, experiencing the same text enables us to explore how we resemble each other as well as how we differ from one another.

What are teachers to make of all this? Experts agree that there is no one correct response to or interpretation of literature. All responses are right if they make sense and if they are true to the text.

Purves and Monson (1984) report that children's overt responses to literature (what they say about it) develop in something like the following stages:

- Deal with literal aspects of the story (He had lots of cats.)
- Make subjective judgments without elaboration (I didn't like it.)
- Identify with characters (He feels bad about it.)
- Make subjective judgments and elaborate (I like it because it sounds like it is true.)
- Make judgments that deal with formal aspects of the work (I like the way it rhymes.)
- Make interpretations of character (He was kind of small but he was stubborn, so . . .)
- Refer to the theme (You can take it literally, but it might mean that you can't trust adults.)

Finally, children are able to make the whole range of responses to literature. They can refer to the subject, characters, plot, conflict, contrasts, identification, structure, tone of voice, and theme.

❖ Teaching the Elements of Literature

In chapter 6 I described approaches to teaching reading through literature. These approaches make provisions for teaching children about literature as well as improving their reading. In response to the material they are reading children naturally refer to people in the stories, what happened, where it happened, and so on. They do not at first use the terms *character, plot, action,* and *setting.* Teachers, however, can use these words in responding to the students—sometimes defining them, sometimes simply using them appropriately, and always using the child's reference to the concept to teach the meaning of the literary term.

The very youngest children allude to more abstract concepts such as tone of voice and theme. Teachers may use the appropriate term in their responses, but will not focus on the term as much as respond to the child's particular reference to the concept. In middle and upper grades, teachers begin to use appropriate terms consistently, point out the reappearance of the same element from story to story, and begin to make these elements the subject of minilessons or group projects.

❖ Teaching Appropriate Responses to Literature

The evidence is overwhelming that children learn to respond to literature by engaging in literature as part of a literate community. Stories are read to them and told to them. They retell favorite stories and make up new ones. They read stories and respond to them, and their responses are validated by their teachers and peers. They write stories which are shared and responded to by their teachers and peers. They come to understand what to expect when listening (and later when reading), and they come to know what is expected when they tell (and later write) stories. According to Applebee (1979)

> . . . the stories which children hear lead them to a rich and highly structured set of expectations about what new stories will be like. They come to expect a consistent structure, with a definite beginning and a definite end which resolves the situation (or problem) in a satisfying way. Associated with this, they develop a set of conventional characters and situations which provide a kind of story shorthand for dealing with complex notions such as wickedness or deceit.
>
> These expectations come to bear when children encounter a new story, and are also brought to bear in the children's own storytelling. They can be used to recount, and in the process reflect upon and organize, the children's everyday experience of the world. They can also be used as a powerful and safe vehicle for exploring somewhat threatening or disturbing ideas, providing both the structure for controlling those ideas and the promise of a happy ending. The storyteller can create a bad character and explore the consequences of "bad" actions, without any of the blame for these evil deeds falling back upon the storyteller. (p. 644)

Reading Aloud to Children

Gordon Wells' (1986) longitudinal study of children's literacy development emphasized the importance of "book and story experiences" in the lives of preschoolers. This study also demonstrated the enormous variability in the number of such experiences in the lives of preschoolers. In his study, one child who was very successful in school had something like 6,000 book and story experiences before beginning school, while another child who was decidedly unsuccessful in school had not had a single one! Other studies have shown that respect for reading in the home is an important variable to predict literacy achievement in school (Thorndike, 1973; Clark, 1976). Noyce and Christie (1989) cite a number of studies that show a positive relationship between preschoolers being read to at home and oral language development, vocabulary knowledge, eagerness to read, and later school reading achievement.

Fortunately, there is evidence that reading aloud to children in the primary grades can have similar beneficial effects even among children who have not had much experience with books and stories in their preschool years. Cullinan, Jaggar, and Strickland (1974) showed that reading aloud to children for only twenty minutes a day and encouraging some response through art, creative drama, and so on, produced significant gains in vocabulary and reading comprehension scores. Imagine what benefits children will reap from a program that finds them awash in literacy events such as the following program described by Huck and Kerstetter (1987).

Kristen Kerstetter is a kindergarten teacher who sees the importance of reading to children. She maintains a classroom library of around 400 titles, some of which she buys with funds supplied by the school PTA and some of which she borrows from the public and school libraries. She changes as many as one-fourth of the titles each month. In preparation for visiting the library, Kristen posts a sheet of paper and asks children to suggest particular books or subjects they would like to read about. When the books arrive, she takes them out one at a time telling the children something about each book and commenting, when appropriate, on who requested the book or books on that subject.

She has the children organize the classroom library—counting books, ABC books, books by Ezra Jack Keats, for example—and she encourages the children to invent their own categories. One class had a shelf of spaghetti books (tall and thin).

Kristen reads to the whole class, to groups of five or six, and to individuals. She reads two or three stories at each session, and she reads two or three times a day. She rereads stories—sometimes she reads the same story twenty times in a month.

When she reads to children, Kristen's objectives are to make the experience pleasurable and instructive. She begins by showing the cover of the book and asking the children to predict what will happen in the story by looking at the title and the picture on the front cover (see the discussion of the directed listening and thinking activity in chapter 7). If appropriate, she asks what other books the class has read by the same author. She sometimes reads two versions of the same story and discusses the differences with the children. She encourages children to respond to the stories by using art, creative dramatics, and building blocks; by cooking; and by reading other stories and poems. She chooses some story books because of their beautiful pictures or rich language and others because they are easy and predictable. Books like *Brown Bear, Brown Bear* can be brought home and "read" by children to their parents.

After reading a story several times, Kristen uses a big book (a published version if available, or she creates her own) to point to words as she reads. This is similar to the shared reading that many children are accustomed to doing with adults at home. Through reading, pointing, and discussion, children learn the concepts of word, letter, and directionality of print. They learn to handle books and to match texts with pictures. Children begin to share books with one another, imitating the shared book experiences they have had with the teacher. (See the discussion of emergent literacy in chapter 6.)

Soon children know books by heart. They respond to favorite well-known texts with variations "Tin Man, Tin Man, who do you see? I see Scarecrow looking at me!" Games of literary trivial pursuit soon begin. "Who lived in a shoe?" "Whose porridge did Goldilocks 'eat all up'?"

During shared writing (described in chapter 6 as the experience story approach to teaching beginning reading) patterns of often read books soon appear. Elements from literature appear as well—princesses go into long sleeps to be awakened by a kiss. The language and phraseology of books appear—"He was the kindest of kings and lived in the beautifulist of castles."

As they grow older, children continue to borrow words, content, and structure from their reading to use in their writing. One child responded when asked if reading made her a better writer, "If you never read a book, you wouldn't know how to write a book" (Jaggar, Carrara, & Weiss, 1986). Burris (1985) reported that third graders combined character themes and plots from different folk tales in creating their own. She concluded that good stories are the best "story starters." Mills (1968) reported that reading or listening to a story followed by discussion as a prewriting activity had a good effect on the writing of fourth graders.

The benefits of reading aloud to students continue in the middle and upper grades. Tiedt (1989) suggests that students learn the following things as they listen to their teacher read aloud. (The book she refers to is *Tom Sawyer*.)

1. What fluent reading sounds like—the cadence of English sentences, the varied intonation appropriate for questions or a sense of excitement, and the way to pronounce words.
2. A positive attitude toward reading and toward being in school—teacher and students are sharing an enjoyable experience. . . .
3. English grammar—what book language sounds like, how English sentences are structured, and sentence variety.
4. Writing style—interesting ways of using language, figurative language, and imagery.
5. Characteristics of one form of writing (narrative)—plot development, characterization, setting, mood, theme, and dialogue.
6. Comprehension abilities—same ones used in reading independently are introduced through listening—vocabulary, inference, generalization, and evaluation.
7. Perception of the author as a writer—information about the man, Samuel Clemens, who wrote this book, the difficulties of his life, his familiarity with the setting, and issues presented. (pp. 17–18)

Tiedt's list implies that the teacher's reading to students is accompanied by a discussion of such matters as plot, characterization, inference, evaluation, and information about the author. This might take the form of minilessons as in a reading workshop (see chapter 6). Reading to students should always be followed by an opportunity for students to respond through discussion, writing, art, and creative dramatics.

Ways into "Critical Response"

Young children have some very interesting ideas about stories (Applebee, 1977). Children start out believing that stories are facts. They will not permit parents to change a story—bowls of cornflakes cannot be substituted for bowls of oatmeal. They cannot cope with the idea that stories have authors and can be changed. When asked how stories might be made better, even seven-year-olds suggest other stories that are better rather than suggesting how the story could be made better. Asked if she could visit Cinderella, a six-year-old answered that she could not, because Cinderella lived too far away.

Applebee explains the difference between the child's experience of literature and a mature experience of literature. The child sees literature as facts to be dealt with as in a conversation to which she or he is a party—listening and responding as a participant. Mature readers view literature from a little distance. (Applebee refers to this as the "spectator role.") They do not ask whether the story is true, but whether it is pleasing to them and consistent with their experience and beliefs. Once again the idea of detachment appears as it did in the discussions of writing and creative dramatics. The mature reader's response to literature is a **critical response.** This does not mean that they criticize in the negative sense of the word, but that they consider the piece from a little distance and from many angles and respond congnitively, emotionally, and aesthetically.

TO THINK ABOUT

Detachment and Communication

Can you find other places in this book where the idea of detachment or distance is mentioned in connection with higher levels of performance in listening, speaking, reading, and writing? Does this suggest a theme to you in terms of an approach to language arts?

At all grade levels it is useful to help students see that stories are created by authors (sometimes anonymous authors, sometimes a series of authors as in legends, but authors nevertheless). Perhaps nothing does this so well as publishing children's writing as described in the process approach to teaching writing.

Another way of doing this is to collect various versions of the same story. Fables, legends, nursery rhymes, and certain children's classics put out by different publishers often have somewhat different texts and they always have different art and illustrations accompanying the text. The words *abridged* or *told by* on the cover are indications that a book contains a variation of a story. Teachers who use basal readers for teaching reading may find that teachers' manuals have lists of other versions of some of the selections that appear in the readers.

Examining different presentations of the same story, comparing them, and discussing which students like best may be a first step in helping students see that stories have authors and can be changed and that one version can be more satisfying than another version. This can be tied in with helping children understand the function of the revising stage of their own writing.

Similarly, classroom libraries can be organized to help children understand that many stories (and poems) are of the same type (genre) or are on the same topic or share the same theme.

Strickland and Feeley (1985) developed "the story structure framework for reading and writing." This involves three stages: exposure to stories within the same genre; retelling and creating stories within the genre; and writing activities focused on the genre. The genre chosen might be Native American legends, mystery stories, fairy tales, and so on.

Exposure

A sixth-grade teacher introduced mysteries to his class by first reading a collection of mystery short stories aloud to his class. He and the librarian presented book talks (brief oral reviews) on mysteries and encouraged the students to choose them for their independent reading. Group discussions and individual conferences focused on these books.

Retelling and Creating

Children responded to the mysteries they read through pantomime, role playing, reader's theater, and story retelling. At times they re-created the stories they read, and at times they changed them or created similar new stories.

Writing

Through retelling and creating, most students develop an implicit knowledge of the features associated with a genre. As a prewriting activity, the teacher elicited what they had learned about mystery stories. He helped make their knowledge of the genre explicit. Their list looked something like this:

What Makes a Mystery Story?

1. It has clues.
2. There is a crime or a puzzling situation.
3. There is one or more detectives.
4. The ending is surprising.
5. The detective uses the clues to find out who committed the crime or to explain the puzzle.
6. There is suspense.

Using such lists, three kinds of writing experiences follow.

- Shared retelling. With the teacher acting as scribe, the class retells a favorite story, comparing it to elements on their list.
- Shared writing. With the teacher acting as scribe, the class creates an original mystery story, comparing it to elements on their list. The teacher models revision and editing.
- Individual writing. Students are encouraged to include the genre in their story-writing efforts and to share their stories with the group.

Additional Ways of Responding to Literature

Write a poem about a character in a book.
In a letter, tell how you feel after reading the book.
Read parts of the book aloud to a younger child. Ask the child what he or she liked best about it.
Write an advertisement and provide an illustration for the book.
Write a radio review of the book.
As a group, create a newspaper about a book. Write news stories, editorials, advertisements, obituaries, and so on.
Write a news story about an incident in the book.
Write a diary for a character in the book.
Dress up like a character from the book and introduce yourself to other students.
Make masks representing the characters.
Use one of the creative dramatics techniques discussed earlier in this chapter—storytelling, movement, pantomime, role playing, reader's theater, playmaking, or puppetry.

❖ Literature and Teaching Reading and Writing

Alwood (1984) suggests that older students write personal accounts that parallel accounts in literature. After reading the story of Prometheus she suggested that students write about a time when they felt rebellious or actually did rebel. She believes this approach helps students appreciate great writing and their own writing as well. Noyce and Christie (1989) suggest using this approach in the middle and upper grades using the following titles:

Paul Danziger's *The Cat Ate My Gym Suit:* Have you made excuses for not doing something you should do?
Betsy Byar's *The Glory Girl:* Have you helped someone avoid danger or trouble?
Patricia MacLachlan's *Sarah, Plain and Tall:* If you were getting a new stepmother, what would you write about yourself in a letter to her?

❖ Using Poetry

The magic of language is nowhere more apparent than in poetry—listening to it, reading it, reciting it, responding to it, and writing it. Appreciation of poetry begins in the high chair and crib with "Patty-Cake" and "This Little Piggy Went to Market." It continues on the playground with "London Bridge" and "Little Sally Saucer" and jump-rope rhymes that children recite and respond to through movement. Choral recitation begins here, too, as children chant formulas and poems that are part of games. In primary grades the teacher's job is to keep it going, to give children permission to continue to enjoy poetry.

Nancy Larrick (1987) suggests that primary teachers start with group singing of familiar songs and move into choral reading, movement, and pantomime as discussed earlier in this chapter. Through these activities children learn to show their emotional responses to poetry physically and vocally by making their voices harsh or tender. Children learn that it is all right to respond in these ways to poetry in school. Larrick suggests the following ways to make poetry fit into every part of the school day:

- Read a poem each day. Print it in a prominent place where students can reread it often.
  Invite children to help choose the poem for the day. Favorites can be repeated.
  Focus your daily poems on a theme—sports, the moon and stars, an upcoming holiday.
  Devote a week to one poet, such as John Ciardi or Aileen Fisher.
- Do impromptu choral reading frequently—not to analyze the poem or to produce a polished performance, but to revel in the language, rhyme, and melody.
- Play music, sing, or hum an appropriate melody or song as a background to reading a poem.
  Use percussion instruments (drum, bells, sticks) to emphasize rhythm.
  Add movement, pantomime, and dance.
  Stage impromptu poetry "happenings" with choral reading, music, movement, pantomime, and dance.

❖ Writing Poetry

As pointed out earlier in this chapter, children's compositions, whether recited orally, dictated to the teacher, or written, reflect the literature they read and hear. In classrooms where children listen to poetry often, read it, perform it, and talk about it, many students will compose poetry without being asked. In shared writing experiences, children can write group poems modeled on poems that have become favorites for reading and reciting. While writing class poems, teachers can call attention to features of language that are often found in poetry, such as rhythm, rhyme, writing in lines and stanzas, the use of words that recall the sounds they represent (the buzzing of bees, the crashing of metal), and the use of words beginning with the same sound (ten terrible tall truckers).

Children enjoy writing poetry based on patterns or formulas. The teacher presents examples, the class composes one or two poems modeled on the examples, and the children are encouraged to write poems in small groups or individually, based on the models and the formula. The results can then be compared with the examples and formula to see if they conform.

The following patterns and formulas are frequently taught in elementary school:

Acrostic

Acrostics are based on names of people, places, or things. The name is written vertically and each letter is used as the first letter in a word in that line. The words should describe the name appearing vertically.

Merry
Outgoing
Laughing
Lovable
Young

A good pal
My partner
Years ahead of her time

List

Lists of short related phrases supply a very loose structure that becomes a poem. Children brainstorm the topic (lies I have told; things that annoy me) as well as the items on the list. Outrageous responses make this a spontaneous and upbeat exercise.

Ten Things That Could Never Happen

I win the lottery
No spelling test on Friday
The Cubs win the pennant
Everyone gets an A
Billy becomes president
Mr. Fradin wins the Mr. Universe contest
Snow in August
Robins in January
Clocks run backward
Water runs uphill

Cinquain

Cinquain can be described as a five-lined poem constructed as follows:

One word, giving the title
Two words, describing the title
Three words, expressing an action
Four words, expressing a feeling
One word, a synonym for the title

Trucks
Big, powerful
Hauling big loads
Their power scares me
Monsters

Lantern

A lantern is a poem that suggests the shape of a Japanese lantern. It is a five line poem with eleven syllables in a one-two-three-four-one pattern.

```
       —              One syllable
     —   —            Two syllables
   —   —   —          Three syllables
 —   —   —   —        Four syllables
       —              One syllable
```

          Tests
          Scary
        Lot to lose
     Not much to gain
          Ouch

Diamente

A diamente is a poem that suggests the shape of a diamond. It has seven lines. It is a poem of contrasts. The first line is noun; the second line has two adjectives describing the noun; the third line has three *-ing* or *-ed* verb forms related to the noun. The fourth line begins to make a transition. It contains four nouns that refer to both the opening noun and the concluding noun (line 7). The noun of the seventh line has an opposite or contrasting meaning to the noun in the first line. The fifth line has three *-ing* or *-ed* verb forms related to the concluding noun. The sixth line has two adjectives related to the concluding noun.

          Skyscraper
         tall, straight
    climbing, reaching, towering
Offices, apartments, shelter, abode
     humbled, crouching, battered
        squat, crooked
          shanty

Limerick

A limerick is a five-lined poem. Lines 1, 2, and 5 rhyme, and lines 3 and 4 rhyme. Lines 1, 2, and 5 are longer than lines 3 and 4.

There once was a fellow named Pat
Who had an outrageous straw hat.
He walked by a cow
Who was hungry and how,
And that was the end of Pat's hat.

The formal characteristics of poetry are often more restricting than the formal requirements of prose. The formulas offered in the preceding section are testimony to that. On the other hand, poetry offers the writer more freedom in many ways. Surprising, logic-defying word choices are often the best ones. There is not the requirement that thoughts be expressed in complete sentences. The demands of grammar and standard usage are relaxed. Perhaps it is this tremendous license coupled with stricter formal demands that makes writing poetry magic.

Short lessons on composing poems that imitate models or that conform to a particular formula gives students the knowledge they need to choose poetry as a form of expression when it is appropriate. Doing poetry in school gives them permission to keep alive the delight in poetry that many children bring to school from the home and playground.

❖ Making Children Literate

One meaning of the word *illiterate* is "unacquainted with literature." Adult Americans who do not know who Mark Twain was or who think Hamlet was a Scottish king might be considered illiterate regardless of whether they could read or write. Ameliorating this form of illiteracy, that is acquainting children with literature, is one of the primary objectives of the schools. A second meaning of the word *illiterate* is "unable to read and write." People who can read and write at a low level of proficiency are also often considered illiterate. Ameliorating this form of illiteracy is perhaps an even more basic objective of the schools. Introducing literature into the elementary-school classroom meets both these objectives. It becomes both an object of study and a vehicle for teaching all the language arts. It unifies the language arts program and it brings the classroom to life.

Strickland (1987) believes that classrooms where literature is given its proper place have the following characteristics:

Students have access to many books in the classroom library, school library, and public library.
Time is set aside every day for children to read books they choose for themselves. Reading literature is not relegated to homework or done when the "real" work of the school is completed.
Teachers read aloud to students frequently, choosing a variety of types of literature—prose and poetry, fables, myths, modern short stories, and so on.
Teachers and librarians give frequent book talks, sharing and discussing books with students.
Reading and writing instruction is related through literature. Literature is used in writing lessons as an example, a model, a story starter, and so on. Responses to literature frequently incorporate writing.
At times teachers focus on aspects of literature itself—character, setting,

theme, and genre. Students need this kind of knowledge in order to appreciate literature and to respond to it properly.

Students are encouraged to respond to literature in many different ways.

LANGUAGE ACROSS THE CURRICULUM: USING THEMATIC UNITS

Language learning takes place across the curriculum. Students speak, listen, read, and write when they conduct science experiments; when they create and discuss concrete examples of mathematical statements such as "five divided by sixteen"; when they attempt to articulate the connection between the women's suffrage movement early in this century and the civil rights struggle of the 1960s; and as they work together on an art project or reflect on individual projects.

Different learning activities across different subjects engage children in various forms of speaking (conversation, discussion, formal presentation), various forms of reading (skimming for information, summarizing, reading for enjoyment, reading graphs, charts, diagrams), and writing at various levels of formality (taking notes, writing up observations, writing reports).

Different disciplines give students varied experiences with using language to inform and be informed, to persuade and be persuaded, to express and feel emotion, to imagine, to be entertained, and to engage in transaction and ritual. Addressing subject-matter learning gives students the opportunity to learn about language, to consider language as an object of study, and to reflect on their own thinking processes and problem-solving strategies. Language learning across the curriculum is enhanced "when children recognize in more explicit ways how linguistic choices are expressed in different genres and how various disciplines reflect various ways of knowing" (Pappas et al., 1990).

Learning language skills through subject matter and learning subject matter through language is further enhanced when children are given the opportunity to focus on things that interest them and when they are given ample time "to explore and think and change their minds, to consider and evaluate different points of view, to decide on their questions and how to resolve them, to read and reread, to write and revise" (Pappas et al., 1990).

Pappas and her colleagues have articulated a perspective on teaching in the elementary school that is based on the foregoing view of the relationship of learning language arts and other subject matter. According to their plan teachers devise thematic units that link many subject areas. These units may last for several days or for many weeks. The topics or themes come from the curriculum and are related to children's interests. They allow for the use of many resources.

For example, in a fourth-grade classroom the teacher focused on the topic of exploration that is part of the social studies curriculum. Brainstorming with colleagues she created a web of topics and ideas that relate to exploration. A small number of these ideas are presented here in outline form.

Exploration

    Exploring with language
        Exploring accents, dialects, regionalism
            Survey TV use of dialect
            Invite a storyteller who can use dialect effectively
        Exploring word origins
            Examine a dictionary of American slang
            List prefixes and meanings
        Codes and special languages
            Explore sign language
            Read a story in two languages
    Scientific exploration
        Exploring the microscope
            Look at life in a drop of water
            Research the invention of the microscope
        Exploring space
            Construct a mural of the known universe
            Write a story about travel to Saturn
    Historic exploration
        The ages of exploration
            Make a time line of historic exploration and discovery
            Write a journal of a journey of your own
    Political exploration
        Invent a good government
        Debate: There should be reparations for Japanese-Americans who were interned during World War II
    Exploring life histories
        Write a biography
        Study biography as a genre
    Personal exploration
        Exploring careers
            Invite people to talk about their work
            Visit worksites and list skills
        Inner journeys
            Make a time line of important events in your life
            Write a plan for things you want to accomplish

The theme, the options, and the activities were introduced and students were encouraged to add to the lists. Over the next twenty days (during the implementation stage) this theme was explored throughout the school day in the various subjects.

Language Arts

Make time lines
Read poetry
Discuss biography
Small groups pinpoint places on a map where group members have visited
Students learn to use primary source material related to the United States westward movement

Social Studies

Role play the decision-making process of a New England family thinking about moving west in 1850

Science

Report on living systems in an aquarium. Use an observation chart
Watch a video on ocean exploration

Math

Work on problems related to time and distance
Calculate time differences between points on the earth

Art

Paint with watercolors after reading a biography of Winslow Homer

There are several distinguishing features of integrated language classrooms:

1. Students and teachers collaborate in meaning making. Children are regularly involved in brainstorming at the outset of a thematic unit and are given choices in daily activities.
2. Teachers and students adopt a different view of "error." Students develop hypotheses and test them. Risk-taking is expected and encouraged.
3. Teachers strive to arrange contexts that engage students in learning. Students are participants, not recipients.
4. Classrooms are filled with a range of materials.
5. The community serves as a resource. Both materials and people are brought in and the students go into the community as part of their learning experience. (Pappas et al., 1990, pp. 161–162)

The integrated language classroom, like the reading workshop and the process approach to teaching writing, is one more manifestation of the holistic, collaborative, integrated approach to teaching. It includes not only language arts, but also all the elementary-school subjects. It is one more approach that results in a language- and literacy-rich classroom community.

> **ACTIVITY**
>
> Plan a thematic unit—from choosing a theme to implementing the unit. Use your classmates as brainstorming and planning partners.
>
> Although the discussion of the thematic unit approach presented here should enable you to do this activity, you will find a much fuller treatment of the topic in *An Integrated Language Perspective in the Elementary School* (Pappas et al., 1990, chaps. 1–4).

Summary

Children are adept at the imaginative and affective use of language long before they enter school. They can switch in and out of discourse styles and real and imaginary activities. They attempt in play what they dare not in everyday activity—linguistically, emotionally, and cognitively. Through play they experience the pervasive ritual of language use, discourse styles, and conventions of literary forms. They are able to detach themselves from actual situations and envisage situations that are not equal.

Using creative dramatics and literature is a way of nurturing the affective and imaginative uses of language that most children bring to school, a way of teaching subject matter, and a way of teaching the conventional forms of literature and drama.

Storytelling is an art practiced by teachers to engage children in speech, wonder, mystery, and creativity. Encouraging storytelling by young students helps them gain facility with concepts that are important in reading and writing, such as sequence and use of dialog. Storytelling is encouraged in the middle and upper grades as an art—a form of literature and performance.

Choral speaking fosters the linguistic, emotional, and cognitive growth of students. It is used as a vehicle for speech improvement. It can be done with groups of any size or age. It emphasizes group effort, provides an opportunity to introduce poetry, offers shy or handicapped students an opportunity to speak, and promotes good speech habits. It is enjoyable and can be combined with rhythmic movement and pantomime.

Creative drama is improvised. It is not intended for performance before an audience. It is engaged in for the purpose of imagining, enacting, and reflecting on human experience. Children's first efforts to try out roles and re-create life situations arise through dramatic play. Movement, pantomime, role playing or improvisation, story drama, and reader's theater are forms of creative drama.

Children's first efforts to try out roles and re-create life situations arise through dramatic play. Children mimic the actions and behaviors of others. Therefore, movement is an entree to creative drama.

Pantomime is the art of conveying ideas without words. It is a vehicle for responding to literature. It encourages close reading. It can be enhanced with movement, music, and sound. Story theater is an activity where one person reads a story or poem while others pantomime the meaning. Role playing and improvisation are two names for the same activity.

Story drama involves five steps: presentation of material, organization, dramatization, evaluation, and replaying. The evaluate and replay cycle is repeated until the group is satisfied that no significant improvement is possible. Reader's theater involves five steps: selection of material, creation of a written script, assigning parts and reading, discussion, and rereading.

Puppets and masks are vehicles for encouraging expression, and they are used as teaching tools. Shy children will often speak for a puppet when they would not otherwise perform. Novelty and fun motivates most children to greater involvement in creative dramatics and to pay greater attention when the teacher uses puppets and masks in teaching.

Creative dramatics is useful in teaching oral language and improving vocabulary. It fosters critical detachment which is necessary for mature writing. The plan-attempt-evaluate-plan cycle of creative dramatics is reminiscent of the writing cycle. Creative dramatics motivates greater attention during reading and improves comprehension.

Literature has six characteristics: It uses language; it portrays emotion, suggests pictures, or gives pleasure; it is organized; it speaks in a voice; it conveys experience; and it invites us to think of other works of literature that are similar. The elements of literature are characters, setting, plot, conflict, contrast, structure, tone, and content (subject and theme).

Rosenblatt describes experiencing literature as a transaction. The reader's experience, personality, and memories are drawn upon and combine with the work to form a new experience. There is therefore no one correct response to or interpretation of literature. Correct responses to literature make sense to the reader and are true to the text.

Children's responses to literature develop in the following stages: dealing with literal aspects; making subjective judgments without elaboration; identifying with characters; making subjective judgments with elaboration; dealing with formal aspects of the work; interpreting characters; and referring to theme.

When young children respond to stories they refer to the elements of literature, but they do not identify them by name. Teachers comment on children's responses using the appropriate terms. In middle and upper grades, teachers begin to use appropriate terms consistently, point out the same elements from story to story, and make the elements of literature the subject of minilessons.

There are positive relationships between children being read to and oral language development, vocabulary, eagerness to read, and reading achievement in school. As children become knowledgeable about literature, elements of literature begin to appear in their spoken and written stories. Reading to students in the middle grades teaches them what fluent reading sounds like; gives them a positive attitude toward reading; and exposes them to the sound of book language, writing style, and characteristics of form. It enhances their comprehension and heightens their perception of authors as writers.

Children must develop detachment from literature in order to respond critically. They must realize that stories have authors and that the stories could have been written differently. This can be accomplished through publishing students' writing, comparing different versions of the same story, comparing stories and poems from the same genre, and studying the characteristics of various genres.

Some additional ways of responding to literature are writing a poem about a character, writing an advertisement for a book, and making a mask to represent a character.

Literature is used to teach writing. Stories themselves are the best story starters. Children often write stories or poems with themes found in literature.

Poetry in the classroom capitalizes on children's happy experiences with rhymes and word games. In school, children experience poetry with group singing of familiar songs, choral reading of poems, and movement and pantomime accompanying poetry.

Many children who experience poetry begin to compose poetry without being asked. Teachers encourage this by calling attention to the features often found in poetry, such as rhyme, rhythm, writing in lines and stanzas, using words that recall the sounds they represent, and using words beginning with the same sound. Children also enjoy writing poems based on patterns or formulas such as acrostic, list, cinquain, lantern, diamente, and limerick.

Literature in the elementary school is both the topic of study and a vehicle for teaching speaking, writing, reading, and listening. In a classroom that gives literature its proper place students have access to many books, time is set aside for reading self-selected material, teachers read aloud to students frequently, teachers share books with students through book talks, literature is used to teach reading and writing, teachers sometimes focus on elements of literature, and students are encouraged to respond to literature in a variety of ways.

Language learning takes place across the entire curriculum. Learning in various subjects engages students in speaking; listening; reading; and writing in many formats, for many purposes, and at various levels of formality. Subject-matter learning involves students in the informative, persuasive, affective, imaginative, and transactional functions of language as reader, writer, speaker, and listener.

Language across the curriculum is a perspective on teaching based on integrating subject matter and language arts in thematic units that last for several days or many weeks. Teachers create a web of topics and ideas related to one area of the curriculum. Students are encouraged to add to the web and to choose activities for exploring the theme. In an integrated language classroom students and teachers collaborate, risk-taking is encouraged, teachers arrange contexts for student learning, there is a wide range of material, and the community serves as a resource.

For Review and Discussion

1. Recall from your experience examples of imaginative, poetic, and dramatic use of language by very young children.
2. What are the characteristics of storytelling, choral speaking, and creative drama?
3. What are the characteristics of movement, pantomime, role playing or improvisation, story drama, and reader's theater?
4. Recall a creative drama or teaching experience that might have been enhanced by the use of puppets or masks.
5. Relate the use of creative drama to teaching writing, reading, speaking, and listening.
6. Choose a popular song, comic strip, soap opera, or situation comedy. Analyze it in terms of the six qualities of literature attributed to Purves and Monson in this chapter.
7. Choose a popular song, comic strip, soap opera, or situation comedy. Discuss the elements of literature in relation to it.
8. Recall the first book or story you vividly remember from childhood. How does Rosenblatt's transactional theory of literature account for your response to this book or story?
9. Contrast storytelling with reading aloud to students. What are the purposes of each in primary grades? In middle and upper grades?
10. What part does the concept of detachment play in critical response to literature and in the writing process? Compare these uses of the concept of detachment to the idea of reflecting on small-group discussion and processing cooperative learning episodes.
11. Choose a popular song, comic strip, soap opera, or situation comedy. How would you foster critical response to this work in an upper-grade classroom?
13. Write poems following each of these patterns or formulas: acrostic, list, cinquain, lantern, diamente, and limerick.
14. What are the characteristics of a classroom where literature has been given its proper place?

For Further Reading

Cariello, M. (1990). "The path to a good poem that lasts forever": Children writing poetry. *Language Arts, 67,* 832–838.
Hill, B. (1989). Books before five revisited. *Language Arts, 66,* 309–317.
King, M., & McKenzie, M. (1988). Research currents: Literary discourse from the child's perspective. *Language Arts, 65,* 304–314.
Langer, J. (1990). Understanding literature. *Language Arts, 67,* 812–816.
McClure, A., & Zitlow, C. (1991). Not just the facts: Aesthetic response in elementary content area studies. *Language Arts, 68,* 27–33.

Mikkelsen, N. (1989). Remembering Ezra Jack Keats and "The Snowy Day": What makes a children's book good? *Language Arts, 66,* 608–624.

Millward, P. (1990). Drama as well-made play. *Language Arts, 67,* 151–162.

O'Neill, C. (1989). Dialogue and drama: The transformation of events, ideas, and teachers. *Language Arts, 66,* 147–159.

Pace, G. (1991). When teachers use literature for literacy instruction: Ways that constrain, ways that free. *Language Arts, 68,* 12–25.

Pappas, C. (1991). Fostering full access to literacy by including information books. *Language Arts, 68,* 449–462.

Rosenblatt, L. M. (1991). Literature-S.O.S.! *Language Arts, 68,* 444–448.

San Jose, C. (1988). Story drama in the content areas. *Language Arts, 65,* 26–33.

Trousdale, A. (1990). Interactive storytelling. Scaffolding children's early narratives. *Language Arts, 67,* 164–173.

Verriour, P. (1986). Creating worlds of dramatic discourse. *Language Arts, 63,* 253–263.

Verriour, P. (1989). "This is drama": The play beyond the play. *Language Arts, 66,* 276–286.

Verriour, P. (1990). Storying and storytelling in drama. *Language Arts, 67,* 144–150.

Wason-Ellam, L. (1988). Using literary patterns: Who's in control of the authorship? *Language Arts, 65,* 291–301.

Wolf, S. (1991). Following the trail of story. *Language Arts, 68,* 388–395.

CHAPTER 11

Grammar, Syntax, Usage, Handwriting, and Spelling

Introduction
Grammar, Syntax, and Usage
Handwriting
Spelling

Summary
For Review and Discussion
For Further Reading

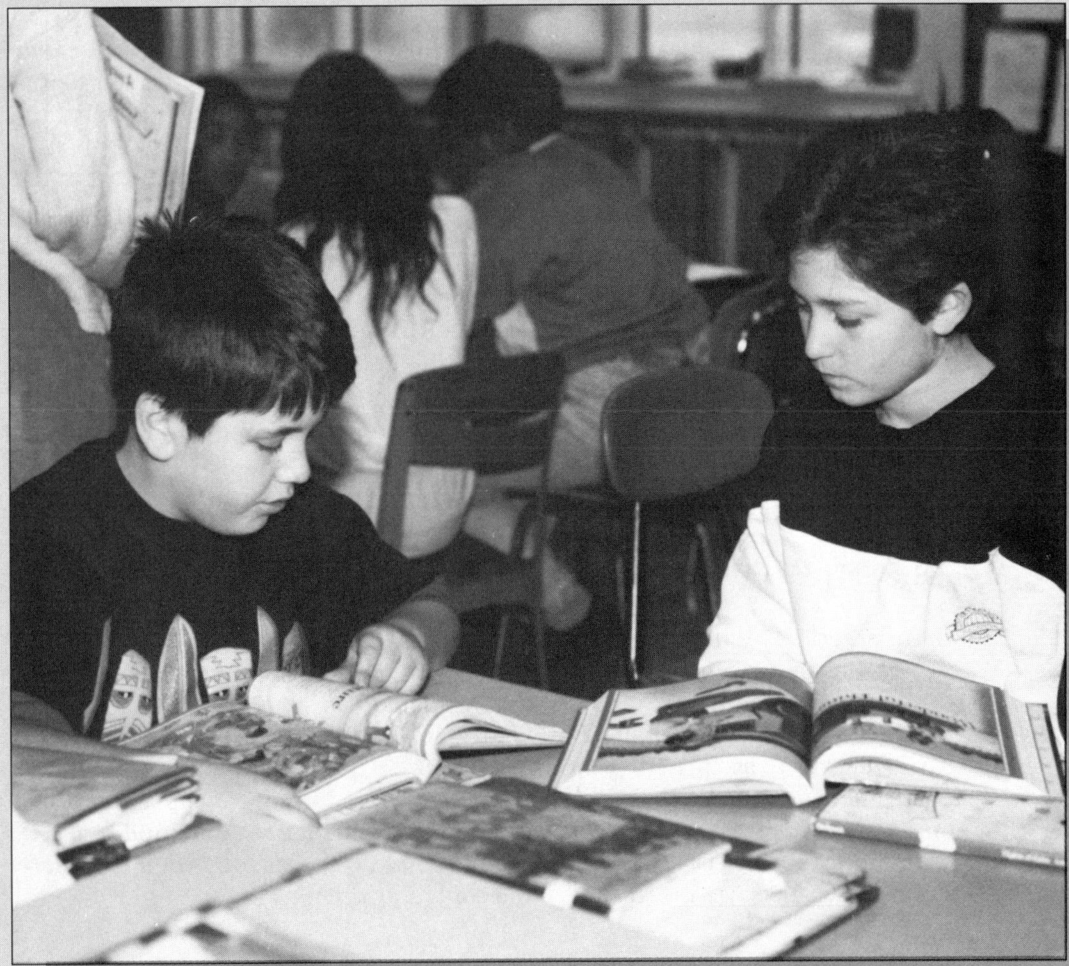

INTRODUCTION

Facility with a full range of syntactic structures and standard usage is of crucial importance in the effective use of language. When language is perceived as immature or inappropriate because of limited syntactic range or nonstandard usage, the informative, persuasive, or other intent may fail. Facility with syntax and standard usage is perhaps even more important in writing than in speech because more complex syntax and formal usage are characteristics of written language. In writing, concerns with handwriting and spelling are added, and all these concerns are addressed in the revising and editing stages. Serious attention from teachers to these matters is essential since they contribute to the effectiveness of the text, and because students who feel insecure in these areas are often unable to put them aside in the writing stage. This chapter deals with spelling, handwriting, standard usage, and facility with syntax. Because of its intimate connection to teaching facility with syntax and standard usage, grammar is discussed as well.

GRAMMAR, SYNTAX, AND USAGE

In this section I will discuss three things: (1) teaching grammar to children; (2) helping children gain facility with the full range of syntactic structures offered by English; and (3) teaching children standard usage. These are three traditional objectives of the language arts curriculum. Unfortunately, all three are at times referred to as "teaching grammar."

If there is any area of teaching language arts that is controversial, it is this one, and confusing these three objectives has made the discussion muddy. I will explain the differences between them and explain why it is important to understand these objectives clearly and avoid confusing them.

❖ ### Defining Terms

Teaching Grammar

When teachers say things like, "In the sentence *My hat is red*, *hat* is the subject. It is a singular noun," they are teaching grammar. A grammar is a set of statements that systematically describe a language. Countless people use language proficiently but do not know any grammar.

Teaching Facility with Syntax

Syntax has to do with the arrangement or order of meaningful parts in phrases or sentences. A child will say "more milk," "more tickle," "more book"—but never "milk more," "tickle more," "book more." An early form of negative utterance may be "No daddy go." Children who use this form never say "Daddy go no." Since the order of words at this stage appears to be rule-governed, we can assert that the child has facility with syntax.

When a child goes from the construction *more book* to *Read the book more* we can say that he shows increased knowledge of English syntax or that his syntax is improving (becoming more conventional by adult standards). Such growth in syntax is expected of children. It is not expected that a child would be able to make statements that describe the differences between the two statements *more book* and *Read the book more.* Such statements would demonstrate knowledge of grammar (language that describes a language).

In everyday speech, however, we say that a four-year-old's grammar is probably more complex than a two-year-old's and everyone knows what we mean—we mean that her or his syntax is more complex. In the popular mind, "grammar" means statements that describe language and it also means "syntax." There is nothing wrong with that. In a discussion of teaching of language arts, however, more precision is necessary. There is considerable opposition to teaching grammar in the elementary school, but giving elementary-school students facility with the full range of syntactic structures available in English is a generally agreed-up objective. Referring to both these activities as teaching grammar is the source of a great deal of confusion.

Teaching Standard Usage

When teachers say things like

- Don't say (or write), "George ain't." Say (or write), "George isn't."
- Don't say (or write), "between him and I." Say (or write), "between him and me."
- Don't say (or write), "Him leaving upset Anna." Say (or write), "His leaving upset Anna."

they are attempting to teach standard usage. Once again, however, such admonitions are often referred to as teaching grammar. In a discussion of teaching language arts, such imprecision is the source of a good deal of confusion since many people who oppose teaching grammar in elementary school favor teaching standard usage.

Teaching Two Things at Once

Aside from the imprecise use of terms, it is difficult to keep these terms separate because grammar is often taught in order to increase children's facility with syntax as in the following example:

> Teacher: Words that describe nouns are called adjectives. [This is a grammatical statement]. Let's take the statement *Jeffrey saw the house.* What adjectives might we use to describe the house?

The objective of this lesson is to give students facility with more complex syntax—phrases with multiple adjectives such as *the big, old, wooden house.*

Grammar is often taught in order to teach standard usage as in the following example:

Teacher: If the subject of a sentence is plural, you use the verb *are* rather than *is*. [This is a grammatical statement.] What should you say, *The boys is here* or *The boys are here*?

The objective of this lesson is to teach standard English usage.

Notice that in both examples the teacher *is* teaching grammar. In both cases, however, teaching grammar is not the ultimate aim of the lesson.

✤ The Obligation of the School

Regarding Grammar

There is widely divided opinion on the question of teaching grammar in elementary schools. Practically no one believes any longer that grammar should be taught to teach logic or improve the mind. Years of experimentation have shown that teaching grammar does not improve students' writing. Judges do not rate the compositions of students who are taught grammar for a period of time any higher than the compositions of comparable students who are not taught grammar for the same period of time.

Those who favor teaching grammar believe that knowledge of grammar facilitates teaching language arts (writing, for example). A standard concern in elementary-school writing classes, for example, is about choosing precise adjectives (not *good* music but *lively, rhythmic* music) or precise verbs (not *walked* but *crept, strode* or *tiptoed*). Practically everyone agrees that if teachers are talking about adjectives they should call them "adjectives" rather than "describing words." Referring to a class of words is making a grammatical statement. Calling them by other than their conventional name does not make such statements less abstract. It may add to the students' confusion.

Of those who favor teaching grammar there is universal agreement that it should be taught in applied situations. A teacher may have a minilesson on identifying adjectives, for example, as part of a discussion of using adjectives in writing. This may be addressed to the whole class, a small group, or an individual child in a conference. The teacher may have a minilesson on identifying subjects and verbs in sentences as part of a discussion of choosing *was* or *were* in sentences with students who use such nonstandard constructions as *we was* and *they was*. Ideally such lessons arise out of collaborating with students who have agreed to work on matters of standard usage that arise in their spoken or written language.

If, in spite of all the foregoing, teachers still feel compelled to teach grammatical concepts as they appear in their school curriculum or in a textbook, they should keep lessons short and relate them to improving students' facility with mature syntax or to teaching standard usage.

Regarding Syntax

It is universally agreed that schools should give all students facility with the full range of syntactic structures that are available to literate, mature speakers.

Regarding Standard Usage

It is nearly universally agreed that schools should give all students facility with standard usage. Students who come from groups where nonstandard usage occurs should learn standard usage as a "second language," not as one to replace the language of their community, but as one that gives them access to mainstream economic and social institutions. I, for example, was raised in a blue-collar, Irish Catholic neighborhood in Chicago. I learned to say *ain't* on the street but not in school. I heard (and perhaps used) *yous* as the plural of *you* on the street, but I learned never to use it in school or formal situations. In college I learned to stress the first syllable of *theater* in mainline groups rather than the second syllable as I had learned in my neighborhood. When I became an editor (after teaching for ten years) I began to pay attention to the distinction between the verbs *lie* and *lay* in my speech (I probably learned to make this distinction in writing in college). Such things were important to my boss, the chief editor, and so they were important to me and I learned them.

I know grammar (one of my favorite subjects in school) and it helped in some cases. I know others (many of my classmates) who do not know grammar (it was not a favorite subject—they just didn't get it) but who have also learned standard usage as a second dialect. I am not convinced that knowledge of grammar is essential to learning standard usage if it is not one's native dialect, but I do believe it helps.

❖ The Impact of Structural Linguistics

In the past fifty years revolutionary developments in the fields outside education have had dramatic effects on the areas of teaching language arts that concern us here. The first of these was an intense interest, around mid-century, in structural linguistics by linguists and anthropologists.

One school of social science takes the position that the social sciences are essentially the same as the physical sciences. Adherents to this school believe the only difference is that the social scientists have not advanced their measurement devices to the point where they can describe their data in terms of mathematical formulas in the way that physical scientists have. Such social scientists are preoccupied with describing, with gathering data, and with measurement. They are interested in the frequency, intensity, and contiguity of events—that is, in measuring how often events occur, how perceptible they are, and what other events occur at the same (or nearly the same) time or place. This tradition in science is known as **empiricism.** In the nineteenth century, linguists of this school were preoccupied with the most physical, observable aspect of language—sound—and the science of phonology.

By the middle of this century, the most prominent linguist in the United States was Leonard Bloomfield (1887–1949), who was an empiricist. His method of studying language became known as **structural linguistics.**

Structural linguistics is an attempt to describe language as data without reference to meaning. Theoretically, linguists applying the principles of structural linguistics could write a grammar of a language they did not know. They did this by collecting a lot of data—transcriptions of language produced by people—and then looking at such things as frequency, intensity, and contiguity—all the classical concerns of the empiricists. They would then begin to write statements that described the language. Such statements are, of course, a grammar.

Suppose anthropologists who did not know English arrived in New York City and wanted to write a grammar of the people. According to the methods of structural linguists, they would first collect a lot of data or copy down in a phonetic notation the speech they heard. One must assume that the anthropologists had a transcription system that was able to capture the sounds and the melody (pitch, rhythm, stress, and juncture) of the language and that this system was good enough to enable them to divide the recorded speech into words, phrases, and sentences.

Imagine what rules (grammar) the researcher would be able to formulate about the structure of English. They might make observations like the following:

- The word *the* is very frequent in this language; it never appears at the end of a sentence, and it frequently appears at the beginning of a phrase.
- They might observe that the syllables we represent in written English as *-ing, -est,* and *-er* appear often at the ends of words. They might surmise that such syllables serve a word-building function. (They are, in fact, common English suffixes.)
- They might surmise that *of, in,* and *on* is a class of words—because of their frequency and the position where they occur in phrases.

When the anthropologist had accumulated a great amount of data, he or she could compile many facts about the structure of English and write a description of this language in terms of these observations. Such a description is a grammar. Notice that there is no mention of the meaning of the language, only a description of the physical data. Since this grammar refers not to meaning but to structure, it is known as structural linguistics.

Other linguists applied the principles of structural linguistics to describing English syntax. Subjects and predicates were defined in terms of their positions in sentences. Nouns were described as words that follow *noun determiners*—that is, words that fit into the slots "a ____," "the ____," and "my ____." Adjectives were described as words that fit into the slots "more ____" and "most ____," or "____er," and "____est." Words such as *because, if,* and *when* came to be called clause markers. Linguists went to great lengths to describe the syntax of English without referring to meaning.

Permissiveness

Several aspects of structural linguistics have had a very real effect on education. Structural linguistics is purely descriptive; it is nonprescriptive and nonjudgmental. When describing data, linguists do not ask whether it is considered correct to say such and such; they write down what is said, and it becomes part of the data. Going back to the earlier example, the linguist who is collecting data on a New York City street would copy down *ain't* and *you wasn't* and be interested only in identifying the frequency (how often it was uttered) and distribution (whether it appeared in certain parts of phrases and sentences and not others). The linguist might observe that *ain't* is a word found in the data from some subjects and not others. He or she might guess that there is a dialect difference involved but would not make any judgment about whether or not the word was "correct."

This is where the notion that modern linguistics is permissive (not concerned with standards) originated. It is a misunderstanding. Linguists such as Bloomfield were not talking about English usage as it traditionally concerned the schools. They were not talking about dialect differences in terms of whether political and economic advantages were attached to particular dialects, nor whether it was the business of the schools to teach some standard dialect. They were talking about studying language as a natural phenomenon—as a physicist or chemist studies matter.

However, the notion of studying language from a nonjudgmental, nonprescriptive point of view had far-reaching effects. Books such as Hall's *Leave Your Language Alone!* (1950) expressed the point of view that one dialect is as good as another, and that, therefore, one should not attempt to switch dialects or to switch anyone else's dialect (one's students', for example). Whether dialect differences play a part in learning to read became a central issue in this debate.

The matter of dialect differences became a politically charged issue in the decades that followed the heyday of structuralism. Attitudes of middle America (particularly of the schools) toward African-American English became a concern in the civil rights struggle.

❖ Structural Linguistics and Teaching Parts of Speech

Many concepts and much of the vocabulary of structural linguistics have been incorporated into methods of teaching grammar in elementary schools. We still use traditional definitions, but we also use structural concepts to identify parts of speech or form classes.

Sentence Frames

A word's part of speech is identified by the position it is able to occupy in phrases or sentences.

Only nouns can occupy the slots in the following sentence frame.

One ____ had many ____.
Examples: One *bird* had many *feathers*.
One *idea* had many *parts*.

Only a preposition can occupy the slot in the following sentence frame.

The (someone/something) moved ____ the (someone/something).
Examples: The airplane moved *toward* the hangar.
The bug moved *under* the door.

Inflectional Suffixes

A word's part of speech is identified by the inflectional suffixes that can be added to it.

Only nouns can take plural inflections (usually *-s* or *-es*).
Examples: boy/boys; match/matches
Only nouns can take possessive inflections.
Examples: girl's hat; hat's brim
Only verbs can take past tense inflections (usually *-ed*).
Examples: walk/walked; believe/believed
Only verbs can take progressive inflections (*-ing*).
Examples: take/taking; try/trying

Derivational Suffixes

Words can be changed from one part of speech to another by adding a derivational suffix. The presence of a derivational suffix, therefore, is a clue to a word's part of speech. For example, words ending in *-age* and *-ment* are often nouns (postage, coverage, employment, government) and words ending in *-ize* and *-ify* are often verbs (socialize, patronize, classify, justify).

Traditional definitions and structural concepts (sentence frames, inflectional suffixes, and derivational suffixes) are used in combination in identifying parts of speech as in Boxes 11.1 through 11.5.

> I. Traditional definition: A noun is a word that names a person, place, or thing.
> II. Nouns can occupy slots in the following test frame.
>   One ____ had many ____ .
>   One *boy* had many *interests*.
> III. Nouns can usually take the following inflectional suffixes.
>   *-s, -es* (plural)   hats, thoughts
>   *-'s* (possessive)   boy's hats, tree's color
> IV. Words with the following derivational suffixes are usually nouns.
>   *-age*   postage, coverage
>   *-ment*   employment, government
>   *-ity*   publicity, scarcity

BOX 11.1 Identifying nouns

> I. Traditional definition: A verb is a word that expresses action or state of being.
> II. Verbs can occupy the slot in the following test frame.
>   The (something/someone) may ____ the (something/someone).
>   The *man* may *believe* the story.
> III. Verbs can usually take the following inflectional suffixes.
>   *-ed* (past tense)   started, played
>   *-ing* (progressive) going, running
> IV. Words with the following derivational suffixes are usually verbs.
>   *-ize*   criticize, idolize
>   *-ify*   mystify, classify

BOX 11.2 Identifying verbs

Using definitions and structural concepts for identifying parts of speech is not without pitfalls. Not all nouns fit in all noun sentence frames, for example. Many words taken out of context can be categorized as more than one part of speech. Nevertheless, structural concepts used in combination with definitions often do give students a handle on the concept of parts of speech that is missing using definitions alone.

> I. Traditional definition: An adjective is a word that describes a noun.
>
> II. Adjectives can occupy the slots in the following sentence frame.
> The _____ (someone/something) was very _____.
> The *tall* boy was very *angry*.
>
> III. Adjectives can usually take the following inflectional suffixes.
> -er bigger, handsomer
> -est biggest, handsomest
>
> IV. Words with the following derivational suffixes are usually adjectives.
> -y   funny, messy
> -ive festive, creative

BOX 11.3 Identifying adjectives

> I. Traditional definition: Adverbs are words that modify verbs, adjectives, or other adverbs.
>
> II. Adverbs are movable. They can occupy many slots in a sentence frame.
> *Sadly* the boy told his story.
> The boy *sadly* told his story.
> The boy told his story *sadly*.
>
> III. Adverbs take no inflectional suffixes.
>
> IV. Words with the following derivational suffix are usually adverbs.
> -ly slowly, quickly

BOX 11.4 Identifying adverbs

> I. Traditional definition: Prepositions are words that show relationships.
>
> II. Prepositions can occupy the slot in the following sentence frame.
> The (someone/something) moved _____ the (someone/something).
> The airplane moved *toward* the hangar.
>
> III. Prepositions take no inflectional endings.
>
> IV. Prepositions are not formed with derivational endings.

BOX 11.5 Identifying prepositions

❖ The Impact of Transformational Grammar

The work of two people, Noam Chomsky and Kellogg Hunt, has had a profound effect on the concept of giving children facility with the full range of syntactic structures in English.

In the late 1950s, Noam Chomsky attacked the basic premise of structural linguists. He showed that one cannot assign structure to a great many English sentences without references to the meaning of the sentence. He further asserted that even in the many sentences where structures can be assigned in terms of frequency, position, stress, and juncture (the physical characteristics of language), meaning is essential to language. To insist on studying language without reference to meaning is pointless.

Chomsky (1957, 1965) proposed a *generative transformational grammar* that was a counterproposal to the grammars proposed by structural linguists. The main feature of this grammar is that every sentence has a deep structure (a structure in the mind of the speaker), as well as a surface structure (a physical manifestation of speech sounds). **Transformational grammar** is an attempt to describe the relationship between the two.

For example, the concept of boy-chase-girl (past) may be in the mind of the speaker. This may be uttered as a number of English sentences.

1. The boy chased the girl.
2. The girl was chased by the boy.
3. It was the boy who chased the girl.

Transformational grammar describes the transformations that change meaning into conventional English syntactic structures. One set of transformations results in a simple declarative active sentence (1). A second set of transformations results in a simple, declarative, passive sentence (2). A third set of transformations results in what is known as a cleft sentence (3).

Kellogg Hunt (1965) studied the syntax of the written language of students in fourth, eighth, and twelfth grades.[1] Earlier studies had shown that sentence length was not a good indication of the maturity of the writer. Hunt showed that young students write very long sentences because they string clauses together with *and* (This happened *and* that happened *and* . . .). He divided the students' writing into units in such a way as to take their immature behavior into account. He divided the texts into what he called **t-units.** His definition of t-unit is somewhat complicated. One frequently sees t-units defined as main clauses with all their modifiers.

---

[1] Hunt titled his study *Grammatical Structures Written at Three Grade Levels.* This is unfortunate from my point of view since I am trying to keep the concepts of syntax and grammar distinct. According to the definitions used here, an accurate title for Hunt's study would have been *Syntactic Structures Written at Three Grade Levels.*

Basic Sentence Patterns

Hunt found that as children mature, the length of both their clauses and t-units increases. He further found that the increased length in clauses and t-units was the result of increased syntactic complexity. Hunt, and others who followed, used transformational grammar to describe this increased syntactic complexity. In the next few pages I will show how transformations result in both increased complexity and greater length in clauses and t-units.

There are five kinds of simple statements one can make in English.

1. Subject + Intransive Verb
   Bill talks.
2. Subject + Transitive Verb + Direct Object
   Bill hit the target.
3. Subject + Transitive Verb + Indirect Object + Direct Object
   Bill gave Mary an apple.
4. Subject + Linking Verb + Predicate Noun
   Bill is president.
5. Subject + Linking Verb + Predicate Adjective
   Bill is brave.

Transformations of Basic Sentence Patterns

These basic sentence patterns can be manipulated by transformations in a number of ways. For example, passive transformations can be applied to types 2 and 3.

> The target was hit by Bill.
> An apple was given to Mary by Bill.

Negative transformations can be applied.

> Bill does not talk.
> Bill is not president.

Yes-no question transformations can be applied.

> Did Bill hit the target?

Wh- question transformations can be applied.

> Who is brave?
> What did Bill give Mary?

Notice that these transformations result in both longer and syntactically more complex sentences.

More than one transformation can be applied to the same basic sentence. For example: Negative and yes-no question transformations can be applied as in the following sentence:

Didn't Bill hit the target?

Passive, negative, and *wh-* question transformations can be applied as in the following sentence:

Wasn't an apple given to Mary by Bill?

Notice again that additional transformations result in both longer and syntactically more complex sentences.

Transformations That Combine Sentences

Transformations account for another option offered by English syntax. We can take meanings that can be represented by more than one basic sentence and transform them into a single sentence. These are called sentence-combining transformations.

Mary has a hat.
    The hat is red.
Mary has a red hat.

My mother is on the stage.
    My mother is wearing a hat.
My mother, who is wearing a hat, is on the stage.

The hat is red.
    The hat is on the table.
The hat on the table is red.

Paul knows something.
    Cheating is unfair.
Paul knows that cheating is unfair.

Something bothers Henry.
    Martha coughs.
Martha's coughing bothers Henry.

The possibilities for increasing the syntactic complexity are limitless.

Alan knows (something).
    The hat is on the table.

        The table in the dining room.
        The dining room is unheated.

Alan knows the hat is on the table in the dining room, which is unheated.

   Hunt discovered that the increase in length and syntactic complexity of children's sentences (technically t-units) can be attributed to increased use of transformations and especially to transformations that combine sentences.
   O'Donnell, Griffin, and Norris (1967) confirmed Hunt's findings and found that the same process occurs in the speech of elementary-school children. Syntactic complexity increases because of increased use of transformations—especially those that combine sentences. These authors also found that in fifth grade most students' written language becomes more complex than their speech.
   Bateman and Zidonis (1966) showed that teaching transformational grammar to ninth and tenth graders increased their facility with syntactic complexity. Soon after, Mellon (1969) and later O'Hare (1973) showed that teaching sentence combining alone, without teaching transformational grammar, produced the same results.
   The idea of sentence combining was around long before the introduction of transformational grammar. As early as 1917, Sterling Leonard (1917) suggested sentence massing, which involves taking two or three statements with a clear relation and combining them, showing the superior effect of putting less important thoughts into phrases. Mildred Dawson (1948) suggested sentence combining for middle grades in 1948. The introduction of transformational grammar did result in giving give us a framework in which to more systematically pursue sentence combining as a technique for increasing students' facility with mature syntactic structures.

❖ Teaching Facility with Syntax

Sentence Combining

   Sentence combining is now a frequently used technique in elementary schools. Exercises for sentence combining have been written by people who have a thorough understanding of transformational grammar, and therefore the variety of syntactic structures possible are systematically introduced (Hailey, 1978; Lawlor, 1983; Strong, 1976, 1981). Teachers can use these exercises without having extensive knowledge of transformational grammar.
   Teachers who understand the concepts behind sentence combining add it to their repertoire of responses to students' writing.
   You say, "We left at 10 o'clock. We left on Sunday." Can you combine those into one sentence?
   You say, "I read the story and it made me sad." How could you say that starting with the word *reading*? "Reading..."

Sentence Reconstruction

Noyce and Christie (1989) suggest taking sentences from literature and decombining them. Students are asked to reconstruct the sentences and then compare their efforts with the originals. Students discover that authors use syntax to produce a desired effect. On the other hand, students sometimes prefer their own versions.

The following is the result of decombining one complex sentence from *The Wind in the Willows* (Grahame, 1908):

> Toad sat straight down.
> He sat in the middle of the road.
> The road was dusty.
> His legs stretched out before him.
> He stared fixedly.
> He stared in the direction of the motor-car.
> The motor-car was disappearing.

After writing their own sentences, students compare them with the original sentence in the book:

> Toad sat straight down in the middle of the dusty road, his legs stretched out before him, and stared fixedly in the direction of the disappearing motor-car.

Modeling

Calling children's attention to passages from literature makes them aware of syntactic options available to them and encourages them to try imitating excellent writing. Teachers sometimes present passages like the following from *Peter Rabbit* and lead a group effort to imitate parts of it.

> But Peter, who was naughty, ran straight to Mr. McGregor's garden and squeezed under the gate. First he ate some lettuce, then some French beans, and then some radishes. Feeling rather sick, he went on a little farther to look for the parsley patch.

The group rewrite might look like the following:

> First she put on her leotards, then her long-sleeved shirt, and then her wool sweater. Feeling rather warm, she went back to the closet to look for her ski pants.

Some authorities suggest having children first write short passages like the one from *Peter Rabbit* from dictation. Blackburn (1985) suggests a less structured approach based on frequent oral reading from literature by the teacher and providing many opportunities for free writing. In her experience children do not imitate the models precisely; they copy patterns of events and sentence structure. Shawn, a first grader, imitated Bill Martin's *Haunted House* by borrowing the idea of a room-by-room progression. However, he introduced his own version of what was found in each room and added his own embellishment to the repeated sentence structure. The child's book was published and put in the reading corner. Other children began to produce books modeled more closely on Shawn's than on Bill Martin's.

❖ Teaching Standard Usage

Defining nonstandard usage can be a very tricky business. There are several problems.

1. Standard usage in speech varies in different parts of the country. Former President Carter's saying "you all" in informal situations might be quite appropriate. "You all" from a native Chicagoan would be suspect. In all but the most informal writing the standard form "you" is more appropriate.
2. The level of formality of the situation must be considered. *Who did you see?* would pass unnoticed in informal, private situations and would probably go unnoticed (except by English teachers) in somewhat formal, public situations. In all but the most informal writing, however, *Whom did you see?* is appropriate.
3. Standards change. "Can I go?" was once considered nonstandard. It is now considered appropriate in speech and informal writing. Saying or writing "May I go?" might be thought prissy in many situations today.
4. Even more subtle elements may enter in. For example, people say "ain't" to be humorous or for stylistic effect.

The language arts teacher has two responsibilities: (1) to make children sensitive to the context variables that effect standards of usage; and (2) to teach particular standard forms to children who do not have facility with them.

Very young children respond to social variables in communication. For example, four-year-old children talk differently to two-year-old children than they do to other four-year-olds or adults. They give two-year-olds direct commands—"Give me that!"—but make requests of other four-year-olds and adults—"Can I have that?"—(Shatz & Gelman, 1973). It is sensitivity to the same kind of variables that might prompt a ten-year-old to say, "I ain't goin'" to a friend and "I'm not going" to a visiting wealthy aunt.

In the middle and upper grades children's usage might be improved in more formal settings by simply making them aware of the process they already engage in unconsciously. Ask students to role play the following situations.

A new student is in the lunchroom line with three other students. The new student would like to be accepted as a friend by the other students. They are discussing the quality of the food.

A girl is telephoning her friend's mother to explain why her friend will be late for dinner.

Three students are being interviewed by the school principal. The principal must decide which two of them will be included on a school-sponsored field trip to a nearby professional baseball team spring training camp.

Standards of usage vary for everyone, not just students. Students might become more aware of this if they role play the following situations.

Two teachers are driving to work together. They are discussing a movie they have both recently seen.

A teacher is being interviewed by two school board members. The school board members must decide whether to buy expensive science equipment that the teacher has requested.

Discussion following such role plays should help students see that standards of correctness of usage are effected by context—for them and for everyone else.

Of course, some children do not have facility with the standard form of expressions such as

youse	that's mines
hisself	have did
have ate	it don't
her and me went	them books
they knowed	we was
haven't no	learn me a song

Even in informal speech and writing, reactions to expressions like these can create great social and economic hardship for the users. Most educators agree that such usages should receive attention in the elementary school. The following guidelines should be adhered to.

1. Individualize instruction. Do not teach lists of standard usage since most people lack facility with only a few usages.
2. Concentrate on two or three at a time. Notations such as *himself* not *hisself*, *haven't any* not *haven't no*, or *we were* not *we was* in a student's writing folder can identify a skill the student will work on in his or her writing. The usage identified will vary from student to student.
3. Advocates of teaching grammar argue that it is useful for a student to know the meaning of the terms *subject*, *verb*, and *nominative case*

when one tries to teach a student to use *she and I went* rather than *her and me went*. However, one should not wait for a child to learn the relevant grammar before attending to such matters. The child would not say *her went* or *me went*, but *she went* and *I went*. Such explanations are often helpful and they do not rely on knowledge of grammar.

HANDWRITING

Emergent Handwriting

A review of the discussion of emergent literacy in chapter 6 will remind you that in a literate society children start with broad concepts about what writing is used for and, if permitted, many children work out the details and learn the conventions of writing as they write. Three-year-olds sign their names as in Figure 6.1. Five-year-olds write stories such as Ashley's "The Runaway Elephant" in Figure 6.2.

Sulzby and colleagues (1989) found that when asked to write, kindergartners produced the following categories of material: drawings, scribbles (wavy), scribbles (letterlike), letterlike units, random letters, patterned letters (often letters in their names), and words copied from the environment.

Clay (1975) observed that in such classrooms (where preschoolers are encouraged to write), evidence of certain principles that underlie adult writing are present in children's earliest attempts.

The Generativity Principle

Writing is a limited set of marks that can be repeated in different combinations generating numerous patterns.

The Linearity Principle

Writing is arranged in horizontal lines across the page.

The Sign Principle

Writing has meaning. It is to be read by others, not just the writer. This principle manifests itself in a curious way with some youngsters who ask adults "What did I write?" They believe they can write, but only adults can read.

The Flexibility Principle

As children begin to discover that writing is conventional they discover that a letter may be written in various ways and remain the same letter such as *J* and *J* but that similar embellishments may result in a different letter as in *I* and *T*.

❖ Handwriting Instruction

Handwriting that is both legible and attractive was once considered a necessity for a career in business and many professions. However, with the wide availability of typewriters and more recently word processors, people are far less interested in the aesthetics of handwriting. The concept of emergent literacy has also greatly reduced the anxiety and sense of importance that once surrounded initial instruction in handwriting. Nevertheless, teaching children to write easily, legibly, and with reasonable speed is still an important part of the language arts program.

Experts agree that formal handwriting instruction should not begin before first grade. There are several handwriting programs that include books, teaching instructions, and materials. The following are among the most widely used:

HBJ Handwriting
Betty Kracht Johnson
Orlando: Harcourt Brace Jovanovich
1987

McDougal, Littell
Handwriting
Evanston, IL: McDougal, Littell & Company
1987

Palmer Method Handwriting
Fred M. King, Ed.D.
Schaumburg, IL: The A.N. Palmer Company
1984

Bowmar/Noble Handwriting
Oklahoma City: The Economy Company
1987

Improving Your Handwriting
Phyllis Anderson Wood
New York: Scholastic Book Services
1980

D'Nealian Handwriting
Donald N. Thurber & Dale R. Jordan
Glenview, IL: Scott Foresman and Company
1978

Zaner-Bloser, Inc. Handwriting
Walter B. Barbe, Ph.D., Virginia H. Lucas, Ph.D., Thomas M. Wasylyk, Clinton S. Hackney, and Lois S. Braun
Columbus, OH: Zaner-Bloser, Inc.
1989

Formal instruction in handwriting should be limited to ten to fifteen minutes a day. As new conventions are introduced and practiced, we expect to see them followed in the children's writing throughout the day. However, as with other communication skills, teachers should focus on the meaning of children's writing while encouraging them to use the skills and conventions of a particular writing system as they are introduced during brief daily lessons and practice sessions.

Schools usually adopt one of these programs on a schoolwide basis so that there will be continuity throughout the elementary-school grades. Teachers should use the same style of writing as that of the program used for formal instruction.

In summary, handwriting instruction should be based on the following principles:

1. Follow one program and its attendant style consistently.
2. Model that style in your teaching and in all writing meant for students to read.
3. Keep periods of direct, formal instruction and practice short—ten to fifteen minutes per day.
4. Encourage students to incorporate conventions and skills as they are introduced, particularly in final drafts.

❖ Left-handed Students

About ten percent of the population is left-handed. Right-handed writers are able to see what they are writing as they write it and can see what they have written as their hand moves away from their writing across the page and down the page. When writing with the left hand, however, the writing hand crowds the field of vision at the point that writing is occurring and hides (and often smears) what was just written.

This causes many left-handed writers to adopt unorthodox postures and methods of holding the pencil. Handwriting experts argue that these remedies can result in added fatigue and are therefore contrary to the objectives of teaching children to write easily and with reasonable speed.

Experts agree that children should be permitted to write with the hand they prefer. Teaching left-handed children to write calls for special attention.

1. Right-handed children are taught to turn the paper so that they write toward the far right-hand corner of the desk with the eraser end of their pencils pointing at their right shoulder. Left-handed children should be taught to turn their paper so that they write toward the near right-hand corner of the desk with the eraser end of their pencils pointing at their left shoulder. (See Figure 11.1.)

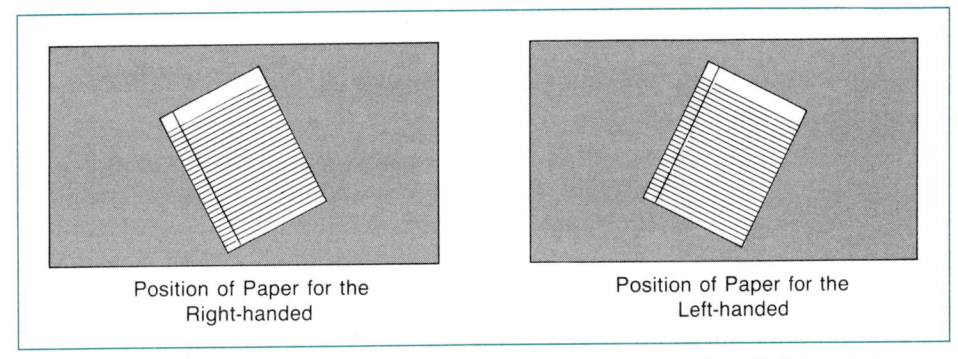

Figure 11.1 Recommended position of paper for the right-handed and left-handed

2. Letter forms that are easily executed by right-handers are sometimes very difficult for left-handers. Legible and more easily executed variations of letter forms should be permitted for left-handers.
3. Whenever possible, teachers and older children who write with their left hand, who write with the desired posture, and who write legibly, should be asked to model handwriting for left-handed students.

❖ Manuscript and Cursive Writing

Children are taught manuscript (print) beginning in first grade. This is the style of writing that approximates the print of published materials—the print they are learning to read. It is customary for children to learn cursive (connected, fluid) handwriting in third grade.

Cursive writing is not superior to manuscript writing in terms of ease, speed, or legibility and, in a very small number of schools, cursive writing is never introduced. The expectation is so strong that children will be taught cursive writing by the end of third grade, however, that this custom is followed nearly universally. The handwriting programs identified in this chapter include instructions on first manuscript and then cursive writing.

❖ Improving and Maintaining Legibility

There are six elements of legibility in handwriting: shape, size and proportion, position, slant, spacing, and stroke. (See Figure 11.2.) Children, especially those whose handwriting is difficult to read, should be encouraged to analyze their own handwriting to discover which element or elements need work. Teachers should be consulted in this process to be certain that the student understands the elements and has correctly identified the element or elements that need attention.

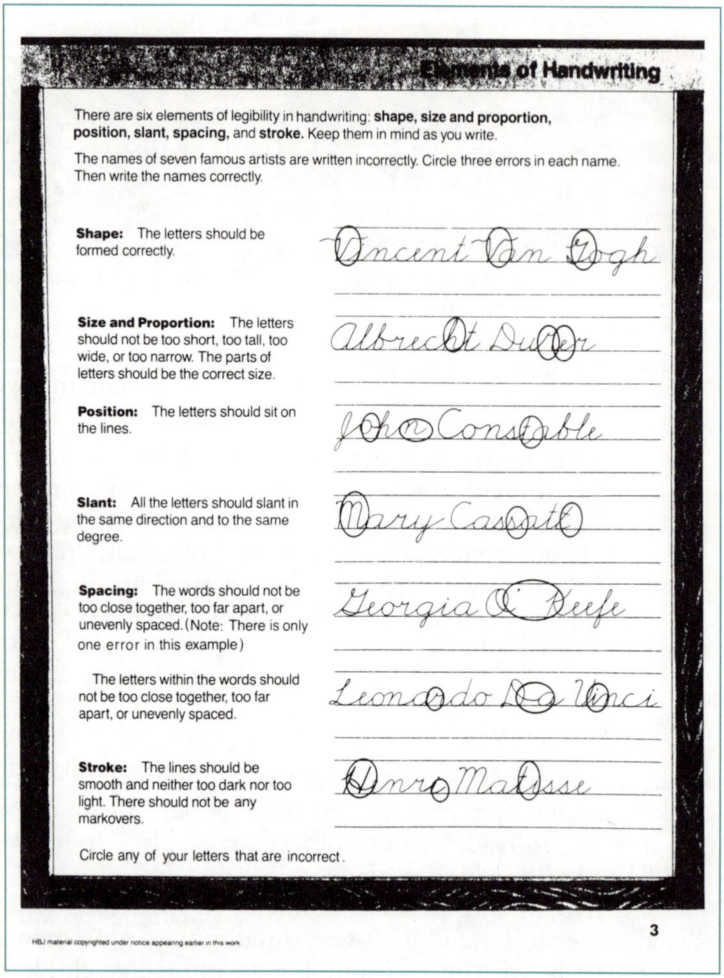

Elements of Handwriting

There are six elements of legibility in handwriting: **shape, size and proportion, position, slant, spacing,** and **stroke.** Keep them in mind as you write.

The names of seven famous artists are written incorrectly. Circle three errors in each name. Then write the names correctly.

Shape: The letters should be formed correctly.

Vincent Van Gogh

Size and Proportion: The letters should not be too short, too tall, too wide, or too narrow. The parts of letters should be the correct size.

Albrecht Durer

Position: The letters should sit on the lines.

John Constable

Slant: All the letters should slant in the same direction and to the same degree.

Mary Cassatt

Spacing: The words should not be too close together, too far apart, or unevenly spaced. (Note: There is only one error in this example)

Georgia O'Keefe

The letters within the words should not be too close together, too far apart, or unevenly spaced.

Leonardo Da Vinci

Stroke: The lines should be smooth and neither too dark nor too light. There should not be any markovers.

Henri Matisse

Circle any of your letters that are incorrect.

3

HBJ material copyrighted under notice appearing earlier in this work

Figure 11.2 Elements of handwriting (*Source:* Table from HBJ HANDWRITING, BOOK 6, TEACHER'S EDITION AND RESOURCE BOOK by Betty Kracht Johnson, copyright © 1987 by Harcourt Brace Jovanich, Inc., reprinted by permission of the publisher.)

Children must write extended text every day if they are to maintain legible handwriting. According to Mina Shaughnessey (1977) average high-school students in the United States write only 350 words a week compared with 1,000 words per week written by the average British high-school student. "The basic writing student is more likely to have written 350 words a semester. It would not be unusual for him [or her] to have written nothing at all" (p. 14).

It can be assumed that if the average high-school student was writing 350 words per week in 1977, the average elementary-school student was writing even less. With the increasing interest in the writing process and the incorporation of the writing process approach, we can hope that students write more text (as compared with filling in blanks) today. The point is, however, that if students do not write extended text on a daily basis, they are not likely to achieve or maintain handwriting that is legible, easy to produce, and produced with acceptable speed.

Separating Working Drafts from Finished Drafts

Shaughnessey (1977) recommends frequent writing in circumstances that encourage a flow of words, such as journal writing and free writing "until the pen seems a natural extension of the hand, and the hand of the mind itself" (p. 16).

Students who do such writing—writing that they will attempt to read at a later date—learn the first reason why writing must be legible: They must be able to read it themselves. They will find that writing that they themselves can read must be very nearly as legible as handwriting that others can read. However, in writing drafts for one's self, the writer need not be as attentive to conventions of neatness. Abbreviations are permissible. The conventions of shape, size and proportion, position, slant, spacing, and stroke are relaxed while the writer focuses on the writing process rather than the handwriting process. Copying over final drafts (perhaps only those that will be published) permits the writer to focus on the elements of legibility and the conventions of neatness. At a certain point these are no longer matters of legibility but matters of convention and courtesy to the reader.

Attending to the Affective and Transactional Functions of Language

In chapter 5 I discussed the fact that people often send messages they do not intend in their oral communication. Inappropriate use of slang and nonstandard usage in formal situations may send messages about the speaker's education, sophistication, and perhaps his or her economic and political power. Matters of legibility and neatness in handwriting may send similar messages. This can be simply stated in minilessons or become the topic of a discussion or role play.

Creating Interest in Handwriting

There are many topics related to handwriting that might be introduced into writing workshops as possible topics or explored in social studies or science. Books on these topics might be suggested or made available in the reading programs.

Some books on calligraphy are the following:

> Korn, Ellen, ed. *Teach Yourself Calligraphy: For Beginners from Eight to Eighty.* New York: Morrow, 1982.

Parkhurst, Christine, and Marian Fellows. *Script Ease: A Step-by-Step Guide from Manuscript to Calligraphy.* Tucson, AZ: Kino Publishing, 1982. (Grades 1–12)

Butterworth, Emma M. *The Complete Book of Calligraphy.* New York: Harper & Row, 1984.

Some books on graphology (handwriting analysis) are the following:

Engel, Joel. *Handwriting Analysis Self-taught.* New York: Elsevier-Nelson Books, 1980.

Mann, Peggy. *The Tell-Tale Line: The Secrets of Handwriting Analysis.* New York: Macmillan, 1976.

Wyland, Johanna L. *Your Paths in Ink: Graphoanalysis and the Personality.* Smithtown, NY: Exposition Press, 1980.

Children in your class (or their parents) may have experience with other alphabets such as Greek, Russian, or Arabic. Asian children (or their parents) may have experience with different (nonalphabetic) writing systems such as Chinese, Korean, or Japanese. Demonstrations of such writing in the classroom serves the dual purpose of fostering an interest in the topic of handwriting and capitalizing on the presence of children from may cultures in the classroom. A student in one of my teacher-preparation classes recently gave a demonstration of how Chinese writing is taught using pens and brushes in Taiwan schools. People with such knowledge are a real asset, and they should be encouraged to share their abilities in classrooms.

SPELLING

❖ The Irregularity of English Spelling

Spelling reformers and others who despair at the irregularity of English spelling often start with a misconception. That misconception is that English spelling is based on a single principle—phonetics. In a phonetic system for transcribing speech into writing there is a one-to-one correspondence between speech sounds and written symbols. Each speech sound is always represented by the same written symbol; each written symbol always represents the same speech sound.

There is indeed a system used by linguists to transcribe the sounds of speech from any language. It is known as the **International Phonetic Alphabet.** A trained phonologist can transcribe the speech of a speaker of Russian, English, or Chinese so that the phonologist could read it back and it would be understood by other speakers of the language. This is not a conventional spelling system, however.

In a phonetic transcription, if the same word is pronounced differently it is represented differently in the transcription. The word *of* in "Of course I'm going" and "a couple of beers" might be stressed in the first case and unstressed in the second. This would result in a change in sound, and therefore different symbols would be used in a phonetic transcription to represent the word. In English spelling, the same word is spelled the same in all environments, even though they may be pronounced differently.

Many words are pronounced differently in different parts of the country. For example, I have heard the word *cards* pronounced "cards" in Chicago, "cords" in St. Louis, and "cods" in Boston. These pronunciations would be represented differently in a phonetic transcription, but there is one standard spelling for this word (and for most words) throughout the country and throughout the English-speaking world.

Before English spelling was standardized, the system probably was more phonetic with scribes transcribing words the way they heard them. This made the task of spelling easier, but imagine the hardships it must have presented to readers, especially readers from different dialect groups.

✤ Factors Affecting English Spelling

The Alphabetic Principle

There is something resembling a phonetic principle in English spelling. It is sometimes called the **alphabetic principle.** The alphabetic principle states that there is a correspondence between speech sounds and written letters, but it is not a perfect one-to-one match.

> The same sound may be represented by different letters as the /s/ sound is represented by *c* in *center* and *s* in *send.*
> Different sounds may be represented by the same letter as the *g* in *give* and *gem.*
> Two letters together may represent one sound as *th* in *the* or *gh* in *enough.*
> Letters sometimes indicate the sound represented by other letters in the same syllable. For example, the *e* indicates the sound represented by the *a* in *mate.*

When one understands the alphabetic principle and how it works in English, the system appears more orderly than when one thinks that English spelling is a purely phonetic system somehow gone awry.

Morphology

English spelling reflects the way words are put together (their morphology) as well as the way words are pronounced. Many English words are made of parts—roots, prefixes, and suffixes. We all recognize the past tense marker *-ed* in the words *walked, weighed,* and *waited.* Most of time we are not conscious of the fact that the past tense morpheme in these three words is pronounced /t/, /d/, and /id/, respectively.

We all recognize the plural marker on the words *boys* and *hats*. Most of the time we are not conscious of the fact that the plural morpheme in these words is pronounced /z/ and /s/, respectively.

In English, the same morpheme (past tense or plural, for example) tends to be spelled the same from word to word even though it may be pronounced differently from word to word.

When derivational suffixes are added to root words, the pronunciation of the root word often changes as in *nation-national, symbol-symbolic,* and *trivial-triviality*. In English spelling, the root word in derived words is spelled the same as the underlying root word, despite changes in the pronunciation from root word to derived form.

English spelling reflects both the pronunciation of words (not through a strict phonetic principle, but through a somewhat more complicated alphabetic principle) *and* the morphology of words. When these two systems come into conflict, morphology is usually reflected in spelling rather than in pronunciation. When one understands this, the English spelling system appears to be much more orderly than at first assumed.

Historical Influences

Knowledge of the history of the English language and the history of writing helps to explain some of the puzzling things about English spelling. For example:

- The *k* in *knife* and *knee* were once pronounced. The pronunciation changed, but the spelling, out of custom, remained the same.
- The *gh* in *night* and *light* represented a sound that was once heard in these words. The pronunciation changed. The spelling remained the same. When the words *tight* and *delight* entered the language, their spelling was modeled on the older English words *night* and *light*.
- *Some* and *son* were once spelled *sum* and *sun*. During the Middle English period the Gothic style of writing made the *u* difficult to read before an *m* or *n*. The spelling was changed to avoid this problem.
- During the revival of interest in Latin during the Renaissance, letters were inserted into many words to show their relation to Latin words although the letters were never pronounced. Spellings like *debt, indict,* and *receipt* resulted.
- Words borrowed from other languages often retain their original spellings. This explains the puzzling spellings of such words as *frijole* and *spiel*.

♣ Invented Spelling

In this section I will focus on what is known about the way spelling emerges in children who are encouraged to try writing in homes and classrooms where the concept of emergent literacy is recognized and encouraged. This phenomenon is referred to as invented spelling. Ehri (1989) summarized several studies of invented spelling and identified four stages of development.

The Precommunication Stage

Children produce scribbles, strings of randomly selected letters and/or numerals to represent words or sentences. They usually produce only a small number of letters, and they often do not differentiate letters from numerals.

The Semiphonetic Stage

Children learn the names and the sounds usually represented by some letters and use this knowledge in their spelling. At first only one or two letters correspond to sounds. With additional experience with print, children learn more and more letter-sound correspondences.

Children at this stage sometimes think the name of the letter *is* the sound it represents. This results in spellings like *hkn* for *chicken*. The child's reasoning appears to be as follows: *chicken* begins with the sound /ch/. The letter *h* is pronounced /āch/. Therefore, *chicken* starts with *h* and is spelled *hcn*. Likewise *wife* may be spelled *yuf* because *wife* begins with /wī/. The letter *y* is pronounced /wī/. Therefore, *wife* starts with *y* and is spelled *yuf*. With additional experience with print, confusion between the names of letters and the sounds usually represented by letters disappears.

Children know very few correct spellings at this stage. Words spelled correctly once may be misspelled at a later time. Memory for correct spellings is unstable.

The Phonetic Stage

Children begin to produce spellings that contain letters for all the sounds in words. The ability to spell vowels increases dramatically. This indicates that the children are able to perform phonetic segmentation—to hear words as a succession of speech sounds and to identify them in order. At this stage children sometimes hear sounds in words that are not represented in conventional spelling and produce such spellings as *doktor*.

The Morphemic Stage

In the morphemic stage, children begin to realize that word parts that have the same function (such as past tense morphemes on verbs and plural morphemes on nouns) are spelled the same even though they are pronounced differently in different words. A child in the phonetic stage might spell *watched* as *wacht*. A child in the morphemic stage might spell *watched* as *wached*.

Similarly, children discover that certain spellings occur only in suffixes. For example, /shun/ is spelled *-tion* in the final unaccented syllable of numerous words such as *nation, motion,* and *reputation*. Many such words were root words plus suffixes in their language of origin.

According to Ehri (1989) conventional spelling emerges when children have the phonetic principle well in hand. That is, they first develop a concept of one-to-one correspondence of speech sound to letter. They then become aware of the alphabetic principle—that there is a correspondence between sounds and letters, but it is not a perfect one-to-one match. Ehri believes that we store correct spellings as phonetic representations with footnotes—*hill* has two *l*'s, *city* is spelled with a *c* not an *s*, there is a silent *t* in *listen*.

With experience, writers make other discoveries associated with morphology which they incorporate as widely applicable rules. For example, the past tense suffix is usually spelled *-ed*, and the final unaccented syllable pronounced /shun/ in many words is spelled *-tion*.

The Persistence of Invented Spelling

The following question sometimes arises regarding emergent literacy and spelling: Does encouraging children to spell words unconventionally cause them to persist in misspelling words? Tierney and colleagues (1990) gave the same twenty-word spelling test to the same child five times during first and second grade.

The spellings of these words were never taught directly to the student. Some examples of the child's successive spellings of words are as follows:

Word	Test 1	Test 2	Test 3	Test 4	Test 5
lid	E	LD	lad	lid	lid
six	6	SS	sis	siks	six
nice	SAT	Nis	nis	nis	nice
track	P	TAK	tac	tac	tack
muffin	KO	MN	mufn	mufin	muffen
wife	1	yuf	wif	wif	wife

The child progressed from the precommunication stage to the semi-phonetic stage to the phonetic stage, and he finally adopted the alphabetic principle and conventional spelling by the end of second grade. His spellings reflect the principles he responded to from stage to stage rather than a commitment to or memory of previous unconventional spellings.

Ehri, Gibbs, and Underwood (1989) taught nonsense words modeled on English spellings to children and college students. Some students were encouraged to write the words before the correct spellings were taught and other students were taught the correct spellings before they were permitted to write the words. Both groups learned the correct spellings with equal success.

❖ Teaching Spelling

Recall the words of Laura from chapter 1:

> Sure I use the textbooks. Of all of them I use the spellers most religiously. I'm convinced that they'd learn to spell most of the words on their weekly spelling list through massive experience with reading and writing, but the parents

expect a spelling program and I just don't think it would be worth the effort to try to convince them that we could do without it.

A wise and prudent teacher, Laura. Spelling is a subject that is near and dear to the hearts of many Americans. Until there is a good deal more evidence that children would learn to spell almost incidentally if they read and wrote enough in a holistic, collaborative, integrated language arts program, we should probably continue to teach spelling as a separate subject—in crisp, short lessons.

Research dating back to Ernest Horn (1919, 1926, 1944) has consistently shown that the most successful approach to teaching spelling includes the use of a predetermined list of frequently written words and stresses the formation of perceptual images (visually and aurally), along with proper habits of study. This is the approach used in many published spelling programs. It is interesting that this same body of research shows that frequent opportunities to use spelling words in writing contribute greatly to the maintenance of spelling ability, and the most important thing about spelling is that it's something writers use. Until writers need to use it, spelling has no value.

Devoting ten to fifteen minutes a day, five days a week, to a crisp spelling program, while students engage in sustained periods of reading and writing in collaboration with teachers and one another, appears to be the ideal approach.

❖ Research on Teaching and Learning Spelling

Commercial spelling textbooks form the basis of spelling programs in most elementary classrooms (Graves, 1977). In this section I will summarize the research on spelling learning and instruction. Teachers should choose spelling textbooks that are consistent with this research and modify teaching procedures if the textbooks they choose are not entirely consistent with research.

Teach Frequently Used Words

Words taught in the spelling curriculum should be selected on the basis of two criteria. First, they should be the words children will need to write frequently in the normal course of their school, home, and community life. Secondly, they should be the words that are written frequently by society at large. The second criteria begins to apply in the upper grades and in high school.

Publishers who choose words based on these criteria consult published word-frequency counts. The following word-frequency studies are based on the writing and speaking vocabularies of schoolchildren.

> Hillerich, R. L. (1978). *A Writing Vocabulary of Elementary Children.* Springfield, IL: Thomas.
> Hopkins, C. J. (1979). The spontaneous oral vocabulary of children in grade one. *Elementary School Journal, 79,* 240–249.
> Horn, E. (1926). *A Basic Writing Vocabulary.* Iowa City: University of Iowa Press.

Moe, A. J., Hopkins, C. J., & Rush, R. T. (1982). *The Vocabulary of First-Grade Children.* Springfield, IL: Charles C. Thomas.

Murphy, H. (1957). The spontaneous speaking vocabulary of children in primary grades. *Journal of Education, 140,* 3–106.

Rinsland, H. D. (1945). *A Basic Writing Vocabulary of Elementary School Children.* New York: Macmillan.

Sherk, J. K. (1973). *A Word-Count of Spoken English of Culturally Disadvantaged Preschool and Elementary Pupils.* Kansas City: University of Missouri.

There are also frequency studies of words written in published materials. They yield an estimate of how likely a person is to encounter a word in reading rather than how likely a person is to want to write a word. But, because they can be considered a way of estimating words' relative frequencies in literate contexts at large, they may be consulted as ways of choosing words that are used in the writing of adults in society.

In 1921 Thorndike (1921) counted word frequencies in a potpourri of English language publications. His study included American and British literature, literature intended for children and adults, and literature that had been published recently as well as literature from the distant past. This study was updated in 1944 (Thorndike & Lorge, 1944).

Since the advent of computers, two important word-frequency counts have been done. Kucera and Francis (1967) counted a million running words of text published in the United States in the year 1961. The count included fifteen categories of writing representing types of journalism, scientific writing, and fiction and nonfiction trade books. This study had an advantage over the Thorndike lists in that it was of contemporary, American, published writing, and was thought to give a better estimate of the probability of a word's being encountered by a contemporary American.

Carroll, Davis, and Richman (1971) published a frequency count of over five million words published in texts and other published materials used in American classrooms in 1969. This highly sophisticated study reports that frequency of words in the entire body of material, their frequency in each of seventeen subject categories (reading, math, library fiction, magazines, and so on), their frequency in each of grades three through nine, and ungraded. The study even reports the probability of one's encountering a word based on how often, as well as where, it was found. A word found fairly often in music books is not as likely to be encountered as a word found equally often in social studies books because more time is spent in school reading social studies than music.

Present Words in Lists

Research shows that it is more efficient to present words in lists than in sentences or paragraphs. Words studied in lists are learned more quickly, remembered longer, and transferred more readily to new contexts (Horn, 1967; Fitzsimmons

& Loomer, 1977). Since words that are introduced as spelling words are frequent words—words that should be known and used by the students—time should not be taken during spelling lessons to teach word meanings.

The Test-Study-Test Approach

The most successful method of teaching spelling is the test-retest method. Traditionally, the method begins with a pretest on Monday, after which the students check their own papers. The words they missed are written on a list for special study and studied on Tuesday. On Wednesday they are tested again on all the words. Those who get all the words right on the Wednesday test are exempted from further testing. The others restudy the words they missed and on Friday have a posttest covering all the words. This method is useful because it focuses children's attention on the words they need to study rather than on those they already know, and it leads to concentrated effort through repeated testing.

The following components must be present to make self-correcting of pretests an effective strategy:

- Pupils should correct their own tests (touching every letter) as the teacher spells the word aloud. This focuses attention on each word misspelled, as well as on the correct spelling of the word.
- Time for the study of the words missed on the test should be provided as soon as possible, preferably immediately after the test has been given and corrected.
- Results on the final tests should be compared with those on the first test to show that progress has been made. (Horn, 1960, in Fitzsimmons & Loomer, 1978)

According to Fitzsimmons and Loomer (1978),

The self-corrected-test procedure, under the direction of the teacher, is the single most important factor in learning to spell. It is clearly appropriate for all ages and abilities and should be implemented within the total spelling program.

Study Strategy

An effective strategy for learning to spell words involves the following steps:

- Look at the word and say it.
- Read each letter in the word.
- Close your eyes and spell the word to yourself.
- Look at the word. Did you spell it correctly?
- Copy the word from your list.
- Cover the word and write it again.
- Look at the word. Did you write it correctly?
- If you made any mistakes, repeat the steps.

This strategy focuses on the whole word and involves visual, auditory, and kinesthetic responses. Teachers should model this strategy and coach students as they attempt it until they have mastered it.

Doubtful Practices

Research fails to support many widespread practices. Fitzsimmons and Loomer's (1977) survey of research reveals the following findings:

- Learning to spell a word should involve the student's formation of a correct visual image of the whole word. The presentation of words in syllables has no advantage over whole-word presentation.
- Drawing attention to the "hard spots" of a word has no value in improving spelling ability. Children learn words as whole units, not individual parts.
- Attempts to teach spelling by phonic rules are questionable.
- The practice of having a child copy a word several times in quick succession has no value in spelling.
- The practice of writing words in the air is of doubtful value since the arm and hand movements are generally not the same as those used in the writing of words.
- Oral spelling lessons should not occur frequently. Spelling ability is defined as the ability to write a word rather than spell it aloud.

❖ Spelling Consciousness

Some poor spellers read very little and have little exposure to the visual representation of words. Some poor spellers are people who are not conscious of spelling. They read and write, but their spelling is weak. They simply do not pay attention to how words are spelled. Most such people do not think correct spelling is important. President Kennedy, a notoriously poor speller, is said to have believed that poor spelling was a mark of intelligence!

The remedy for the first class of poor spellers is obvious. They should be encouraged to partake fully in the entire language arts program—speaking, listening, reading, and writing—since all are connected. All of the information and advice in this book should be brought to bear in the effort to make such students readers and writers, part of the literate community.

The second class of poor spellers must be helped to develop a spelling consciousness. There are two fronts on which to attack the problem. One is to help the student to see that poor spelling sends a message to the reader that the writer does not intend. Many readers attribute poor spelling to a lack of intelligence, lack of education, and illiteracy. The reader's negative reactions can get in the way of his or her dealing with the substance of the writing. I have discussed this phenomenon in connection with oral languages in chapter 5, and in connection with nonstandard usage and handwriting earlier in this chapter.

On the second front, students should be helped to see that correct spelling is simply a courtesy to the reader. A reader who can get past poor spelling and respond to the substance of the writing, might still have negative feelings toward the writer because the writer did not seem to care enough to spell correctly. I sometimes experience this reaction when reading college students' papers. Both ideas—that readers might not get to the substance of the paper because they dismiss the writer's ability and that they may respond appropriately to the substance of the paper but feel the writer has not treated them courteously—are matters of audience awareness. Encouraging students to write frequently and publish regularly is the best way to develop audience awareness.

Proofreading for spelling errors is essential in developing spelling consciousness. With the demands of the composing process, it is not surprising that students misspell words that they do, in fact, know how to spell. They also use words in writing that they do not know how to spell. During the drafting stage of the writing process, students are concerned with expressing ideas. It is important that they complete the process by editing their work for spelling and other errors after the drafting and revisions are complete.

In chapter 9 I discussed teaching and learning during the editing stage. Attention to spelling was repeatedly mentioned in connection with editing and with teaching strategies associated with editing. Misspelled words were introduced into daily edits. A specialized editing committee on spelling was suggested.

During teacher-editing, the teacher can identify students for whom spelling is a particular problem. Attention to confusion among *they're* and *their* and *there* or *to, too,* and *two* can be listed as a skill in the "taught" column of the students' folders and checked from paper to paper. Lists of frequently misspelled words (such as *comeing* for *coming*) can be added to the folder so that the student can become conscious of them.

Students should not avoid using new words because they do not know how to spell them. They should be aware that such words should be looked up or checked out with a good speller. Developing spelling consciousness can be addressed in the editing and publishing stages of the writing process.

Summary

Teaching students to make statements about language using words like *noun* and *direct object* is teaching grammar.

Syntax has to do with the arrangement or order of meaningful parts in phrases and sentences. Giving children facility with the full range of syntactic structures available in English is an important objective of the language arts curriculum.

Suggesting that in some situations the use of a phrase like "I'm not" is preferable to "I ain't" is teaching standard usage. These three teaching objectives are often referred to by the same words: "teaching grammar." This is the source of much confusion, because many educators are opposed to teaching grammar (as defined above), but they are in favor of increasing students' facility with syntax and teaching standard usage. Grammar is often taught as a brief but necessary part of lessons whose purpose is to increase facility with syntax or to teach standard usage. Most educators approve of teaching grammar under these conditions.

The concepts of structural linguistics and transformational grammar have had significant effects on teaching grammar, syntax, and usage in schools. Structural linguistics is an attempt to describe language without reference to meaning. The structure of the language is discovered an described in terms of frequency, intensity, and contiguity of speech elements. Structural linguistics is purely descriptive and nonjudgmental. The notion of studying language from a nonprescriptive and nonjudgmental point of view had far-reaching effects. Books were published attacking the concept of standard English and asserting that no one dialect was superior to another. This led to a period of time when the idea of teaching standard usage was under attack. A less controversial and more pervasive effect is that structural concepts have been incorporated into the way grammar is taught. Sentence frames, the presence of derivational suffixes, and the possibility of adding inflectional suffixes are now widely used as tests to determine words' parts of speech.

Later, transformational grammar overshadowed structural linguistics. Transformational grammar is based on the assumption that consideration of meaning is essential to grammar. One important feature of this grammar is that it shows how meanings expressed in simple sentences can be expressed within larger sentences. Sentences are joined together with conjunctions, or they are reduced to words, phrases, and clauses and imbedded in other sentences. This process accounts for all the syntactic possibilities of English.

Researches found that teaching transformational grammar to students generally resulted in their using more complex syntax in their writing. Later research found that teaching a technique known as sentence combining (without teaching grammar) yielded similar results. Sentence combining has become a widely used technique for improving students' facility with syntax.

In regard to standard usage, the teacher has two responsibilities: (1) to make students sensitive to the context variables that affect standards of usage, and (2) to teach particular standard forms (such as *you* for *youse* or *teach me* for *learn me*) to children who do not use the appropriate forms. Guidelines for such lessons are (1) individualize instruction, (2) concentrate on only two or three usages at a time, and (3) address the problem while (not after) teaching the grammatical concepts involved.

Children who are encouraged to write as preschoolers frequently discover the following principles about handwriting without formal instruction: generativity, linearity, sign, and flexibility.

Teaching students to write easily, legibly, and with reasonable speed is an important objective of the language arts curriculum. Sound handwriting instruction is based on the following principles: (1) Follow one program consistently; (2) model that style for students; (3) keep periods of direct, formal instruction short; and (4) expect students to incorporate conventions and skills into final drafts as they are introduced.

Teaching left-handed students calls for special attention. The page should be oriented differently, more easily formed variations of letters should be permitted, and good left-handed writers should be provided as models.

Children are taught manuscript writing in first grade because of its similarity to print. Although cursive writing is not superior to manuscript in any way, it is customary to teach children cursive writing in third grade.

Methods of improving and maintaining legibility are (1) separating working drafts from finished drafts, (2) attending to the affective and transactional functions of language in relation to handwriting, and (3) creating student interest in handwriting.

English spelling is affected by the alphabetic principle (there is a correspondence between speech sounds and written letters, but it is not a perfect one-to-one match), morphology (the way parts—affixes and root words—are combined), and historical influences.

For students who are encouraged to try invented spelling, conventional spelling emerges in four stages: (1) precommunication, (2) semiphonetic, (3) phonetic, and (4) morphemic. There is no evidence that invented spelling persists among children who are encouraged to produce it.

Research shows that successful teaching of spelling includes the use of lists of frequently written words and proper study habits. The most successful method of teaching spelling is by the test-study-test approach. Frequent need to spell words correctly in writing contributes to maintenance of spelling facility. Devoting ten to fifteen minutes a day to a crisp spelling program together with massive experience with reading and writing appears to be the ideal approach. Research fails to support many widespread practices, such as teaching spelling by phonic rules and copying words several times in lists.

Poor spellers are often not conscious of spelling. Such students must become more aware of their audience. Poor spelling may cause a negative reaction in readers. Good spelling is simply a matter of courtesy to the reader.

For Review and Discussion

1. Define "teaching grammar," "enhancing students' facility with syntax," and "teaching standard usage." Why is it important to understand the differences between these three objectives?

2. Discuss usages that you employ in informal settings, but not in formal settings. If your usage has changed over the course of your life, describe how it has changed and what motivated the change.

3. Using sentence frames and information about inflectional and derivational suffixes, determine the probable part of speech of each of these words: *criticize, glove, over, pensive, sadly, shipment, tall, through,* and *walk*.

4. Write your version of the passage from *The Wind in the Willows* that was decombined in this chapter. Compare your version with the original. Find other passages from literature and create an exercise like this.

5. Write a paragraph imitating the passage from *Peter Rabbit* in this chapter. Think aloud while doing it, stating the decisions you make.

6. Imagine you are a fifth-grade teacher with students from diverse backgrounds. A student says, "axed" for "asked," or "Me and Janet went." Other students criticize her or him for "saying it wrong." What would you do immediately? As a long-range plan?

7. Name and explain the four principles identified by Clay that appear in children's earliest attempts at writing.

8. Discuss the principles of handwriting instruction, teaching writing to left-handed students, teaching cursive writing, and methods of maintaining handwriting legibility.

9. Discuss the alphabetic principle, morphology, and historical influences in relation to English spelling.

10. Describe the stages of invented spelling.

11. Describe an ideal spelling program.

12. List four doubtful but widespread practices connected with teaching spelling.

13. Discuss ways of developing spelling consciousness. If your spelling consciousness has improved over the years, relate your experience.

For Further Reading

Anderson, K. F. (1985). The development of spelling ability and linguistic strategies. *The Reading Teacher, 39,* 140–147.

Davis, F. (1984). In defense of grammar. *English Education, 16,* 151–164.

Haley-James, S. (Ed.). (1981). *Perspectives on Writing in Grades 1–8.* Urbana, IL: National Council of Teachers of English.

Hudson, B. A. (1980). Moving language around: Helping students become aware of language structure. *Language Arts, 57,* 614–620.

Johnson, T. D., Langford, K. G. & Quorn, K. C. (1981). Characteristics of an affective spelling program. *Language Arts, 58,* 581–588.

Koenke, K. (1986). Handwriting instruction: What do we know? *The Reading Teacher, 40,* 214–216.

Stewing, T. W. (1987). Students' spelling errors. *Clearinghouse, 61,* 34–37.

Strong, W. (1986). *Creative Approaches to Sentence Combining.* Urbana, IL: ERIC Clearinghouse on Reading and Communication Skills and the National Council of Teachers of English.

Taylor, K. K., & Kidder, E. B. (1988). The development of spelling skills: From first grade through eighth grade. *Written Communication, 5,* 222–244.

Tompkins, G. E. (1980). Let's go on a bear hunt! A fresh approach to penmanship drill. *Language Arts, 57,* 782–786.

Tompkins, G. E., & McGee, L. M. (1983). Launching nonstandard speakers into standard English. *Language Arts, 60,* 463–469.

CHAPTER 12

Language Arts in the Multicultural Classroom

Jean V. Yepes

Introduction: The Increasingly
  Diverse Student Population
Second Language Acquisition
Effective Language Arts
  Programs for Culturally
  Diverse Students
Structuring the Class to Help
  English as a Second
  Language Students
  Activities
TO THINK ABOUT: Sharing
  Cultures

Strategies for Fostering
  Language Development
  in the Multicultural
  Classroom
Language Arts as a Way of
  Empowering Culturally
  Diverse Students
  Activities
Summary
For Review and Discussion
For Further Reading

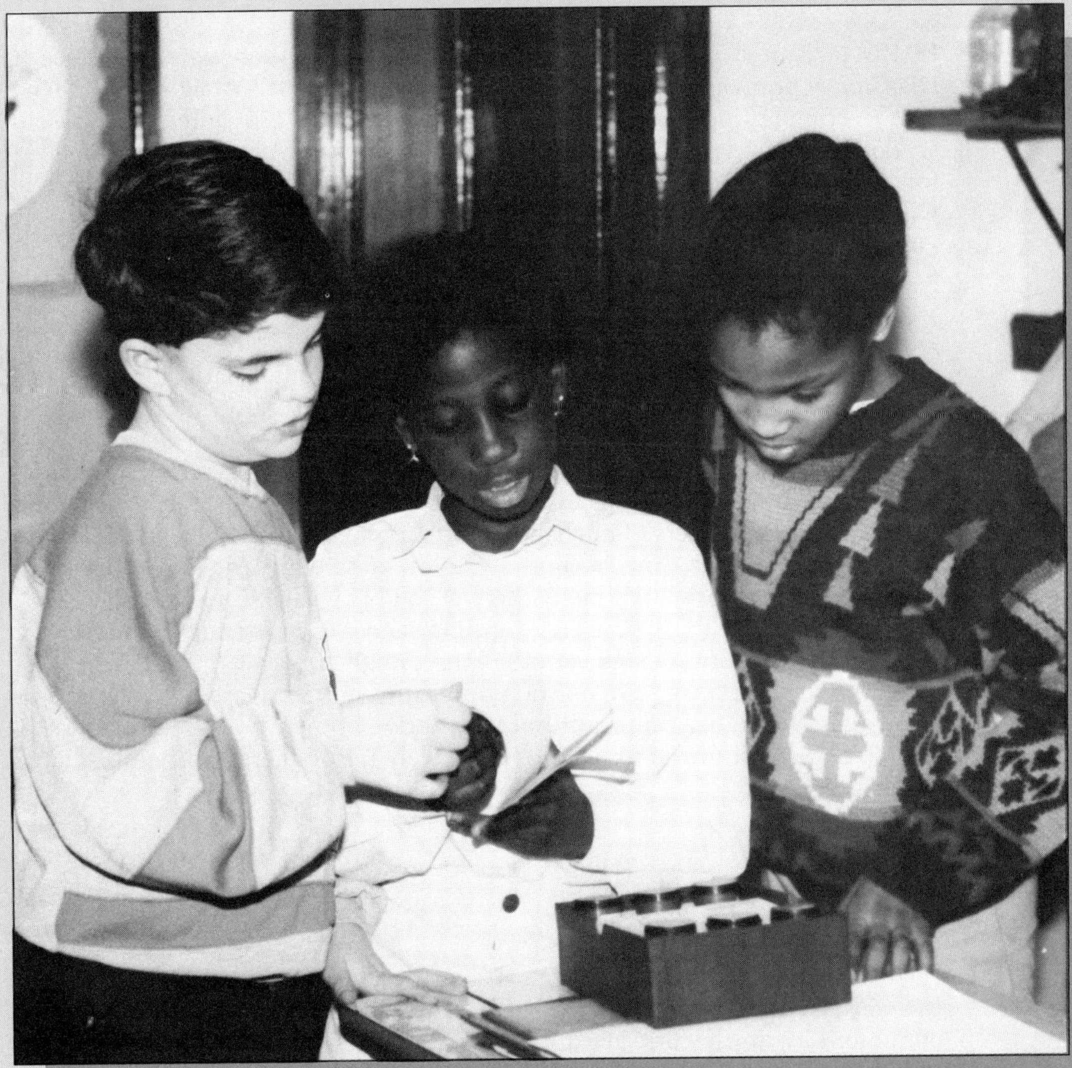

INTRODUCTION: THE INCREASINGLY DIVERSE STUDENT POPULATION

In 1990, 25 percent of the United States population defined themselves as Hispanic or nonwhite. In New York Sate, 40 percent of school-aged children belong to ethnic minority groups. In California, the total Hispanic and nonwhite school-aged population was 51.3 percent. Given current rates of birth and immigration, by the end of this century both the Hispanic and Asian populations will have grown by over 20 percent, the black population by about 12 percent. During this same period, the white population is estimated to grow by about 2 percent. By the year 2020, the Hispanic and nonwhite population will double to an estimated 115 million, over one-third of the total population. No growth is expected in the white population (*Time*, April 1, 1990).

What are the implications of this demographic information for language arts teachers? First, those teachers who now have culturally and linguistically diverse students must implement a language arts program that is sensitive to these students' backgrounds and needs. Second, it means that all teachers must be prepared to work with this ever-growing new population. The international organization of Teachers of English to Speakers of Other Languages (TESOL) estimates that at some time in their career all classroom teachers will have at least one student for whom English is a second language (Rigg & Allen, 1989). In 1986, there were more than eight million school-aged American children living in homes where a language other than English was spoken. Third, even teachers who currently have no such minorities in their classrooms must consciously incorporate a multicultural perspective in their classrooms if they are to prepare their students to interact effectively in the increasingly multicultural U.S. society.

❖ Implications for Classroom Teaching

As discussed in chapter 2, the society we live in affects the way we think and the way we use language. In her study of three culturally different American communities, Shirley Brice Heath points out how different lifestyles and child-rearing practices will result in children's coming to school with radically different literacy experiences (see chapter 2 for a synopsis).

If the American families in the Heath study had such dramatically different experiences with printed language in their English-speaking homes, we can imagine the diversity of experiences of children from other than English-speaking homes. What background experiences do the children of the Hmong farmers of the mountain regions of Laos bring to the language arts class? How do their experiences compare with those of the Ethiopian child who sat in an Amharic class of sixty, writing on and memorizing from a four-by-six-inch slate? What does the Jewish boy from the Soviet Union, trained rigorously in religious studies as well as academic subjects, bring to his new language arts class? For him, as for the Flemish-speaking child from Belgium who may not know any English when he enters the classroom, English will not be a second language. It will be a third. The former can already read and write in both Hebrew and Russian, the latter in French and Dutch. Their Puerto Rican classmate may speak English well but read and write neither English nor Spanish.

Culturally and linguistically diverse children come to the classroom with a broad range of language and literacy experiences. They are a diverse group, each of whom has had many experiences upon which to build. Each has already learned to communicate in one language, and each is a child who wants to use English to do what all children want to do with language—to make friends; to share ideas, feelings, and experiences; to make jokes; to record information; and to read for pleasure.

In this chapter, all students whose native tongues are not English will be referred to as **English as a second language** (ESL) students. Those who have not yet achieved a level of English proficiency to perform academic tasks successfully in English will be referred to as **limited English proficient.**

Throughout the history of the United States, different immigrant groups have met with varying degrees of success in American educational institutions, depending on their previous cultural experiences, the expectations they and their parents brought to the school setting, and the expectations teachers had for them (see Seller, 1988, for a thorough treatment of this topic). In their study of effective schools for Mexican-American children, Hakuta and Garcia (1989) found that the most effective classrooms for these children have a discourse style that is similar to the one they know at home. The give-and-take of cooperative learning is not unknown to these children. They are used to valuing the group effort and learning in a warm, responsive environment. The best schools for these children have a child-centered, integrated curriculum that is responsive to children's needs. All schools nominated for this study had to have at least 25 percent limited English proficient students. It is interesting to note that of the seventeen schools nominated, the three that were chosen based on academic achievement all gave children in grades k–3 the opportunity to develop literacy in their dominant language first.

Clearly, the second-grade teacher with one Punjabi speaker will not be able to help this student learn to read in Punjabi first. However, the classroom teacher can convey an interest in and appreciation for the child's home language and culture, inviting the child and his or her family to share stories, songs, and holiday rituals with the class. The teacher can invite the child to bring a native language book from home to put on display or to read during sustained silent reading time. The teacher can find out about the child's home culture and language from parents and other sources. By finding out which aspects of the classroom environment are most alien to the child's home culture and language, the teacher helps make the child and parents more at ease by modifying expectations and by slowly working on areas of special need. For instance, even after five or more years in the United States, a Korean may not use articles or verbs correctly because there are no articles in Korean and verbs are not inflected for tense or number. Likewise, a Chinese fifth grader who has been in school since kindergarten may still not participate fully in group decision making and discussion tasks. Chinese children are taught not speak out unless called on and to follow adults' directions. Collaborative learning techniques run counter to their home culture.

The most effective classroom for an Asian student might not be that described in the Hakuta and Garcia study. Most Asian students are not familiar with the active student-centered classroom. They expect a definite social distance between the teacher and the student, and they look down when spoken to. They have been taught to remain in their assigned seats. For such students, class participation and discussion appear to indicate disrespect for authority and can make them uncomfortable. In general, Asians value factual information and want their children to learn facts. A great deal of homework is expected (Cheng, 1987). In fact, there is a great discrepancy between the informal, open atmosphere of the American classroom and the expectations of the Asian child and parent. Although not all Asians have the same value system, and awareness of their general cultural and linguistic values is vital to the teacher of an Asian child.

SECOND LANGUAGE ACQUISITION

✤ Parallels to First Language Acquisition

As discussed in chapter 2, children develop language in a predictable way through their interactions with others, particularly the primary and secondary caregivers. When two-year-old Mark tells his mother, "Jubs bread," as they watch the birds eating, his mother follows the child's lead by paraphrasing his thought (see chapter 2). She knows that *jubs* is his word for bird and that *bread* is a generalization meaning "food."

"Oh, look. They're eating *berries*, aren't they?" responds the mother. Like any good mother, she does not explain that the real word for birds is *birds* or go into a definition of *bread*. Neither does she worry that "Jubs bread" is not grammatically correct. She responds to the communication by seeing what the child wants her to look at and by expanding on his utterance. By placing extra stress on "berries," perhaps a new word for Mark, she draws it to his attention in a meaningful context at a time he is interested and receptive. With her toddler, this mother talks about the here and now, speaks in short, clearly enunciated sentences and uses an exaggerated intonation pattern. These adaptations are characteristic of caretaker speech, sometimes called "motherese."

There are striking parallels between the adaptations made by people who interact effectively with limited English proficient speakers and those described for caretaker speech. English spoken by such children is syntactically less complex, idiomatic expressions are avoided, words are enunciated clearly, and the rate of speech is slower than normal. When interacting with non-English and very limited English proficient speakers, topics are limited to the here and now. Objects or pictures are used to aid communication and as a way to extend the here and now to include other situations, just as shared picture-book reading between adults and young language learners extends the here and now. Such strategies promote second language growth by providing what Krashen (1982) calls comprehensible input.

In a toddler's world, most communication is embedded in a rich context. The child learns to associate names with the concrete objects they stand for. If Dad says, "Do you want a cookie?" as he holds one out in his hand, the child will associate this object with the name "cookie." At first, the toddler's category for "cookie" may not match that of the adult—it might include other snacks like crackers and pretzels—but little by little it will approximate that of the adult.

Similarly, English as a second language (ESL) students will quickly learn the words presented to them in context-embedded situations. On the playground, a classmate shouts, "Catch the ball!" As the ball sails toward her, newly arrived Ana will learn the meaning of both *catch* and *ball*. She may not be able to use these words immediately, but she can understand them.

Just as the baby builds up a large receptive vocabulary before beginning to speak, so, too, can the limited English proficient student understand many things before being able say much. This stage is often called preproduction or the silent period. Like the parent of a very young child, the English as a second language teacher does not force the limited English proficient student to speak until he or she feels ready to do so. In the meantime, the student listens and tries to make sense of what others are saying to him or her.

As is true of children learning their first language, second language speakers' first utterances are telegraphic in nature. A noun and something else (perhaps a verb or another noun) stand for the whole thought. Roger Brown's (1970) chart of two-word sentences for native speakers gives examples such as

Joey shoe. (Joey is putting on his shoe.)
Book table. (The book is on the table.)

Limited English proficient students' first utterances will be similar. For example:

Come on!
Oh my gosh!
Me bathroom. (May I go to the bathroom, please?)
Billy sandwich. (Billy took my sandwich in the lunch room and threw it in the garbage.)

Also like first language learners, second language learners will overgeneralize categories and rules. All printed materials may be called "book." All past tense verbs will end in *-ed*, as in "I goed home." Some of these problems are complicated by first language characteristics. For instance, a Spanish speaker may call all of the children in the class "boys" because in Spanish this term covers boys and girls. Similarly, in Spanish a *galleta* could be either a cookie or a cracker. To make the distinction, one would specify whether it is sweet or salty. Speakers of some Asian languages may not use any past tense verbs at all since there are no past tense inflections in their languages.

The same characteristics of interactions that facilitate language development in young children as set forth in chapter 2 (intentionality, proximal development, collaboration, internalization, and continuous development) apply to children learning English as a second language. Like all other children, limited English proficient students try to communicate for a purpose. When Ana says with fury and urgency, "Billy sandwich," the teacher may not understand the full meaning of the utterance but can assume that it does not just mean, "Billy has a sandwich." A few well-chosen questions and lead-ins, such as suggesting that Ana show what happened to the sandwich, will help to uncover that the real purpose of this utterance is to communicate this message:

> That pesky kid, Billy, is bothering me again, Teacher. And this time he even threw out my entire lunch. I think you should make him sit on the bench all during recess for what he did to me.

Through collaboration by means of such questions and context clues—in this case her tone of voice and teary eyes—it is possible to help the child communicate much more than she might be able to alone. This is the idea of proximal development. It is also similar to Krashen's idea of ideal input. Krashen expresses the ideal input situation with the formula *I + 1*. *I* stands for the input the child is currently capable of understanding and *+ 1* means that this input should be slightly beyond the current capability. *I + 1* is, therefore, what Krashen means by comprehensible input. According to current second language acquisition research, with comprehensible input and a rich variety of opportunities for real language use, people can acquire a second language just as toddlers and preschoolers acquire their first language—without memorizing verb conjugations and pronoun rules.

The language learner is always learning more, with successively closer approximations of the rule system and lexicon of the literate adult. It is this continuous development that surprises us into really thinking about how our language works. When the six-year-old native English speaker says, "It's pitch hot," the teach knows she is trying to use *pitch* as an intensifier like *very* after having heard it as an intensifier with *dark*. The speech of students whose first language is not English is full of such surprises because the students are not beginning language students. They already have a rule system and lexicon to apply to the language learning situation. They already know a lot about language. Some other repercussions of this background knowledge will be discussed further in this chapter under The Linguistic Interdependence Principle.

✣ How Long Does It Take to Learn English?

The question of how long it takes to learn English must be broken down into parts. What do we mean by "learn English"? To be able to carry on a conversation with classmates in the playground about the game they are playing? To be able to read an unillustrated sixth-grade history text? To be able to write an effective persuasive paper about why there should be no dress code in the middle school?

Research shows that it usually takes about two years for limited English proficient students to become fluent in everyday conversation such as the playground talk described above. Gaining academic language skills, such as those required for the context-reduced reading and persuasive writing tasks suggested above can take five or more years (Cummins, 1984; Wong-Fillmore, 1983). In other words, very different time periods are required for ESL students to achieve the level of their peers in conversation than are for academic language skills.

The Linguistic Interdependence Principle

Another important consideration in discussing the length of time needed to learn English is the degree of literacy of the student in the primary language (L1). A child who can already read and write in L1 will have a much easier time learning to read and write in English. The Flemish boy who reads fluently in both French and Dutch and can write well-organized, engaging compositions in those languages may be able to read and write in English within a year or two. Another classmate whose first language is not English may struggle with reading and writing tasks for five years or more. Why the difference? Cummins (1981) explains this variability with his **linguistic interdependence principle.** According to this principle, cognitive/academic, or literacy skills transfer from one language to another. For example, if a child knows how to find the main idea and supporting details in a passage in French, as soon as he has developed the language required to read the English passage he will be able to find the main idea and supporting details in English. He will need no instruction in this skill because he already understands the organizing principle. In other words, although the surface structure (grammar, vocabulary, pronunciation) of the two languages are different, there is an underlying academic language proficiency common to both.

Just as this linguistic interdependence principle helps to explain why students with strong academic backgrounds often seem to pick up the language and the content area knowledge with amazing speed, it also serves to clarify why students from societies with no tradition of school literacy may need years of support by language specialists and culture-sensitive classroom teachers to achieve these same goals.

EFFECTIVE LANGUAGE ARTS PROGRAMS FOR CULTURALLY DIVERSE STUDENTS

❖ Terrell's Natural Approach

Current foreign and second language acquisition research findings are consistent with the research findings in first language learning discussed throughout this book. This research suggests that people learn language holistically, in a top-down rather than bottom-up way. This top-down language acquisition is in marked contrast to the foreign language training most current teachers received in which we first learned verb conjugations:

```
yo estoy          nosotros estamos
tu estás          Usted está
el   ⎫ está      Ustedes están
ella ⎭
```

then practiced them in little dialogues:

¿Como está Usted?
Muy bien, gracias. ¿Y Usted?

If we were lucky, after a few years of this sort of training we might actually speak to a native speaker and try out a few of our memorized phrases. However this approach simply did not produce people who were able to communicate effectively in the target language.

Current language teachers are concerned with developing communicative competence rather than a passive knowledge of grammar and vocabulary. Having communicative competence means being able to use the language for real day-to-day interactions with native speakers. They understand that language develops globally instead of linearly. As Rigg and Allen (1989, p. xi) explain:

> Language is not learned as a jigsaw of tiny bits of mastered skills, each fitting into a pattern, but rather as an entire picture that is at first blurred, only gradually coming into focus.

Terrell's Natural Approach to second language acquisition (1977) is based on this global view of language learning. It incorporates the silent period many researchers and observers have noted when students first arrive in the new language milieu. This preproduction or silent period may last three months or longer. Therefore, the natural approach starts with listening comprehension tasks, using Total Physical Response (Asher, 1969), a technique in which the student need only follow commands nonverbally. The child's game Simon Says is an example of a TPR task.

Another common approach is Sheltered English (Northcutt & Watson, 1986), in which students are taught age-appropriate lessons in a setting designed to maximize comprehensible input. Lots of visuals, clear speech, and hands-on activities provide a context-rich environment for learning. Errors are expected and student anxiety is kept to a minimum by keeping the focus on the communication (function) itself rather than on the form.

Both of these approaches have many of the characteristics of the parent-child interaction that facilitates language development as described in chapter 2.

STRUCTURING THE CLASS TO HELP ENGLISH AS A SECOND LANGUAGE STUDENTS

♣ Organizing the Physical Environment

Like children learning their first language, students for whom English is a second language learn English best through interactions in which they can communicate real wants, needs, and feelings in a safe environment. Therefore, the grouping of students in small clusters with desks pushed together or gathered at small round tables will help foster oral communication in comfortable settings.

Listening centers with tape recorders, headphones, and sets including tapes with books or song lyrics are a valuable part of any multicultural language arts classroom. Another important consideration in the physical structuring of a classroom for listening comprehension is the creation of quiet spots and time for listening activities. This provision must include monitoring the general noise level of the class. In a primary class, one child could be assigned the role of noise-level monitor. If activities get too loud, the child rings the bell. Such monitoring is especially important for students learning English as a second language because they often cannot fill in the gaps in messages they have only partially heard because of background noise interference. Unlike native speakers who can use the redundancy in a message to fill in the missing pieces, limited English proficient students do not know the structural rules of the language and the vocabulary well enough to predict the parts of the message they lost. Anyone who has tried to communicate in a not-yet-mastered foreign language at a noisy cocktail party knows how frustrating such situations can be.

Like the necessity of quiet times and places for listening comprehension to ensure that the maximum amount of the message comes through, it is essential that any written materials copied for limited English proficient students be clear, dark, and perfectly legible. A light mimeo or photocopy that is difficult for most students to read will almost surely be indecipherable for these ESL students. Since cursive writing differs considerably from country to country, newly arrived students who can read typed or printed words may not be able to read some handwriting.

A print-rich environment is helpful to limited English proficient students. Big calendars with the months and days of the week printed in boldface letters can serve as a constant reminder for student headings. Titles of bulletin board displays often become part of the students' new vocabulary. Lists of procedural and classroom rules, classmates' names and special subject names and times can all serve as ready references. Even labels on boxes and shelves help students learn the words as well as find the needed materials. Vital school words like *paste, ruler,* and *dictionary* are reinforced each time the student checks the label of the shelf or drawer.

When students are given ownership of part of the display areas or are asked for suggestions for displays and titles, the printed word around the classroom takes on new meaning. In his second week in school, a recent immigrant from Colombia suggested the title for a display of free writing: "Escribir y Pensar." The translated title, "Writing and Thinking," went up the next day. He promptly wrote it across his journal.

Groups of students can be assigned their own bulletin board space. The group becomes responsible for planning, acquiring and presenting display materials. Displays could be an illustrated group writing project, photos of family and pets (with descriptions,) or a story about their recent field trip.

Whether or not the class is ethnically and culturally diverse, teachers can send positive messages about cultural diversity by displaying photos and other visuals showing people of varying backgrounds engaged in appealing activities. School librarians may have such poster-sized photos published by UNESCO, for instance, in their geography files.

All multicultural classrooms need good world maps and globes. Children can put flags on the region of the map they or their ancestors are from. This activity could be part of a class oral history project, for example. Even very young children enjoy pointing out where they are from on a soft pillow-like globe and seeing how far away it is from their new home. Older children need maps of the country, state, and region. As they read books, children can see where the authors or characters are from and mark them on the map as well.

ACTIVITY

Visit an elementary-school classroom or analyze your own classroom.

A. What are the racial, cultural, linguistic, and socioeconomic groups represented in the student body? How do you know?
B. To what extent are these groups represented in the classroom environment by decorations, photographs, posters, displays, and toys?
C. To what extent are they represented in classroom books?
D. Which groups are overrepresented and which groups are underrepresented in b and c? (Task adapted from Yepes-Baraya, 1990.)
E. List changes that could be made to make the physical surroundings more representative and accepting of culturally diverse students.

> **ACTIVITY**
>
> Do A above for your college class.
> If your class were a fifth grade, how would you do B, C, D, and E?

Classroom library books should be surveyed to make sure there are adequate numbers of books in which culturally diverse characters are represented and different cultures are treated in a positive way.

In addition, limited English proficient students need concrete objects to work with as they start learning the language. When describing their room at home, for example, they might begin by showing with dollhouse furniture how the room is set up. Classmates can help them learn prepositional phrases such a "next to," "on the other side of," and "above" that they will need to describe their room. Any time a reading or writing task can be introduced using real objects it will become more accessible to students learning English as a second language.

❖ Organizing Interaction

When a new student for whom English is a second language arrives, one of the first things that can be done to help the child become part of the class is to assign him or her to a pal. This pal is an empathetic classmate—perhaps one who expresses an interest in having this role. Pals should be briefed on their roles, which will include not only helping the new student figure out what to do in class but also helping when the teacher is not around. Pals can discuss what these situations might include—buying lunch, entering playground games, figuring out bus rules and routines, and finding out about after-school activities. If there are a number of ESL students who need pals, it might be worthwhile to organize a Pal Club with bi-monthly lunchtime meetings to discuss the challenges of being a pal, exchange helpful hints, and exchange information on their pals' cultures (Janda, 1989).

Becoming part of a stable cooperative learning group can also help new students make friends by giving them a smaller, more comfortable way into their new peer group. The structuring of cooperative learning tasks where each person's contribution is valuable and necessary will keep the group's attention on getting the meaning across to their new classmates, keeping them actively involved (Kagan, 1986; Coelho, in press). Suppose, for example, the group has an activity requiring that they find someone who has an unusual pet, an unusual hobby, and an unusual possession. Each group must interview its members and write up its findings. The group would make every effort to find out all it could about their classmates' pets, hobbies and possessions. If the Cambodian child has a gilded headdress worn in a traditional Cambodian dance, this special possession becomes an asset to the child and the group for the task at hand. Moreover, sharing this special cultural tradition can give the class a greater appreciation of the ESL student and his or her culture.

> **ACTIVITY**
>
> Work in small groups.
> A. Develop a cooperative learning task for a group of four students that could elicit special skills or cultural or linguistic knowledge that English as a second language students might have. Make sure that the task requires that students share their information and work together in order to successfully complete the task.
> B. Ask your classmates how this task could fit into a larger thematic unit of study.
> C. Discuss ways to adapt the task for primary, intermediate, and upper grades.

The more verbal interaction limited English proficient students can participate in, the faster they will gain communicative competence and grammatical competence as well. Unlike the foreign language programs most present-day teachers went through, up-to-date ESL programs do not consider knowledge of English grammar a prerequisite for communicative ability. Neither do they structure lessons around a graded sequence of grammatical structures. In traditional foreign language programs the student would never be asked, "What would you like to be when you grow up?" in the first week. This verb tense would be saved until much later in the curriculum. In current second language eduction, however, the topic determines the verb tenses to be taught. Grammatical structures are developed as they are needed to express ideas about topics of real concern. In a class unit on occupations, students might be asked to interview their parents about their jobs, asking questions such as

> What is your job?
> What do you do in this job?
> What tools do you use for your job?
> What do you like about your job?

In this task, students practice asking present tense *wh-* questions and receive present tense statement answers. They use these structures because the topic requires them. In the following group assignment, when students discuss what profession or occupation they would like to have, the question will be

What would you like to be?
Why would you like to be a _____ ?

This structure is practiced next, not because it follows the present tense in the syllabus, but because it is needed to discuss the topic at hand. In other words, the language arts teacher can develop a topic-driven ESL grammar lesson using the current content matter of the class.

> **ACTIVITY**
>
> For a given communicative setting and interaction, design a small-group assignment requiring that students use one of the following grammatical patterns:
>
> to be going + infinitive
> (We are going to have supper.)
> to like + infinitive
> (John likes to swim.)
> to have + past participle + for
> (I have lived here for three years.)
> to have + past participle + since
> (I have lived here since May.)
> subject + simple present tense + time
> (He comes home at three o'clock.)
>
> Explain the situation and how it fits into a thematic unit of study.

One effective way of integrating ESL students into the classroom is by incorporating these students' languages and cultures into classroom life. Add picture books in their languages to the classroom library, even if its necessary to borrow them from the students' families. Have each student teach the class a song or a game from his or her homeland. Find out each child's special cultural knowledge and use it as a resource. A girl from India might be able to demonstrate how to wrap a sari. A boy from China might play a Chinese flute using a twelve-tone scale. This latter demonstration might fit in well with an elementary physics unit on making musical instruments. In a multicultural classroom, one such demonstration might lead to a number of other undiscovered musicians coming forward—the Colombian student bringing in his tiple, a guitarlike instrument, and the Danish boy his accordion.

As these students get to share their expertise with their classmates, they will gain self confidence and will be increasingly respected by their peers.

12: Language Arts in the Multicultural Classroom

---TO THINK ABOUT---

Sharing Cultures

Share something particularly "ethnic" with the class—a folk song, a trinket, or a craft. How might this activity work if your class were third grade? Seventh grade?

♣ Affective Considerations

Newly arrived limited English proficient students usually feel uncertain and insecure. What may not be as obvious is that for a long time, students who are just starting to learn English may feel anxious about speaking out. As mentioned previously, the preproduction—or listening—phase may last for three months or longer. Even students with excellent listening comprehension who have been in the United States for several years may feel very uncomfortable about speaking out in class. For this reason, new arrivals should not be forced to speak until they are ready. Rather, they can be asked to perform nonverbal tasks like pointing to the correct picture or placing sequence cards in the right order to tell a story. Children who are still quiet after several years in the system can be helped to perform the required oral tasks by initially giving presentations to a small supportive group of peers, perhaps after a little teacher or one-to-one peer coaching. The pantomime and puppet activities discussed in chapter 10 can also be valuable for these students.

Often children who speak little or no English feel extremely frustrated by their inability to communicate with their peers. They feel that their classmates will think they are just stupid. Being able to express these feelings in their own language is helpful. While the other children are writing in their journals, new limited English proficient students could write down feelings and impressions in their native language. If a bilingual teacher, aide, or someone from the community is available, passages that the student wants to share with others could be translated. One fifth grader from Colombia wrote this journal entry (in Spanish) two months after arriving at a school where he and his sisters were the only Spanish speakers:

My Thoughts

How I would love to have a book to read for fun, reading and looking at the pictures. But I don't have one. I'm happy to be here, but i don't have any Spanish books. Also, I would like to learn English so I can talk to everybody and read in English. Before I hated books, but now I think it is better to have a book because all the books are in English. Do you agree? If you were on another continent in another country and you didn't have any books in English, how would you feel?

The reading aloud and posting of this translation not only helped this boy's classmates to better understand his feelings, but also turned up a little collection of Spanish storybooks for him to borrow.

Being new immigrants is usually not an entirely happy stress-free situation for the family either. Often the child's family is struggling to make all the necessary adjustments to a radically different life. Some new arrivals were forced to leave their country because of political upheavals that made it unsafe to remain. In 1991 alone the United States accepted 121,000 refugees under the United Nations refugee resettlement program. Such families have often spent years in refugee camps before coming to the United Sates. Many of them have had harrowing experiences occasioned by war and civil unrest. Economic conditions have forced many newcomers to leave everything and everyone they knew and try their luck at making a new and better life for themselves. Perhaps in doing so some family members were left behind. Some children come to the United States to become adoptive members of an American family. They have to make the adjustments not only to school but also to their new family life.

Although they may not want to share such experiences in the large group, children with such traumatic backgrounds may find that the writing workshop gives them a way of communicating and working through some of the pain and hurt they feel.

If students for whom English is a second language are to be successful in school, they need a language arts program that will empower them to take their place among their classmates as valuable members of the classroom community. They should be given many varied experiences to draw upon in the learning process and many opportunities to share their unique experiences and background knowledge with their classmates. Viewed in this way, such students can work to fill the gaps in their own background knowledge with courage and enthusiasm. This approach differs considerably from the remediation model which starts with a test—in English—to see what the student does not know.

Most of all, teachers need to remember that language minority children are children—children who have the same needs, and hopes, and ups and downs as all other children. They are also children who have language. The non-English-speaking child who scores zero on the language section of the kindergarten screening is not a child with no language. If she is made to feel like a special member of the class who knows another language and who will soon have two languages, she and her classmates will all gain from this multicultural perspective.

STRATEGIES FOR FOSTERING LANGUAGE DEVELOPMENT IN THE MULTICULTURAL CLASSROOM

❖ Providing Opportunities for Real Language Use

The approach to teaching language arts advocated in this book makes great sense for linguistically diverse students because it creates settings in which children have a myriad of opportunities to use language for real communicative purposes. Such authentic communication is fostered through cooperative learning, the language experience approach, language arts in content area studies, and process writing.

Cooperative Learning

As discussed previously cooperative learning tasks will create settings in which limited English proficient students need to make their ideas and feelings known to the members of the group. Likewise, the group has a vested interest in making every part of their discussion clear to the limited English proficient students because the group's success hinges upon the successful collaboration of all members. In a jigsaw word puzzle (Coelho, 1989), for example, a group of four students are given the same jigsaw gird, but each one has a different set of clues, none of which is sufficient alone to allow the player to guess the word. The clues for one six-letter word might be

— — — — — —

1. It's big.
2. It begins with a T.
3. It is a bird.
4. People see it on Thanksgiving.

In heterogeneous groups of native and non-native speakers of English working on tasks like the one described above, the limited English proficient student gets to interact with peers who can serve as language models, much as the child inviting Ana to play ball on the playground served as a language model. There is a real need to communicate in both circumstances. Students in such tasks have a clear purpose and goal. While engaged in cooperative learning tasks, they get a chance to explore ideas with nonjudgmental peers. The exploratory talk in this type of reciprocal interaction helps all students develop the higher-level cognitive skills of analysis, evaluation, and synthesis (Cummins, 1989; Coelho, 1988). Moreover, these cooperative learning tasks will help all students—native and non-native English speakers alike—become better communicators.

The Language Experience Approach

The language experience approach (LEA) is well-suited to the needs of students for whom English is a second language. It builds on the children's own experience. The class collectively generates its own text based on real happenings. When the class goes on a trip downtown, they can all retell the story of their trip. One boy is most impressed by the metro and draws a detailed diagram of the subway, marking the stations. The Korean child remembers her immigration hearing in the courthouse they walked by. Everyone can contribute something to the class book about the trip.

As discussed in chapter 6, the language experience approach gives children control over the language that will become their reading text. In some ways it is like the home in which the parent follows the young child's interest and leads from behind. In this way, LEA gives limited English proficient children the vocabulary they need to talk, write, and read about their current interests. If Whitey, the class mouse in chapter 6, were to escape, and the class talked and wrote about it in the daily news, the ESL learner would listen intently and perhaps later be able to communicate this exciting event to his seatmate on the bus home.

Language Arts in Content Area Studies

When limited English proficient students can study thematically organized units in which the other content areas become part of the language arts program, they can develop language skills while learning math, science, and history. According to Hakuta and Garcia (1989), one common characteristic of classrooms that are effective in teaching Hispanic children is that they have an "integrated 'child-centered' curriculum" in which there are no specific times for reading and writing. Rather, literacy is pervasive in all aspects of instruction. The students in such programs have an opportunity to learn in depth about subjects that are important to them.

Process Writing

The writing process approach to teaching writing gives students who are learning English as a second language the opportunity to use writing as a way of communicating. As previously mentioned, with intermediate-grade limited English proficient students, initial writings may be in the native language. The teacher, an aide, another student, or a community member may serve as translator for pieces to share. Primary-grade students may start labeling pictures in their journals with English words from around the room early on. After the first big snow, one newly arrived first grader in Buffalo, New York, took a piece of blue construction paper, drew lots of snowflakes and a snowman, copying "SNOWY" across the top from the weather chart.

More advanced second language learners find the process writing approach much more motivating than traditional methods of teaching composition and grammar. As one student explained, "I always wrote as little as I could because I could not stand to see my ideas covered with red spiderwebs." When students get the idea that it is the thoughts and feelings that matter most, they will be willing to risk exposing their lack of knowledge of English grammar, spelling, and vocabulary.

Process writing is especially successful with culturally and linguistically diverse students because of its feature of ownership of one's writing. As discussed in chapter 8, students in a writers' workshop are frequently free to choose their own topics and forms of expression. Having the power to work on self-selected topics, limited English proficient students can make the most of their own background knowledge, working on topics they feel comfortable with and perhaps have considerable insight into. The important feature of ownership will be discussed in depth later in this chapter.

Accessing Prior Knowledge

Parent-child interactions that facilitate language development help the child express things he could not manage to express alone. By asking leading questions in an effort to negotiate meaning, the parent helps the child learn through speaking. This parental building on what the child can currently do and say is consistent with Vygotsky's idea that instruction entails identifying the child's zone of proximal development and assisting them in the solution of problems that are currently just beyond their reach (see chapter 2 for discussion). A similar concept in reading is schema. The teacher's role in the schema-building process is to access prior knowledge that the child will need before being able to understand a passage and to see how the child's own experiences can be used as a springboard to the topic or concept in question. Accessing prior knowledge is helping to set the stage for the new material by leading children to consider related experiences or actually creating such experiences in the classroom.

Some recent models of comprehension (Baker & Brown, 1984) consider comprehension to be "an active process of hypothesis testing or schema building." As readers gather more information, they modify or refine their hypotheses. When an adequate set of hypotheses cannot be derived, there is a lack of comprehension. This failure to understand occurs basically in three situations: first, when readers cannot interpret the text because they lack background knowledge; second, when the authors have not conveyed their ideas clearly enough; and third, when readers misinterpret the text (Baker & Brown, 1984).

Baker and Brown point out that learners, regardless of age, "are more likely to take active control of their own cognitive endeavors when they are faced with tasks of intermediate difficulty." Limited English proficient students may sometimes cease comprehension-monitoring activities if the reading is too difficult. In other words, they may not pause if what they are reading does not make sense nor will they backtrack if they missed the author's point. The subject is unfamiliar to them, there is too much new vocabulary, or the sentence structure is too complex. They simply give up. For instance, after a Korean sixth grader, Kwang-hi, was required to read about the Sumerians in her social studies text, she was asked what she understood as she read. She could not say, nor did she have any idea what strategies to use to help her understand. Even after several days spent raising background knowledge by looking at filmstrips and pictures of civilization in the Fertile Crescent, she could make no sense of the passage. The reading was simply too difficult. This illustration supports Brown's contention (Baker & Brown, 1984) that lack of both strategic knowledge and world knowledge can impede effective reading and that the two forms of knowledge interact in complex ways. Necessary reading strategies include identifying the main idea and the supporting detail and determining the structure of the argument by looking at transitional expressions such as "on the other hand" and "in addition." However, if the reader has no knowledge of the topic of the reading—if it is not within his or her knowledge of the world—strategy use alone may not enable the reader to make sense of the passage.

Another illustration of the importance of world knowledge is the difficulty a skillful middle-school reader from China had with a simple passage on maple syrup and how it is made. This Chinese girl had never had syrup, pancakes, waffles, or French toast. She had never seen a maple tree, maple sugar candy, maple syrup, or sap. She did not know the word *bucket* or *faucet* (used to explain how the spigot works). In short, like Kwang-hi, this student had no experience with anything mentioned in the passage she was asked to read. If limited English proficient students are to feel successful in independent reading assignments they should, whenever possible, be offered a library of reading materials which will not entail inordinate amounts of time spent in raising background knowledge.

In contrast to her performance on the Sumerian reading, when given picture books with predictable story lines Kwang-hi was able to tell exactly where she had doubts and problems. Moreover, she had a repertoire of strategies to use in dealing with the difficult parts. When reading *One Fine Day* by Nonny Hogrogian, she quickly realized that the tale was cumulative; each time the fox asked someone or something for a certain item to help him get his tail back, the reply would be, "Yes, if you do X." Kwang-hi said, "Now the fox ask for something." She did not recognize the words *begged* or *jug,* but kept going with the idea that further on in the story she would find out what *jug* means. Sure enough, on the next page there was a picture of a girl with a jug. As she read, "The fox found a fair maiden," she said, "Oh, that [girl] is a fair maiden with a jug."

❖ Providing Experiences with REAL Written Discourse

A holistic, integrated language arts program provides ESL students with many opportunities to work with authentic written language in meaningful ways. Some of these opportunities include the "shared books experience," directed reading and thinking activities, language experience lessons, reader's theater, and the reading/writing workshop.

When the teacher reads aloud to the class (raising background knowledge before the reading and discussing the story's meaning with the class), minority students get to have one of the important literacy experiences they may never have had before coming to school—a bedtime story (Heath, 1982). With each directed reading lesson, the teacher helps children see what they need to know in order to understand the story (see chapter 7). Children learn through techniques like semantic mapping to make connections among the things they know that will help them make sense of a reading. All of this work with readings will help culturally and linguistically diverse students learn how school discourse works.

Participation in a reading/writing workshop will make ESL students into full members of the group. Even if they are reading picture books, they are members of the workshop, and often come up with beautiful stories and pieces to share. After one ESL student shared the story of *Mufaro's Beautiful Daughters* by John Steptoe, many of her classmates, who were reading *Sweet Valley Twins* or the *Babysitter's Club* books, asked to borrow this poignant African tale. A twelve-year-old Taiwanese boy in the United States for one year surprised his classmates when he shared this first draft of a poem written after a field trip to the local art gallery:

Abstract [Art]

Abstract is very nice
Abstract is coloerful   [colorful]
Abstract is very fun,
it has many things in it
Abstract is very strage   [strange]
Abstract is very net   [neat]
Abstract is buteful   [beautiful]
that's why I cuce Abstract.   [choose]

Since language develops holistically, limited English proficient students benefit from reading and writing experiences right from the beginning. In a language arts class that gives them opportunities for comprehensible written input, and writing experiences where they are free to make the kinds of errors any language learner will make while communicating things they want to say, ESL students will grow. They will gradually learn to make sense of school discourse practices and become proficient English listeners, speakers, readers, and writers.

LANGUAGE ARTS AS A WAY OF EMPOWERING CULTURALLY DIVERSE STUDENTS

♣ Students Take Ownership

Throughout this book a holistic, collaborative, integrated approach to teaching language arts is developed. Each of these characteristics help students take control of their own learning. This taking control of one's learning is what Bereiter and Scardamalia (1985) call intentional learning. Having a real purpose, using language in the classroom to really share ideas, creating a story, a book, a puppet show, are all ways of empowering students. As participants in such integrated, collaborative classrooms, students learning English as a second language and other minority children are empowered. Four ways in which students take ownership in such classes will be described—the use of self-selected topics, instruction in metacognitive skills, peer tutoring, and later, under a Multicultural Perspective, students as resources.

♣ Self-selected Topics

Atwell (1987) shares with her eight-grade writers the fact that "most published first novels are semi-autobiographical" and that by starting with what they know best, writers convey conviction, involvement, and voice, which are all characteristics of engaging writing (p. 89). By starting with a writing topic that they know personally, limited English proficient writers, too, can feel in command. They become the authorities who can teach their readers about their area of expertise. The teacher can help empower linguistically and culturally diverse students by guiding them in determining what they know to write about and what they want to find out more about through the writing process.

Similarly, self-selected reading helps turn the control and responsibility for learning over to readers whose first language is not English. It is important that the reading be of interest to the readers. There are a number of reasons why giving students a choice, or allowing for self-selection of reading material, makes sense for linguistically diverse students. It optimizes reading strategy use. For example, if students are familiar with the subject matter, they are better able to guess word meaning from context, to make predictions, to monitor comprehension, and to identify the main ideas and supporting information. It makes sense according to current theory; both schema theory and in terms of fostering intentional learning. When selecting their own readings, children are apt to have adequate schemata; they choose topics they already have an interest in and probably know something about. By making their own choice on readings, children are able to take ownership of the reading activity and can pursue their own learning goals. By taking executive control of their reading material, readers are able to take responsibility for their own learning.

In the Sumerian reading, Kwang-hi had insufficient background knowledge and no intrinsic motivation for the reading. She was not really interested in ancient civilization. It was a reading topic imposed upon her. In contrast, in a search for current periodicals with pictures of Korea, Kwang-hi found an issue of *Cricket* (September, 1986), a children's literary magazine, with folktales from Korea. She was fascinated and asked if she could read some of the tales in class. Although these Korean tales were more difficult than most of the readings she had worked on, Kwang-hi was able to guess meaning from context, get the gist of the story, and forge ahead. After reading "The Pheasant's Bell" through once, she wanted to read it again to see if she could get the parts she had not understood the first time. The underlying structure of the story was so much in keeping with her story schema that she could use it to predict what should happen next. In addition, the symbolism of these folktales, the snake in "The Pheasant's Bell" and the tiger in "The Magic of Maengho" were so familiar to her that she got the implied meaning of the text faster than the teacher could and later helped the teacher figure out the moral of the stories.

The self-selection of tales for which the limited English proficient reader has a wealth of background knowledge, makes them manageable despite their syntactic and semantic difficulty. Similarly, many ESL students select books in which they can use the pictures to help get the gist of the story and to determine the meaning of specific words. When reading *Big Max* by Kin Platt, one fourth grader looked ahead to see what would happen and then looked carefully at the pictures for the page she was on to help guess unfamiliar words. The illustrations served as a motivator, giving her confidence that she could manage to get through the hard parts.

More advanced ESL students may rely on the grammatical and semantic contexts to figure out sections of text that they do not understand. Sokha and Raj, Cambodian and Indian fourth graders, were reading a poem called "The New Kid on the Block" by Jack Prelutsky. Two lines from this poem are "That new kid tweaked my arm," and "That new kid swiped my ball." They discussed "tweaked" and "swiped" and although neither knew what the words meant, they decided not to worry about it because, "It's something bad like pulled or kicked." Throughout the poem, the new kid is causing trouble, so these readers got the idea from the context.

Another way linguistically diverse children are able to deal with parts they do not understand or cannot read is if the story or poem they are reading is in rhyme. When a first grader who had been in the country about six months read *A Fly Went By*, many words that she would not otherwise have deciphered where in rhyme so she was able to predict them. She loved reading *The Berenstain Bears and the Spooky Old Tree* and *Old Hat, New Hat* for this reason.

Another way these children help themselves deal with reading is by choosing books in a series. For example, third grader Maria read one Frog and Toad book, and she took another for her next choice. Frog and Toad each have consistent personalities. Moreover, the writing style and even some vocabulary and structures carry over from one Frog and Toad story to the next.

In summary, by allowing limited English proficient children to choose their own writing topics and their own reading materials, teachers empower these children and help them learn to take control of their own learning. Students for whom English is a second language get many of the same benefits that other students get from the self-selection, but the practice is especially important for these students because it helps them build the necessary background knowledge, validating and letting them use the special background knowledge they have as a point of departure. It also insures that all students are working at their zone of proximal development, even if it is different from the norm.

✤ Instruction in Metacognitive Skills

The freedom of ownership also helps students who may not be fluent in English to develop the vital metacognitive skills of learning, "those involved in the regulation and orchestration of the various activities that must be carried out in order for learning to be successful" (Shuell, 1986). In other words, this kind of self-directed writing demands that students know how to plan and use problem-solving strategies to achieve their goal (Bereiter & Scardamalla, 1985).

One method that can help develop the metacognitive strategies required for successful writing is conferencing (see chapters 8 and 9). The kind of conferencing Graves (1983) and Atwell (1987) advocate changes the focus of the student-teacher relationship. Instead of trying to match the student text to the teacher's preconceived notion of the ideal text, the student tries to get the piece of writing to match his or her intended meaning as closely as possible. This central focus on trying to determine the writer's intended meaning not only gives students greater incentive to write but also makes the teacher's response more relevant. An underlying assumption of this approach is that limited English proficient writers, too, have a purpose and a sense of logic. It is empowering to the student that what he or she wants to communicate is the central focus rather than how it is expressed.

This approach requires multidraft writing because the intended meaning can only come out through progressive fine-tuning, through successive approximations. This approach of conferencing on drafts-in-progress contrasts sharply with the after-the-fact correction of the traditional approach to giving feedback. It is much closer to the parent's leading from behind. In a face-to-face conference about writing-in-progress, writers whose first language is not English have the opportunity to try out their works on a small, supportive audience. By asking questions, the teacher or peer reader can initiate a process of negotiating meaning. As discussed in chapter 9, the teacher can collaborate with the author, helping the writer see the piece through the eyes of the audience. Together the reader and writer can consider the relationship between the writer's intent and the outcome as perceived by the reader. Is the teacher or peer reader's response that intended by the writer? Does each section of the text help sustain the writer's intentions? Is there any part that needs more clarification or elaboration? By asking such questions of the writer, the teacher or peer reader gives control of decision making to the writer while developing the metacognitive skills of monitoring and evaluating, looking at the text from the perspective of the audience. In this way, the reader gives the child author a motive for improving the text. Without such input, limited English proficient writers (like any other beginning writers) will often assume that they have communicated their intended message on the first draft, so they will not see any need to change the substance of their text. Through conferencing, these young writers should see ways to help their readers better understand the ideas they had hoped to communicate. They should learn to predict how the reader will react, monitor how their message is coming across, and make plans about how to better achieve their goal.

Peer Tutoring

When a reading partner, aged eight, was reading *The Bremen Town Musicians* to a five-year-old Cambodian boy, she stopped to ask him what was going to happen when the donkey, the dog, and the cat met the rooster. He had no idea. She turned back to the previous page and pointed to the picture. "What happened when the donkey met the cat?" The boy shrugged his shoulders. "Well, look at the next page then." She turned to the page beyond the one they were reading. His eyes lit up. "He go, too." The reading partner had shared her strategies of using information already given or looking ahead to predict. The five-year-old had not yet learned to employ such strategies. Children paired across classes or within classes can read to one another and also serve as audience and critic for each other's writing. The use of peer tutors is an excellent way to deal with the multilevel linguistically and culturally diverse class. It not only gives children more one-to-one interaction and feedback but also helps integrate limited English proficient students. Moreover, the bilingual, biliterate child can be a valuable peer translator/interpreter for new students of the same language background.

This peer tutoring experience has great benefits for the tutor as well. As the teacher, the child must learn to clearly articulate questions, explain unclear points, and draw parallels. These tasks all require high-order thinking and mastery of the topic at hand. Working as a peer tutor with a limited English proficient student may have the added benefit of increasing the tutor's interest in the other's culture and language.

✤ Focus on Multicultural Perspective

In his powerful book *Empowering Minority Students* (1989), Jim Cummins makes the point that classroom teachers play an important role in the kind of education that culturally diverse students experience.

> Classroom teachers convey crucial messages in subtle ways to minority students about the validity (or lack of validity) of their language and cultural identity; they can provide (or fail to provide) opportunities for students to express this identity through sharing their experiences with other students and adults by means of the active use of written and oral language; in addition, classroom teachers have a choice with respect to the extent to which they collaborate with minority parents as partners in a shared enterprise; specifically, they can either explore with parents ways of promoting children's literacy at home or alternatively, they can ignore any potential contribution parents might make to their children's academic growth. (p. 4)

One of the reasons why parental involvement is vital to the success of a language arts program for children learning English as a second language is that there are often great incongruities between the American teacher's expectations and the parents' expectations. Asian parents' expectations are a case in point. Generally speaking, they want their children to be quiet and obedient and to learn through memorization and observation. Facts are important. Fantasy is not important. Reading is decoding of information and facts (summarized from Cheng, 1987). Most Asian parents would probably view the language arts classroom advocated in this book as confusing and undisciplined. It is important to discuss with such parents what the child is doing and why. Although a request for a conference may be interpreted as shameful—their child must be misbehaving—it is important to explain to Asian parents the rationale and goals for the language arts class, lest they think the teacher is incompetent for not giving sufficient grammar and vocabulary drillwork!

Parents whose native language is not English may benefit greatly from workshops in which the teacher models the kinds of activities done with the children to foster literacy. Through a series of participatory, intergenerational activities, one group of educators designed a language arts workshop series for Hispanic parents (Quintero & Huerta-Macias, 1990). Each thematically organized session included an initial inquiry, a learning activity, a language experience activity, a storybook demonstration, and a home activity. Through such interventions, culturally diverse parents can learn to understand what the teacher is doing in the language arts class and why. Moreover, they can become collaborators in the literacy development of their children, providing the "multicultural link to the classroom both in terms of social and emotional support and in terms of providing teachers with important factual information about [the] language and culture [of the child]" (p. 312).

In order to empower culturally and linguistically different students, the teacher must be a promoter of pluralistic point of view. Such a view is simply an extension of the position that Graves and Atwell have taken in their reading and writing workshops. Each child's personal experience is a valuable resource in the academic setting, and a point of departure for both reading comprehension and writing.

Understanding among culturally and linguistically diverse people requires respect for others' cultures and an ability to see others' perspectives and to interpret their actions within their own context (Ramsey, 1987). Even primary-school children can learn to consider another child's feelings This consideration of the other child's feelings is a good starting point for helping children to see what they have in common with children who seem different. The newly arrived Nigerian first grader is timid and afraid. The teacher might ask the class to think back to when they started kindergarten. How did they feel? Did they know anybody? A child who moved into the district and did not know anybody could share her feelings. What if they had been new and did not know the language either? Young children can empathize with the predict the feelings of others, and this ability can help them to bridge cross-cultural and cross-linguistic gaps.

For older children and adults, learning more about the minority child's language and culture is important. One way teachers might incorporate discussion of and appreciation for the child's culture is through read-aloud sessions devoted to literature related to that child's—or simply various culturally diverse children's—background. The class of any Southeast Asian refugee child could benefit from hearing M. Surat's *Angel Child. Dragon Child*, the story of a Vietnamese girl's first months in an American school. *Aekyung's Dream*, by M. Paek, a story of a Korean child and her adjustment to the United States is in both Korean and English.

ACTIVITY

Work in small groups.
A. Each person will select a picture book to read aloud to the group. This book should have a main character from a minority cultural group. After

> **ACTIVITY (continued)**
>
> sharing the books, each group will discuss the following questions:
> 1. Which cultural or ethnic group is represented?
> 2. Are the characters portrayed in a positive light?
> 3. Does the book reinforce or dispel ethnic stereotypes?
> 4. Does the story have universal appeal?
> 5. Will the reader empathize with the main character?
> 6. What can the reader learn from this story?
> 7. Would this book be a worthwhile addition to the classroom library?
> 8. How could it be incorporated in a thematic unit?
>
> B. Each group will pick one or two of the best picture books to share with the whole group. This large-group sharing can be the basis for discussion of the chosen books' merits, using the questions listed above as a point of departure.

Culturally diverse children and their families are also great classroom resources. If a child is literate in the first language, he or she might read a story for the others. The class could get an idea what it is like to listen to English all day as a newcomer. Children whose first language is not English could teach the class how to say or write a few things in their languages or to sing a song. At Thanksgiving they could explain about harvest festivals or special feast days in their countries. (This activity could also help the minority child see how Thanksgiving is not just for the Pilgrims and their descendants.) At Christmas they could tell about a major religious holiday and show the symbols connected with it. Parents could be asked to show how to make a traditional dish or craft.

> **ACTIVITY**
>
> A. Design a class activity for which culturally diverse students or their parents could teach or demonstrate some traditional skill, cultural practice or aspect of their language. Explain how this lesson would fit into a larger unit of study. Describe class preparation or follow-up activities that might be included.
> B. Share your activity with a small group of classmates. The group will select one or two activities to share with the whole class.
> C. In the large group, discuss the appropriateness of these activities for primary, intermediate and upper-grade students and any adaptations that might be needed for each.

The more the teacher collaborates with culturally and linguistically diverse students in a holistic, integrated language arts class, learning about their home cultures and languages while they learn English, the more interesting having such children in class becomes and the richer the experience for everyone involved.

Summary

This chapter discusses the rationale for preparing all teachers to work with culturally and linguistically diverse students. It examines some classroom implications of the current demographic changes in the United States and offers teachers background on the second language acquisition process as well as suggestions for appropriate language learning strategies to use in the language acquisition process as well as suggestions for appropriate language learning strategies to use in the language arts classroom.

After comparing the first and second language acquisition processes, some of the characteristics of interaction that foster language development are set forth. These include the offering of comprehensible input and a variety of opportunities to use the language for real communication purposes. In dealing with the question of how long it takes to learn English, a distinction is made between the time it takes to learn to carry on everyday conversations and that needed to learn to use the language for cognitively demanding academic purposes. Related to this issue is the degree of literacy children have in their primary language. The relationship of first language literacy to second language acquisition is discussed in terms of Cummins's (1981) linguistic interdependence principle.

What are the components of an effective language arts program for culturally diverse students? Consistent with the research findings in first language acquisition discussed throughout this book, current foreign and second language acquisition research suggest that people learn language in a holistic, top-down rather than bottom-up way. Terrell's Natural Approach (1977), Asher's Total Physical Response (1969), and Northcutt and Watson's Sheltered English (1986) are mentioned as approaches that help second language learners through the preproduction phase of language learning. Practical suggestions are offered on how to structure the physical environment and the social interaction in the language arts classroom to help students for whom English is a second language.

Discussion of the physical environment includes both such aspects as setting up seating to ensure that these students can hear and the more subtle considerations of having a classroom library that presents a pluralistic perspective, one in which culturally diverse characters are represented and different cultures are portrayed in a positive light. Organizing interaction includes the arranging for peer pals to help the newly arrived student through daily routines, including lunch lines and recess as well as classroom procedures. It includes helping limited English proficient students become part of a stable cooperative-learning group.

This chapter presents strategies for fostering language development in a multicultural classroom through the provision of opportunities for REAL language use. In addition to the development of cooperative-learning tasks, the language experience approach, language through content area study and process writing are discussed. The important of accessing prior knowledge and providing experience with REAL written discourse through a holistic, integrated language arts program are stressed as vital ways of creating positive environments for second language learners. Like the home in which the parent leads from behind by following the young child's interest and by building on personal experience, the teacher who uses the above-mention approaches allows second language learners to use their prior knowledge, read and write about things they have experienced, use their own language as text for reading, and study about new topics thematically. These are all components of what Hakuta and Garica (1989) call the "integrated 'child-centered' curriculum" which they found to be a common characteristic of effective schools for Hispanic children.

Finally, this chapter stresses the need to involve parents in any effective language arts program for children learning English as a second language. The teacher must learn about the parents' views of education and try to explain any practices that are new and baffling to the parents so that they understand the rationale and goals of the language arts class. In this way, they can become collaborators in the literacy development of their children. This chapter also stresses the need for the classroom teacher to be a promoter of a pluralistic point of view. As Ramsey (1987) remarks, understanding among culturally and linguistically diverse people requires respect for others' cultures and an ability to see others' perspectives.

For Review and Discussion

1. How is second language acquisition similar to first language acquisition? How is it different?
2. Why are cooperative learning and process writing especially appropriate for students who are learning English as a second language?
3. Explain the role of accessing prior knowledge in helping limited English proficient students develop listening and reading comprehension. Identify the related model of reading comprehension.
4. Discuss ways in which the classroom teacher can help foster a pluralistic perspective in the language arts class.
5. Discuss ways in which the teacher can collaborate with parents of limited English proficient students in the development of their children's literacy skills.

For Further Reading

Early, M. (1990). Enabling first and second language learners in the classroom. *Language Arts, 67,* 567–581.

Flores, B., Tefft, C., & Diaz, E. (1991). Transforming deficit myths about learning, language and culture. *Language Arts, 68*, 369–379.

Gunkel, J. (1991) "Please teach America": Kersuke's journey into a language community. *Language Arts, 68*, 303–310.

Language Arts in Multilingual/Multicultural Education. (1989, September). *Language Arts, 66* (5).

Mikkelsen, N. (1990). Toward greater equity in literacy education. Storymaking and non-mainstream students. *Language Arts, 67*, 556–566.

Moll, L. (1988). Some key issues in teaching Latino students. *Language Arts, 65*, 465–472.

Pellegrini, A. (1991). A critique of the concept of at risk as applied to emergent literacy. *Language Arts, 68*, 380–385.

Slavin, R., Madden, N., Karwitn, N., Dolan, L., & Wasik, B. (1991). Research directions: Success for all: Ending reading failure from the beginning. *Language Arts, 68*, 404–409.

Walsh, C. (1987). Language, meaning, and voice: Puerto Rican students' struggle for a speaking consciousness. *Language Arts, 64*, 196–206.

References

Aaronson, E. (1978). *The jigsaw classroom.* Beverly Hills, CA: Sage Publications.
Alach, N. (1987). *Handbook for nonviolent action.* New York: War Resisters League.
Alwood, J. E. (1984). Polly doesn't want just another cracker. *English Journal, 73,* 68–70.
Anderson, A., Brown, G., Shillcock, R., & Yule, G. (1984). *Teaching talk—Strategies for production and assessment.* Cambridge: Cambridge University Press.
Anderson, R. C., Hiebert, E. C., Scott, J. A., & Wilkinson, I. A. G. (1985). *Becoming a nation of readers.* Washington: National Institute of Education, U.S. Department of Education.
Anderson, V., Bereiter, C., & Smart, D. (1980). *Activation of semantic networks in writing: Teaching students how to do it themselves.* Paper presented at Annual Meeting of the American Educational Research Association.
Ankney, P., & McClurg, P. (1981). Testing Manzo's guided reading procedure. *The Reading Teacher, 34,* 681–685.
Applebee, A. (1977). *The child's concept of story: Ages two to seventeen.* Chicago: University of Chicago Press.
Applebee, A. (1979). Children and stories: Learning the rules of the game. *Language Arts, 56,* 641–646.
Applebee, A., & Langer J. (1984). Instructional scaffolding: Reading and writing as natural language activities. In J. M. Jenson (Ed.), *Composing and comprehending* (pp. 185–190). Urbana, IL: National Council on Research in English.
Asher, J. (1969). The total physical response approach to second language learning. *Modern Language Journal, 50,* 79–84.
Atwell, N. (1987). *In the middle: Writing, reading and learning with adolescents.* Portsmouth, NH: Heinemann.
Baker, L., & Brown, A. (1980). *Metacognitive skills and reading* (Technical Report No. 188). Urbana, IL: Center for the Study of Reading.
Baker, L. & Brown, A. (1984). Metacognitive skills and reading. In P. D. Pearson (Ed.), *Handbook of reading research* (pp. 353–394). White Plains, NY: Longman.
Barnes, D., & Todd, F. (1977). *Communication and learning in small groups.* London: Routledge and Kegan Paul.

Bateman, D., & Zisonis, F. (1966). *The effect of a study of transformational grammar on the writing of ninth and tenth graders.* Champaign, IL: National Council of Teachers of English.

Bechtel, J. (1979). *Videotape analysis of the composing processes of six male college freshmen writers.* Paper presented at the Annual Meeting of the Midwest Regional Conference on English in the Two-Year College (ERIC Document ED 177 558).

Beck, I., McKeown, M., McCaslin, E., & Burkes, A. (1979). *Instructional dimensions that may affect reading comprehension: Examples from two commercial reading programs.* Pittsburgh: Learning Research and Development Center, University of Pittsburgh (ERIC Document ED 197322).

Bellanca, J., & Fogerty, R. (1990). *Blueprints for thinking in the cooperative classroom.* Palatine, IL: Skylight Publishing.

Bereiter, C., & Scardamalia, M. (1982). From conversation to composition: The role of instruction in a developmental process. In R. Glaser (Ed.), *Advances in instructional psychology*, Vol. 2 (pp. 1–64). Hillsdale, NJ: Lawrence Erlbaum Associates.

Bereiter, C., & Scardamalia, M. (1985). *Intentional learning in school contexts. Unpublished report,* Intentional Learning Project: Center for Applied Cognitive Science, Toronto, Ontario Institute for Studies in Education.

Bereiter, C., & Scardamalia, M. (in press). Intentional learning as a goal of instruction. In L. Resnick (Ed.), *Knowing and learning: Issues for a cognitive science of instruction.* Hillsdale, NJ: Lawrence Erlbaum Associates.

Berenstain, S. (1978). *The Berenstain Bears and the spooky old tree.* New York: Random House.

Berkenkotter, C. (1981). Understanding a writer's awareness of audience. *College Composition and Communication, 32,* 388–99.

Bernstein, B. (1972). Education cannot compensate for society. In D. Rubinstein & C. Stoneman (Eds.), *Evolution of the comprehensive school* (pp. 61–66). London: Routledge and Kegan Paul.

Bernstein, B. (1973). A brief account of the theory of codes. In H. P. Dreitzel (Ed.), *Childhood and socialization* (pp. 213–239). New York: Macmillan.

Bernstein, B. (1975). *Class, codes, & control: Theoretical studies towards a sociology of language,* Vol. 3. (2nd ed.). London: Routledge and Kegan Paul.

Bickmore, K. (1984). *Alternatives to violence.* Akron, OH: Peace Grows.

Bissex, G. L. (1979). *Patterns of development in writing: Case study of a child from five to ten years old.* Paper presented at the annual meeting of the National Conference on Language Arts in the Elementary School.

Blackburn, E. (1985). Stories never end. In J. Hansen, T. Newkirk, & D. Graves (Eds.), *Breaking ground: Teachers relate reading and writing in the elementary school* (pp. 3–13). Portsmouth, NH: Heinemann.

Block, E. (1980). The comprehension strategies of second language readers. *TESOL Quarterly, 14,* 353–363.

Bloom, L., & Lahey, M. (1978). *Language development and language disorders.* New York: Wiley.

Bock, D., & Bock, E. H. (1981). *Evaluating classroom speaking.* Urbana, IL: ERIC Clearinghouse on Reading and Communication Skills.

Boiarsky, C. (1980). A cognitive map for teachers of writing. *English Education, 12,* 77–81.

Book, C., & Galvin, K. (1975). *Instruction in and about small group discussion.* Urbana, IL: ERIC Clearinghouse on Reading and Communication Skills.

Bortnick, R., & Lopardo, G. S. (1973). An instructional application of the close procedure. *Journal of Reading, 6,* 296–300.

Bridges, D. (1979). *Education, democracy and discussion.* Windsor, U.K.: NFER Publishing Company, Ltd. (Humanities Press, Inc., Atlantic Highlands, NJ).

Bridwell, L. (1980). Revising strategies in twelfth grade students' transactional writing. *Research in the Teaching of English, 14,* 197–222.

Brilhart, J. (1986). *Effective group discussion.* Dubuque, IA: William C. Brown Publishers.

Britton, J. (1970). *Languages and learning.* Harmondsworth, England: Penguin.

Britton, J. (1971). What's the use? In A. M. Wilkinson (Ed.), The context of language, *Educational Review, 23.*

Britton, J., Burgess, T., Martin, N., McLeod, A., & Rosen, H. (1975). *The development of writing abilities (11–18).* London: Macmillan Education.

Brown, A. (1980). Metacognitive development and reading. In R. Spiro, B. Bruce, & W. Brewer (Eds.), *Theoretical issues in reading comprehension* (pp. 453–481). Hillsdale, NJ: Lawrence Erlbaum Associates.

Brown, A., & Palicsar, A. (1982). Inducing strategic learning from texts by means of informed self-control training. *Topics in learning and learning disabilities, 2,* 1–17.

Brown, C., & Lytle, S. (1988). Merging assessment and instruction: Protocols in the classroom. In S. M. Glazer, L. W. Searfoss, & L. M. Gentile (Eds.), *Reexamining reading diagnosis* (pp. 94–102). Newark, DE: International Reading Association.

Brown, M., & Krensky, S. (1983). *Perfect pigs: An introduction to manners.* Boston: Atlantic-Little.

Brown, R., & Hanlon, C. (1970). Derivational complexity and order of acquisition in child speech. In J. R. Hayes (Ed.), *Cognition and the development of languages.* New York: Wiley.

Buckhalt, J., Rutherford, R., & Goldberg, K. (1978). Verbal and nonverbal interactions of mothers with their Down's syndrome and nonretarded infants. *American Journal of Mental Deficiency, 82,* 337–43.

Burgess, C. (1968). *Goops and how to be them.* New York: Dover.

Burgess, C., Burgess, T., Cartland, L., Chambers, R., Hedgeland, F., Levine, N., Mole, J., Newsome, B., Smith, T., & Torbe, M. (1973). *Understanding children writing.* New York: Penguin.

Burris, N. (1985). Third-graders write folk-tales. *Educational Horizons, 64,* 32–35.

Byren, D. (1981). *Inquiries into child language.* Boston: Allyn and Bacon.

California State Department of Education (1986). *Beyond language: Social and cultural factors in schooling language minority students.* Los Angeles: California State University, Evaluation, Dissemination and Assessment Center.

Calkins, L. M. (1980a). Children learn the writer's craft. *Language Arts, 57,* 207–213.

Calkins, L. M. (1980b). Children's rewriting strategies. *Research in the Teaching of English, 14,* 331–341.

Calkins, L. (1983). *Lessons from a child: On the teaching and learning of writing.* Portsmouth, NH: Heinemann Educational Books.

Carlson, R. (1970). *Writing aides through the grades.* New York: Teachers College Press.

Carroll, J., Davies, P., & Richman, B. (1971). *The American heritage word frequency book.* Boston: Houghton Mifflin.

Carver, R. P. (1981). *Reading comprehension and reading theory.* Springfield, IL: Charles C. Thomas.

Cazden, C. B. (1972). *Child language and education*. New York: Holt, Rinehart, and Winston.
Cazden, C., Cordeiro, P., & Giacobbe, M. (1985). Spontaneous and scientific concepts: Young children's learning of punctuation. In G. Wells & J. Nicholls (Eds.), *Language and learning: An interactional perspective* (pp. 107–124). London: Falmer Press.
Chenfeld, M. (1978). *Teaching language arts creatively*. New York: Harcourt Brace Jovanovich.
Cheng, L. (1987). *Assessing Asian language performance: Guidelines for evaluating limited-English proficient students*. Rockville, MD: Aspen Publishers.
Chomsky, C. (1981). Research update: Linguistic consciousness-raising in children. *Language Arts, 58*, 607–612.
Chomsky, N. (1957). *Syntactic structures*. The Hague: Mouton.
Chomsky, N. (1965). *Aspects of the theory of syntax*. Cambridge, MA: MIT Press.
Christenbury, N. (1985). Meeting the Martians. In J. N. Cyrren (Ed.), *Ideas plus* (pp. 9–11). Urbana, IL: National Council of Teachers of English.
Clark, H., & Haviland, S. (1977). Comprehension and the given-new contract. In R. Freedle (Ed.), *Discourse production and comprehension* (pp. 1–40). Norwood, NJ: Ablex.
Clark, M. (1976). *Young fluent readers*. Portsmouth, NH: Heinemann.
Clay, M. (1975). *What did I write?* Portsmouth, NH: Heinemann.
Clay, M. (1979). *The early detection of reading difficulties: A diagnostic survey with recovery procedures* (2nd ed.). Lexington, MA: Ginn.
Clay, M. M. (1972). *Reading: The patterning of complex behavior*. London: Heinemann.
Coelho, E. (1989). *The jigsaw kit*. Toronto: Dominie Press.
Coelho, E. (in press). *The cooperative classroom and language learner*. Hayward, CA: Alemany Press.
Cohen, E., & Scardamalia, M. (undated). *The effects of instructional intervention in the revision of essays by grade six children*. Downsview, Ontario: York University.
Courlander, H. (1962). The wedding of the hawk. *The king's drum & other African stories*. New York: Harcourt Brace Jovanovich.
Cramer, R.L. (1977). Pass out the red pencils. *Instructor, 87*(1), 80–84.
Cricket. (1986). *14* (1). Peru, IL: Open Court.
Cross, T. (1977). Mothers' speech adjustments: The contribution of selected child listener variables. In C. E. Snow & C. A. Ferguson (Eds.), *Talking to children: Language input and acquisition* (pp. 151–188). Cambridge: Cambridge University Press.
Crowhurst, M. (1979). The writing workshop: An experiment in peer response to writing. *Language Arts, 56*, 757–762.
Cullinan, B. E., Jaggar, A., & Strickland, D. (1974). Language expansion for black children in the primary grades: A research report. *Young Children, 29*, 98–112.
Cummins, J. (1981). *Bilingualism and minority language children*. Toronto: OISE Press.
Cummins, J. (1984). *Bilingualism and special education: Issues in assessment and pedagogy*. Clevedon, England: Multilingual Matters.
Cummins, J. (1989). *Empowering minority students*. Sacramento, CA: California Association for Bilingual Education.
Cunningham, P. (1981). Story dramatization. *The Reading Teacher, 34*, 466–468.
Dawson, M. A. (1948). Maximum essentials in english. *Elementary English Review, 25*, 35–38, 63.
De Gasztold, C. B. (1962). *Prayers from the Ark*. New York: Viking.

Delia, J. G., Kline, S. L., & Burleson, B. R. (1979). Development of persuasive communication strategies in kindergartners through twelfth graders. *Communication Monographs, 46,* 255.

Dewey, J. (1933). *How we think.* Boston: D.C. Heath.

Dixon, J. (1967). *Growth through English.* London: Cox & Wyman.

Dobson, L. (1989). Connections in learning to write and read: A study of children's developments through kindergarten and first grade. In J. Mason (Ed.), *Reading and writing connections* (pp. 83–104). Boston: Allyn and Bacon.

Dulay, H., Burt, M., & Krashen, S. (1982). *Language two.* Oxford: Oxford University Press.

Dyson, A. H. (1984). Research currents: Who controls classroom writing contexts? *Language Arts, 61,* 618–626.

Ede, J., & Williamson, J. (1980). *Talking, listening, and learning: The development of children's language.* London: Longman.

Ehri, L. C. (1986). Sources of difficulty in learning to spell and read words. In M. L. Wolraich & D. Routh (Eds.), *Advances in developmental and behavioral pediatrics* (pp. 121–195). Greenwich, CT: JAI Press.

Ehri, L. C. (1989). Movement into word reading and spelling. In J. Mason (Ed.), *Reading and writing connections* (pp. 65–82). Boston: Allyn and Bacon.

Ehri, L. C., Gibbs, A., & Underwood, T. (1988). Influence of errors in learning the spellings of English words. *Contemporary Educational Psychology, 13,* 236–253.

Eimas, P. D., Siqueland, E. R., Jusczyk, P., & Vigorito, J. (1971). Speech perception in infants. *Science, 171,* 303–306.

Eisner, E. (1976). *The arts, human development and education.* Berkeley: McCutheon.

Elbow, P. (1973). *Writing without teachers.* London: Oxford University Press.

Elbow, P. (1981). *Writing with power: Techniques for mastering the writing process.* New York: Oxford University Press.

Emig, J. (1981). *The composing processes of twelfth graders.* Urbana, IL: National Council of Teachers of English.

Enright, D., & McCloskey, M. (1988). *Integrating English: Developing English language and literacy in the multilingual classroom.* Reading, MA: Addison-Wesley.

Faigley, L. L., & Witte, S. P. (1986). Analyzing revision. *College Comprehension and Communication, 32,* 400–414.

Farr, R., Fay, L., & Negley, H. (1978). *Then and now: Reading achievement in Indiana (1944–45, and 1976).* Bloomington: School of Education, Indiana University.

Fitzgerald, J. (1983). Helping readers gain self control over reading comprehension. *Reading Teacher, 37,* 249–253.

Fitzsimmons, R. J., & Loomer, B. M. (1977). *Spelling research and practice.* Iowa City: University of Iowa Press.

Fitzsimmons, R. J., & Loomer, B. M. (1978). *Spelling: Learning and instruction.* Iowa City: Iowa State Department of Public Instruction and The University of Iowa.

Flavell, J. H., Speer, J. R., Green, F. L., & August, D. L. (1981). *The development of comprehension monitoring and knowledge about communication.* Chicago: University of Chicago Press.

Flower, L. S. (1979). Writer-based prose: A cognitive basis for problems in writing. *College English, 41,* 19–37.

Flower, L. S., & Hayes, J. R. (1981). A cognitive process theory of writing. *College composition and communication, 32,* 365–387.

References

Flowers, B. S. (1981). Madman, architect, carpenter, judge: Roles and the writing process. *Language Arts, 58,* 834–836.

Foresta, A., Lantieri, L., & Roderick, T. (1987). *Resolving conflict creatively: A draft teaching guide for grades kindergarten through six.* New York: New York City Board of Education.

Fox, C. (1983). Talking like a book, young children's early narrations. In M. Meek (Ed.), *Opening moves, Bedford Way papers, 17.* London: London University Institute of Education.

Fradd, S. (1987). Accommodating the needs of limited English proficient students in regular classrooms. In S. Fradd & W. Tikunoff (Eds.), *Bilingual education and bilingual special education* (pp. 133–181). Boston: Little, Brown.

Friedman, Paul G. (1986). *Listening processes: Attention, understanding evaluation* (2nd ed.). Washington D. C.: National Education Association.

Galton, M., & Simon, B. (1980). Effective teaching in the primary classroom. In M. Glaton & B. Simon (Eds.), *Progress and performance in the primary classroom* (pp. 179–212). London: Routlege and Kegan Paul.

Garnica, O. K. (1977). Some prosodic and paralinguistic features of speech to young children. In C. Snow & C. Ferguson (Eds.), *Talking to children* (pp. 63–68). London: Cambridge University Press.

Gee, J. (1985). The narrativization of experience in the oral style. *Journal of Education, 167*(1), 9–35.

Gee, J. (1986). Orality and literacy: From the savage mind to ways with words. *TESOL Quarterly, 20,* 719–746.

Gibbs, J. (1987). *Tribes.* Santa Rosa, CA: Center Source Publications.

Gillet, J. W., & Temple C. (1989). *Language arts: Learning processes and teaching practices* (2nd ed.). Glenview, IL: Scott, Foresman.

Gleason, J. B. (1977). Talking to children: Some notes on feedback. In C. E. Snow & C. A. Ferguson (Eds.), *Talking to children: Language input and acquisition* (pp. 199–218). Cambridge: Cambridge University Press.

Goodlad, J. I. (1984). *A place called school.* New York: McGraw-Hill.

Goody, E. N. (1977). Towards a theory of questions. In E. N. Goody (Ed.), *Questions and politeness: Strategies in social interaction.* Cambridge: Cambridge University Press.

Grahame, K. (1908). *The wind in the willows.* New York: Scribners.

Graser, E. R. (1983). *Teaching writing: A process approach.* Dubuque, IA: Kendall/Hunt.

Graves, D. H. (1975). An examination of the writing process of seven year old children. *Research in Teaching English, 9,* 227–241.

Graves, D. H. (1977). Research update: Spelling texts and structural analysis methods. *Language Arts, 54,* 86–90.

Graves, D. H. (1978). We won't let them write. *Language Arts, 55,* 635–640.

Graves, D. H. (Ed.). (1981). *A case study observing the development of primary children's composing, spelling and motor behaviors during the writing process.* (Final report, NIE grant No. G–78–0174). Durham, NH: University of New Hampshire.

Graves, D. H. (Ed.). (1982). Research update: How do writers develop? *Language Arts, 59,* 173–179.

Graves, D. (1983). *Writing: Teachers and children at work.* Portsmouth, NH: Heinemann.

REFERENCES

Graves, D., & Hansen, J. (1984). The author's chair. In J. M. Jensen (Ed.), *Composing and comprehending* (pp. 69–76). Urbana, IL: National Council of Teachers of English.

Graves, N., & Graves, T. (1988). San Francsico's community board's conflict manager's program, *Cooperation in Education*, Nov–Dec., p. 14.

Greenberg, M. D., McAndrews, D., & Meterski, M. (1975). In C. Cooper (Ed.), *Getting it together: A sentence combining workbook.* Adapted by T. Callahan and M. Sullivan. Mimeographed. State University of New York at Buffalo, Department of Instruction, Buffalo.

Greenlinger-Harless, C. S. (1987). A new cross-referenced index to U.S. reading series, grades K–8. *The Reading Teacher, 41,* 293–303.

Grice, H. P. (1975). Logic and conversation. In P. Cole & J. L. Morgan (Eds.), *Syntax and semantics: Vol. III.* New York: Academic Press.

Griffin, W. J., O'Donnell, R. C., & Norris, R. C. (1967). *Syntax of kindergarten and elementary school children: A transformational analysis.* Champaign, IL: National Council of Teachers of English.

Hailey, J. (1978). *Teaching writing K–8.* Berkeley: University of California Press.

Hakuta, K. (1986). *Mirror of language: The debate on bilingualism.* New York: Basic Books.

Hakuta, K., & Garcia, E. (1989). Bilingualism and education. *American Psychologist, 44,* 374–379.

Haley-James, S. (Ed.). (1981). *Perspectives on writing in grades 1–8.* Urbana, IL: National Council of Teachers of English.

Hall, M. A. (1981). *Teaching reading as a language experience* (3rd ed.). Columbus, OH: Charles E. Merrill.

Hall, N., & Duffy, R. (1987). Every child has a story to tell. *Language Arts, 64,* 523–529.

Hall, R. A. (1950). *Leave your languages alone.* Ithaca, NY: Linguistica.

Halliday, M. A. K. (1975). *Learning how to mean: Explorations in the study of language.* London: Edward Arnold Publishers.

Hansen, J. (1987). *When writers read.* Portsmouth, NH: Heinemann.

Harste, J. C., Woodward, V. A., & Burke, C. L. (1984). *Language stories and literacy lessons.* Portsmouth, NH: Heinemann.

Havelock, E. (1963). *Preface to Plato.* Cambridge, MA: Harvard University Press.

Heath, S. B. (1982). What no bedtime story means: Narrative skills at home and school. *Language and Society, 11*(2), 49–76.

Heath, S. B. (1983). *Ways with words.* Cambridge: Cambridge University Press.

Heath, S. B. (1986). Separating things of the imagination from life: Learning to read and write. In W. Teale & E. Sulzby (Eds.), *Emergent literacy* (pp. 156–172). Norwood, NJ: Ablex.

Heimlich, J. E., & Pittelman, S. D. (1986). *Semantic mapping: Classroom applications.* Newark, DE: International Reading Association.

Hennings, D. G. (1986). *Communication in action* (3rd ed.). Boston: Houghton Mifflin.

Henry W. III. (1990, April 1). Beyond the melting pot. *Time,* pp. 28–31.

Hidi, S., & Hildyard, A. (1983). The comparison of oral and written productions of two discourse types. *Discourse Processes, 6,* 91–105.

Hillocks, G., Jr. (1986). *Research on written composition.* Urbana, IL: ERIC Clearinghouse on Reading and Communication Skills National Conference on Research in English.

Hogrogian, N. (1971). *One fine day.* New York: Macmillan.

Hollman, M. J. (1981). Learning about writing from the public. *English Journal, 70*(3), 26–31.

Horn, E. (1919, February). Principles of methods in teaching spelling as derived from scientific investigation. *Eighteenth Yearbook of National Society for the Study of Education, Part II.* Bloomington, IL.

Horn, E. (1926). *A basic writing vocabulary.* Iowa City: University of Iowa Press.

Horn, E. (1944). Research in spelling. *The Elementary English Review, 21,* pp. 6–13.

Horn, E. (1960). Spelling. In C. W. Harris (Ed.), *Encyclopedia of educational research* (3rd ed.) (pp. 1337–1354). New York: Macmillan.

Hubbell, P. (1965). *8 A.M. Shadows.* New York: Atheneum.

Huck, C. S., & Kerstetter, K. J. (1987). Developing readers. In B. E. Cullinan (Ed.), *Children's literature in the reading program.* Newark, DE: International Reading Association.

Hunt, K. W. (1965). *Grammatical structures written at three grade levels.* Champaign, IL: National Council of Teachers of English.

Jaggar, A. M., Carrara, D. H., & Weiss, S. E. (1986). The influence of reading on children's narrative writing (and vice versa). *Language Arts, 63,* 292–300.

Janda, C. (1989). *Sharing with colleagues: Giving an inservice course.* Unpublished presentation at NYSTESOL Annual Conference, Rochester, NY.

Johnson, D. W., & Johnson, F. P. (1982). *Joining together: Group theory and group skills* (2nd ed.). Englewood Cliffs, NJ: Prentice-Hall.

Johnson, D. W., & Johnson, R. (1984). *Circles of learning: Cooperation in the classroom.* Alexandria, VA: Association of Supervision and Curriculum Development.

Jongsma, E. (1971). *The close procedure as a teaching technique.* Newark, DE: International Reading Association.

Joslin, S. (1958). *What do you say, dear?* Reading, MA: Addison-Wesley.

Kagan, S. (1986). Cooperative learning and sociocultural factors in schooling. In *Beyond Language: Social and Cultural Factors in Schooling Minority Students* (pp. 231–298). Los Angeles: California State University: Evaluation, Dissemination, and Assessment Center.

Kaiser, A. (1985). *Preschool children's responses to two styles of story telling.* Unpublished master's thesis, University of Florida.

Kantor, K. J., & Rubin, D. L. (1981). Between speaking and writing: Processes of differentiation. In M. Kross & R. J. Vann (Eds.), *Exploring speaking-writing relationships* (pp. 55–81). Urbana, IL: National Council of Teachers of Education.

Keats, E. J. (1966). *Jennie's hat.* New York: Harper & Row.

King, M. (1989). Speech to writing: Children's growth in writing potential. In J. Mason (Ed.), *Reading and writing connections* (pp. 7–30). Boston: Allyn and Bacon.

Kinneavy, J. L. (1971). *A theory of discourse: The aims of discourse.* Englewood Cliffs, NJ: Prentice-Hall.

Koch, C., & Brazil, J. M. (1975). *Strategies for teaching the composition process.* Urbana, IL: National Council of Teachers of English.

Kock, R. A. (1972). A study of free association as a technique to improve student writing. *Dissertation Abstracts International, 32,* 6292A.

Krashen, S. (1982). *Principles and practice in second language acquisition.* New York: Pergamon.

Krashen, S. D. (1984). *Writing: Research, theory, and applications.* New York: Pergamon.

REFERENCES

Krashen, S. D., & Terrell, T. D. (1983). *The natural approach: Language acquisition in the classroom*. Hayward, CA: Alemany Press.

Kreidler, W. J. (1984). *Creative conflict resolution*. Glenview, IL: Scott, Foresman.

Kucera, H., & Francis, W. N. (1967). *Computational analysis of present-day American English*. Providence, RI: Brown University Press.

Kukla, K. (1987). David Booth: Drama as a way of knowing. *Language Arts, 64*, 73–78.

La Brant, L. L. (1934). The changing sentence structure of children. *The Elementary English Review, 11*, 59–65, 86.

LaBrant, L. L. (1955). Inducing students to write. *English Journal, 44*, 70–74.

Lam, J. A. (1988). *The impact of conflict resolution programs on schools*. Amherst, MA: National Association for Mediation in Education.

LaRaus, R., & Remy, R. (1978). *Citizen decision making for grades 4–6*. Reading, MA: Addison-Wesley.

Larrick, N. (1987). Keep a poem in your pocket. In B. E. Cullinan (Ed.), *Children's literature in the reading program* (pp. 20–28). Newark, DE: International Reading Association.

Lawlor, J. (1983). Sentence combining: A sequence for instruction. *Elementary School Journal, 84*(1), 53–61.

Leonard, S. A. (1917). *English composition as a social problem*. Cambridge, MA: Houghton Mifflin.

Lobel, A. (1972a). *Frog and toad all year*. New York: Harper & Row.

Lobel, A. (1972b). *Frog and toad are friends*. New York: Harper & Row.

Lobel, A. (1972c). *Frog and toad together*. New York: Harper & Row.

Luria, A. R., (1976). *Cognitive development: Its cultural and social foundations*. Cambridge, MA: Harvard University Press.

McCaslin, N. (1990). *Creative drama in the classroom*. White Plains, NY: Longman.

McClintock, M. (1958). *A fly went by*. New York: Random House.

McCormick, J. (1965). *Etti-Cat, the courtesy cat*. New York: Hastings.

McCrosky, J. C. (1977). *Quiet children and the classroom teacher*. Urbana, IL: ERIC Clearinghouse on Reading and Communication Skills.

McCurdy, M. (1984). Writing on their own: Kindergarten and first grade. In N. Gordon (Ed.), *Classroom experiences: The writing process in action* (pp. 1–23). Portsmouth, NH: Heinemann.

Manzo, A. (1975). Guided reading procedure. *Journal of Reading, 18*, 287–291.

Maratsos, M. (1973). Non-egocentric communication abilities in preschool children. *Child Development, 44*, 697–700.

Martin, B. (1970). *The haunted house*. New York: Holt, Rinehart, and Winston.

Martin, N., Williams, P., Wilding, J., Hemmings, S., & Medway, P. (1976). *Understanding children talking*. New York: Penguin Books.

Matthews, M. M. (1966). *Teaching to read*. Chicago: University of Chicago Press.

Meek, M. (1985). Play and paradoxes: Some considerations of imagination and language. In G. Wells & J. Nichols (Eds.), *Language and learning: An interactional perspective* (pp. 41–58). London: The Falmer Press.

Mellon, J. C. (1969). *Transformational sentence combining: A method for enhancing the development of syntactic fluency in English composition*. Urbana, IL: National Council of Teachers of English.

Meng-Peterson, C. (1975). The modification of communicative behavior in preschool-aged children as a function of the listener's perspective. *Child Development, 46*, 1015–1018.

References

Menyuk, P. (1988). *Language development, knowledge and use.* Glenview, IL: Scott, Foresman.

Metis Associates. (1990). *The resolving conflict creatively programs 1988–89: Summary of significant findings.* New York: Author.

Metzger, E. A. (1977). Cases of failure to learn to write: Exploratory case studies at grade seven, grade ten and college level. *Dissertation Abstract International, 38,* 3346A.

Michaels, S. (1986). Narrative presentations: An oral preparation for literacy with first graders. In J. C. Gumperz (Ed.), *The social construction of literacy.* Cambridge: Cambridge University Press.

Mills, E. B. (1968). An experimental study in the use of literacy models in written composition. *Dissertation Abstracts International, 28,* 3900A.

Moffett, J. (1968). *Teaching the universe of discourse.* Boston: Houghton Mifflin.

Monschein, E. (undated). *Living together under the law.* Albany, NY: New York State Bar Association and New York State Education Department.

Monson, D. L., & Purves, A. C. (1984). *Experiencing children's literature.* Glenview, IL: Scott, Foresman.

Morain, G. G. (1978). *Language and education: Theory and practice 7. Dialect and nonstandard English.* Arlington, VA: Center for Applied Linguistics.

Murray, D. M. (1968). *A writer teaches writing: A practical method of teaching composition.* Boston: Houghton Mifflin.

Murray, D. M. (1973). Why teach writing and how? *English Journal, 62,* 1234–1237.

Murray, D. M. (1978). Internal revision: A process of discovery. In C. R. Cooper & L. Odell (Eds.), *Research on composing: Points of departure* (pp. 83–103). Urbana, IL: National Council Teachers of English.

Murray, D. M. (1980). How writing finds its own meaning. In T. R. Donovan & B. W. McClelland (Eds.), *Eight approaches to teaching composition.* Urbana, IL: National Council of Teachers of English.

Murray, D. M. (1985). *A writer teaches writing* (2nd ed.). Boston: Houghton Mifflin.

Myers, M. (1983). Approaches to the teaching of composition. In M. Myers & J. Gray (Eds.), *Theory and practice in the teaching of composition* (pp. 3–43). Urbana, IL: National Council of Teachers of English.

Nelson, D. (1976). D. and E.: Show and tell, grown up. *Language Arts, 53,* 203–205.

Northcutt, L., & Watson, D. (1986). *Sheltered English teaching handbook.* Carlsbad, CA: Northcutt, Watson & Gonzales.

Noyce, R. M., & Christine, J. F. (1989). *Integrating reading and writing instruction.* Boston: Allyn and Bacon.

O'Donnell, R. C. (1967). A transformational analysis of oral and written grammatical structures in the language of children in grades three, five and seven. *Journal of Educational Research, 61,* 35–39.

O'Donnell, R. C., Griffin, W. J., & Norris, R. C. (1967). *Syntax of kindergarten and elementary school children: A transformational analysis* (NCTE Research Report No. 8.). Champaign, IL: National Council of Teachers of English.

O'Hare, F. (1973). *Sentence combining: Improving student writing without formal grammar instruction.* Urbana, IL: National Council of Teachers of English.

O'Neill, C., & Lambert, A. (1982). *Drama structures: A practical handbook for teachers.* London: Heinemann Educational Books.

Ong, W. (1982). *Orality and literacy: The technologizings of the word.* New York: Methuen.

REFERENCES

Paek, M. (1978). *Aekyung's dream.* Chicago, IL: Children's Book Press.

Palincsar, A. (1984). The quest from expository text: A teacher-guided journey. In G. Duffy, L. Roehler, & J. Mason (Eds.), *Comprehension instruction: Perspectives and suggestions* (pp. 261–264). White Plains, NY: Longman.

Palincsar, A. S., & Brown, A. L. (1986). Interactive teaching to promote independent learning from the text. *The Reading Teacher, 39,* 771–777.

Pappas, C., Kiefer, B., & Levstik, L. (1990). *An integrated language perspective in the elementary school: Theory into action.* White Plains, NY: Longman.

Pearson, P. D., & Camperell, K. (1981). Comprehension of text structures. In J. Guthrie (Ed.), *Comprehension and teaching: Research reviews* (pp. 27–54). Newark, DE: International Reading Association.

Peck, M. S. (1978). *The road less traveled.* New York: Simon and Schuster.

Perl, S. (1980). A look at basic writers in the process of composing. In L. N. Kasden & D. R. Hoeber (Eds.), *Basic writing: Essays for teachers, researchers and administrators* (pp. 13–32). Urbana, IL: National Council of Teachers of English.

Phillips, T. (1985). Beyond lip-service: Discourse development after the age of nine. In G. Weels & J. Nichols (Eds.), *Language and learning: An interactional perspective* (pp. 59–82). Philadelphia: The Falmer Press.

Pianko, S. H. (1979). A description of the composing processes of college freshman writers. *Research in Teaching English, 13,* 5–22.

Picard, C. A. (1988). *Woodroffe high school peer mediation project.* Ottawa, ONT: Woodroffe High School.

Pinnell, G. S. (1975). *Language functions of first grade students observed in informal classroom environments.* Unpublished doctoral dissertation, Ohio State University.

Platt, K. (1965). *Big Max.* New York: Harper & Row.

Plume, I. (Reteller and Illustrator) (1980). *The Bremen town musicians.* Garden City, NY: Doubleday.

Prelutsky, J. (1984). *The new kid on the block: Poems by Jack Prelutsky: drawings by James Stevenson.* New York: Greenwillow Books.

Purves, A., & Monson, D. (1984). *Experiencing children's literature.* Glenview, IL: Scott, Foresman.

Quintero, E., & Huerta-Macias, A. (1990). All in the family: Bilingualism and biliteracy. *The Reading Teacher, 44,* 306–312.

Ramsey, P. (1987). *Teaching and learning in a diverse world: Mutlicultural education for young children.* New York: Teachers College Press.

Raphael, T. E. (1982). Question-answering strategies for children. *The Reading Teacher, 36,* 186–190.

Raphael, T. E., & Wannacott, C. A. (1985). Heightening fourth-grade students sensitivity to sources of information for answering comprehension questions. *Reading Research Quarterly, 20,* 282–296.

Rigg, P., & Allen, V. (1989). *When they don't all speak English: Integrating the ESL student into the regular classroom.* Urbana, IL: National Council of Teachers of English.

Robinson, F. P. (1970). *Effective reading.* New York: Harper and Row (originally 1961).

Rosenblatt, L. S. (1978). *The reader, the text, the poem: The transactional theory of the literary work.* Carbondale, IL: Southern Illinois University Press.

References

Russell, C. (1983). Putting research into practice: Conferencing with young writers. *Language Arts, 60,* 333–340.

Russell, D. H., & Russell E. F. (1979). *Listening aids through the grades.* New York: Teachers College Press.

Sager, C. (1973). Improving the quality of written composition through pupil use of rating scale. *Dissertation Abstract International, 34,* 1496A.

Sawkins, M. W. (1971). The oral responses of selected fifth grade children to questions concerning their written expression. *Dissertation Abstracts International, 31,* 6287A.

Schiff, N. (1976). *The development of form and meaning in the language of hearing children of deaf parents.* Unpublished doctoral dissertation, Columbia University, New York.

Schniedewind, N., & Davidson, E. (1987). *Cooperative learning, cooperative lives.* Dubuque, IA: William C. Brown.

Schoen, D. A. (1984). *The reflective practitioner: How professionals think in action.* New York: Basic Books.

Schribner, S., & Cole, M. (1981). *The psychology of literacy.* Cambridge, MA: Harvard University Press.

Sebesta, S. L. (1987). Enriching the arts and humanities through children's books, In B. E. Cullinan (Ed.), *Children's literature in the reading program* (pp. 77–88). Newark, DE: International Reading Association.

Seller, M. S. (1988). *To seek America: A history of ethnic life in the United States.* Englewood, NJ: Jerome S. Oser.

Shatz, M., & Gelman, R. (1973). The development of communication skills: Modifications in the speech of young children as a function of listener. *Monographs of the Society for Research in Child Development, 28*(5 Serial No. 152).

Shatzman L., & Strauss, A. (1955). Social class and modes of communication. *American Journal of Sociology, 60,* 329–339.

Shaughnessy, M. P. (1977). *Errors and expectations: A guide for the teacher of basic writing.* New York: Oxford University Press.

Shuell, T. (1986). Cognitive conceptions of learning. *Review of Educational Research, 56,* 411–436.

Silo-Miller, J. (1984). Expanding ideas: Fourth grade. In N. Gordon (Ed.), *Classroom experiences: The writing process in action* (pp. 49–62). Portsmouth, NH: Heinemann.

Slaughter, J. P. (1983). Big books for little kids: Another fad or new approach for teaching beginning reading. *The Reading Teacher, 36,* 758–763.

Slavin, R. E. (1983). *Cooperative learning.* White Plains, NY: Longman.

Slobodkin, L. (1957). *Thank you, you're welcome.* New York: Vanguard.

Smith, F. (1982). *Writers and writing.* New York: Holt, Rinehart and Winston.

Smith, F. (1983). Reading like a writer. *Language Arts, 60,* 558–567.

Smith, M. (1933a). Grammatical errors in the speech of preschool children. *Child Development, 4,* 183–190.

Smith, M. (1933b). The influence of age, sex and situation on the frequency, form and function of questions asked by preschool children. *Child Development, 4,* 201–213.

Snow, C. E. (1977). The development of conversation between mothers and babies. *Journal of Child Language, 4,* 1–22.

Sowers, S. (1979). A six-year-old's writing process: The first half of first grade. *Language Arts, 56,* 829–35.

Sowers, S. (1981). Young writers' preference for non-narrative modes of composition. In D. H. Graves (Ed.), *A case study observing the development of primary children's composing, spelling and motor behaviors during the writing process* (NIE Grant No. G-78-0174, pp. 189–206). Durham, NH: University of New Hampshire.

Spencer, M. (1976). Stories are for telling. *English in Education, 10*(1), 16–23.

Stanford, G. (1977). *Developing effective classroom groups.* New York: Hart Publishing.

Stauffer, R. G. (1980). *The language experience approach to the teaching of reading* (rev. ed.). New York: Harper & Row.

Steil, L. K., Summerfield, J., & deMare, G. (1983). *Listening: It can change your life.* New York: Roland Press.

Steptoe, J. (1987). *Mufaro's beautiful daughters.* New York: Lothrup, Lee & Shepard.

Stern, L. (1987). *Joint educational development share.* Havertown, PA: United Church Press.

Sticht, T. G., Beck, L. J., Hauke, R. N., Kleiman, G. M., & James, J. H. (1979). *Auding and reading.* Alexandria, VA: Human Resources Research Organization.

Stiles, E. E. (1977). A case study of remedial writers in selected two-year colleges in East Tennessee. *Dissertation Abstracts International, 37,* 7004A.

Street, B. V. (1984). *Literacy in theory and practice.* Cambridge: Cambridge University Press.

Strickland, D. (1987). Literature: Key element in the language and reading program. In B. Cullinan (Ed.), *Children's literature in the reading programs* (pp. 68–76). Newark, DE: International Reading Association.

Strickland, D., & Feeley, J. (1985). Using children's concept of story to improve reading and writing. In T. L. Harris & E. J. Cooper (Eds.), *Reading, thinking and concept development.* New York: College Board.

Strong, W. (1976). Close-up sentence combining: Back to basics and beyond. *English Journal, 65*(2), 54–56.

Strong, W. (1981). *Sentence combining and paragraph building.* New York: Random House.

Strong, W. (1986). *Creative approaches to sentence combining.* Urbana, IL: National Council of Teachers of English.

Stubbs, M. (1980). *Language and literacy.* London: Routledge and Kegan Paul.

Sulzby, E. (1985). Children's emergent reading of favorite storybooks: A developmental study. *Reading Research Quarterly, 20,* 458–481.

Sulzby, E., Barnhart, J., & Hieshima, J. A. (1989). Forms of writing and prereading from writing a preliminary report. In J. Mason (Ed.), *Reading and writing connections* (pp. 31–64). Boston: Allyn and Bacon.

Surat, M. (1983). *Angel child, dragon child.* Milwaukee, WI: Raintree Publishers.

Teale, R. H., & Sulzby, E. (1986). Introduction: Emergent literacy as a perspective for examining how young children become writers and readers. In W. H. Teale & E. Sulzby (Eds.), *Emergent literacy* (pp. vii–xxv). Norwood, NJ: Ablex.

Terrell, T. (1977). A natural approach to second language acquisition and learning. *Modern Language Journal, 6,* 325–337.

Thorndike, E. L. (1921). *The teacher's word book.* Columbia University, New York: Bureau of Publications, Teachers College.

Thorndike, E. L., & Lorge, I. (1944). *The teacher's word book of 30,000 words.* Columbia University, New York: Teachers College Press.

Thorndike, R. L. (1973). *Reading comprehension education in 15 countries.* New York: Wiley.

Tiedt, I. (1989). *Reading/thinking/writing: A holistic language and literacy program for the K–8 classroom.* Boston: Allyn and Bacon.

Tiedt, I., Bruemmer, S., Jane, S., Stelwagon, P., Watanabe, K., & Williams, M. (1983). *Teaching writing in K–8 classrooms: The time has come.* Englewood Cliffs, NJ: Prentice-Hall.

Tierney, R., Caplan, R., Ehri, L., Healy, M. K., & Hurdlow, M. (1990). Writing and reading working together. In A. H. Dyson (Ed.), *Writing and reading: Collaboration in the classroom.* Urbana, IL: National Council of Teachers of English.

Trevarthn, C. (1979). Communication and cooperation in early infancy: A description of primary intersubjectivity. In Bullowa, M. (Ed.), *Before speech, the beginning of interpersonal communication* (pp. 307–320). London: Cambridge University Press.

Van Allen, R. (1976). *Language experiences in communication.* Boston: Houghton Mifflin.

Vanderbilt, A. (1978). *The Amy Vanderbilt complete book of etiquette: A guide to contemporary living.* Garden City, NY: Doubleday.

VanLeeuwen, J. (1979). *Tales of Oliver Pig.* New York: Dial Books for Young Readers.

Veatch, J. (1978). *Reading in the elementary school* (2nd ed.). New York: Wiley.

Vygotsky, L. (1962). *Thought and language.* Cambridge, MA: MIT Press.

Vygotsky, L. (1978). *Mind in society.* Cambridge, MA: Harvard University Press.

Wagner, B. J. (1976). *Dorothy Heathcote—Drama as a learning medium.* Washington, D.C.: National Education Association Press.

Wallas, G. (1926). *The art of thought.* New York: Harcourt Brace Jovanovich.

Wells, G. (1973). *Coding manual for the description of child speech.* Bristol, England: University of Bristol, School of Education.

Wells, G. (1981). *Language as interaction.* In Wells, G. (Ed.), *Learning through interaction* (pp. 22–72). Cambridge: Cambridge University Press.

Wells, G. (1986). *The meaning makers: Children learning language and using language to learn.* Portsmouth: Heinemann.

Wells, G. (1987). *Meaning makers—children learning language and using language to learn.* London: Hodder and Stoughton.

Wenden, A., & Rubin, J. (1987). *Learner strategies in language learning.* Englewood Cliffs, NJ: Prentice-Hall.

Wigginton, E. (1985). *Sometimes a shining moment: The Foxfire experience.* Garden City, NY: Anchor Press/Doublday.

Wong-Fillmore, L. (1983). The language learner as an individual. In M. A. Clarke & J. Handscombe (Eds.), *On TESOL '82: Pacific perspectives on language and teaching* (pp. 157–173). Washington, D.C.: TESOL.

Wong-Fillmore, L., & Valadez, C. (1986). Teaching bilingual learners. In M. C. Wittrock, *Handbook of research on teaching* (pp. 648–685). Washington, D.C.: American Education Research Association.

Wood, B. S. (1977). *Development of functional communication competencies: Pre K–grade 6.* Urbana, IL: ERIC Clearinghouse on Reading and Communication Skills.

Yepes-Baraya, M. (1990). *Class assignment for multicultural education; teaching and learning with culturally diverse children.* Unpublished paper, SUNY Fredonia, NY, Nov. 8, 1990.

Glossary

Alphabet knowledge. Students' ability to discriminate between letters, to name letters, and to identify letter-sound correspondences.

Alphabetic principle. States that although there is not an invariable one-to-one relationship between written letters and speech sounds, there is a fairly reliable relationship between letters and the sounds they represent. In English, letter-sound correspondences are affected by other factors such as the position of a letter in a syllable and letters following it in a syllable. Words beginning with the letter *b* begin with the initial sound in *ball*; however, *b* does not always represent the initial sound in *ball*. Both these statements are consistent with the alphabetic principle.

Auditory discrimination. Students' ability to demonstrate that they can hear differences between sounds, particularly language sounds like the initial sounds in *cat* and *bat* or the final sounds in *leaf* and *leave*.

Cloze technique. A procedure first used to measure the reading difficulty of a written text. Every *n*th (usually fifth) word is deleted and replaced with a blank line. Students are required to write in the words they believe were deleted. The technique is also used to stimulate discussion of the thought processes used to guess the missing words thereby promoting metalinguistic awareness and comprehension.

Communication model. A construct for analyzing the components of oral communication. It includes a speaker, listener, topic, and context. This permits one to focus on one component without forgetting that the components constantly affect each other.

Communication stress. Results from factors that make effective listening and speaking difficult. For example, speaking to an audience of strangers causes more communication stress than talking to a friend.

Cooperative principle. One of four rules that make it possible to create meaning collaboratively in conversation. Speakers try to be informative, truthful, relevant, and clear. Listeners interpret what is said accordingly.

Critical response. The ability to view a text, not like a conversation in which one is immersed, but from a distance. It is the ability to evaluate the text with detachment asking, for example, whether it is true, pleasing, clever, cheerful, gloomy, well-written or consistent with one's experience. It is the ability to reflect on one's own emotional reactions to a text as if observing another person's reactions. This is similar to the concept of critical detachment in writing.

English as a second language (ESL). An approach to teaching English in American schools to students whose native tongue is not English. Students in such programs are frequently referred to as ESL students.

Environmental mode. A method of teaching writing demonstrating the following characteristics: 1. There are clear and specific objectives, but they may not be explicitly stated. 2. Problems and materials engage students with one another in processes important to writing. 3. Students engage in these activities before writing. 4. Lecture and teacher-led discussion is used minimally to introduce the lesson and to summarize and draw generalizations from the activities. 5. Principles and concepts are approached through concrete problems and materials. 6. Students get feedback from peers in small groups.

Given-new contract. One of four rules that make it possible to create meaning collaboratively in conversation. Participants presume that new information offered by others is related to meaning already established and that the most likely relationship is the correct one, unless the speaker explicitly states a different one.

Goal structures. A concept that specifies how individual student's learning goals are related to each other students' learning goals. In a cooperative structure, each student's goal achievement depends on other students' achieving their goals. In a competitive structure, a student's achieving his or her goal depends on other students failing to reach theirs. In an individual structure, a students achieving his or her goals is unrelated to other student's achievement.

Holistic, collaborative, integrated approach. Focuses first on large concepts that learners apprehend regarding language and literacy learning—for example, that one can convey meaning through marks on paper, that words in print are related to words in speech, and that language can be used for many functions such as to inform, persuade, and express feelings. Skills are taught as students need them to accomplish language tasks they are attempting, and so it is a collaborative rather than directive approach. Since language tasks often involve combinations of listening, speaking, reading, and writing, it is an integrated approach.

Insert sentence. In sentence combining, the sentence which is reduced and inserted into a matrix sentence. In the following sentence combining problem *The hat is red* is an insert sentence.

            Mary has a hat.
                The hat is red.
                    Combined: Mary has a red hat.
International Phonetic Alphabet. A set of symbols devised by the International Phonetic Association for transcribing the speech sounds of any language into writing.
Limited English proficiency. A category of students in American schools who are not necessarily in ESL programs but whose mastery of English is limited because it is not their native tongue. Students are usually so categorized as the result of tests of English proficiency.
Linguistic interdependence principle. The idea that mastery of certain cognitive skills in one's first language transfer to a second language. For example, students who are able arrive at an unfamiliar word's meaning from context in their native tongue soon begin to use this skill in a second language as they learn it.
Matrix sentence. In sentence combining, the sentence into which other sentences are inserted. In the following sentence combining problem *Mary has a hat* is the matrix sentence.
            Mary has a hat.
                The hat is red.
                    Combined: Mary has a red hat.
Metacomprehension. The ability to think about and make statements about one's own comprehension processes. The ability to state what one knows, what one does not know, and what one needs to know to make sense of a text one has read is evidence of metacomprehension. Repair strategies, such as rereading for missing crucial information, are also evidence of metacomprehension.
Metalinguistic awareness. The ability to reflect on language and make statements about what it is, how it works, and what one can do with it.
Presentational mode. A method of teaching writing demonstrating the following characteristics: 1. The lesson has clear, explicitly stated objectives. 2. Concepts are presented through lecture or teacher-led discussion. 3. Models and materials are presented for study. 4. Students are given specific writing assignments. 5. Teachers supply feedback through corrections and comments on written assignments.
Proto-conversation. An early form of infant-caretaker communication. A cycle of mutual gaze and looking away is repeated. In a more developed stage participants follow one another's lead in looking at something in the environment during the "looking away" phase. This is thought to be the forerunner of conversation with two participants taking turns and referring to a topic.
QARs (Question Answer Relationships). A method for promoting metacomprehension wherein students not only answer questions about a text, they state whether the question can be answered from information in a single sentence (Right There Questions), from information from more than one sentence (Think and

Search Questions), or whether the question requires them to reflect on prior knowledge (On My Own Questions).

Reading readiness. The belief and practices arising from it that learning to read can begin only after the child has mastered prerequisite skills, abilities, and knowledge such as visual discrimination and alphabet knowledge. Whereas emergent literacy is compatible with the holistic, collaborative, integrated approach to teaching language arts, reading readiness is compatible with the skills emphasis approach.

School discourse practices. Practices associated with the language of the schools and the public language of politically and economically powerful groups. Such practices include being explicit, not context-dependent, not redundant, concise, impersonal, abstract, and expository.

Semantic mapping. A technique where the teacher (or leader) writes a word on the board and circles it, and students suggest words or phrases that are associated with it. Each association is written on the board, circled, and connected with the stimulus word with a line. Associations are sometimes rearranged into groups having common characteristics. The technique is used to teach new vocabulary, to marshall prior knowledge on a topic before reading, and to generate ideas for writing. It is sometimes used as a first step to outlining or summarizing.

Skills emphasis approach. An approach to teaching language arts that focuses first on "outer" aspects of language such as letter recognition and knowledge of letter-sound correspondences, spelling, and punctuation. It is, therefore, an atomistic rather than a wholistic approach. Advocates of this approach divide the language arts into discrete steps ordered from easy to more difficult and teach all students each step in fixed order. Therefore, it is a highly teacher-directed approach. Skills involved in listening, speaking, reading, and writing are conceived of and taught separately.

Structural linguistics. A method of studying language by observing the frequency and position of words and word parts in discourse and discovering generalizations that describe the structure of the language—how its parts relate to one another. Defining parts of speech in terms of sentence frames and suffixes is an outcome of interest in structural linguistics. Because structural linguistics does not consider questions of correctness it is blamed by some for a putative decline of standards in English usage.

T-units (minimal terminable units). A main clause and all its modifiers. Since longer t-units tend to be more complex syntactically than short ones, the average number of words per t-unit is frequently used as a measure of the syntactic complexity of written English texts.

Time-space match. An indication that emergent readers understand that there is a relationship between the amount of print and the number of words in a story. While "reading" they track the print with their gaze and hurry up or slow down their speech and/or tracking so that they come to the end of the print when they finish talking.

Transformational grammar. A grammar based on the premise that meaning in "deep structure" (in the mind) is a series of unelaborated propositions (kernel sentences) with notations attached expressing relations between them and stating such details as "tense" and "negative." Transformational grammar attempts to state the rules that transform this deep structure meaning into acceptable English sentences. Sentence combining is an outcome of interest in transformational grammar.

Visual discrimination. Students' ability to demonstrate that they can see differences between shapes such as squares and circles or the letters *b* and *d*.

Whole language. A fairly uncompromising holistic, collaborative, integrated approach to teaching language arts. It usually includes the process approach to teaching writing and the literature workshop approach to teaching reading. One would not expect to find basal readers or regularly scheduled time set aside for such subjects as spelling, standard English usage, or handwriting in a whole language classroom since these would be seen as evidence of a teacher directed rather than a collaborative curriculum and method.

Zone of proximal development. The place in a hierarchy of concept or skill complexity where learning occurs. The most advanced skills or concepts learners can deal with on their own marks the lower limit of the zone. Concepts or skills that learners can deal with only in collaboration with more experienced learners (teachers) are in the zone. Further advanced concepts or skills that learners cannot deal with even in collaboration with more experienced learners are beyond the zone.

Index

Aaronson, Elliot, 109, 110
Acrostics, 321
Active learning, 10–11
Active listening, 115–116
Adjectives, 342
Adverbs, 342
Affective function of language
   classroom function supporting
     use of, 139–143
   discussion of, 137–139
Affirmation activities, 113, 114
Alphabetic principle, 357
Alphabet knowledge, 173–174
Alternatives to Violence program, 119–120
Alwood, J. E., 319
Anderson, A., 55, 82
Anderson, R. C., 292
Announcements, class and school, 83
Applebee, A., 26, 27, 314, 317
Argumentational talk, 96–97
Arguments, 133
Asian-Americans, 372, 374
Atomistic teaching approach, 11–12. *See also* Skills emphasis approach
Attitudes, 137–143
Atwell, Nancie, 170, 241–245, 278, 390, 392
Audiences, 83, 84
Auditory discrimination, 173
Authority
   language use and exercise of, 31
   as method of decision making, 117
Author's Chair, 282–283

Baker, L., 388
Barnes, D., 93, 95
Barnhart, J., 232
Basal reading programs
   eclectic, 178–179, 188
   explanation of, 177–178
   phonics or skills emphasis, 178, 188
   teaching in groups using eclectic, 180–182
Bassing, Eileen, 227
Bateman, D., 346
Beardsley, Robert, 107
Bellanca, J., 110, 112
Bereiter, C., 390
Berkenkotter, C., 235
Bernstein, B., 31
Blackburn, E., 347–348
Bloomfield, Leonard, 338, 339
Bluestone, Max, 227
Bock, D., 83
Bock, E. H., 83
Boiarsky, C., 270
Book reports, 67, 81
Brainstorming, 259–260
Brainwetting, 260–261
Bridges, D., 73–75
Bridwell, L., 271–272
Brilhart, J., 103
Britton, J., 236, 237
Brown, A., 219, 388
Brown, Roger, 375
Bruner, Jerome, 226
Bryen, D., 58
Burgess, C., 236
Burke, C. L., 157

Burleson, B. R., 133
Burris, N., 316

Calkins, L. M., 244, 271
Calligraphy, 355–356
Carroll, J., 362
Cazden, C. B., 234
Chenfeld, M., 81
Children. *See also* Infants; Preschool children
   egocentricity in, 233–235
   imaginative and affective use of language by, 290–292
   interactional view of language acquisition in, 18–22
   language development and interactions between parents and, 22–27
Chinese-Americans, 374
Chomsky, Noam, 270, 343
Choral speaking, 295–297
Christie, J. F., 261, 280, 302–304, 319, 347
Ciardi, John, 226
Cinquain, 321
Circle Strategy, 276
Clarification, 75
Clark, H., 69
Classrooms. *See* Culturally diverse classrooms
Clay, M., 190, 350
Cloze technique, 200
Cognitive theory, 18
Cohen, E., 274
Cohesion, 69
COIK (Clear Only If Known), 62

421

Collaborative informative
    language, 128
Collaborative talk
  directive vs., 93
  support for, 42–44
Collaborative teaching approach.
    See also Holistic, collaborative, integrated approach
  as aspect of natural language learning, 27
  directive vs., 10–11
  example of, 4–10
  varieties in, 9–10
Communication. *See also* Conversation; Discussion; Formal speaking; Oral language
  conflict resolution and, 115–116
  early acquisition of strategies for, 19
  meaningful and intentional, 20
  meaningful but unintentional, 19–22
  role of culture in, 55
Communication model, 54
Communicative acts, 147
Communicative stress, 54
  from listener's point of view, 60–63
  from speaker's point of view, 55–57
Competitive goal structure, 105
Composition
  emergent literacy and, 156–158
  stages of, 226
Comprehension
  description of, 388
  directed listening and thinking activities to aid, 212
  directed reading and thinking activities to aid, 210–212
  directed reading lesson to foster, 214–217
  group reading procedure to aid, 213–214
  promotion of, 206–207
  reciprocal teaching to foster, 217–220
  approach to assist in, 212–213
  and use of semantic mapping, 207–210
Computer software, 283, 284
Computer use, 283–284
Conferences
  with oneself, 278
  reading, 167–170
  writing, 241–248, 266
Conflict
  activities to help children deal with, 137–138
  in small-group discussion, 95
Conflict Manager Program, 121

Conflict resolution
  affirmation activities and, 113, 114
  decision making and, 117–120
  explanation of, 113
  in language arts curriculum, 121
  oral communication skills and, 115–116
Conformity, 31
Consensus, 117–118
Content, in literature, 311–312
Content conferences
  revision through, 274–275
  during writing workshops, 243
Context
  communicative stress and characteristics of, 56, 57
  and listening success, 61–62
Conversation
  communicative stress and, 56, 57
  emergence of, 19
  rules of, 68–69, 71
  skills in, 70–73
Conversational style, 42–44
Cooperative learning
  assignments in, 110–112
  characteristics of, 108
  contrasting goal structures and, 105–106
  effective lessons applying, 112–113
  for ESL students, 286
  examples of lessons applying, 106–108
  models of, 109–110
  small groups and, 110
Cooperative principle, 69
Cramer, R. L., 281
Creative drama
  explanation of, 297
  fostering imagination in, 299–301
  movement in, 298–299
  pantomime in, 299, 300, 302
  role of teacher in, 304
  role playing or improvisation as, 301–302
  teaching through use of, 307–309
  types of, 301–304
Criticism, 75–76
Crowhurst, M., 276
Cubing, 264
Cullinan, B. E., 314–315
Cultural journalism, 36–37
Culturally diverse students
  as classroom resource, 396
  experiences with written discourse by, 389–390
  implications for teaching, 372–374

language arts as way of empowering, 390–397
language arts programs for, 378–379
opportunities for real language use by, 385–389
second language acquisition in, 374–377. *See also* ESL students
use of dialects by, 33
Culture, communication and, 55
Cummins, Jim, 394
Cunningham, P., 309
Curriculum, 324–326
Cursive writing, 353

Dale, Edgar, 62
Dartmouth Conference (1966), 240
Davidson, E., 106
Davis, P., 362
Decision making
  methods of, 117–119
  roles in, 119–120
Delia, J. G., 133
Demonstrate and Evaluate, 81
Derivational suffixes, 340
Development, zone of proximal, 18
Dewey, J., 216
Dialects
  choral speaking and, 295
  politics and, 339
  standard English vs. nonstandard, 33, 348
  used by culturally diverse students, 33
Dialogue journals, 267
Diamente, 322
Dictation, 268
Directed listening and thinking activity, 212
Directed reading and thinking activity, 210–212
Directed reading lesson, 214–217
Direction following, 65–66
Directive informative language, 128
Directive teaching styles
  collaborative vs., 10–11
  use of, 41–42
Discourse. *See also* Topic-associating discourse; Topic-centered discourse
  modes of, 236–238
  topic-centered vs. topic-associating, 33–34
Discovery strategies, 262–265
Discussion
  attitudes and values necessary for, 74–75

INDEX

characteristics of, 73–74
to clarify thoughts, 75
criticism and, 75–76
neutrality in teacher-led, 78
during prewriting stage, 262
reflection on and evaluation of, 78–80
role of teachers in, 100–101
small-group. *See* Small-group discussion
stages and procedures in, 74
study of recorded, 101–103
techniques for teacher-led, 76–77
Dobson, L., 158
Drama, 9. *See also* Creative drama
Duffy, R., 267
Dyson, A. H., 245

Eclectic basal reading approach
description of, 178–179
holistic, top-down assumptions and, 188
used in groups, 180–182
use of whole word method by, 193
Editing. *See* Rewriting stage: editing
Editing committees, 281
Egocentricity
concept of, 233–234
in older students, 234–235
in writing, 233, 247, 266
Ehri, L. C., 359, 360
Eisner, E., 292
Elbow, P., 247, 261, 277
Eliot, T. S., 35
Emergent literacy
individualized reading program for, 165–167
language experience approach to, 163–165
middle-school reading workshops for, 170–171
observations regarding, 154–159
reading conference concept for, 167–170
reading readiness vs., 173
underlying assumptions in, 160
writing process approach to, 161–163
Emig, Janet, 226, 227, 230, 236
Emotions
communication of, 137–143
evoked by speakers, 61
Empiricism, 338
Empowerment, 390–397
English as second language students. *See* ESL students
English language. *See* Standard English

Environmental mode of writing instruction, 251–253, 269
ESL students
affective considerations for, 384–385
context-embedded situations for, 375
definition of, 373
organizing interaction for, 381–384
organizing physical environment for, 379–381
Ethnographers, 37–38
Evaluation
of addresses to audiences, 83
of discussion, 78–80, 102, 103
Experiential talk, 96
Explicit language
development of skills in, 116, 117
life styles and demands for, 29–31
in speech, 46
use of, 29
Expositional talk, 99
Expressive language
characteristics of, 236–237
encouragement of use of, 137–138
modification of, 237–238
External revision, 270

Faigley, L. L., 272
Feeley, J., 318
Fitzgerald, J., 205
Fitzsimmons, R. J., 363, 364
Flower, L. S., 234
Flowers, Betty, 228, 273
Focused free writing, 261
Fogerty, R., 110, 112
Formal speaking
in classroom, 80–81
speaker-audience format for, 81–84
Formal writing. *See* Institutional writing
Fox, C., 291
Francis, W. N., 362
Free association, 260
Free writing, 261
Friedman, Paul G., 63
Friend Crests, 64–65

Galton, M., 172
Garcia, E., 373, 387
Gee, J., 30, 32, 34–36
Generative transformational grammar, 343
Gibbs, A., 360
Given-new contract, 69
Globes, 380

Goal structures, 105–106
Goodlad, J. I., 292
Grammar
explanation of, 334
impact of transformational, 343–346
opinions regarding teaching of, 336–337
teaching syntax with, 335–336
Graphology, 356
Graser, E. R., 264
Graves, Donald, 161, 227, 240, 245, 265, 267, 271, 279, 282, 392
Greenlinger-Harless, C. S., 178
Griffin, W. J., 232, 346
Group discussion. *See* Discussion; Small-group discussion
Group paper revision, 276
Groups, 117–118. *See also* Small groups
Group share, 244, 245
Guided reading procedure, 213–214

Hakuta, K., 373, 387
Hall, Mary Ann, 165
Hall, N., 267
Hall, R. A., 339
Halliday, Michael A. K., 20, 147, 236, 239
Handwriting
emergent, 350
instruction in, 351–352
in left-handed students, 352–353
legibility in, 353–355
manuscript and cursive, 353
Hansen, J., 167–169, 172, 282
Harste, J. C., 157
Haviland, S., 69
Heath, Shirley Brice, 27, 37, 372
Hennings, Dorothy, 81
Heuristics, 262–263. *See also* Discovery strategies
Hidi, S., 232
Hieshima, J. A., 232
Hillocks, G., Jr., 228, 235, 240, 249, 252, 266
Hillyard, A., 232
Hispanic-Americans, 372, 387
Holistic, collaborative, integrated approach. *See also* Collaborative teaching approach
atomistic vs., 11–12
characteristics of, 27
example of, 4–10
explanation of, 13
strategies used in, 33
structure and, 172
Hollman, M. J., 258

Index

Holmes, Oliver Wendell, 110
Horn, Ernest, 361
Hunt, Kellogg, 343
Hypothetical talk, 96

I Can Type, 284
Idea Fair, 81–82
Imagination, 299–301
Imaginative language
 classroom characteristics
  supporting use of, 143
 purposes of, 143
 skills related to use of, 144
Implicit language
 teaching styles and use of, 31–32
 use of, 29, 30
Improvisation, 301–302. *See also*
 Creative drama
Individual goal structure, 105–106
Individualized reading program,
 165–167
Infants
 choral-speaking games used by,
  296
 early communication strategies
  of, 19
 imaginative and affective use of
  language by, 290, 291
Inflectional suffixes, 340
Informational gap, 55
Informative language
 classroom activities supporting
  use of, 129–132
 discussion of, 128–129
Insert sentences, 201–202
Institutional writing
 characteristics of, 45–46
 development of, 46
 elements of, 232
Integrated teaching style. *See also*
 Holistic, collaborative,
 integrated approach
 example of, 4–10
 for language arts, 12–13, 324–326
Intentionality, 27
Intentional learning, 390
Interactive writing, 267–268
Internalization process, 278
Internal revision, 270
International Phonetic Alphabet,
 356
Invented spelling, 358–360

Jaggar, A., 314–315
Johnson, D. W., 105, 109
Johnson, F. P., 105, 109
Journals. *See* Professional journals
Joyce, James, 35

Kantor, K. J., 234
Kennedy, John F., 364

Kerstetter, Kristen, 315
Key words, 260
King, Stephen, 320
Kinneavy, J. L., 237, 238
Kline, S. L., 133
Knowledge
 access to prior, 388–389
 effective listening and lack of, 62
Krashen, S. D., 275, 375
Kreidler, William, 135
Kucera, H., 362
Kukla, K., 309

Langer, J., 26, 27
Language. *See also* Explicit language; Expressive language
 across curriculum, 324–326
 affective function of, 137–143
 emergence of meaningful, 21
 emergence of unconventional,
  20–21
 essence of teaching, 47
 and home and school culture,
  292–293
 imaginative and affective use of,
  290–292
 imaginative function of, 143–
  144
 informative use of, 128–131
 life styles and demands for
  explicit, 29–30
 persuasive use of, 132–137
 poetic function of, 237
 transactional function of, 237,
  355
 use of explicit, 29
 written vs. spoken, 232
Language acquisition. *See also*
 Second language acquisi-
 tion
 interactional view of, 18–22
 role of parent-child interaction
  in, 22–27
Language arts
 approaches to teaching, 3–11
 goal structures for teaching,
  105–106
 integration of, 12–13, 44–47
 issues to define approaches to,
  10–13
Language arts curriculum, 121
Language experience approach
 (LEA)
 for ESL students, 386–387
 explanation of, 163–165
 reflections on, 165
 to word recognition, 193
Lantern, 322
Larrick, Nancy, 298, 320
Leading from behind, 23, 24. *See
 also* Scaffolding

Learning. *See also* Cooperative
 learning
 aspects of natural language, 27
 definition of, 18
 intentional, 390
 passive vs. active, 10–11
 social view of, 18
Left-handed students, 352–353
Limerick, 322
Limited English proficient students, 373. *See also* ESL
 students
Linguistic interdependence
 principle, 377
Linguistics. *See* Structural
 linguistics
Listeners
 characteristics of, 62
 communicative stress and
  characteristics of, 55–57
 communicative stress from
  point of view of, 60–63
 in listening-reacting groups, 82
Listening
 affective function and, 138–139
 components of, 63, 64
 demands of, 58
 informative function and,
  128–129
 persuasive function and, 133–134
 in school, 60
 transactional functions of,
  144–147
Listening centers
 for ESL students, 379
 establishment of, 68
Listening instruction
 activities to aid in, 64–68
 approaches to teaching, 4–5,
  63–64
Lists
 for poems, 321
 for prewriting stage, 263
 studies of words presented in,
  362–363
Literacy. *See also* Emergent
 literacy
 and classroom use of literature,
  323–324
 school discourse practices and,
  32–33
Literature. *See also* Poetry
 children's vs. mature experiences with, 316–317
 in classroom, 323–324
 elements of, 310–312
 qualities of, 309–310
 and reading and writing
  instruction, 319
 teaching appropriate responses
  to, 314–319

INDEX

teaching elements of, 313
transactional view of, 312–313
use of creative drama with, 300
Loomer, B. M., 363, 364
Lost on the Moon, 97–98

Manuscript writing, 353
Maps, 380
Martin, Bill, 348
Martin, N., 75
Masks, 305–307
Matrix sentence, 201
McCaslin, N., 296, 299, 305, 308
McCroskey, J. C., 70
McCurdy, Marla, 161
Meek, M., 292
Mellon, J. C., 346
Meng-Peterson, C., 234
Menyuk, P., 234
Metacognitive skills, 392–393
Metacomprehension
  activities that foster, 217
  description of, 203–204
  question-answer relationships to increase, 205–206
  use of modeling comprehension to foster, 205
Metalinguistic awareness
  cloze technique to promote, 200
  explanation of, 199–200
  sentence combining to promote, 201–202
Mexican-Americans, 373
Michaels, S., 33, 36
Microtype: The Wonderful World of Paws, 284
Milliken, Helen, 106
Mills, E. B., 316
Modeling comprehension, 205
Moffett, J., 235
Monson, D., 309, 313
Morphology, 357–358
Movement, 298–299
Muppet Learning Keys, 284
Murray, D. M., 245, 259
Myers, M., 261

Nelson, Dorothy, 81
Neutrality, 78
Newman, Samuel P., 236
Nonverbal communication
  affective function and, 139
  associated with rituals and transactions, 145
Norris, R. C., 232, 346
Nouns, 341
Noyce, R. M., 261, 280, 302–304, 319, 347

O'Connor, Sandra Day, 54
O'Donnell, R. C., 232, 346
O'Hare, F., 346
O'Neill, Cecily, 308
Operational talk, 98–99
Oral communication skills, 115–116
Oral language. *See also* Communication; Conversation; Discussion; Formal speaking
  creative drama used to teach, 308
  dialogue journals to link writing with, 267
  examples of children's use of, 39–42
  experienced at school, 38–39
  learning to use explicit language in, 46
  preschool children's experiences with, 38
Ownership of topics, 245–246, 390–392

Paek, M., 395
Palincsar, A., 217, 219
Pantomime, 299, 300, 302
Pappas, C., 324
Parent-child interactions
  language development and, 22–27, 275, 388
  studies of, 27–29
Parent-child register, 58–59
Passive learning, 10–11
Peck, M. Scott, 62
Peer conferences
  facilitating revision through, 276–278
  used in writing workshops, 243
Peer-mediation programs, 121
Peer tutoring, 393–394
Perl, Sondra, 228
Persuasive language
  classroom activities supporting use of, 134–137
  discussion of, 132–134
Phillips, T., 96, 99
Phonetics, 356, 357
Phonics emphasis approach
  pros and cons of, 193–194
  to reading instruction, 176–177
  using basal readers, 178, 188
Physical environment, 379–381
Piaget, Jean, 132, 233, 234
Platt, Kim, 391
Playlike writing, 267
Plot, 311
Poetry
  approaches to teaching, 9
  benefits of using, 319–320
  requirements of, 323
  use of movement with, 298–299
  writing, 320–323

Point of view, 61
Prelutsky, Jack, 392
Preschool children
  imaginative and affective use of language by, 290–292
  oral language experiences of, 38
  reading aloud to, 314
Presentational mode of writing instruction, 248–251
Prewriting stage
  choice of topic during, 258–259
  discovery strategies for, 262–265
  for emerging writers, 229–230
  explanation of, 258
  planning during, 259–262
Print, 188–189
Prior knowledge, 388–389
Process approach to writing instruction
  characteristics of, 245–246
  conferences used in, 241–248
  description of, 239–240, 268
  for ESL students, 387
  reflections on, 162–163
  used in fourth grade, 240–241
  used in middle schools, 241–245
  used to teach reading, 161–162
Professional journals, 284
Propositions, 342
Props, 294
Proto-conversation, 19
Proximal development, 27
Publishing
  as stage in writing process, 282–284
  during writing workshops, 244–245
Puppets, 305–307
Purves, A., 309, 313

Question-Answer-Evaluate format, 60
Question-Answer Relationships (QARs), 205–206

Raphael, T. E., 205, 206
Reactive writers, 265
Reader's theater, 303–304
Reading
  creative drama used to teach, 309
  emergent literacy in, 154–156
  and metacomprehension, 203–206
  and metalinguistic awareness, 199–202
Reading aloud, 314–316
Reading conferences, 167–170
Reading groups, 180–182
Reading instruction
  approaches to, 5–6, 292

Reading instruction (*continued*)
and comprehension. *See*
Comprehension
and concepts related to print, 188–189
and concepts related to storybooks, 191, 192
individualized reading program approach to, 165–167
language experience approach to, 163–165
reading conference approach to, 167–170
reading workshops approach to, 170–172
structure and holistic, collaborative, integrated approaches to, 172
using basal readers. *See* Basal reading programs
vocabulary and, 189–190
and word recognition, 193–198
writing process approach to, 161–163
Reading readiness
applications of, 174–175
assumptions that underlie concept of, 175–176
phonics or skills emphasis approach to, 176–177
traditional concept of, 172–173
traditional skills of, 173–174
Reading workshops, 170–172
Reciprocal teaching, 217–220
Redirection, 77
Reflective listening, 115–116
Reflective writers, 265, 266
Resolving Conflict Creatively Program (RCCP), 121
Revision. *See* Rewriting stage: revising
Rewriting stage: editing
discussion of, 280
importance of teaching at, 278–279
teacher editing during, 281–282
teaching one or two conventions during, 279
teaching strategies for, 280–281
Rewriting stage: revising
content conferences used during, 274–276
observations during, 270–272
peer conferences used during, 276–278
process of, 269–270
teaching strategies for, 272–274
Richman, B., 362
Right-handed students, 352, 353
Rituals
activities using, 146–147
in classrooms, 145

discussion of, 144–145
knowledge and skills associated with use of, 145
Robinson, F. P., 212, 213
Role playing, 301–302. *See also* Creative drama
Rosenblatt, Louise, 312
Rosie's Walk (Hutchins), 154–155
Rubin, D. L., 234
Russell, C., 276
Russell, D. H., 63, 134
Russell, E. F., 63, 134

Sager, C., 268
Scaffolding
example of, 26
explanation of, 23, 24
of young children's language attempts, 278
Scardamalia, M., 274, 390
Schniedewind, N., 106
School discourse practices
approaches to teach, 36–38
development of, 31–32, 36
explanation of, 30
literacy and, 32–33
need for facility with, 35, 39, 47
school success and facility with, 44–46
Scrimshaw, Kris, 156
Seating arrangements, 76
Sebesta, S. L., 300
Second language acquisition
first language vs., 374–376
time involved in, 377
Semantic mapping
discussion of, 207–208
as form of list making, 263
illustrations of, 207–210
Sendak, Maurice, 301
Sentence combining
explanation of, 201–202
teaching, 346
transformations and, 345–346
Sentence frames, 340
Sentence patterns, 344–345
Sentence reconstruction, 347
Sharing, 81
Sharing/publishing stage, 282–284
Sharing-time stories, 33–34
Shatzman, L., 29–30
Shaughnessey, Mina, 354, 355
Sheltered English, 378–379
Show and Tell, 81
Silo-Miller, Irene, 240–241
Simon, B., 172
Skills emphasis approach
example of, 4–10
explanation of, 13
rationale for use of, 32
to reading instruction, 176–177

using basal readers, 178
Skinner, B. F., 227
Slavin, R. E., 109, 110
Small-group discussion. *See also* discussion
example of, 92–93
expressing feelings in, 137
negative aspects of, 95–96, 104–105
ritualistic use of language in, 145
role of teachers in, 100–101
study of recorded, 101–103
success in, 95
task presentation and, 94
types of talk in, 96–99
Small groups
activities to improve oral language in, 148–149
cooperative learning and, 110
familiarity among group members in, 93–94
size of, 93
Smith, Frank, 261, 265, 274, 275
Sowers, Susan, 229
Speakers
communicative stress stemming from, 61
listening to professional, 67
Speaking
affective function and, 137–138
choral, 295–297
informative function and, 128
instructional approaches to, 4–5
persuasive function and, 132–133
transactional functions of, 144–147
Spelling
development of consciousness regarding, 364–365
factors affecting, 357–358
invented, 358–360
irregularity of English, 356–357
research in teaching and learning, 361–364
teaching, 360–361, 363
during writing stage, 266
Spencer, M., 291
Spoken language, 232
SQ3R, 212–213
STAD (Student Teams-Achievement Divisions), 109
Standard English
nonstandard dialect vs., 33
opinions regarding teaching of, 337
role of teacher in acquisition of. *See* Standard English teaching, 335, 348–350
Stanford, G., 76
Stauffer, R. G., 165
Stein, Gertrude, 35, 226

INDEX

Steptoe, John, 389
Storybooks, 191, 192
Story drama, 302–303
Story form, 156–158
Storytelling
  discussion of, 293–294
  lesson plans for, 294–295
  responding to topic-associated, 35–36
Story theater, 301
Strauss, A., 29–30
Strickland, D., 314–315, 318, 323
Structural linguistics
  explanation of, 338
  impact of, 337–339
  and teaching parts of speech, 340–342
Structure
  and holistic, collaborative, integrated approach, 172
  in literature, 311
Stubbs, M., 45, 46
Students. See Culturally diverse students
Suffixes, 340
Sulzby, E., 157, 160, 172–173, 175, 232, 350
Surat, M., 395
Survey QRRR, 213
Syntax
  opinions regarding teaching of, 337
  teaching facility with, 334–335, 346–348
  teaching grammar with, 335–336

Teachers
  multicultural perspective of, 394–397
  relationship between practices and beliefs of, 2–3
  responsibilities of language arts, 348
  types of talk used by, 99–100
Teachers of English to Speakers of Other Languages (TESOL), 372
Teacher-student register, 58–59
Teacher-to-student teaching model, 11
Teaching
  integration of language arts and, 46–47
  underlying assumptions in, 3–4
Teale, R. H., 160, 172–173, 175
Terrell, T., 378–379
Textbooks, 8–9. See also Basal reading programs
Thematic units
  for ESL students, 387
  linking subject areas, 324–326

Theme, 312
Thorndike, E. L., 362
Three-Story Intellect Model, 110–112
Tiedt, I., 301, 316
Tierney, R., 360
Time-space match, 158
Todd, F., 93, 95
Topic-associating discourse
  characteristics of, 35
  responding to, 35–36
  use of, 33–34
Topic-centered discourse
  characteristics of, 35
  teacher responses to, 293
  use of, 33–34
Topics
  communicative stress and characteristics of, 56, 57
  modeling choice of, 258–259
  ownership of, 245–246, 390–392
  problems in listening resulting from, 61
Total Physical Response, 378
Transformational grammar, 343
T-units, 343
Turn-taking, 68–69
Tutoring, peer, 393–394

Underwood, T., 360

Vader, Donald, 176, 178
Van Allen, Roach, 165
Veatch, J., 165
Verbal Activity Scale, 70, 71
Verbs, 341
Videotapes, 101–103
Vocabulary
  knowledge of, 174
  of reading instruction, 189–191
Voice
  in literature, 311
Voting, 117
Vygotsky, Lev, 18, 388

Wells, Gordon, 20, 39, 68, 314
Whole language approach, 13
Whole word method, 193
Wigginton, Eliot, 36, 37
Witte, S. P., 272
Woodward, V. A., 157
Woolf, Virginia, 35
Word-learning tasks, 174
Word recognition
  phonics method of, 193–194
  and study of word structure, 194–197
  using context for, 197–198
  whole word method of, 193
Words, frequency studies of, 361–362

Word structure, 194–197
Writers
  critical detachment in, 235
  egocentricity in, 232–235
  modes of discourse used by, 236–238
  observations of accomplished, 230–231
  observations of emerging, 229–230
  reactive, 265
  reflective, 265, 266
  what we know about professional, 226–227
Writer's folders, 246
Writing
  connection between reading and, 46–47
  creative drama used to teach, 308–309
  dimensions of growth in, 231–232
  emergent literacy in, 155–156
  formal aspects of, 158, 159
  functional, 267
  institutional, 45–46, 232
  interactive, 267–268
  ownership of, 245–246
  playlike, 267
  spoken language and, 232
  stages of. See Prewriting stage; Rewriting stage: editing; Rewriting stage: revising; Sharing/publishing stage; Writing stage
Writing instruction
  approaches to teaching, 6–8
  environmental mode of, 251–253, 269
  presentational mode of, 248–251
  process approach to. See Process approach to writing instruction
Writing process
  description of, 227–228, 245
  detachment regarding, 247
  in maturing writers, 231–232
  in young writers, 232
Writing stage
  conferencing during, 266
  development of criteria for good writing during, 268–269
  development of fluency during, 267–268
  discussion of, 265–266
Writing workshops, 240

Zidonis, F., 346
Zone of proximal development
  explanation of, 18